AMERICAN WOMEN HISTORIANS, 1700s–1990s

A BIOGRAPHICAL DICTIONARY

JENNIFER SCANLON
AND
SHAARON COSNER

GREENWOOD PRESS
WESTPORT, CONNECTICUT • LONDON

Library of Congress Cataloging-in-Publication Data

Scanlon, Jennifer.
    American women historians, 1700s–1990s : a biographical dictionary
/ Jennifer Scanlon and Shaaron Cosner.
        p.   cm.
    Includes bibliographical references (p.   ) and index.
    ISBN 0–313–29664–2 (alk. paper)
        1. Women historians—United States—Biography—Dictionaries.
    I. Cosner, Shaaron.   II. Title.
    E175.45.S27   1996
    973'.072022—dc20
    [B]   96–2538

British Library Cataloguing in Publication Data is available.

Library of Congress Catalog Card Number: 96–2538
ISBN: 0–313–29664–2

First published in 1996

Greenwood Press, 88 Post Road West, Westport, CT 06881
An imprint of Greenwood Publishing Group, Inc.

Printed in the United States of America

The paper used in this book complies with the
Permanent Paper Standard issued by the National
Information Standards Organization (Z39.48–1984).

10 9 8 7 6 5 4 3 2 1

*For Michael Arthur and Asha Arthur
and for Victoria Cornell*

CONTENTS

Photo essay follows page 148.

PREFACE

This work provides biographical and bibliographical portraits of roughly two hundred women who have practiced the craft of history in the United States. For the most part, these women have been neglected by the very field they have practiced. Reference works written to memorialize the names and works of scholars in general and historians in particular have largely ignored women historians. *American Women Historians, 1700s–1990s* begins the work of reclaiming these women's lives and professional accomplishments. In doing so, however, it leaves out as many women as it includes, and the authors hope that this book will inspire others to continue the process of highlighting the work of women historians.

This select group of deceased and living women historians covers a variety of occupations, including public history, academia, archival work, and popular history writing; and a variety of fields, including biography, art history, and history based primarily on issues of region, gender, race, ethnicity, class, or sexuality. Inclusion in this volume was based primarily on publications, but the authors considered other criteria as well, including participation in defining a field of study, influence on other historians or related scholars, cross-disciplinary achievements, and contributions to the work of others. In fact, this work includes several women whose training was in a field other than history but whose work has contributed greatly to our understanding of our own field.

In making our final decisions, the authors relied on suggestions made by a wide variety of people, and we are pleased to have the opportunity to express our gratitude. Several historians acted as consultants on the project, and we owe them special thanks: they are Hasia Diner, Evelyn Hu-Dehart, Nikki Keddie, and Virginia Sanchez Korrol. Many others, historians and related scholars, made suggestions about women historians in their fields, and we offer thanks to Vincent Carey, Robert Daniels, Phyllis McGibbon, Elizabeth Perry, and Monica van Beusekom. Finally, each of the living women historians included in the volume was given the opportunity to suggest other women for inclusion. We often followed suggestions they made, broadening our base in many fields and, just as often, finding suggestions that opened up our work to new fields and extraordinary historians. We are enormously grateful to those who helped in a variety of ways in determining who would be included and who would be left out; the authors, of course, take final responsibility for the collection.

We are also grateful to those who helped with the research and computer work: they are Robin Prenoveau, Pamela Bigelow, Louise Bigelow, Elaine Bristol, and Dawn Fogelberg. Shaaron Cosner also offers special thanks to the Social Science Educational Consortium in Boulder, Colorado, and in particular James R. Giese, Betsy Glade, Barbara Miller, Sylvia Thomas, Lori Eastman, Gary Holthaus, and Elliott Wiest, for providing inspiration and encouragement for this project.

INTRODUCTION

This book chronicles the lives and work of roughly two hundred American women historians from the 1700s to the 1990s. The earliest writer included, Hannah Adams, was born in 1755 in Medfield, Massachusetts; the most recent, Vicki Ruiz, was born in 1955 in Atlanta, Georgia. Two full centuries fall between these women's birthdates, and in the intervening years thousands of women have chosen to practice the craft of history in the United States. The small group of historians included here, all American by birth or by citizenship, represents a much larger group in terms of diversity, personal strength, and professional accomplishment.

The stories of Hannah Adams and Vicki Ruiz, however, do frame the text both in chronology and in diversity. In effect, their life stories provide a framework for understanding women's relationships to history in the United States. Hannah Adams began compiling historical information while she worked as a bobbin lace weaver. A religious historian, she published her first work, *Alphabetical Compendium of the Various Sects,* as a way to remain economically independent in a time when marriage provided the most direct and certain means of economic survival for women. Adams remained unmarried throughout her life and eventually wrote ten books, the last one published posthumously. She became known as the first woman in the United States who sought to support herself through her writing.

Vicki Ruiz, a third generation Chicana, began her academic training at a community college in Florida and completed her studies at Stanford University. Although she faced discrimination as a Mexican-American girl and woman, Ruiz focused her work on the strengths and struggles, rather than simply the victimization, of working-class Mexican-American women in southern California. Her most recent edited work, *Unequal Sisters: A Multicultural Reader in U.S. Women's History,* has been hailed as the first collection in the field that provides for a more inclusive, multicultural women's history.

Between Hannah Adams and Vicki Ruiz the reader will encounter women historians of diverse backgrounds, motivations, and accomplishments. They became historians because they longed to, and, some felt, because they had to. They produced work that helped them earn a living, secured their niche in the profession, or, perhaps, changed the course of historical writing. Some always loved history; others arrived at history after working in other fields and finding themselves drawn to the questions historians asked, the perspectives historians held. Many of the women, however popular their works were while they were alive, died in obscurity; others have achieved international reputations that will help keep their names and work alive.

The women included here have something to say to the readers and to each other. Women historians will recognize mutual struggles to make legitimate a field of study, obtain higher education against the odds, and break through barriers of gender, race, and ethnicity. Readers will likely appreciate the works of these historians even more once they are familiar with the larger stories of the women's lives. All readers will marvel at the impressive accomplishments of women who have often managed to maintain hobbies and strong family relationships in addition to completing the work to which they are clearly dedicated.

These women have asked a variety of questions about the world around them and their role in it. Many of the earliest women historians, denied access to higher education, struggled to carve out careers pursuing local history, popular history, and biography. More recent historians have carved out new fields of study and demanded new definitions of history and of the historian. This work reveals some of the questions they asked as well as some of the answers they have provided through their work.

These historians often felt the push or pull of family ties, some in positive and others in negative ways. Many received intellectual encouragement from their parents or grandparents. "There was never a moment in our family," Helen Gray Edmonds recalls, "that higher education wasn't stressed." Barbara Engel, Natalie Zemon Davis, and Sucheng Chan remember reading as an important household activity when they were young. Constance McLaughlin Green won the Pulitzer Prize in history in 1963, twenty-seven years after her father had received the same award. Others were less fortunate and felt they escaped their family lives through their studies. When Sharlot Hall was awarded an honorary degree from the University of Arizona, she did not tell her father, believing "he would not understand and would be contemptuous of any institution that thought I had any sense." Economic and personal hardships in Mary Frances Berry's family, combined with the racism she faced from the white community, created what she later called a young life like a "horror story." And Susan Ramirez claims that her father's refusal to allow her to attend college because she was a girl was "the most crucial thing that ever happened to me."

Still other women found that their accomplishments would be overshadowed by those of their historian husbands: Mary Ritter Beard, Mary Flug Handlin, and Elizabeth Schlesinger received little encouragement and few accolades while they lived and wrote. And some of the women were largely without family. Irene Aloha Wright, for example, left Colorado in 1895 at age sixteen to see the world, protected by the money her mother had sewn into her petticoat.

Whatever their personal circumstances, this group of women all became historians. In doing so they made claim to a profession and, for many, a way of life. They were and are award-winning writers and award-winning teachers. The Pulitzer Prize winners include Margaret Antoinette Clapp, Constance McLaughlin Green, Laurel Thatcher Ulrich, Barbara Tuchman, and Ola Elizabeth Winslow. Bernice Johnson Reagon was awarded a MacArthur Foundation "Genius" fellowship, and many of the women were awarded fellowships and grants from the most prestigious granting agencies in the United States. Others have received international awards and international acclaim. Their works have been translated into French, German, Italian, Japanese, Persian, Portuguese, and Spanish, and issued in Braille.

These women were and are dedicated community members as well as respected scholars. Letitia Woods Brown helped train the first group of Peace Corps volunteers, at the University of California, in the 1960s, and Alice Kessler-Harris testified for women plaintiffs in a landmark employment discrimination case pursued by the federal Equal Employment Opportunity Commission. Samella Sanders Lewis founded a gallery dedicated to showcasing the art of young black artists, and Virginia Sanchez Korrol has initiated enrichment and outreach programs to connect her university with the Latino communities of New York City.

Several of these women were "firsts" in some ways. Mary Louise Booth wrote the first comprehensive history of the city of New York, published in 1859. Mary Barnes was the first female faculty member in the history department at Stanford University, appointed in 1892. Louise Phelps Kellogg was the first woman president of the Mississippi Valley Historical Association, now the Organization of American Historians, assuming that post in 1930. In 1932 Merze Tate became the first African-American woman to matriculate at Oxford University; she earned a bachelor's degree there in 1935. Mary Frances Berry assumed the position of chancellor of the University of Maryland in 1976 and became the first black woman to join the ranks of presidents and chancellors at major research universities in the United States.

Whether they were "firsts" or not, however, each of these women provides a compelling and impressive example of the historian at work. Contemporary women historians have followed, often unwittingly, in the footsteps of those who came before them. This work offers them, and all readers, the opportunity to explore women historians' motivations, accomplishments, and, above all, rich legacies. All of the women profiled here, varied as they are by circumstances of birth and by life choices, leave the legacies of hard work, determination, a sense of responsibility to the past and to the future, and the sense that a more accurate history is one which encompasses marginalized as well as privileged characters, women as well as men, writers of as well as actors in history.

ABBREVIATIONS

Alli	Allibone: *A Critical Dictionary of English Literature*
AmAu	*American Authors, 1600–1900*
AmAu&B	*American Authors and Books*
AmBi	*American Biographies*
AmLY	*The American Literary Yearbook*
AmWom	*American Women*
AmWomWr	*American Women Writers*
AmWr	*American Writers*
AnCL	*Anthology of Children's Literature*
ApCAB	*Appleton's Cyclopaedia of American Biography*
ArizL	*Arizona in Literature*
ArtsAmW	*Artists of the American West*
AuBYP	*Authors of Books for Young People*
Au&Wr	*The Author's and Writer's Who's Who*
BbD	*The Bibliophile Dictionary*
BiCAW	*The Biographical Cyclopaedia of American Women*
BiDAmEd	*Biographical Dictionary of American Educators*
BiDAmLL	*Biographical Dictionary of American Labor Leaders*
BiD&SB	*Biographical Dictionary and Synopsis of Books*
BiDrLUS	*A Biographical Directory of Librarians in the United States and Canada*
BiDSA	*Biographical Dictionary of Southern Authors*
BiE&WWA	*The Biographical Encyclopedia and Who's Who of the American Theatre*

BiIn	*Biographical Index*
BkC	*The Book of Catholic Authors*
BlkWrNE	*Black Writers of the Northeast*
CanNov	*Canadian Novelists, 1920–1945*
CarSB	*The Carolyn Sherwin Bailey Historical Collection of Children's Books*
CathA	*Catholic Authors*
CelR	*Celebrity Register*
ChPo	*Childhood in Poetry*
CnDAL	*Concise Dictionary of American Literature*
ConAu	*Contemporary Authors*
ConBlkW	*Contributions of Black Women*
CurBio	*Current Biography*
CyAL	*Cyclopaedia of American Literature*
DcAmAu	*Dictionary of American Authors*
DcAmB	*Dictionary of American Biography*
DcEnL	*Dictionary of English Literature*
DcLB	*Dictionary of Literary Biography*
DcLEL	*A Dictionary of Literature in the English Language*
DcMAH	*Dictionary of Mexican American History*
DcNAA	*A Dictionary of North American Authors*
Drake	Drake: *Dictionary of American Biography*
DrAS	*Directory of American Scholars*
EncAAH	*Encyclopedia of American Agricultural History*
EncBlAu	*Encyclopedia of Black Americans*
EncAB	*Encyclopedia of American Biography*
FemStud	*Feminist Studies*
FilmgC	*The Filmgoers Companion*
ForWC	*Foremost Women in Communications*
GoodHS	*The Good Housekeeping Woman's Almanac*
HarEnUS	*Harper's Encyclopedia of United States History*
HerW	*Her Way*
HsB&A	*The House of Beadle and Adams and Its Dime and Nickel Novels*
IntAu&W	*International Authors and Writers Who's Who*
IntDcWB	*International Dictionary of Women's Biography*
IntWW	*The International Who's Who*

InWom	*Index to Women*
JBA	*The Junior Book of Authors*
LEduc	*Leaders in Education*
LibW	*Liberty's Women*
LinLibL	*The Lincoln Library of Language Arts*
LinLibS	*The Lincoln Library of Social Studies*
McGEWB	*The McGraw-Hill Encyclopedia of World Biography*
MexAmB	*Mexican American Biographies*
MorJA	*More Junior Authors*
NatCAB	*The National Cyclopaedia of American Biography*
NewYT	*New York Times*
NewYTBE	*The New York Times Biographical Edition*
NewYTBS	*The New York Times Biographical Service*
NotAW	*Notable American Women*
NotAW: Mod	*Notable American Women: The Modern Period*
NotBlkAmWom	*Notable Black American Women*
NotHSAW	*Notable Hispanic American Women*
NotNAT	*Notable Names in the American Theatre*
OhA&B	*Ohio Authors and Their Books*
OxAm	*The Oxford Companion to American Literature*
OxCan	*The Oxford Companion to Canadian History and Literature*
OxFilm	*The Oxford Companion to Film*
REn	*The Reader's Encyclopedia*
REnAL	*The Reader's Encyclopedia of American Literature*
REnAW	*The Reader's Encyclopedia of the American West*
ScF&FL	*Science Fiction and Fantasy Literature*
SmATA	*Something About the Author*
Str&VC	*Story and Verse for Children*
TexWr	*Texas Writers of Today*
TwCA	*Twentieth Century Authors*
TwCBDA	*The Twentieth Century Biographical Dictionary of Notable Americans*
WebAB	*Webster's American Biographies*
WhAm	*Who Was Who in America*
WhAmHS	*Who Was Who in America, Historical Volume, 1607–1896*
WhE&EA	*Who Was Who Among English and European Authors*
WhLit	*Who Was Who in Literature*

WhNAA	*Who Was Who Among North American Authors*
Who	*Who's Who*
WhoAm	*Who's Who in America*
WhoAmA	*Who's Who in American Art*
WhoAmJ	*Who's Who in American Jewry*
WhoAmW	*Who's Who of American Women*
WhoE	*Who's Who in the East*
WhoGov	*Who's Who in Government*
WhoPNW	*Who's Who Among Pacific Northwest Authors*
WhoWest	*Who's Who in the West*
WhoWor	*Who's Who in the World*
WhoWorJ	*Who's Who in World Jewry*
WisWr	*Wisconsin Writers*
WomPO	*Women in Public Office*
WomWWA	*Woman's Who's Who of America*
WorAu	*World Authors*
WrDr	*The Writer's Directory*
YABC	*Yesterday's Authors of Books for Children*

A

ABEL, ANNIE HELOISE
(1873–1947)
Native American History

Annie Heloise Abel was born in Fernhurst, Sussex, England, on February 18, 1873, the first daughter and the third of seven children of George and Amelia Anne (Hogban) Abel. The Abels had immigrated to the United States in 1871 and then returned to England. They immigrated again in 1884 and settled in Salina, Kansas, where Annie joined them the following year.

Abel graduated from Salina High School in 1893 and taught for two years before entering the University of Kansas. She received a B.A. degree in 1898, then served for a year as manuscript reader in the English department. She entered graduate school in history, and her thesis, "Indian Reservations in Kansas and the Extinguishment of Their Title," resulted in an M.A. degree in 1900. She continued to research and write on Native American affairs while furthering her education at Cornell University, where she received her Ph.D. in 1905. She was awarded the Justin Winsor Prize in 1906 for her dissertation, "The History of Events Resulting in Indian Consolidation West of the Mississippi," which was published in the Annual Report of the American Historical Association.

In 1905 Abel began teaching history at Wells College. She then taught at the Woman's College of Baltimore (Goucher College) as an instructor, associate professor (1908), and professor and head of the department (1914). She also taught English history at the Teachers College of Johns Hopkins University from 1910 to 1915. She joined the faculty of Smith College in 1915 and served as an associate professor and professor until 1922.

Abel continued to research and write on Native American history while teaching. She published the first volume of *The Slaveholding Indians,* entitled *The American Indian as Slaveholder and Secessionist: An Omitted Chapter in the Diplomatic History of the Southern Confederacy,* in 1915. The second volume,

The American Indian as Participant in the Civil War, was published in 1919, and the third, *The American Indian Under Reconstruction,* in 1925. She also edited *The Official Correspondence of James S. Calhoun While Indian Agent at Santa Fe and Superintendent of Indian Affairs in New Mexico* in 1915 and *A Report from Natchitoches in 1807 by Dr. John Sibley* in 1922.

In addition to her research on Native Americans, Abel also actively researched the development of the British Empire. She received a sabbatical from Smith College in 1921–1922 and went to London, New Zealand, and Australia. While researching in the University of Adelaide library in Australia, she met historian George Cockburn Henderson. She returned to her teaching position at Smith College briefly, then returned to Australia to marry Henderson on October 27, 1922. Unfortunately, Abel-Henderson was described as "disturbed and unhappy" after the marriage, and her husband was hospitalized for insomnia and depression. His mental health declined and he insisted on a divorce.

Abel-Henderson returned to the United States and settled in Aberdeen, Washington, where she was acting professor of history at Sweet Briar College for the school year 1924–25. She spent two winters in Canada studying British policy toward the aborigines and spent another year in England. The result was *A Sidelight on Anglo-American Relations, 1839–1858,* written with Frank J. Klingberg in 1927. She published an edition of the correspondence of Lewis Tappan entitled *Chardon's Journal at Fort Clark, 1834–1839* in 1932, and *Tabeau's Narrative of Loisel's Expedition to the Upper Missouri* in 1939. In between she wrote critical reviews for the *American Historical Review* and the *Mississippi Valley Historical Review.*

Abel-Henderson's personal life was devoted to various causes. She was president of the Maryland branch of the College Equal Suffrage League from 1913 to 1915. She was active in the Washington State Society of Daughters of the British Empire and served as president for two years. Her work during World War II with the British-American War Relief Association in Seattle resulted in a decoration from the British government in September 1946.

Abel-Henderson died of cancer at Aberdeen, Washington, in 1947 after a long illness. Most of her research notes are at Washington State University.

ADDITIONAL SOURCES

AmWomWr; LibW; NotAW; WomWWA 14; DcAmB, Supp. v. 4; *Bio-Base.*

ACOMB, FRANCES DOROTHY
(1907–1984)
French History

Frances Dorothy Acomb was born in Donora, Pennsylvania, on October 15, 1907. She received an A.B. from Wellesley College in 1928, an A.M. from Smith College in 1932, and a Ph.D. from the University of Chicago in 1943. She taught mostly on the high school level until 1936. She then became a research assistant at the University of Chicago, where she worked until 1943.

After receiving her Ph.D., Acomb was an instructor at New York State Teachers College in Albany, New York. She was a historian for the War Department during World War II and then assistant professor and professor at Duke University. She wrote *Anglophobia in France, 1763–1789: An Essay in the History of Constitutionalism and Nationalism* in 1950 and *Mallet du Pan, 1749–1800: A Career in Political Journalism* in 1973. She died in 1984.
ADDITIONAL SOURCES
WhoAmW 58, 61; DrAS 74H, 78H; *Bio-Base.*

ADAMS, HANNAH
(1755–1831)
Religious History

Hannah Adams was born in Medfield, Massachusetts, to Thomas and Elizabeth (Clark) Adams on October 2, 1755. Although she had no formal education, her father was interested in education and read constantly. Hannah suffered from frail health, and he encouraged her, too, to read to make up for her sporadic schooling. When her father's business failed, the family was forced to take in boarders; one taught her Latin and Greek, and another interested her in history by reading from *An Historical Dictionary of All Religions* by Thomas Broughton, an English clergyman. She began compiling her own information about various denominations while working at weaving bobbin lace and tutoring young men preparing for college.

In 1784, in an effort to make more money, she published her manuscript, *Alphabetical Compendium of the Various Sects.* The book went through several editions in both the United States and England, and the author was able to gain some financial stability as well as the title ''the first American woman who sought to support herself by her pen,'' given to her by *Notable American Women.*

In 1791 Adams published *A View of Religions.* In 1799 she published *A Summary History of New-England.* Though this book proved less popular, she was able to recoup her money on a shortened version she wrote for the schools in 1804. Unfortunately, the book resulted in an ongoing controversy between Adams and two other authors on the same topic, the Rev. Jedidiah Morse and the Rev. Elijah Parish. Adams heard that Morse and Parish were working on the same topic, and she wrote to Morse seeking assurance that their work would not interfere with hers. He told her it would not, then later wrote that his collaborator was upset with her plans to publish her history. When several influential friends became involved (James Freeman, minister of King's Chapel, Boston; William S. Shaw, director of the Boston Athenaeum; the Rev. Joseph Stevens Buckminster, owner of a 3,000-volume collection of books), Morse and Parish decided to place the matter before three referees. Meanwhile, as publication was held up, Adams was unable to earn money on the book. The argument was eventually placed before the referees, who decided that Morse had done nothing legally wrong, but that morally he was responsible for Adams's suffering financially and should repay her. He did offer an apology, then made the matter public in 1814 when he published a book outlining the ten-year controversy.

Through annuities given her by her friends, Adams was able to continue her work. In 1804 she published *The Truth and Excellence of the Christian Religion Exhibited,* a compilation of biographical sketches of Christian apologists, followed by *An Abridgement of the History of New-England, for the Use of Young Persons* in 1807. She then wrote *History of the Jews* in 1812 and *A Dictionary of All Religions and Religious Denominations* in 1817. She wrote *Leipzig* in 1819–20, followed by *Letters on the Gospels* in 1824. *A Memoir of Miss Hannah Adams, Written by Herself,* written mainly to raise money for her ailing younger sister, was published posthumously in 1832. Hannah Adams died December 15, 1831, in Brookline, Massachusetts.

ADDITIONAL SOURCES

Manuscript materials in Massachusetts Historical Society, Morse Papers at Yale University, and New York Public Library; AmBi; AmWomWr; BiIn 3, 9; DcAmB; Drake; InWom; LibW; NotAW; TwCBDA; WhAM HS; Alli; AmAu; AmAu&B; AmWom; ApCAB; BbD; BiD&SB; CyAL; DcAmAu; DcEnL; DcNAA; LinLibL; NatCAB 5; OxAm; REn; REnAL; *Bio-Base.*

ALLEN, HOPE EMILY
(1883–1960)
Medieval History

Hope Emily Allen, known as an "independent scholar," was born in Kenwood, Oneida, New York, in 1883. She attended Niagara Falls (Ontario) Collegiate Institute, then graduated with distinction from Bryn Mawr College in 1905 with a B.A. degree. She continued her master's work at Radcliffe College and Newnham College at the University of Cambridge.

Allen's main area of interest was mystical literature of the fourteenth and fifteenth centuries and the writing of Richard Rolle in particular. In 1910 she contributed to a volume of the *Radcliffe Monographs* in which she presented evidence that proved Rolle was not the author of the *Prick of Conscience.* In 1927 she published *Writings Ascribed to Richard Rolle, Hermit of Hampole, and Materials for His Biography* in the third volume of the Monograph Series of the Modern Language Association of America. She was awarded the Rose Mary Crawshay Prize of the British Academy in 1929 for this work. She published *English Writings of Richard Rolle, Hermit of Hampole* in 1931.

Allen was the assistant editor of the *Early Modern English Dictionary* at the University of Michigan from 1933 to 1938. She then became interested in researching the "eccentric fifteenth-century mystic and ardent feminist" Margery Kempe and was responsible for the discovery of an autobiography written more than 500 years ago by Kempe. She and Sanford Meech completed a biography of Kempe in 1940. Allen was awarded an honorary degree by Smith College in 1946 for her "deep appreciation of the spiritual values" of the Middle Ages.

Allen died on July 1, 1960, at Oneida, New York.

ADDITIONAL SOURCES

WhE&EA; BiIn 5, 6; WhAm 4; obituary in *Speculum* 36: 535, July 1961; obituary in NewYT, July 2, 1960, p. 17, *Bio-Base.*

ANDERSON, EVA GREENSLIT
(1889–1972)
Local History

Eva Greenslit Anderson was born on May 20, 1889, in Surprise, Nebraska, to Walter Henry and Catherine (Ammerman) Greenslit. She received a B.A. from Nebraska Wesleyan University in 1910, then moved to Washington State in 1912 to teach high school in Wenatchee. She married Leonard O. Anderson on June 10, 1915. Eva was superintendent of the Douglas County School from 1919 to 1921, then superintendent of Waterville Public Schools. She received an M.A. from the University of Washington in 1926. She was an instructor at the University of Oregon, then returned to Wenatchee High School as girls' advisor. In 1934 she was Washington State Supervisor of Adult Education. Anderson received a Ph.D. at the University of Washington in 1937. She was named Washington's "Woman of Achievement" in 1949. In 1954 she became a member of the Board of Curators of the Washington State Historical Society. Eva Anderson received the Washington State Press Women's Pioneer Writers' Award in 1963. In 1968 the Social Science Building at Wenatchee Valley College was named Anderson Hall.

Anderson became interested in the history of the Pacific Northwest and began writing local history books such as *A Child's Story of Washington* in 1938, *Dog Team Doctor* in 1940, and *Chief Seattle* in 1943. In 1943 she also began to write a series of books with a co-author, Dean Collins. They published *Indian Boy on the Columbia River* and *Pioneer Days in Old Oregon* in 1943, *The Wenatachee Kid* in 1947, and *Stories of Oregon* in 1949 (later revised in 1967 as *Oregon Stories*). Anderson also wrote *The Varied and Colorful Career of Jack Rogers* (1947), *An Orchid for Grandma Little* (1950), *Charley Wright— True Pioneer* (1950), *Rails over the Cascades* (1952), *George Adams, Indian Legislator* (1953), *E. O. Pybus, Ingenious Pioneer* (1954), *Charles Keiser—With a Yen for Work* (1954), *The Spirit of the Big Bend* (1955), *George Adams, Indian Legislator* (1956), and *Dr. Isaac Hubbard—Pioneer Doctor* (1956). Eva Anderson died in 1972.

ADDITIONAL SOURCES

Who's Who in Washington, 1963; WhoWest, 1947–1956; WhoAmW, 1968; *Pacific Northwest Quarterly,* Oct. 1943; *Pacific Northwest Quarterly,* Jan. 1941.

ANTHONY, KATHARINE SUSAN
(1877–?)
Biography

Katharine Susan Anthony was born on November 27, 1877, at Roseville, Arkansas. She was the daughter of Ernest Augustus and Susan Jane (Cathey) Anthony. She attended Peabody College for Teachers in Nashville, Tennessee, from 1895 to 1897 before leaving for the universities of Heidelberg and Freiburg in Germany. She returned to the United States and received a Ph.D. degree in 1905 from the University of Chicago.

Anthony taught in public schools in Arkansas before becoming an English instructor at Wellesley College in 1907–8. She moved to New York City in 1908 and entered a career in social service with the Russell Sage Foundation and other social organizations. She began writing books on social issues, such as *Mothers Who Must Earn* (1914), *Feminism in Germany and Scandinavia* (1916), and *Labor Laws of New York* (1917). In 1920 she began writing biographies, beginning with *Margaret Fuller: A Psychological Biography*. This was followed by *Catherine the Great* (1925), *Queen Elizabeth* (1929), *Marie Antoinette* (1933), and *Louisa May Alcott* (1938). She was also co-author of *Civilization in the United States—An Inquiry by Thirty Americans* (1921). The biographies on Catherine the Great, Marie Antoinette, and Queen Elizabeth were researched in Russia, France, and England, and all received favorable reviews.
ADDITIONAL SOURCES
ConAu 25R; WhE&EA; AmAu&B; BiIn 4, 7; ChPo 52; DcAmB 57; InWom; TwCA; TwCA Supp.; WhAm 4, 5; WhNAA; WomWWA 14; obituary in NewYT, Nov. 22, 1965; *Time,* Dec. 3, 1965; *Antiquarian Bookman,* Dec. 13, 1965; *Bio-Base;* Raven, Susan. *Women of Achievement: Thirty-five Centuries of History.* N.Y.: Harmony Books, 1981, p. 84.

APPLEBY, JOYCE OLDHAM
(1929–   )
History of Modern Political Thought

Joyce Oldham Appleby was born on April 29, 1929, in Omaha, Nebraska, of English, Scotch-Irish, and Norwegian ancestry. She attended public schools in Omaha, Dallas, Kansas City, Evanston, Phoenix, and Pasadena. Her father was in business, her mother a full-time homemaker. Joyce's older sister, she reports, had a great influence on her as a child, "raising a standard of excellence and generally bullying me into caring for intellectual virtues."

Appleby attended Stanford University as an undergraduate student, earning the bachelor's degree in 1950. She worked for *Mademoiselle* magazine, the *Pasadena Star-News,* and in advertising before obtaining her first academic job. Appleby attended the University of Santa Barbara and Clarement Graduate School, earning the master's degree and then the Ph.D. in history in 1959 and 1966. She decided to become a historian because of "a very early, unexamined fascination with the complexity of human beings and their social enactments.'' She loves the coherence, she reports, ''that can sometimes be achieved in reconstructing the past, despite the complexity of causes and influences playing upon events.''

From 1967 to 1981 Appleby taught at San Diego State University, attaining the ranks of professor of history and associate dean of the College of Arts and Letters. In 1981 she took a job as professor of history at the University of California at Los Angeles. She served as department chair from 1987 to 1988, and in 1991 was named Harmsworth Professor of American History at Oxford for the academic year. Appleby continues to teach at UCLA.

Among her most significant achievements, Appleby counts the innovative program she directed for general education requirements in the social sciences and a course she developed, ''Knowledge and Postmodernism in Historical Perspective,'' which graduate students teach to undergraduates. Appleby was also instrumental in getting Congress to appropriate $2 million for sending collections of works on the United States to foreign universities and colleges that have American studies courses but inadequate resources for building libraries.

The author, co-author, or editor of five books and over thirty articles, Appleby is an award-winning writer as well as teacher, having received the Berkshire Prize for her second book, *Economic Thought and Ideology in Seventeenth-Century England.* Her most recent book, *Telling the Truth About History,* has brought Appleby and co-authors Lynn Hunt and Margaret Jacob further scholarly attention. An account of the historical profession's encounters with postmodernism and multiculturalism, *Telling the Truth* looks to a modified reawakening of Enlightenment sensibilities in order to create a history sufficiently far-reaching and inclusive to be a ''true'' accounting.

Former president of the Organization of American Historians, Appleby is also an elected member of the American Philosophical Society and the American Academy of Arts and Sciences. She has served on the editorial boards of numerous journals and other publications, including the *American Historical Review,* the *William and Mary Quarterly,* and the *Journal of American Studies.* Her most recent fellowship was with the Guggenheim Foundation, and she currently serves on the editorial boards of *American National Biography,* the *Journal of Interdisciplinary History, Revue Française d'Etudes Américaines,* and the *Journal of the American Republic.* She also serves on the advisory committees for the Papers of Thomas Jefferson and the Adams Papers.

Now a widow, Joyce Oldham Appleby was married to Andrew Bell Appleby, a historian of modern Europe at San Diego State University. She has three children and two granddaughters. Her principal hobby is gardening, although her interests include politics and literature. She also enjoys her active participation in the Organization of American Historians and the American Historical Association. Appleby, recipient of UCLA's College of Science and Letters Distinguished Professor Award in 1993, lectures widely.

BOOKS BY JOYCE APPLEBY

With Lynn Hunt and Margaret Jacob. *Telling the Truth About History.* New York: W. W. Norton, 1994.

Liberalism and Republicanism in the Historical Imagination. Cambridge, MA: Harvard University Press, 1992.

Capitalism and a New Social Order: The Republican Vision of the 1790s. New York: New York University Press, 1984.

Economic Thought and Ideology in Seventeenth-Century England. Princeton, NJ: Princeton University Press, 1978; Italian translation, 1983.

Editor. *Materials and Morality in the American Past: Themes and Sources, 1600–1800.* Redding, MA: Addison-Wesley, 1974.

ADDITIONAL SOURCES

Hollinger, David. Rev. of *Telling the Truth About History. New York Times Book Review,* March 27, 1994, p. 16.

Questionnaire completed by the subject for *American Women Historians, 1700s–1990s: A Biographical Dictionary.*

ATKINSON, DOROTHY GILLIS
(1929–   )
Russian History

Dorothy Gillis Atkinson was born in Malden, Massachusetts, on August 5, 1929, of Scotch-Italian ancestry. Her mother was a full-time homemaker, her father a labor-union leader. As a child she attended public schools in Massachusetts, New York, and California. The oldest of six children and the only girl, Atkinson was an avid reader who did well in school, as she puts it, "without much effort." At around age eight, she was promised a new bicycle if she earned all A's. "Yes, I was bribed," she states, "and it worked. I learned that extra effort pays off."

Atkinson attended Barnard College, Columbia University, as an undergraduate. She decided as a teenager that her highest values were people and time, and she felt that the study and practice of history fit well with those values. After graduating with a bachelor's degree in 1951, she attended the University of California at Berkeley, earning a master's degree in 1953 and then Stanford University, earning a Ph.D. in 1971.

Professor Atkinson's first academic appointment was at Stanford University, where she was assistant professor of history from 1973 to 1982. From 1984 to 1985, she was visiting associate professor of history at the University of California at Berkeley. From 1983 to 1986, Atkinson was also director of the Stanford Summer Institute for Soviet and East European Studies. In 1981, she was named executive director of the American Association for the Advancement of Slavic Studies, a post she held until her retirement in 1995. Atkinson remains the AAASS representative on the International Council for Central and East European Studies.

Dr. Atkinson has published widely in Russian history. Her work includes *The*

End of the Russian Land Commune, 1905–1930 (1983), and a co-edited work, *Women in Russia* (1977). Critic Roberta Manning, arguing that *The End of the Russian Land Commune* was the first comprehensive account of the commune in the twentieth century, called it "an outstanding work of scholarship that should be read by all serious students of twentieth-century Russia and of agrarian development in general." Dorothy Atkinson has also written approximately fifty articles, book chapters, and reviews. She has been the recipient of many awards, including fellowships from the U.S. Fulbright-Hays Foundation, the Ford Foundation, the Hoover Institution, and the Mellon Foundation. She also received a Faculty Exchange with the USSR Ministry of Higher Education, a Cory Scholarship Award, and a Pulitzer Scholarship.

Her work includes service to the International Council for Central and East European Studies, the American Historical Association, the American Council of Learned Societies, the National Council for Area Studies Associations, and the U.S. Department of State Advisory Committee on Russian, Eurasian, and East European Studies.

Dorothy Atkinson was married to Sterling K. Atkinson from 1950 to 1982, when they divorced. She has two children, a daughter, Kim Leslie Atkinson Fudenberg, and a son, Paul David Atkinson. She also has two "extraordinary" granddaughters, Amy and Keri, her daughter's children. Her hobbies include gardening and travel.

BOOKS BY DOROTHY GILLIS ATKINSON

The End of the Russian Land Commune, 1905–1930. Stanford, CA: Stanford University Press, 1983.

Editor, with Alexander Dallin and Gail Warshofsky Lapidus. *Women in Russia.* Stanford, CA: Stanford University Press, 1977.

ADDITIONAL SOURCES

Manning, Roberta. Rev. of *The End of the Russian Land Commune,* by Dorothy Atkinson. *The Historian,* Vol. 46 (August 1984): 622–623.

Questionnaire completed by the subject for *American Women Historians, 1700s–1990s: A Biographical Dictionary.*

B

BAKER, CHARLOTTE ALICE
(1833–1909)
New England History

Charlotte Baker was born in Springfield, Massachusetts, on April 11, 1833. She was the daughter of Dr. Matthew Bridge and Catharine (Catlin) Baker. The family on her mother's side descended from Rowland Stebbins, one of the founders of Springfield. Because Baker was believed to be a delicate child, she did not attend school regularly until about age eleven, when she entered Misses Stone's School in Greenfield, Massachusetts, and later Deerfield Academy, where she and another young woman were the only females. She eventually became an assistant teacher and in 1856 opened a school in Chicago with life-long friend Susan Minot Lane. The school was discontinued in 1864, when Baker returned to Cambridge to help her mother. She began writing book reviews and newspaper and magazine articles on botany, art, and women's work. She also wrote a series for children, *Pictures from French and English History.* She became interested in white settlers kidnapped by Indians and read a paper entitled "Eunice Williams, the Captive" before the Pocomtock Valley Memorial Association in Deerfield.

In 1897 Charlotte Baker printed a volume of thirteen papers entitled *True Stories of New England Captives Carried to Canada During the Old French and Indian Wars.* During the course of her research she traveled to Canada several times to locate the official records of Montreal and Quebec and to visit villages and Indian missions. She found eighteen Deerfield captives and identified many more whose fate had been unknown. She became known as an expert in New England history and was invited to join the New York, Cambridge, and Montreal Historical Societies. Another historian, Mary Hemenway, asked her to teach early American history to Boston children, and she prepared a series of lectures. Charlotte Baker died in 1909.

ADDITIONAL SOURCES
Alli Supp; BiCAW; DcNAA; OxCan; *Bio-Base.*

BALL, EVE
(1890–1984)
Western U.S. History

Katherine Evelyn Daly Ball was born March 14, 1890, in Clarksdale, Tennessee, to Samuel Richard and Gazelle (Gibbs) Daly. Her mother was the first woman to practice medicine in Kansas, where the family eventually made their home. Eve received a B.S. in education from Kansas State Teachers' College in Pittsburg, Kansas, in 1918, an M.A. in education at Kansas State University in 1934, and an honorary doctorate in the humanities from Artesia College in 1972.

Ball taught most of her life, eventually residing in Ruidoso, New Mexico, where she became interested in the Southwest and Native Americans; she did not begin her historical career until about age sixty. She had amassed an extensive oral history of southwestern pioneers and the Apache Indians at a time when such work was not valued. Ball preferred to concentrate on unknown figures, and her work earned her the Golden Spur Award in 1975 from the Western Writers of America for best nonfiction short story. In 1981 she won the Saddleman's Award for *Indeh, an Apache Odyssey,* a compilation of interviews with some sixty-seven Apaches. In 1982 she was inducted into the Cowgirl Hall of Fame and Western Heritage Center in Hereford, Texas. Eve Ball died at her home in Ruidoso, New Mexico, on December 24, 1984.

ADDITIONAL SOURCES
WhoAmW 81, 83; Kimberly Moore Buchanan, "Eve Ball," in *Historians of the American Frontier: A Bio-Bibliographical Sourcebook,* John R. Wonder (ed.). New York: Greenwood Press, 1988; Lynda A. Sanchez, "Eve Ball," *New Mexico Magazine,* Apr. 1981, p. 33.

BANCROFT, CAROLINE
(1900–1985)
Local History

Caroline Bancroft was born September 11, 1900, in Denver, Colorado, the daughter of George Jarvis Bancroft, a mining engineer, and Ethel (Norton) Bancroft. She received a B.A. from Smith College in 1923 and an M.A. from the University of Denver in 1943. She was literary editor for the *Denver Post* from 1928 to 1933 and writer of its "Literary Flashlights" column. She was also a creative writing instructor at the University of Colorado Extension and the University of Denver Extension from 1931 to 1935. From 1947 to 1951 she taught Colorado history at Randell School in Denver.

Bancroft is most famous for her original work on Colorado history, on which the opera *The Ballad of Baby Doe* and the musical *The Unsinkable Molly Brown* were based. Her works include *Silver Queen: The Fabulous Story of Baby Doe*

Tabor (1950); *Famous Aspen: Its Fabulous Past—Its Lively Present* (1954); *The Brown Place in Denver* (1955); *The Unsinkable Mrs. Brown: S.S. Titantic Heroine* (1956); *Gulch of Gold: A History of Central City* (1958); *Colorful Colorado* (1959); *Tabor's Matchless Mines and Lusty Leadville* (1960); *Unique Ghost Towns and Mountain Spots* (1961); *Colorado's Lost Gold Mine* (with Mary B. Wills, 1965); *The Unsinkable Molly Brown Cookbook* (1966); *Two Burros of Fairplay: Morsels of History for Young and Old* (1968); and *Trail Ridge Country: Estes Park and Grand Lake* (1969). She also wrote a play for the television biographical series of the American Telephone and Telegraph Company, produced by the American Broadcasting Company network in 1956–1957. She wrote articles for the *New York Evening Post, New York Herald Tribune, New York Times, Town and Country, Woman's Home Companion, Western Folklore Quarterly, Colorado Westerner's Brand Book,* and other magazines and newspapers.

Caroline Bancroft died on October 8, 1985.

ADDITIONAL SOURCES

ConAu P-2; WhoAmW 72, 74; *Bio-Base.*

BARNES, MARY DOWNING SHELDON
(1850–1898)
Educational History

Mary Barnes was born at Oswego, New York, on September 15, 1850. Her father was Edward Austin Sheldon, founder of a "ragged school" (schools for the poor first developed in Great Britain in the nineteenth century) in Oswego and a proponent of the educational philosophies of the Swiss educator, Johann Heinrich Pestalozzi. Mary's mother was Frances Anna Bradford (Stiles).

Barnes was educated in public schools and in 1868–69 studied classical and advanced courses at the Oswego Normal and Training School, where her father was principal. She taught at the school for two years before entering the University of Michigan in 1871 as one of the first women students. She had enrolled to study the natural sciences, but together with Lucy Maynard Salmon and Alice Freeman (Palmer), who would also eventually pioneer in history education, she took a course in history with Charles Kendall Adams, a pioneer in the German seminary method of instruction.

Barnes graduated in 1874, then taught history, Latin, Greek, and botany for $1,000 a year at the Oswego Normal School. At this time she began to apply the scientific methods of her science classes to history and later turned down a chance to teach chemistry at Wellesley, instead becoming a history professor at Wellesley in 1876 and perfecting the source method of teaching, using primary sources for critical study instead of textbooks.

Mary Barnes was a lifelong learner. When internal strife at Wellesley and ill health led to her resignation in 1879, she traveled to Europe until 1882 and studied at Newnham College, Cambridge, under John R. Seeley. She returned to Oswego Normal as history instructor and wrote her groundbreaking book, *Studies in General History,* in 1885. In August of that year she married Earl Barnes, a professor of history at Indiana University. The two spent seven years studying, travelling, and writing, with Mary concentrating on a study of historian Andrew Dickson White, recently retired president of Cornell.

In 1891 Earl Barnes accepted a position at the newly founded Stanford University as head of the department of education, and in March 1892 Mary became an assistant professor of history, the first woman to be appointed a member of the faculty. She taught nineteenth-century European history and the history of the Pacific Slope. While there, the Barneses wrote *Studies in American History* (1891), a text for eighth graders, and in 1896 Mary published *Studies in Historical Method.*

In 1897 the Barneses resigned their posts at Stanford and left for Europe, where they studied and traveled for two more years before Mary's organic heart disease took its toll. After weeks of suffering and an unsuccessful operation, she died in London on August 27, 1898.

ADDITIONAL SOURCES

DcAmAu; DcNAA; AmWom; AmWomWr; BiDAmEd; DcAmB; NotAW; WhAmHS; *Bio-Base.*

BARRY, IRIS
(1895–1969)
Film History

Iris Barry was born in Washwood Heath, near Birmingham, England, in 1895 (month unknown). She was the daughter of Alfred Charles Crump, a brass founder, and Annie Crump, a dairy farmer known for her fortune-telling and crystal-gazing. Alfred Crump abandoned the family, but Iris's mother and grandparents managed to send her to convent schools in England and Belgium. Her education ended there because of World War I, although she had passed the qualifying examinations for Oxford in 1911.

Always interested in writing, Barry began corresponding with Ezra Pound in 1916 or 1917, then moved to London and proceeded to socialize with a variety of artists and writers. She had an affair with the author and painter Wyndham Lewis; they had two children who were raised by Barry's mother.

During this time, Iris Barry went to the movies every day and was eventually given the job of reviewing films for theaters controlled by Sidney Bernstein, a businessman also interested in films. In 1923 she became a film reviewer for the *Spectator,* and was the first woman film critic in England. She married the magazine literary editor and poet Alan Porter. In 1925 she founded the London Film Society and changed jobs to become the film critic for the *Daily Mail.*

In 1930 Barry's job and marriage ended, and she immigrated to the United States. She made friends with a variety of influential art patrons, and in 1932 she was hired to begin the library at the Museum of Modern Art. Three years later, she established the Film Library and became its first curator. She traveled to Hollywood and Europe, collecting films, lecturing, teaching, and developing film programs for colleges and museums. In 1938 she translated *The History of Motion Pictures* by Maurice Bardèche and Robert Brasillach, and in 1939 she became the founder and president of the International Federation of Film Archives. In 1940 she wrote *D. W. Griffith, American Film Master.*

In 1941 Barry married John E. "Dick" Abbot, a Wall Street financier and director of the Film Library at the Museum of Modern Art. Barry returned to Europe in 1949, and the two divorced the next year. She was made a Chevalier of the Legion of Honor for her work on behalf of French film, and she eventually settled in Fayence, Var, in the south of France. In 1969, when she was ill, alone, and poor, her American friends came to her aid. She died of cancer in Marseilles in 1969.

ADDITIONAL SOURCES
BiIn 8; FilmgC; OxFilm; NotAW Supp. v. 1; *Bio-Base.*

BEARD, MARY RITTER
(1876–1958)
U.S. Women's History

Mary Ritter Beard was born in Indianapolis, Indiana, on August 5, 1876, to Eli Foster Ritter, a lawyer, and Narcissa (Lockwood) Ritter, a school teacher. At age sixteen Mary attended DePauw University in Asbury, Indiana, where she met her future husband, Charles Austin Beard. She graduated in 1897 and taught high school German in Indiana until her marriage to Beard in 1900. The Beards moved to Oxford, where Mary became involved in the women's suffrage movement and Charles studied history and helped form the workingman's college Ruskin Hall.

The Beards returned to New York in 1902, and Mary enrolled at Columbia University. She failed to graduate but spent the remainder of her life on self-study. While in New York, she continued her work with women's suffrage and the unions, but in 1915 turned to writing and lecturing instead of activism. Her first book was a social study called *Woman's Work in Municipalities,* and her second was historical, *A Short History of The American Labor Movement.* She soon became an expert on the history of women with *On Understanding Women* (1931), *America Through Women's Eyes* (1933), *Women's Humor in America* (1934), and *Women as a Force in History* (1946). She also became well known for a study guide called "A Changing Political Economy as It Affects Women" and a critique in 1942 on the omissions and distortions about women in the *Encyclopaedia Britannica.* In the 1930s she attempted to establish a World Center for Women's Archives to preserve the records of women's lives, but it failed because of lack of funds.

During this time, Beard was also collaborating with her husband on a variety of historical projects, including three textbooks. They wrote *The Rise of Amer-*

ican Civilization in 1927, a series of volumes on American history, as well as *America in Mid-Passage* (1939) and *The American Spirit: A Study of the Idea of Civilization in the United States* (1942).

Throughout her life, Beard faced hostility from male academics as well as professional women, but she continued to lecture and write to combat the hypothesis that history was only the story of men. Mary Beard continued to write into old age, and at age seventy, published *Woman as Force in History.* She outlived her husband by ten years and died of kidney failure in Phoenix, Arizona, in 1958 after a long illness.

ADDITIONAL SOURCES

Ann J. Lane, "Mary Ritter Beard: Woman as Force," in *Feminist Theorists* (Pantheon Books, 1983), pp. 335–347; B. G. Smith, "Seeing Mary Beard," *Fem. Studies* 10: 399–416, Fall 1984; NotAW—Mod. Per.; CurBio 41, 58, 59; BiIn 1, 2, 4, 5; DcAmB 54; DcNAA; InWom; NatCAB 35; WhAm 2; WhoAmW 58; AmAu&B; AmWomWr; DcAmB 56; DcLEL; OxAm; REnAL; TwCA; TwCA Supp.; WhAm 3; WhNAA; WomWWA 14; obituaries: 1959; *American Historical Review* 64: 532, Jan. 1959; CurBio 19: 6, Nov. 1958; CurBio Yrbk 1959: 32, 1960; NewYT, Aug. 15, 1958, p. 20; *Newsweek* 52: 61, Aug. 25, 1958; *Publishers Weekly* 174: 21, Aug. 25, 1958; *Time,* 72: 66, Aug. 25, 1958; *Wilson Library Bulletin* 33: 92, Oct. 1958; papers at the Sophia Smith Collection, Smith College; Archives of De Pauw University and Schlesinger Library in Cambridge, Massachusetts; Arthur and Elizabeth Schlesinger Library on the History of Women in America, Radcliffe College, *The Manuscript Inventories and the Catalogs of the Manuscripts, Books and Pictures,* Vol. 3 (Boston: G. K. Hall, 1973); Mary Ritter Beard, *A Woman Making History; Mary Ritter Beard Through Her Letters,* ed. Nancy F. Cott (New Haven, CT: Yale University Press, 1991).

BEASLEY, DELILAH LEONTIUM
(1867–1934)
African-American History

Delilah Leontium Beasley rose from masseuse to one of the foremost authorities on black history in California. She was believed to have been born around 1867 in Cincinnati, Ohio, to Daniel Beasley, probably a semi-skilled worker, and Margaret (Heines) Beasley. She had a promising beginning as an adolescent, publishing a piece of her writing in the *Cleveland Gazette* when she was twelve and then writing a column called "Mosaics" in the Sunday *Cincinnati Enquirer.* She learned newspaper work at the *Colored Catholic Tribune* while still in her teens. When both her parents died within nine months of each other, she was forced to take a job as a domestic for a judge, then moved to Chicago, where she enjoyed a successful career as a masseuse.

During her spare time, Beasley frequented private libraries, trying to learn all she could about black history. She was particularly interested in the history of blacks in California and moved there in 1910 as a nurse and therapist to a former patient. She began examining all the California newspapers at the Bancroft Library Archives at the University of California at Berkeley from 1848 to the

1890s and all the black newspapers, from the first in 1855 through 1919. Beasley inspected records throughout the state and recorded oral histories. Despite a serious illness, monetary help from friends allowed her to complete her research and publish *The Negro Trail Blazers of California* in 1919.

Beasley began lecturing on black history and wrote seven articles in 1915 for the *Oakland Tribune,* which had protested the stereotypes contained in the movie *The Birth of a Nation.* Through a column, "Activities Among Negroes," she campaigned for black dignity and rights. In addition to her writing, Beasley was involved in campaigning to abolish derogatory terms referring to blacks and organized and supported interracial activities. In 1929 she organized a display for Negro History Week at the Oakland Free Library, and it became a yearly celebration.

Delilah Beasley died of arteriosclerotic heart disease in San Leandro, California, on August 18, 1934.

ADDITIONAL SOURCES

Biln 8; Richard Dillon, *Humbugs and Heroes* (New York: Doubleday, 1970), pp. 32–36; *Bio-Base.*

BENÉT, LAURA
(1884–1979)
Biography

Laura Benét was born on June 13, 1884, at Fort Hamilton, Brooklyn, New York. Her father, James Walker Benét, was an army officer, and her mother was Frances Neill (Rose) Benét. Laura graduated from the Emma Willard School in 1903 and received an A.B. from Vassar College in 1907. She was a social worker in her early career days, working as a settlement worker in New York from 1913 to 1916 and as an inspector for the Red Cross Sanitary Commission during World War I. When her brother, William Rose, a writer, died in the influenza epidemic of 1919, Benét returned home to help her mother with William's three children. She submitted occasional verse and reviews to *Literary Review,* began writing for children, and then graduated to adult biographies. She was also a newspaper editor with the *New York Sun* and later with the *New York Times.* Her first biography was *The Boy Shelley* (1937).

Over the next forty-two years, Laura Benét wrote *Enchanting Jenny Lind* (1939); *Young Edgar Allan Poe* (1941); *Washington Irving* (1944); *Thackeray* (1947); *Coleridge, Poet of Wild Enchantment* (1952); a biographical introduction to *Tales by Edgar Allan Poe* (1952); a biographical introduction to *Thackeray's Henry Esmond* (1952); *Stanley, Invincible Explorer* (1955); and biographies of her famous brothers, William and Stephen Vincent. She also wrote compilations of biographies such as *Famous American Poets* (1950); *Famous American Humorists* (1959); *Famous Poets for Young People* (1964); *Famous English and American Essayists* (1966); *Famous Storytellers for Young People* (1968); and

Famous New England Authors (1970). She wrote her memoirs in *When William Rose, Stephen Vincent, and I Were Young* in 1976.

Laura Benét died on February 17, 1979, in New York.

ADDITIONAL SOURCES

BiIn 2, 8, 9, 10, 11; InWom; WhoAM 74; WhoAmW 58, 61, 64, 66, 68, 70, 72, 74; WhoE 74; AmAu&B; AuBYP; ChPO; ChPO S3; ConAu 9R; JBA 51; LinLibL; REn; REnAL; ScF & FL 1, 2, 3; SmATA; WhE&EA; obituary in ConAu 85–88; *Authors of Books for Young People* (Scarecrow, 1971); obituary in NewYT, Feb. 19, 1979; Kunitz and Haycraft (eds.), *Junior Books of Authors*, 1951; *Bio-Base*.

BERGER, IRIS BROWN
(1941–   )
African History

Iris Brown Berger was born on October 12, 1941, in Chicago, of Eastern European Jewish ancestry. Her mother was an English teacher at Loop Junior College in Chicago; her father was a workers' compensation arbitrator for the Illinois Industrial Commission. Iris attended elementary school at the LeMoyne School and the Eugene Field School in Chicago, then Evanston Township High School. She remembers that her politically active family, especially her parents, encouraged her intellectual pursuits. Berger's mother, who returned to college in the 1960s, was the first returning woman student Berger knew. "Her example prompted me, at the age of 3 or 4," she writes, "to instruct a playmate, 'I'll be the mommy and go to a meeting; you be the daddy and stay home with the baby.' " The old magazines her father brought home, she recalls, contributed unwittingly to her penchant for historical documents. Her father's knowledge of Chicago's changing neighborhoods, which he shared with his young daughter, also contributed to her interest in cultural diversity.

Iris Berger attended the University of Michigan, earning a bachelor's degree with distinction in 1963. At the University of Wisconsin she received a master's degree in African history in 1967 and a Ph.D. in African history/comparative Third World history in 1973. Her interest in history was shaped by spending her junior year of college in France, where, she states, "the legacy of the past seemed ever-present"; by an undergraduate course with Sylvia Thrupp, the only woman role model of her academic career; and by two years of teaching at a girls' high school in Kenya "during the early, hopeful years after independence." Berger was also influenced, during her undergraduate years, by the civil rights movement, the early student movement, and her work on the *Michigan Daily*. "As for many women of my generation," she writes, "involvement in the women's movement led to my research and teaching interests in women's history."

Berger started her teaching career in Kenya, teaching at the Kaaga Elementary School, the Kenya-Israel School of Social Work, and the Machakos Girls' High School. When she returned to the United States she accepted a position as assistant professor at Wellesley College. She taught part-time at Hartwick College and the State University of New York College at Oneonta before accepting a position at the State University of New York at Albany, where she was named visiting assistant professor in 1981, assistant professor in 1984, associate professor in 1989, and professor in 1993. She is currently professor of history, Africana studies and women's studies.

Berger has also acted as an administrator. As director of women's studies from 1981 to 1984, she developed the M.A. Certificate Program in Women and Public Policy, implemented the newly approved minor in women's studies, and collaborated with faculty in designing internship programs. From 1991 to 1995 Berger was director of the Institute for Research on Women (IROW). She was the co-organizer of several conferences and a faculty work group, and the co-founder of Initiatives for Women, a campuswide fund-raising effort to benefit women faculty, students, and staff.

Iris Berger has published three books, one of which she edited with Claire Robertson. Her most recent book is *Threads of Solidarity: Women in South African Industry, 1900–1980.* As reviewer T. Dunbar Moodie argues, Berger contributes substantially to our understanding of women's lives in South African social history by exploring women's relationships to labor unions. She recently edited a special issue of *Signs* on "Postcolonial, Emergent and Indigenous Feminisms." She has also published sixteen scholarly articles, on race, class, and gender issues in African history and historiography.

Aside from her teaching and publications, Berger takes pride in several other accomplishments. She was elected president of the African Studies Association for 1995–1996. She has also provided service to the American Historical Association, the Fulbright Scholars Program, the National Endowment for the Humanities, and the Social Science Research Council. She has received fellowships from many foundations, including the National Endowment for the Humanities, the Rockefeller Foundation, and the Ford Foundation. As director of IROW, Berger co-directed several projects sponsored by the Ford Foundation, including an international conference of scholars and labor activists on "Women in the Global Economy: Making Connections." Berger also regularly provides community service, speaking to community groups about South Africa, past and present.

Iris Brown Berger is married to historian and writer Ronald Mark Berger; they have two daughters, Allison and Anna. She is an "obsessive" swimmer who also enjoys running, hiking, skiing, canoeing, cycling, gardening, and traveling.

BOOKS BY IRIS BERGER

Threads of Solidarity: Women in South African Industry, 1900–1980. Bloomington: Indiana University Press, 1992.

Editor, with Claire Robertson. *Women and Class in Africa.* New York: Holmes and Meier/Africana Publishing Co., 1986.

Religion and Resistance: East African Kingdoms in the Precolonial Period. Tervuren,

Belgium: Musée Royal de l'Afrique Centrale; Butare, Rwanda: Institut National de Recherche Scientifique, 1981.

ADDITIONAL SOURCES

Moodie, T. Dunbar. Rev. of *Threads of Solidarity: Women in South African Industry, 1900–1980,* by Iris Berger. *American Historical Review* 99 (Feb. 1994): 279–280.

Questionnaire completed by the subject for *American Women Historians, 1700s–1990s: A Biographical Dictionary.*

BERRY, MARY FRANCES
(1938–   )
U.S. Constitutional History

Mary Frances Berry was born on February 17, 1938, in Nashville, Tennessee, of African-American ancestry. She is the daughter of Frances Southall Berry and George Ford Berry. The family's economic and personal hardships resulted in the placement of Mary and one of her two siblings, George, in an orphanage for a time. The combination of poverty, cruelty, and racism created for Mary what she would later call a life like a "horror story."

One of Berry's high school teachers, Minerva Hawkins, saw in Berry a "diamond in the rough," and she sought to help the young girl reach her potential. As an African American, Hawkins understood Berry's struggles with racism, and they talked about those struggles and about academic success and planning for the future. As a result of her teacher's encouragement and her mother's faith and hard work, Berry pursued her studies. "You have a responsibility to use your mind," her mother told her, "and to go as far as it will take you." Mary Frances Berry graduated from high school with honors in 1956.

Berry attended Fisk University and then Howard University, earning a bachelor's degree in 1961 and a master's degree in 1962. She credits professors Rayford W. Logan and Merze Tate with teaching her historical methodology and historiography and pushing her toward becoming a scholar. Berry's immediate and then lifelong interest would be the black experience in U.S. history. After finishing at Howard, Berry attended the University of Michigan, earning the Ph.D. in 1966. She went on to become an expert on constitutional history and an internationally recognized public servant and civil and human rights activist.

Berry's first academic appointment was as assistant professor at Central Michigan University. At Central, and then as assistant and associate professor at Eastern Michigan University, Berry also studied for a juris doctor degree at the University of Michigan Law School. She completed her law degree in 1970. Berry took a job as associate professor at the University of Maryland in 1969. While there she served as acting director of Afro-American Studies from 1970 to 1972. From 1972 to 1974 she was director of Afro-American Studies at the University of Colorado at Boulder. In 1973 she was appointed chair and then provost of the Division of Behavioral and Social Sciences at the University of

Maryland, and in 1976 she became chancellor. Berry gained national attention with this appointment; she was the first black woman, and one of only two women, to join the ranks of presidents and chancellors at major research universities in the United States.

From 1980 through 1987 Berry was professor of history and law and senior fellow in the Institute for the Study of Educational Policy at Howard University. In 1987 she was named Geraldine A. Segal Professor of American Social Thought at the University of Pennsylvania.

Berry has served in many governmental as well as academic positions. She was assistant secretary for education in the Department of Health, Education and Welfare from 1977 to 1980, the first black woman appointed to this position. Berry created the Graduate and Professional Opportunities Program, augmenting graduate opportunities for racial minorities and white women. She also advocated for raising the budget substantially for educational programs for the disabled. She served under President Jimmy Carter on the U.S. Commission on Civil Rights. An outspoken advocate for civil rights, Berry was targeted for removal from her position by President Ronald Reagan. She fought the Reagan administration in court, and won. She became known as "the woman the president could not fire." Berry was also an outspoken opponent of apartheid in South Africa and one of the founders of the Free South Africa Movement. As biographer Genna Rae McNeil puts it, "Berry both writes and makes history."

The author of seven major books and dozens of scholarly articles, Berry is known internationally for her contributions to U.S. constitutional and black American history. In *Military Necessity and Civil Rights Policy: Black Citizenship and the Constitution, 1861–1868,* she argues that black Americans have made the greatest gains in civil rights during times of national crises, when their contributions are both valued and recognized. In *Why the ERA Failed,* she explores the political, social, and strategic reasons the amendment for women's equality under the law failed to be passed. In her most recent book, *The Politics of Parenthood: Child Care, Women's Rights, and the Myth of the Good Mother,* Berry reviews the social history of the American family and argues that women cannot achieve personal or economic fulfillment unless child care is a shared responsibility.

Berry's professional academic service includes positions with the Organization of American Historians, the Association for the Study of Afro-American Life and History, and the American Historical Association, for which she served as vice president. She was associate editor of the *Journal of Negro History* and an honorary member of the Coalition of 100 Black Women and Delta Sigma Theta. Berry has received honorary degrees from more than eighteen colleges and universities, including Howard University, Oberlin College, and DePaul University. She has received numerous civil rights awards, including the Rosa Parks Award, Black Achievement Award from *Ebony* magazine, and Woman of the Year Award from *Ms* magazine. One of the most eminent civil and human rights advocates in the United States, Mary Frances Berry is clear about her role: "When it comes to the cause of justice," she stated, "I take no prisoners and I don't believe in compromising."

BOOKS BY MARY FRANCES BERRY

The Politics of Parenthood: Child Care, Women's Rights, and the Myth of the Good Mother. New York: Viking, 1993.

Why the ERA Failed: Women's Rights and the Amending Process of the Constitution. Bloomington: University of Indiana Press, 1986.

With John Blassingame. *Long Memory: The Black Experience in America.* New York: Oxford University Press, 1982.

Editor, with Joseph R. Washington. *Blacks in the Year 2000.* Philadelphia: University of Pennsylvania, 1981.

Stability, Security, and Continuity. Westport, CT: Greenwood Press, 1978.

Military Necessity and Civil Rights Policy: Black Citizenship and the Constitution, 1861–1868. Port Washington, NY: Kennikat Press, 1977.

Black Resistance/White Law: A History of Constitutional Racism in America. New York: Appleton-Century-Crofts, 1971; reprint Penguin, 1994.

ADDITIONAL SOURCES

The Moorland-Spingarn Research Center at Howard University houses Mary Frances Berry's papers.

Lanker, Brian. *I Dream a World.* New York: Stewart, Tabori and Chang, 1989.

McNeil, Genna Rae. "Mary Frances Berry." *Notable Black American Women.* Ed. Jessie Carney Smith. Detroit: Gale Research, 1992, 80–86.

BERRY, SARA S.
(1940–)
African History

Sara Berry was born on March 21, 1940, in Washington, D.C., and attended public and private schools in western Massachusetts and southern California. Her mother worked full time as a homemaker; her father worked as a professor. After receiving a bachelor's degree in history from Radcliffe College in 1961, Berry went on to pursue graduate work in economics, earning a master's degree and then a doctorate in economics from the University of Michigan. But her search for what she calls an "effective academic niche" from which she could pursue interdisciplinary interests led her to the field of history.

Berry started her teaching career in 1967, at Indiana University, as a lecturer, then assistant, then associate professor of economics. She worked as visiting professor at the University of Ife in Nigeria and at Virginia Commonwealth and Boston Universities. In 1978 she accepted a position as associate professor of history and economics at Boston University, a position she held until 1991. While at Boston University Berry served one year as acting associate director of the African Studies Center and spent a year as a Noyes Fellow at Radcliffe College's Bunting Institute. She left Boston University to accept an appointment as professor of history at Johns Hopkins University, a position she held until 1995, when she accepted a position as Melville J. Herskovits Professor of African Affairs at Northwestern University.

Berry's three books and more than thirty-five scholarly articles explore agricultural policy and economic development in Africa. Her most recent book, *No Condition Is Permanent: The Social Dynamics of Agrarian Change in Sub-Saharan Africa,* explores the conflicts that have led to a drop rather than the expected increase in per-capita food production in Africa. Reviewer Leroy Vail argued that if Berry's book "is received as it deserves to be, it will serve as a signal blow against the ever-present tendency to deny to Africans historical change and to posit for them a blind adherence, close to irrationality, to unchanging customs." Sara Berry's second book, *Fathers Work for Their Sons: Accumulation, Mobility and Class Formation in an Extended Yoruba Community,* won her the Herskovits Award from the African Studies Association for the best book on Africa published in 1985.

Berry has also contributed a great deal to her field through her consulting activities, which include serving as consultant to the Rockefeller Foundation, first to evaluate applications for a program of fellowships entitled Exploring the Long-term Implications of Changing Gender Roles, and then to review the state of the art on socioeconomics of cassava cultivation in Africa. Berry was commissioned to write review papers on agricultural change in Africa for the Joint Committee on African Studies, the U.S. Agency for International Development, and the Ford-Rockefeller Foundation. She has also received fellowships or awards from the Fulbright Senior Scholars Program, the Social Science Research Council, the Guggenheim Foundation, and the Mary Ingraham Bunting Institute at Radcliffe College. Her professional service includes serving on review panels for the Ford Foundation, the Woodrow Wilson Center, the National Endowment for the Humanities, and the Herskovits Book Awards Committee. In keeping with her interdisciplinary approach to her work, Berry has supervised over forty Ph.D. theses in history, economics, anthropology, political science, and sociology.

BOOKS BY SARA S. BERRY

No Condition Is Permanent: The Social Dynamics of Agrarian Change in Sub-Saharan Africa. Madison: University of Wisconsin Press, 1993.

Fathers Work for Their Sons: Accumulation, Mobility and Class Formation in an Extended Yoruba Community. Berkeley: University of California Press, 1985.

Cocoa, Custom and Socioeconomic Change in Rural Western Nigeria. Oxford: Clarendon Press, 1975.

ADDITIONAL SOURCES

Questionnaire completed by the subject for *American Women Historians, 1700s–1990s: A Biographical Dictionary.*

Vail, Leroy. Rev. of *No Condition Is Permanent."* *American Historical Review* 100, no. 1 (Feb. 1995): 201.

BIEBER, MARGARETE
(1879–1978)
Art History

Margarete Bieber, a leading authority on Greek and Roman art, was born July 31, 1879, in Schoenau, West Prussia (now Preshowo, Poland). Her father was

Jacob Bieber, an industrialist, and her mother was Vally (Bukofer) Bieber. Margarete attended Berlin University from 1901 to 1904 and received a Ph.D. from Bonn University in 1907. She became an assistant at the German Archaeological Institute in Athens, Greece, in 1910 before returning to Germany in 1913, where she worked in various museums and taught in various universities until she fled to England to escape Hitler's regime.

Bieber was an honorary fellow at Somerville College at Oxford, England, for the 1933–34 school year and then traveled to the United States to become a lecturer at Barnard College in New York from 1934 to 1936. From 1936 to 1948 she was associate professor of fine arts and archaeology at Columbia University in New York. She continued as a member of the department of art at Princeton University in New Jersey from 1949 to 1951 and at the Institute of General Studies at Columbia University from 1948 to 1956. She was involved in Associate University Seminars for the department of classical civilization from 1960 to 1974.

Bieber's first publications for American markets were *The History of the Greek and Roman Theatre* (1939) and *Laocoon: The Influence of the Group Since Its Rediscovery* (1942). She edited *German Readings in the History and Theory of Fine Arts* in 1946; it was later published as *A Short Survey of Greek and Roman Art for Students of German and Fine Arts* in 1958. She wrote *The Sculpture of the Hellenistic Age* in 1955; *A Bronze Statuette in Cincinnati and Its Place in the History of the Asklepios Type* in 1957, and *Roman Men in Greek Himation* in 1959. She also published *The Copies of the Herculaneum Women* in 1962. Bieber wrote *The Greek and Roman Portraits of Alexander the Great* in 1964, and *Graeco-Roman Copies* in 1975. *The History of Greek, Etruscan and Roman Clothing* was published that same year, and her last book, *A Contribution to the History of Graeco-Roman Sculpture,* was published when she was ninety-six years old. Margarete Bieber died two years later, on February 23, 1978.

ADDITIONAL SOURCES
IntWW 79; BiE & WWA; ConAu 17R; DrAS 74H; IntAu&W 76, 77; IntWW 74, 75, 76, 77, 78; NotNAT; BiIn 10, 11; ConAu 77; WhoAmA 78N, 80N; NewYTBE 71; obituary in NewYTBS 9: 155, Feb. 1978; "Award for Distinguished Archaeological Achievement," *Archaeology* 28: 74–75, Apr. 1975; *Bio-Base.*

BLACK, MARY CHILDS
(1922–1992)
Art History

Mary Childs Black was born in Pittsfield, Massachusetts, on April 7, 1922, to George and Isabelle (Merrill) Childs. She received a B.A. from the University of North Carolina in 1943 and served in the U.S. Navy Women's Reserve (WAVES) from 1943 to 1946 as a lieutenant junior grade. She married Richard Winthrop Black on April 7, 1947. In 1951 she received an M.A. from George Washington University.

From 1956 to 1957 Black was a research assistant at Colonial Williamsburg, Williamsburg, Virginia. She was registrar for the Abby Aldrich Rockefeller Folk Art Collection at Williamsburg from 1957 to 1958, curator from 1958 to 1960, and director and curator from 1960 to 1963. She was director of the Museum of American Folk Art from 1964 until 1969, when she became curator of painting, sculpture, and decorative arts for the New-York Historical Society in New York City. She was divorced in 1970 and remained with the Historical Society until 1982, when she was suddenly dismissed by James B. Bell, the director. Black filed a complaint with federal and state agencies for sex and age discrimination, and the society settled out of court. She was awarded back pay and vacation, plus a full pension.

During these years, Mary Childs Black completed several books. She wrote *American Folk Paintings* with Jean Lipman in 1966. She identified portraits attributed to four different unidentified painters as the work of one man, Ammi Phillips, an itinerant artist, and wrote *Ammi Phillips* with Barbara and Lawrence Holdridge, folk art collectors, in 1969. She wrote *What Is American in American Art* in 1971 and *Old New York in Early Photographs* in 1973. In 1984 she wrote *New York City's Gracie Mansion: A History of The Mayor's House* for the Gracie Mansion Conservancy. In addition, Black worked on a number of publications for the New-York Historical Society on various topics, including Edward Hicks, Erastus Salisbury Field, aspects of Jewish life in New York, Dutch paintings, advertising posters, Federal furniture and decorative arts, and Belmont Park.

Mary Childs Black died of cancer in Germantown, New York, at age sixty-nine. At the time of her death, she was working on an exhibition of Colonial American painters for the New-York Historical Society.

ADDITIONAL SOURCES

Obituary in NewYT, Feb. 29, 1992, p. 30; obituary in NewYTBS 23: 240, Feb. 1992; obituary in *Art America* 80: 158, May 1992; obituary in *Art News*, 91: 271, May 1992; obituary in *Clarion* 17: 62–63, Summer 1992; WhoAmA 76, 78, 80; ConAu 21R; WomPO 78; WhoAm 80; WhoAmW 70, 72, 74, 77; *Bio-Base*.

BLUM, STELLA
(1916–1985)
Curator, Fashion History

Stella Blum was born in Schenectady, New York, on October 19, 1916, to Joseph Biercuk, a machinist, and Mary (Kiskiel) Biercuk. She graduated from Syracuse University in 1938 with a B.F.A., then attended New York University, Queens College (now City University of New York), and the New York Institute of Fine Arts. She married George A. Blum, a travel agent, in 1939. In 1940 she was on the staff of the Museum of Costume Art in New York. Blum left in 1942 to raise two sons, then returned in 1953. (The Museum of Costume Art had been renamed the Costume Institute and had become part of the Metropolitan Museum.) Blum was assistant curator at the museum from 1953 to 1970, associate curator from 1970 to 1972, and curator of costumes for the Costume Institute from 1970 to 1973.

Blum published *Victorian Fashion Costumes as Seen in Harper's Bazaar 1867–98* in 1974; *Designs by Erté* in 1976. She edited and wrote the introduction to *Ackermann's Costume Plates: Women's Fashions in England, 1818–1828* by Rudolph Ackermann in 1978. She also wrote *Everyday Fashions of the Twenties as Pictured in Sears and Other Catalogues, 1919–31* in 1982 and *Everyday Fashions of the Thirties as Pictured in Sears and Other Catalogues, 1919–31,* which was published posthumously in 1986. She began cataloguing exhibitions in Australia, Switzerland, and Japan and was guest curator for the Detroit Institute of Arts, Flint Institute of Arts, Portland Museum of Art, and St. Louis Museum. She left the Metropolitan Museum to open a new center for the decorative arts and costumes at Kent State University in Ohio from 1983 to 1985. Stella Blum died of cancer in Ravenna, Ohio, on July 31, 1985.

ADDITIONAL SOURCES

ConAu 97; *Bio-Base.*

BOLTON, SARAH KNOWLES
(1841–1916)
Popular History

Sarah Knowles Bolton was born in Farmington, Connecticut, on September 15, 1841, daughter of John Segar and Elizabeth Mary (Miller) Knowles and descendant of Joseph Jenckes, governor of Rhode Island from 1727 to 1732, and Col. John Ally, a historian of the Pequot War. Her father died when she was eleven, and she and her mother went to live with an uncle, Samuel Miller, and later another uncle, Col. H. L. Miller, a Hartford lawyer.

Sarah was considered a precocious and gifted child; she published a poem at age fifteen. She graduated from Catharine Beecher's Hartford Female Seminary in 1860 and taught in Natchez, Mississippi, until the outbreak of the Civil War, when she returned to Connecticut and taught in Meriden.

On October 16, 1866, Sarah married Charles E. Bolton and moved to Cleveland, where she became active in the temperance movement and humanitarian reforms. She wrote a book for the cause, *The Present Problem*, in 1874. From 1878 to 1881 she was on the editorial staff of the Boston *Congregationalist,* then traveled for two years in Europe studying higher education and better working conditions for women. Upon her return Bolton became secretary of the Woman's Christian Association and assistant corresponding secretary to Frances E. Willard in the Woman's Christian Union.

In addition to her activities in political movements, Sarah Bolton wrote fiction and poetry, and in 1885 began a series of successful, popular biographies with inspirational titles such as *Lives of Poor Boys Who Became Famous* (1885), *Lives of Girls Who Became Famous* (1886), *Famous American Authors* (1887),

Famous American Statesmen (1888), *Successful Women* (1888), *Famous Men of Science* (1889), *Famous English Authors of the Nineteenth Century* (1890), *Famous English Statesmen of Queen Victoria's Reign* (1891), *Famous Types of Womanhood* (1892), *Famous Voyagers and Explorers* (1893), *Famous Leaders Among Men* (1894), *Famous Leaders Among Women* (1895), and *Famous Givers and Their Gifts* (1896). She also published a biography of Ralph Waldo Emerson in 1904.

Bolton died on February 1, 1916.

ADDITIONAL SOURCES

Sarah K. Bolton: Pages from an Intimate Autobiography, Edited by Her Son (Boston, 1928); C. K. Bolton, *The Boltons in Old and New England;* ApCAB; Alli Supp.; AmAu; AmAu 7; AmBi; AmWom; AmWomWr; BbD; Biln 7 SB; CarSB; ChPo; ChPo S1 & S2; DcAmAu; DcAmB; DcNAA; NatCAB; OhA&B; TwCBDA; WhAM 1; WomWWA 14; *Bio-Base.*

BOOTH, MARY LOUISE
(1831–1889)
Popular History

Mary Louise Booth was born on April 19, 1831, in Millville (later Yaphank), Long Island, New York, to William Chatfield Booth, descendant of John, who in 1652 took title to Shelter Island, off Long Island, and Nancy (Monsell) Booth, granddaughter of a French Revolutionary emigrant. Mary Louise was largely self-taught but was considered to be very precocious; she was said to have read the Bible and Plutarch at five and Racine at seven. Around 1845–46, she taught in the Third District School in Williamsburgh, where her father was principal. At age eighteen she moved to Manhattan, where she sewed vests during the day and studied and wrote at night. She published without pay until she became a piece-rate reporter for the *New York Times,* writing on education and women's topics. She became friends with Susan B. Anthony and joined the women's rights movement, serving as secretary at the conventions in Saratoga, New York, in 1855 and New York City in 1860.

Booth was especially gifted in translating French, and her first publication, *Marble-Workers' Manual* (1856), led to her translating nearly forty volumes of literary and historical works. During this time, she also began her own historical writing. Her *History of the City of New York* (1859) was the first comprehensive history of the city to be published. The one large volume was so well received that the publisher proposed she go abroad and write popular histories of the great European capitals—London, Paris, Berlin, and Vienna. War intervened, however. A second edition of the New York history was published in 1867, and a third in 1880. A large paper edition was extended and illustrated with supplementary interleaved pages. One copy was enlarged to folio and extended into nine volumes by several thousand maps, letters, and other illustrations.

During the Civil War, Booth used her translating abilities to aid the North. She received an advance copy of a French work by Count Agenor de Gasparin, *The Uprising of a Great People: The United States in 1861,* and, convinced that it would boost the morale of people in the North, talked New York publisher Charles Scribner into publishing an American edition. He agreed only if she could translate the book in one week in case the war ended suddenly. She worked twenty hours a day to complete the work, and during the next two years of the war she continued translating French works on American subjects, for which she received praise from President Lincoln and Charles Sumner.

After the war, Booth continued to produce translations, including one of Henri Martin's *History of France.* In 1867 she became editor of *Harper's Bazaar,* a position she held until her death from heart problems on March 5, 1889.

ADDITIONAL SOURCES

Harriet Prescott Spofford, "Mary Louise Booth," in *Our Famous Women: An Authorized Record of the Lives and Deeds of Distinguished Women of Our Times* (Freeport, NY: Books for Libraries Press, 1883); *Bio-Base;* AmBi; AmWom; AmWomWr; ApCAB; BiIn 4; DcAmAu; DcAmB; Drake; HarEnUS; InWom; LibW; NatCAB 7; NotAW; TwCBDA; WhAmHS; Alli Supp.; AmAu&B; BlD&SB; CyAL 2; DcNAA.

BORG, DOROTHY
(1902–1993)
East Asian History

Dorothy Borg was born on September 4, 1902, in Elberon, New Jersey, to Sidney C., a banker, and Madeleine (Beer) Borg. She graduated from Wellesley College in 1923 and obtained a master's degree in 1931 and a doctorate in 1946 at Columbia University. She became a researcher at Harvard University, and during the 1960s she helped organize programs that trained scholars in American and East Asian history. Borg spent two years in Beijing and Shanghai as a staff member of the American Council of the Institute of Pacific Relations. The institute was targeted by Senator Joseph R. McCarthy to find out "who lost China" to the Communists, and Borg helped defend Owen Lattimore, a fellow historian, against the senator's attacks.

In 1965 Dorothy Borg published *United States and the Far Eastern Crisis of 1933–1938* and was awarded the Bancroft Prize in American History by Columbia. From 1966 until her retirement, she was senior research associate at Columbia's East Asian Institute. In 1973 she published *Pearl Harbor as History: Japanese-American Relations 1931–1941,* followed by *Uncertain Years: Chinese American Relations, 1947–1950,* co-authored with Waldo Henrichs. Dorothy Borg was ninety-one years old when she died on October 21, 1993.

ADDITIONAL SOURCES

AmWomWr; ConAu 21R; DrAS 74H, 78H; WhoAm 74, 76, 78, 80; WhoAmW 68, 70, 72, 74, 77, 79; *Bio-Base;* NewYTBS.

BOWEN, CATHARINE SHOBER DRINKER
(1897–1973)
Biography

Catharine Shober Drinker Bowen was born on the Haverford (Pennsylvania) College campus on January 1, 1897, to Henry Sturgis and Aimee Ernesta

(Beaux) Drinker. The Drinker family motto was "Excellence is the starting point," and among Catharine's five siblings were a lawyer (Harry), the inventor of the iron lung (Philip), and a dean of the Harvard School of Public Health (Cecil). Her aunt, Cecilia Beaux, was a well-known portrait painter.

Catharine's father, general solicitor of the Lehigh Valley Railroad, was named president of Lehigh University in 1905, at which time the family moved to Bethlehem, Pennsylvania. Catharine was sent to Miss Kellogg's dame school and then to Moravian Academy and St. Timothy's School in Catonsville, Maryland. Although her formal education was sporadic because she traveled with her family, she trained for a career as a violinist at the Peabody Conservatory in Baltimore and the Institute of Musical Art (later Juilliard) in New York.

In 1919 Catharine married Ezra Bowen, an associate professor of economics at Lehigh University. The next year the couple moved to Easton, Pennsylvania, when Ezra became head of the economics department at Lafayette College. Catharine began her writing career by winning ten dollars in an *Easton Express* contest. She sold stories and wrote a daily column for the *Express* before writing *A History of Lehigh University.*

The Bowens were divorced in 1936. Catharine's one novel, *Rufus Storbuch's Wife* (1932), was a (probably semi-autobiographical) account of two talented people living together. In 1935 her career took a turn that was to make her famous. She published a book of essays on music and amateur musicians, *Friends and Fiddlers.* This led to *"Beloved Friend": The Story of Tchaikowsky and Nadejda Von Meck* (1937) and *Free Artist: The Story of Anton and Nicholas Rubinstein* (1939). In 1939 she married Thomas McKean Downs, a surgeon.

In 1944 Catharine Bowen's interests concentrated on men who had formed and interpreted the constitutional government of the United States. Her first book in this series was *Yankee from Olympus: Justice Holmes and His Family.* Holmes's literary executors refused Bowen permission to read unpublished material, but the book was well received. She was also refused access to unpublished material for *John Adams and the American Revolution* (1950) and was criticized for writing "fictionalized biography."

After *John Adams,* Catharine decided to trace the foundations of U.S. constitutional government in seventeenth- and eighteenth-century England with a biography of Edward Coke. She continued to meet with resistance while researching at Cambridge but completed *The Lion and the Throne: The Life and Times of Sir Edward Coke, 1552–1634* (1957). She received the Phillips Prize from the American Philosophical Society for "the best essay . . . on the science and philosophy of jurisprudence" and was offered membership in the society. In 1958 she won the National Book Award.

The Coke biography was followed by *Francis Bacon: The Temper of a Man* (1963); a biography of the Bowen family, *Family Portrait* (1970); and *The Most Dangerous Man in America: Scenes from the Life of Benjamin Franklin* (1974), published after her death from cancer on November 1, 1973. Catharine Bowen also wrote a series of essays on the craft of biographical writing, published in

The Writing of Biography (1951), *Adventures of a Biographer* (1959), and *Biography: The Craft and Calling* (1969).
ADDITIONAL SOURCES
Bio-Base; BiIn 2, 4, 5, 6, 8, 10; CurBio 44; NewYTBE 73; Who 74; WhoAm 74; WhE&EA; WhoAmW 58, 64, 66, 68, 70, 72, 74; WhoGov 72; WhoWor 74; AmAu&B; AmWomWr; ConAu 5R; ConAu 44; CurBio 73N; LinLibL 2; OxAm; REn; REnAL; SmATA 7; TwCA Supp.; WhAm 6; InWom.

BRODIE, FAWN (McKAY)
(1915–1981)
Biography

Fawn Brodie was born September 15, 1915, in Ogden, Utah, the daughter of Thomas E. and Fawn (Brimhall) McKay. Her uncle, David O. McKay, was president of the Church of Jesus Christ of Latter-Day Saints in the fifties and sixties, and her maternal grandfather, George H. Brimhall, was once president of Brigham Young University. Fawn graduated from Weber College (then a junior college) at age fourteen and from the University of Utah at age eighteen. She returned to Weber College and taught for a year (1934–35) before travelling east to pursue graduate work at the University of Chicago, where she received an M.A. in English in 1935 at age twenty. That same year she married Bernard Brodie, a fellow student who eventually became a professor of political science.

In 1945 Brodie published a biography of Joseph Smith, founder of the Mormon Church, entitled *No Man Knows My History.* While the book received wide praise from the public, Brodie was condemned by some Mormons who believed it undermined the Mormon religion. She received hate mail from the public, and her family urged her to "repent." She was criticized for not using manuscript materials available in the church historian's office; she later explained that she did not want to involve her uncle in any controversy. She was also criticized for using fictional techniques similar to those used by Catharine Drinker Bowen. Brodie requested and was granted excommunication by the Mormon Church in May 1946.

In 1959 Fawn Brodie wrote *Thaddeus Stevens, Scourge of the South,* which won the medal in history from the Commonwealth Club of California in 1960. In 1962 she published *From Cross-Bow to H-Bomb.* In 1967 she wrote *The Devil Drives: A Life of Sir Richard Burton.* The same year she became a member of the history department of the University of California at Los Angeles, where she remained until 1976. In 1974 she wrote *Thomas Jefferson: An Intimate History,* which, like her Joseph Smith book, was controversial. In it, she wrote that an intimate relationship existed between Jefferson and one of his slaves, Sally Hemings. Fawn Brodie's last biography, *Richard Nixon: The Shaping of His Character,* was published in 1981 as she was dying of cancer.
ADDITIONAL SOURCES
Newell G. Bringhurst, "Fawn Brodie and Her Quest for Independence," *Dialogue* 22 (Summer 1989); Newell G. Bringhurst, "Applause, Attack and Ambivalence—Varied

Responses to Fawn M. Brodie's *No Man Knows My History,*" *Utah Historical Quarterly*
57 (Winter 1989); John Phillip Walker, ed., *Dale Morgan on Early Mormonism: Correspondence and a New History* (1986); Newell G. Bringhurst, "Fawn M. Brodie—Her
Biographies as Autobiography," *Pacific Historical Review* (Summer 1990); Newell G.
Bringhurst, "Fawn Brodie," in *Utah History Encyclopedia,* ed. Allan Kent Powell;
ConAu 17R; WhoAm 80; *Bio-Base.*

BROOKS, JUANITA LEAVITT
(1898–?)
Biography

Juanita Leavitt Brooks was born on January 15, 1898, in Bunkerville, Nevada,
to Henry and Mary Ann Hafen Leavitt. She attended one year of normal school
before becoming a teacher at age nineteen. She was married to Leonard Ernest
Pulsipher for sixteen months before he died in 1922 of cancer of the lymphatic
system, leaving her to care for one young son. She completed her education at
Dixie College in St. George, Utah, and Brigham Young University, and received
a master's degree in English at Columbia. She became an English teacher and
dean of women at Dixie College. In 1933 she married county sheriff William
Brooks; between them they had nine children. Despite her busy life, Brooks
began a diary-collecting project for the Works Project Administration (WPA) in
the 1930s; the typescripts from this project were eventually deposited in the
Library of Congress.

In 1941 Juanita Brooks completed a biography of her grandfather, Dudley
Leavitt. In 1944 she published *Indian Relations on the Mormon Frontier.* She
became a field fellow for the Henry E. Huntington Library in San Marino,
California. For five years she poured over diaries donated to the library and
received a Rockefeller Foundation grant to research the Mountain Meadows
Masacre, resulting in a book by the same name in 1950. She and Robert Cleland
began editing the diaries of John D. Lee, resulting in *A Mormon Chronicle: The
Diaries of John D. Lee.* In 1961 Brooks edited *On the Mormon Frontier: The
Diary of Hosea Stout,* and in 1970 she wrote a biography of her husband entitled
Uncle Will Tells His Story.

Like Fawn Brodie, Juanita Brooks was often controversial, and was forced to
defend her work. She was especially criticized for writing about the Mountain
Meadows Massacre, which some felt showed the Morman Church in a bad light.
She was blacklisted from church periodicals, and she and her husband were left
out of certain church activities. Despite this, she was a member of the Utah
Board of State History and was given the distinguished service award from the
Utah Academy of Sciences, Arts and Letters. She was also awarded honorary
degrees from Utah State University and the University of Utah. Juanita Leavitt
Brooks was placed in a nursing home in 1988; the date of her death is uncertain.

ADDITIONAL SOURCES

Levi S. Peterson, *Juanita Brooks: Mormon Woman Historian* (Salt Lake City: University
of Utah Press, 1988); Levi S. Peterson, "Juanita Brooks," in *Utah History Encyclopedia,*

ed. Allan Kent Powell; WomPO 76, 78; REnAW; WhoAmW 61, 68; ConAu 114; BiIn 16; Davis Bitton and Leonard J. Arrington, *Mormons and Their Historians* (Salt Lake City: University of Utah Press, 1988); *Bio-Base.*

BROWN, ANNE SEDDON KINSOLVING
(1906–1985)
Military History

Anne S. K. Brown, one of the few women military historians, was born March 25, 1906, in Brooklyn, New York, to Arthur B. Kinsolving, a clergyman and Sally (Bruce) Kinsolving. She attended Bryn Mawr School in Baltimore, Maryland, and graduated in 1924. From 1925 until 1930, when she married John Nicholas Brown, Anne was a feature writer, columnist, and music critic. After her marriage she continued her interest in music, serving on several boards and acting as program chair. As her interest in military history developed, she began serving on boards such as the national board of the U.S. Navy Relief Society (1946–1949), the advisory board for Fort Ticonderoga (1959–1963), and the advisory board of the U.S. Army Military History Research Collection (1970–1985).

Brown was a co-founder of the Company of Military Collectors and Historians in 1949 and also belonged to the American Military Institute, National Society of Colonial Dames of America, Society for Army Historical Research, and several foreign societies. For her work in these and other organizations she received the L.H.D. from Brown University in 1962; the Rhode Island Governor's Award for Excellence in the Arts in 1969; the Chinard Prize in 1972 for the leading publication in the Franco-American field; the Award of Merit; the American Association for State and Local History in 1973, and the National Daughters of the American Revolution Medal of Honor in 1973. That same year, she was awarded a Certificate of Merit from the State of Rhode Island Bicentennial Commission.

Brown published several books in her field, including *The Anatomy of Glory: Napoleon and His Guard* (with Henry Lachouque, 1961) and *The American Campaigns of Rochambeau's Army: 1780–1783,* (1972). She was a compiler, with R. G. Thurburn, of the *Index to British Military Costume Prints, 1500–1914* in 1972 and a contributor to many military and historical journals. Anne S. K. Brown died in 1985.

ADDITIONAL SOURCES

ConAu 17R; IntAu& W 77; WhoAmW 61, 64, 66, 68, 70, 72, 74, 77; WhoE 74; *Bio-Base.*

BROWN, LETITIA WOODS
(1915–1976)
African-American History

The only full-time black faculty member at George Washington University from 1971 to 1976, Letitia Woods Brown was born on October 24, 1915, in Tuskegee,

Alabama, to Mathew and Evadne (Adam) Woods, both members of the Tuskegee Institute (now University). She obtained a bachelor's degree from Tuskegee in 1935, a master's degree from Ohio State University in 1937, and a Ph.D. from Harvard University in 1966.

From 1935 to 1936 Brown was a teacher in Macon County, Alabama. She then became an instructor in history at Tuskegee Institute from 1937 to 1940. From 1940 to 1945 she was a tutor at LeMoyne-Owen College in Memphis, Tennessee. She married Theodore E. Brown, an economist with the State Department, in 1947. In 1968 she was senior Fulbright lecturer at Monash University and Australia National University. Brown was also a consultant to the Federal Executive Institute from 1971 to 1973.

While professor of history and American civilization at George Washington University in Washington, D.C., from 1971 until her death in 1976, Letitia Woods Brown helped preserve historical sites of the black community as a member of the Committee on Landmarks of the National Capital. She also wrote several books on the capital. In 1971 she wrote *Washington from Banneker to Douglass, 1791–1870* with Elsie M. Lewis. The next year she wrote *Washington in the New Era, 1870–1970*, also with Lewis, and *Free Negroes in the District of Columbia, 1790–1846*, with Richard Wade. Letitia Woods Brown died of cancer on August 3, 1976, in Washington, D.C.

ADDITIONAL SOURCES

Encyc Black Am; NotBlkAmWom; DrAS 74H; ConAu 69–73; *Bio-Base; Contributions of Black Women to America.* Vol. 2. Ed., Marianna W. Davis (Columbia, SC: Kenday Press, 1981).

BROWN, LOUISE FARGO
(1878–1955)
British History

Louise Fargo Brown was born in Buffalo, New York, in 1878 to Albert Tower and Eva Perry (Fargo) Brown. She received a B.A. degree from Cornell University in 1903 and entered the graduate school there in 1905. She was twice awarded the Andrew White Traveling Fellowship, which enabled her to study in London, Oxford, Basel, Zurich, and Geneva. The results of her research during those years were published in the *English Historical Review*. She received a Ph.D. from Cornell in 1909.

Except for one spring semester at Vassar in 1905, Brown was an instructor in history at Wellesley from 1909 to 1915. In 1911 she published *The Political Activities of the Baptists and Fifth Monarchy Men in England During the Interregnum*, which received the Herbert Baxter Adams Prize from the American Historical Association for the best monograph of the year in modern European history.

From 1915 to 1917 Louise Brown was dean of women and professor of history at the University of Nevada. When the United States entered World War

I in 1917, she became a sergeant in the Marine Corps and did research on the corps. In 1919 she returned to Vassar, where she taught until her retirement in 1944. During this time, Brown published *The First Earl of Shaftesbury* (1933) for the American Historical Association and wrote *Apostle of Democracy: The Life of Lucy Maynard Salmon* in 1943. She was a fellow of the Royal Historical Society, and in 1930 was a co-founder of the Berkshire Historical Conference of Women Historians. After her retirement, Brown published *Men and Centuries of European Civilization,* co-authored with George B. Carson (1948). At the time of her death on May 1, 1955, at Norfolk, Virginia, Louise Fargo Brown was working on a study of the role of informers in English and early American history.

ADDITIONAL SOURCES

WhE&EA; WhAm 3; BiIn 3, 4; obituary in NewYT, May 5, 1955, p. 33; obituary in *American Historical Review* 61: 525–526, Jan. 1956; obituary in *Wilson Library Bulletin* 30: 18, Sept. 1955; *Bio-Base.*

BRUCE, KATHLEEN (EVELETH)
(1885–1950)
U.S. History

Kathleen Eveleth Bruce was born October 21, 1885, in Richmond, Virginia, to Thomas Seddon and Mary Bruce (Anderson). She received her early education at Miss Ellett's Private School in Richmond before moving west to Tucson, Arizona, and El Paso, Texas. She attended Radcliffe College and received an A.B. in 1918, an A.M. in 1919, and a Ph.D. in 1924.

From 1924 to 1926 Bruce taught history and government at Wheaton College, and from 1926 to 1928 she was on the faculty of William and Mary College. She received a grant from the National Research Council for 1928–29 and did research in Washington, D.C., and at Johns Hopkins University on the social, cultural, and business lives of the planters in the South before the Civil War. From 1930 to 1932 Bruce researched at the Museum of Science and Industry in Chicago for the McCormick Biographical Association. In 1932–33 she was on the staff of the Nettie Fowler McCormick Foundation. Bruce was a contributor to the *Dictionary of American Biography* and in 1931 wrote *Virginia Iron Manufacture in the Slave Era* and "Massachusetts Women of the Revolution (1716–1789)," a chapter in *The Commonwealth of Massachusetts Colony, Province and State (1927–30),* edited by Albert B. Hart.

In 1933 Kathleen Bruce returned to teaching at Hollins College in Virginia. From 1936 to 1941 she served as state supervisor of federal archives and records in Virginia and researched the agricultural records of Berry Hill Plantation in Halifax County, Virginia. From 1943 to 1946 she was assistant professor of history at Sophie Newcomb College in New Orleans, Louisiana. She returned to Richmond in 1946, where she did research contrasting conditions following the Civil War with those following World Wars I and II. In 1948 Bruce was professor of history at Westhampton College of the University of Richmond. In January 1949 ill health forced her to abandon her research. At the time of her death on April 26, 1950, Kathleen Eveleth Bruce left the house she built and designed, along with her historical library, to the university as a residence for women faculty members at Westhampton College.

ADDITIONAL SOURCES

NatCAB v. 42; Bio In 2, 5; obituary in *Agricultural History* 24: 239, Oct. 1950: *American Historical Review* 55: 1041–1042, July, 1950; NewYT, Apr. 30, p. 102, 1950, *School & Society* 71: 285, May 6, 1950; *Bio-Base.*

BYNUM, CAROLINE WALKER
(1941–)
Medieval History

Caroline Walker Bynum was born on May 10, 1941, in Atlanta, Georgia, of Scotch-Irish and southern U.S. ancestry. Her father was a college professor; her mother was a college professor for nine years and then a full-time homemaker for twenty years. Bynum attended public grammar school and high school in Atlanta. Her early influences included her parents: her father as an academic, her mother as a frustrated former academic. She was also influenced by growing up in the South, "a region with an intense sense of history." Bynum's father came from a poor family and wanted desperately, as she puts it, "to leave southern prejudice behind." For both parents, conversion from southern fundamentalism to Episcopalianism was important. Their intense religiosity was something Caroline both internalized and rebelled against.

Bynum attended Radcliffe College and then the University of Michigan; she earned a bachelor's degree with high honors in 1962. She continued her studies at Harvard University, earning a master's degree in 1963 and a Ph.D. in 1969. Bynum was motivated to become a historian because she wanted to teach and she wanted a field with "both details and concepts." She studied philosophy and literature before she settled on history, hoping then to work on great ideas within a social context. Bynum's first academic appointment was at Harvard University, in the history department from 1969 to 1973, and in the Divinity School from 1973 to 1976. She then taught at the University of Washington from 1976 to 1988, as associate professor and professor. Since 1988 Bynum has been at Columbia University, where she holds the Morris A. and Alma Schapiro Chair in History. From 1993 to 1994 she was also dean of the School of General Studies and associate vice president of arts and sciences for undergraduate education at Columbia. She has taught all aspects of late antique and medieval history, including political, military, social, economic, religious, and economic history.

Caroline Walker Bynum is the author of five books, editor or co-editor of three books, and author of twenty-five articles, several of which have won prestigious awards. *Holy Feast and Holy Fast: The Religious Significance of Food to Medieval Women,* published in 1987, won the Governor's Award of the State of Washington in 1988 and the Philip Schaff Prize of the American Society for Church History in 1989. *Fragmentation and Redemption: Essays on Gender and the Human Body in Medieval Religion* won the Trilling Prize in 1992 and the American Academy of Religion Award for Excellence in the Study of Religion: Analytical-Descriptive Category in 1992. Bynum has written award-winning articles as well. "Women Mystics and Eucharistic Devotion in the Thirteenth Century" won the Berkshire Prize for Best Historical Article Written by a Woman in 1985, and "The Body of Christ in the Later Middle Ages: A Reply to Leo Steinberg" won the Nelson Prize, awarded by the Renaissance Society of America, for the best article of 1986. As reviewer Amy Hollywood argues, "The source of Bynum's strength as an historian lies in her careful attention to differences and the necessity of understanding such differences, both those between the medieval world and our own and those within medieval culture itself." Her most recent work, *The Resurrection of the Body in Western Christianity, 200 to 1336,* links philosophy, social history, and theology and explores the dimensions of the body-soul dilemma in Christian thought.

Bynum has been the recipient of numerous fellowships and awards, among them fellowships from the American Council of Learned Societies, the National Endowment for the Humanities, the MacArthur Foundation, and the Bunting Institute of Radcliffe College. She has served as president of the Medieval Association of the Pacific, president of the American Catholic Historical Association, president-elect of the American Historical Association, and second vice-president, and future president, of the Medieval Academy of America.

Bynum served on the boards of editors of *Harvard Theological Review, Women's Studies: An Interdisciplinary Journal, Genders: A Journal of Gender and Society, Common Knowledge, Magistra, Encyclopedia of Women in World Religions,* and *Journal of the American Academy of Religion.* Her professional commitments include service to the Medieval Association of the Pacific, the American Historical Association, the American Society for the Study of Religion, the American Catholic Historical Association, the National Humanities Center, and the Medieval Academy of America.

Bynum is married and has one child, an adopted daughter from South America. Her interests include travel, foreign languages, art history, reading fiction and poetry, and music, especially opera.

BOOKS BY CAROLINE WALKER BYNUM

The Resurrection of the Body in Western Christianity, 200 to 1336. New York: Columbia
University Press, 1995.

*Fragmentation and Redemption: Essays on Gender and the Human Body in Medieval
Religion.* New York: Urzone, 1991; German translation, Surhkamp, 1995.

Holy Feast and Holy Fast: The Religious Significance of Food to Medieval Women.
Berkeley: University of California Press, 1987; French translation, Editions du
Cerf, 1994.

Editor, with Stevan Harrell and Paula Richman. *Gender and Religion: On the Complexity
of Symbols.* Boston: Beacon Press, 1986.

Jesus as Mother: Studies in the Spirituality of the High Middle Ages. Berkeley: University
of California Press, 1982.

Docere Verbo et Exemplo: An Aspect of Twelfth-Century Spirituality. Missoula, MT: Scholars Press, 1979.

Editor, with T. Leccisotti. *Statuta Casinensia,* edition of custumals of Monte Cassino. In *Corpus Consuetudinum Monasticarum.* Vol. 4. Siegburg: Francis Schmitt, 1972.

Editor, Bynum et al. *A Select Bibliography of History.* 3rd ed. Cambridge, MA: Henry Adams History Club, History Department, Harvard University, 1966.

ADDITIONAL SOURCES

Hollywood, Amy M. Review of *Fragmentation and Redemption: Essays on Gender and the Human Body in Medieval Religion,* by Caroline Walker Bynum. *Journal of Religion* 72 (Oct. 1992): 632–633.

Questionnaire completed by the subject for *American Women Historians, 1700s–1990s: A Biographical Dictionary.*

C

CAULKINS, FRANCES MANWARING
(1795–1869)
Local History

The first woman elected to membership in the oldest historical society in the United States, Frances Manwaring Caulkins was born in New London, Connecticut, on April 26, 1795, to Joshua and Fanny (Manwaring) Caulkins. Even at an early age, while attending school, she was fascinated with historical and genealogical research. After finishing school, she lived for seven years in New London with an uncle, Christopher Manwaring, and began contributing articles to local newspapers on historical people and events in the area. The death of her stepfather left the family destitute, and Frances became a schoolteacher. From 1820 to 1829 and 1832 to 1834 she ran a girls' school in Norwichtown; from 1830 to 1832 she was a principal in New London. Thereafter she lived with various relatives doing evangelical work. In 1845 Caulkins published *History of Norwich;* it was rewritten for a second edition in 1866. In 1852 she wrote *History of New London.*

Caulkins was nominated as corresponding secretary of the Massachusetts Historical Society on March 29, 1849. She was voted in on April 26 and became the first woman elected to the society and the only one for over a century. She died in 1869, in New London, probably from pneumonia.

ADDITIONAL SOURCES

Alli; Alli Supp.; ApCAB; DcAmAu; AmWomWr; Drake; NotAW; TwCBDA; *Bio-Base.*

CHAN, SUCHENG
(1941–)
Comparative History of Asian International Migration, Asian-American Economic History

Born on April 16, 1941, in Shanghai, China, of Chinese parents, Sucheng Chan attended elementary school in China, Hong Kong, and Malaysia; junior high school in Singapore; and high school in New York City. Her father, an engineer, later worked as a high school physics teacher in Malaysia and as a waiter in the United States. Her mother worked as a social worker in China, a high school history teacher in Malaysia, and a bookkeeper in the United States. Her early memories are of war in China and of learning to read at a young age. Her father taught her to read historical novels, and once she had learned English at age nine, Sucheng read novels from the United States aimed at young adults, which had become available to her in Malaysia and Singapore. Since she had polio at age four, she spent much of her childhood alone. "Hence books, rather than people," Chan states, "were my main influences."

Sucheng Chan attended Swarthmore College, earning a bachelor's degree in economics in 1963. She received a master's degree in Asian studies from the University of Hawaii in 1965 and a Ph.D. in political science from the University of California at Berkeley in 1973. "I was not trained as a historian at all," writes Chan. "However, when I started teaching Asian American studies, an interdisciplinary field, I realized that many questions that I and my students had about the contemporary conditions faced by people of color could only be answered by examining history." Chan trained herself to be a historian, sitting on the floor of the stacks of the University of California at Berkeley library, reading all the articles in the major history journals for the past ten years and learning about how historians think. "I still like working with quantitative data," she argues, "but I now try to wrap such information in palatable prose. History seems to be the only discipline left where good, clear writing is still valued."

Chan started her academic employment in 1971, as assistant professor of ethnic studies at California State University at Sonoma. In 1974 she took a job as assistant professor of Asian American studies at the University of California at Berkeley, where she attained the rank of associate professor. In 1984 Chan was hired as professor of history and American studies at the University of California at Santa Cruz. Since 1988 she has taught at the University of California at Santa Barbara, where she is currently chair of Asian American studies and affiliate professor of history.

Of all her accomplishments, Sucheng Chan takes special pride in having been the first Asian American woman to serve as a provost in the University of California system, in her role as founding editor of the first book series in Asian American studies, and in having served as chair of the first department of Asian American studies at a major research university in the United States. She is also proud of her teaching success in history: Chan has won several teaching awards, including, most recently, the Asian American Faculty and Staff Association's Distinguished Lecturer Award at the University at Santa Barbara.

Author, editor, or co-editor of nine published books and eight books in progress, Chan has explored the histories of several groups of Asians and Asian Americans in the United States, including Koreans, Laotians, Chinese, Japanese, Vietnamese, and Cambodians. Her first book, *This Bittersweet Soil: The Chinese in California Agriculture, 1860–1910,* won four distinguished awards, including the Association for Asian American Studies Outstanding Book Award. Two of her other books, *Quiet Odyssey: A Pioneer Korean Woman in America* and *Asian Americans: An Interpretive History,* have also won awards. Chan is the founding editor of the twenty-volume Asian American History and Culture Series published by Temple University Press, and the editor of *Hmong Means Free: Life in Laos and America,* published in 1994. In a review of one of Chan's works, Nadine Ishitani Hata praises the "growing depth and breadth" of Chan's influence on the historiography of Asian Americans.

Chan is the recipient of many postdoctoral fellowships, including those with the National Endowment for the Humanities, the Institute of American Cultures, and the Guggenheim Foundation. She received a grant from the National Endowment for the Humanities to develop curricular materials and courses in Asian American studies, as well as several research and conference development grants. She has served on the board of editors of the *Journal of American Ethnic History, Pacific Historical Review,* and *Agricultural Review.* Her service is not limited to academe, however; Chan has also worked as a consultant on community film, oral history, and museum projects.

Married to Mark Juergensmeyer, professor of sociology at the University of California at Santa Barbara, Chan has several "wonderful canine children": Brandenburg, Rajah, and Cotufa. She enjoys reading books and articles outside her field, carpentry and sewing, and playing with her dogs. Because she now suffers from post-polio syndrome, however, Chan has had to withdraw from many of her personal and professional activities.

BOOKS BY SUCHENG CHAN

Editor. *Hmong Means Free: Life in Laos and America.* Philadelphia: Temple University Press, 1994.

Editor, with D. Daniels, M. Garcia, and T. Wilson. *Peoples of Color in the American West.* Lexington, MA: D. C. Heath, 1993.

Asian Americans: An Interpretive History. Boston: Twayne, 1991.

Asian Californians. San Francisco: Boyd and Fraser, 1991.

Editor. *Entry Denied: Exclusion and the Chinese Community in America, 1882–1943.* Philadelphia: Temple University Press, 1991.

Editor. *Income and Status Differences Between White and Minority Americans: A Persistent Inequality.* Lewiston, NY: Edwin Mellen Press, 1990.

Editor. *Quiet Odyssey: A Pioneer Korean Woman in America.* Seattle: University of Washington Press, 1990.

Editor. *Social and Gender Boundaries in the United States.* Lewiston, NY: Edwin Mellen Press, 1989.

This Bittersweet Soil: The Chinese in California Agriculture, 1860–1910. Berkeley: University of California Press, 1986.

ADDITIONAL SOURCES

Hata, Nadine Ishitani. Rev. of *Quiet Odyssey: A Pioneer Korean Woman in America,* by Sucheng Chan. *Journal of American History* 79, no. 2 (Sept. 1992): 700.

Questionnaire completed by the subject for *American Women Historians, 1700s–1990s: A Biographical Dictionary.*

CLAPP, MARGARET ANTOINETTE
(1910–1974)
U.S. History

Winner of the Pulitzer Prize for *Forgotten First Citizen: John Bigelow* and eighth president of Wellesley College, Margaret Antoinette Clapp was born to Alfred Chapin and Anna (Roth) Clapp in East Orange, New Jersey, on April 11, 1910. In 1926 she attended Wellesley College on a scholarship and received an A.B. in economics in 1930. Because of the Depression, Clapp was forced to defer graduate work and became a teacher at Todhunter, a private girls' school in Manhattan. She earned an A.M. in history from Columbia University in 1937. She left Todhunter (then Dalton) in 1942 for a variety of teaching jobs in the history departments of City College of New York (1942–1944), Douglass College (1945–1946), and Columbia University's general sessions (1946–1947) while pursuing her doctorate at Columbia, which she was awarded in 1946. Her dissertation was on John Bigelow, a nineteenth-century editor, reformer, and diplomat.

In 1947, while working as a government researcher in Washington, D.C., she published *Forgotten First Citizen* and was offered an assistant professorship at Brooklyn College. In May 1948 she was informed that her biography had won the Pulitzer Prize. She was offered the presidency of Wellesley College and became one of only five women presidents of major liberal arts colleges. She remained at Wellesley until 1966. After retirement, she became interim head of Lady Doak, a women's college in Mandurai, South India; she resigned one year later. Clapp traveled around India as cultural attaché for the United States Information Agency from 1968 to 1971; she was the first woman ever to hold the post of minister councilor of public affairs. Margaret Clapp resigned in 1971 and returned to Tyringham, Massachusetts, living with her sister until her death from cancer in 1974.

ADDITIONAL SOURCES

CurBio 48; NewYTBS 74; IntWW 74; WhoAmW 58, 61, 64, 66, 68, 70, 72; WhoGov 72; BioIn 1, 2, 3, 4, 7, 10; CurBio 74N; InWom; AmAu&B; AmWomWr; BiDAmEd; ConAu 49; OxAm; REnAL; TwCA Supp. 55; WhAm 6; CurBio 9; CurBio Yrbk 49; *National Encyclopedia of America Biography* 52; TwCA; "Alumna Makes Good," *Newsweek* 33: 81, June 13, 1949; "Lively Lady," *Time* 53: 46, June 13, 1949; "Point in Time at Wellesley," *Time* 86: 55–56, Aug. 20, 1965; "Stopping in Midstream," *Newsweek* 66: 72–73, Aug. 23, 1965; "Just Well-Rounded," *Time* 54: 74–76, Oct. 10, 1949; NotAW Mod. Period, pp. 150–151; obituary in CurBio 35: 44, June 1974; CurBio Yrbk, 1974: 456, 1975; NewYT, May 4, 1974, p. 44; *Newsweek* 83: 113, May 13, 1974; *Time* 103: 100, May 13, 1974; *Bio-Base.*

CLINE, GLORIA GRIFFEN
(1929–1973)
U.S. History

Gloria Griffen Cline was born on March 21, 1929, in San Francisco, California, to Robert A. and Grace G. Griffen. She received her B.A. and M.A. in history from the University of Nevada. She went to the University of California for her Ph.D. in 1958; her dissertation, "A History of the Great Basin," was published as *Exploring the Great Basin* by the University of Oklahoma and nominated for a Pulitzer Prize in 1963. Cline also contributed to two volumes of *Mountain Men and the Fur Trade* by LeRoy R. Hafen and wrote a biography, *Peter Skene Ogden and the Hudson Bay Company,* which was published posthumously by the University of Oklahoma Press.

Cline was assistant professor and associate professor of history at Sacramento State College in California and a visiting lecturer at the University of Nevada, the University of Southern California, and Indiana University. She also organized the course in Canadian-American history at the University of Alberta at Edmonton. She was the first woman to win the faculty research award at Sacramento State (1965). Gloria Cline was a lecturer at Cambridge University at the time of her death in Ireland on April 12, 1973. In her honor, her parents created the Gloria Griffen Collection at the library of the University of Nevada, Reno, which holds several thousand volumes of Western Americana.
ADDITIONAL SOURCES
WhoAmW 66, 68; EncAAH; *Bio-Base.*

COLIE, ROSALIE L.
(1924–1972)
European History

Rosalie L. Colie, an expert in the cultural history of early modern Europe, was born in New York City in 1924 to Frederic R. and Rosalie L. Colie. She obtained a B.A. in 1944 at Vassar College, an M.A. from Columbia in 1946, and a Ph.D. in history and English in 1950. During this time she began teaching English at Douglass College and from 1949 to 1961 taught English and humanities at Barnard College. She then became professor of history at Wesleyan University and professor of history and English at the University of Iowa until 1966. She was a visiting professor at Lady Margaret Hall, Oxford, and a professor of English at Victoria College in the University of Toronto. In 1969 she was named Nancy Duke Lewis Professor at Brown University and was chair of the department of comparative literature.

In 1956 Colie wrote *Some Thankfulnesse to Constantine,* a biography of the Dutch virtuoso Contantijn Huygens. The next year she published *Light and Enlightenment,* a study of "the thought of the Cambridge Platonists and the Dutch Arminians." *Paradoxia Epidemica* was published in 1966, a result of research on the use of the paradox in sixteenth- and seventeenth-century liter-

ature. Rosalie Colie drowned on July 7, 1972, when her canoe overturned in the Lieutenant River near her home in Old Lyme, Connecticut.
ADDITIONAL SOURCES
WhoAmW 58, 74; BiIn 9; WhAm 5; *Bio-Base.*

COLLIER-THOMAS, BETTYE M.
(1941–)
African-American History, Archives Founder and Director

The daughter of Joseph Thomas and Katherine (Bishop) Collier, Bettye Marie Collier was born on February 18, 1941, in Macon, Georgia, the second of three children. Her father, the recipient of a B.S. degree in business from Florida A&M College and a master's degree from Georgia College, was a business executive and public school teacher. Her mother attended Florida A&M College and later completed her education at Hunter College. For a number of years she was employed as a teacher by the Board of Education of the City of New York. Bettye Collier attended elementary schools in New York, Georgia, and Florida, and high school in Jamaica, New York.

As a third-generation college graduate, Collier-Thomas was born into a family of educators, administrators, morticians, artisans, and small business owners, graduates of Fort Valley State College, Howard University, Florida A&M College, Harvard University, Boston University, and other professional schools. Her progenitors include her great-uncle Frank Richard Veal, a graduate of Howard and Boston Universities, a noted African Methodist Episcopal minister and president of several colleges and universities; her grandfather William T. Collier, one of the first blacks to work as a building subcontractor in Georgia and the first to serve on a grand jury in Milledgeville, Georgia; her great-uncle George Williams, the only black to own and operate a barber shop on the main street in Milledgeville; and her grandmother Luzella Veal Collier, a teacher and nurse. Collier-Thomas initially thought she would pursue a career in law, but in the eleventh grade she was inspired by a history teacher at John Adams High School in Jamaica, New York, to become a historian.

Bettye Collier-Thomas received a bachelor's degree from Allen University in Columbia, South Carolina, and a master's degree from Atlanta University. In 1974 she became the first black woman to receive a Ph.D. in history from George Washington University. During her college career she received many academic awards and honors, including induction into Alpha Kappa Mu National Honor Society, which was the black Phi Beta Kappa organization during segregation; and Who's Who in American Colleges and Universities. Collier-Thomas received a Presidential Scholarship to attend Atlanta University and a Ford Foundation Fellowship for doctoral studies at George Washington University.

An educator and administrator for thirty years, from 1966 to 1976 Collier-Thomas served as a professor and administrator at Howard University and held faculty positions at Washington Technical Institute and the University of Maryland, Baltimore County. From 1977 to 1981 she was a special consultant to the National Endowment for the Humanities, developing the agency's first program of technical assistance to black museums and historical organizations. From 1977 to 1989 Collier-Thomas served as founding executive director of the Bethune Museum and Archives (BMA). In 1982 Congress designated this institution a National Historic Site, and in 1993 President George Bush signed legislation formally incorporating it into the Department of the Interior. From 1989 to the present Collier-Thomas has served as associate professor of history and director of the Temple University Center for African American History and Culture.

The recipient of many awards and honors, in November 1994 Collier-Thomas received the Department of the Interior's Conservation Service Award, in recognition of outstanding contributions to the preservation and interpretation of African-American women's history. This award, one of the highest granted to a private citizen, recognized her singular achievement in the creation and development of the Bethune Museum and Archives. In tribute to her work, Bruce Babbitt of the Department of the Interior stated that "Dr. Collier-Thomas has established the only repository in the country solely devoted to the collection and preservation of materials relating to African-American women in America. Other repositories may collect materials on black history or on women's history, but no other repository gives black women their principal attention."

In 1985 President Ronald Reagan appointed Collier-Thomas to the National Afro-American History and Culture Commission. She has received scholarships, fellowships, and major grants from the Ford Foundation, the Lilly Endowment, the Rockefeller Foundation, and the National Endowment for the Humanities. She was featured in the 1986 special issue of *Dollars and Sense* as one of "America's Top 100 Black Business and Professional Women."

During her career Collier-Thomas has rendered extensive professional service. She conceived and developed two pathbreaking conferences, The First National Scholarly Research Conference on Black Women, in 1979, and A National Conference on Black Museums: Interpreting the Humanities, in 1980. Funded by the National Endowment for the Humanities, these conferences were covered by the national and international media and gave visibility to black women's studies and black museums, both in their infancy at the time. She has served on boards and committees and has been an advisor to many professional organizations, including the Association for the Study of Afro-American Life and History, Association for State and Local History, American Historical Association, and Organization of American Historians. During its early years, she worked closely with the African American Museums Association, helping to organize the association, identifying funding, and providing housing for the organization at the Bethune Museum.

Educated as an urban historian specializing in African-American and American social history, during the early 1970s Collier-Thomas began to explore new methodologies for researching African-American cultural, institutional, and women's history. She was introduced to the rich historical African-American intellectual and historical tradition, which continues to inform her work, by scholar mentors such as Clarence A. Bacote, Samuel DuBois Cook, John Hope Franklin, and Nell Irvin Painter. By 1977 she had defined several areas for long-term research. These included a history of black theater development and black women's organizations. Undaunted by the paucity of research and extant records in these areas, she determined to research these topics systematically. Following the founding of BMA, as she struggled to advance and articulate African-American women's history, she took to related areas of social and cultural history, including religion and the philosophy of theology articulated by black women. Having amassed extensive data in these areas, Collier-Thomas is now writing several books. Forthcoming publications include *Over the Footlights: A History of Black Theater Development, Encyclopedia of Black Entertainment,* and *Daughters of Thunder: Black Women Preachers and Their Sermons.* Other works in progress include a biography of Frances Ellen Watkins Harper and "African American Women and the Church, 1780–1970" (a five-year project funded by the Lilly Endowment). She has published numerous articles and educational materials.

Bettye Collier-Thomas is married to Charles J. Thomas, a retired educator and writer. Among her hobbies is fashion designing.

ADDITIONAL SOURCES

Plummer, Betty. "Thomas, Bettye." In *African American Women: A Biographical Dictionary.* Ed. Dorothy C. Salem. NY: Garland, 1993, 507–508.

Questionnaire completed by the subject for *American Women Historians, 1700s–1990s: A Biographical Dictionary.*

COMAN, KATHARINE
(1857–1915)
Economic History

When Katharine Coman was born on November 23, 1857, in Newark, Ohio, her father, a graduate of Hamilton College and the father of three sons, declared he would show educators how a girl should be educated. Katharine's mother was a graduate of a female seminary in Ohio, and Katharine was educated mainly at home by her parents. She eventually joined her brother Will at the University of Michigan, which she attended for two years. She taught in Ottawa, Illinois, for two years, then returned to college and graduated in 1880. Coman was hired to teach rhetoric at Wellesley College, then transferred to a professorship in the history department. In 1900 she organized the department of economics. It was at Wellesley that she met Katharine Lee Bates, an English instructor and future author of "America the Beautiful." The two would live, work, and travel together for the rest of their lives.

Between the years 1886 and 1894, Coman made several trips to England that resulted in a *Short History of England for School Use,* written with Elizabeth Kendall in 1902. During this time, Coman also became interested in the settlement and labor movements and became a lifelong friend of Jane Addams. Upon her return to the United States, she resided at Hull-House in Chicago. In 1892 she opened Denison House, a center for labor-organizing activities in the South End of Boston. She worked with immigrant women in the Boston sweatshops and organized an "Evening Club for Tailoresses." She set up a tailoring shop as an alternative to sweatshops, but it failed after six weeks because she refused to pay bribery money to foremen and owners of the larger shops. Coman became president of the electoral board and chairman of the standing committee of the National College Settlements Association in 1900.

During this time Coman published *The Industrial History of the United States,* which was reprinted nine times between 1905 and 1915. She also became interested in the problems of the American West and had the honor of writing the first article in the new *American Economic Review,* "Some Unsettled Problems of Irrigation." In 1912 she published *Economic Beginnings of the Far West,* a two-volume study of the history of the economy of the West. That same year, she tripped over a wire and fell, striking her breast heavily. A malignant tumor was found and cancer had spread throughout her system. Meanwhile, Jane Addams had asked her to study the social insurance program in Europe in hopes of initiating similar programs in the United States. Coman studied operations of programs in England, Spain, Denmark, and Sweden before bad health forced her to return to Wellesley. She died there on January 11, 1915. "Unemployment Insurance: A Summary of European Systems" was published posthumously in the same year.

ADDITIONAL SOURCES

Judith Schwartz, "*Yellow Clover:* Katharine Lee Bates and Katharine Coman," *Frontiers* 4, no. 1 (1979): 59–67; NotAW; Olga S. Halsey, "Katharine Coman: 1857–1915," *The Survey* (Jan. 23, 1915): 451; Katharine Lee Bates, "Starry Runaway," in *Yellow Clover: A Book of Remembrance* (New York: E. P. Dutton & Co., 1922); AmWomWr; OhA&B; WhAm 1; WomWWA 14; DcAmAu; DcNAA; InWom; *Bio-Base.*

CONANT, HANNAH O'BRIEN CHAPLIN
(1809–1865)
Religious History

Hannah O'Brien Chaplin Conant was born on September 5, 1809, to the Rev. Jeremiah Chaplin and Marcia S. O'Brien in Danvers, Massachusetts. At the time of her birth, her father was pastor of the Baptist Church in Danvers and later became the first president of Waterville (now Colby) College in Waterville, Maine. She attended public schools and under the tutelage of her father became an expert in oriental languages.

Chaplin was married on July 12, 1830, to Rev. Thomas Jefferson Conant, and despite assisting him in much of his work and raising ten children, she managed to carve out a career of her own. In 1839, after relocating in Hamilton, New

York, she became editor of the *Mother's Monthly Journal,* published in Utica, and remained editor almost her entire life. She also began historical research and in 1855 wrote *The Earnest Man; A Sketch of the Character and Labors of Dr. A. Judson, the First Missionary to Burmah.* The next year Conant wrote *The English Bible; A Popular History of the Translation of the Holy Scriptures into the English Tongue.*

In addition to oriental languages, Hannah Conant also spoke German and French fluently and translated a number of German works including *Lea; Or, The Baptism in Jordan* (1844), by G.F.A. Strauss; *The Epistle of Paul to the Philippians Practically Explained* (1851), by A. Neander; *The First Epistle of John Practically Explained* (1852), by A. Neander; *Erna, the Forest Princess; Or Pilgrimage of the Three Wise Men to Bethlehem* (1855), by G. Niertiz; and *The New England Theocracy; A History of the Congregationalists in New England to the Revivals of 1740* (1859), by F. H. Uhden. Hannah Conant died on February 18, 1865.

ADDITIONAL SOURCES

NatCAB; DcAmAu; DcAmBio; NotAW; TwCBDA; CyAL 2; Alli Supp.; ChPo; DcNAA; AmWomWr; ApCAB; NatCAB 22; WhAm HS; Drake; *Bio-Base.*

CONWAY, JILL KER
(1934–)
U.S. History, Autobiography

Jill Ker Conway was born October 9, 1934, to William Innis Ker and Evelyn Mary (Adames) Ker in New South Wales, Australia. Historians and general readers both are familiar with her childhood story, which she recounted in her best-selling autobiography, *The Road from Coorain.* In the book she recalls growing up on Coorain, a sheep station named by the aboriginal people of Australia to mean "windy place." Her father, of Scottish descent, raised thousands of sheep on this land granted to him as a veteran of World War I. Her mother, of English descent, was a trained nurse and a "modern feminist," according to her daughter, who made of their isolated outback ranch a comfortable and charming home.

After five years of drought on the sheep farm, her family faced despair. When Conway was eleven years old, her father drowned, either by accident or by suicide, and she and her mother moved to Sydney. Since she had learned to value education, "a gift beyond price" on a chore-filled farm, Conway excelled in her first school experience, a private girls' school in Sydney. Her academic success, however, did not bring social success. "My family and school friends agreed that I was 'brainy,' " she later wrote. "This was a bad thing to be in Australia. People distrusted intellectuals."

At the end of her first full year of study at the University of Sydney, which she attended holding a Commonwealth Scholarship, Jill Ker Conway led her class in history. She became interested in the history of Australia, which had been fairly neglected. Because of her interest in Australia's role in postwar international politics, she, along with two male friends, applied for admission to the Australian Department of External Affairs as a trainee. Of the three equally qualified candidates, the two men were accepted; Conway was not. She was, she learned, "too good looking" for the job. "This one blow of fate," she recalled in her autobiography, "made me identify with other women and prompted me, long before it was fashionable to do so, to try to understand their lives."

Jill Ker Conway graduated from the University of Sydney with a bachelor's degree and a University Medal in 1958; she returned there for a master's degree in Australian history, and then left Australia to pursue a Ph.D. at Harvard University; she earned the degree in 1969. Conway's first academic job was at the University of Toronto, where she moved up the ranks to associate professor. She also served as the university's first vice president for internal affairs.

Much of Conway's scholarship has focused on women's lives. Her dissertation, later published, was *The First Generation of American Women Graduates.* Another of her interests, mythic images, led to a series of lectures on myths and national culture. In 1975, because of her academic accomplishments and advocacy for female faculty and female students, Conway was named president of Smith College. She was the first female president at Smith, the nation's largest privately endowed women's liberal arts college. While there she established the Society of Scholars Studying Women's Higher-Education History, raised funds for the education at Smith of welfare recipients, and increased Smith's endowment from $82 million to $220 million. After a decade at Smith she left to become visiting scholar and professor at the Massachusetts Institute of Technology.

Jill Ker Conway has been widely recognized for her accomplishments, having been granted honorary degrees from sixteen colleges and universities in Canada and the United States. She is also a trustee of Hampshire College, the Northfield Mount Hermon School, the New England Medical Center, and the Kresge Foundation. The work she will most likely be best remembered for, however, remains *The Road from Coorain,* which fellow academic and popular writer Carolyn Heilbrun called "one of the few heroic stories of girlhood."

Jill Ker married John James Conway, a professor she worked with at Harvard, in 1962. She became a naturalized citizen of the United States in 1982. She has been back to Coorain only twice since 1960, feeling that leaving was the right thing to do, "but I still feel very deeply rooted in the back country and the bush."

BOOKS BY JILL KER CONWAY

True North: A Memoir. New York: Knopf, 1994.

Editor, with Susan C. Bourque. *The Politics of Women's Education.* Ann Arbor: University of Michigan Press, 1993.

The Road from Coorain. New York: Random House, 1990.
Editor, with Susan Bourque and Joan Scott. *Learning About Women: Gender, Politics, and Power.* Ann Arbor: University of Michigan Press, 1989.
The First Generation of Women Graduates. New York: Garland, 1987.
ADDITIONAL SOURCE
"Conway, Jill Ker." In *Current Biography Yearbook,* 1991.

COTT, NANCY F.
(1945–   )
U.S. Social, Intellectual, and Women's History

Nancy F. Cott, one of the founders of the field of U.S. women's history, was born on November 8, 1945, in Philadelphia, Pennsylvania, of Jewish, Austro-Hungarian ancestry. Her father was a textile manufacturer; her mother was a full-time homemaker. Cott attended public schools in Cheltenham Township, Pennsylvania, before attending Cornell University as an undergraduate. She received a bachelor's degree in history, magna cum laude, in 1967. Her graduate work in history of American civilization was at Brandeis University, where she earned a master's degree in 1969 and a Ph.D. in 1974. Cott was motivated to become a historian because of her involvement in the women's movement. Feminism, in combination with the new social history movement, encouraged her to study women's lives in the United States.

Nancy Cott taught as a part-time instructor at Wheaton College, Clark University, and Wellesley College while in graduate school. She then taught for a year at the Boston Public Library as a lecturer in the National Endowment for the Humanities Learning Library Program. Cott was appointed assistant professor of history and American studies at Yale University in 1975. In 1979 she was named associate professor, and in 1986 she was named professor. Since 1990 she has been Stanley Woodward Professor of History and American Studies at Yale. Cott also served as chair of women's studies from 1980 to 1987, and since 1994 she has served as chair of American studies.

Cott is the author or editor of five books, author of nearly twenty scholarly articles and seven review articles, and editor of the twenty-volume series *History of Women in the United States.* The series includes nearly 500 outstanding articles that cover women's history from the Revolutionary War era through the 1960s. Cott's most recent book, *A Woman Making History: Mary Ritter Beard Through Her Letters,* explores the life and thought of the woman who founded the field of women's history. "There is much here to ponder," historian Anne Firor Scott writes about Cott's work. "All one can do is to urge the book upon all manner of historians with the assurance that they will not be disappointed." Cott has also written on family life in the Colonial period, the growth of and tensions within feminism in the early twentieth century, and nineteenth-century notions of female sexuality. She is also currently editor of an eleven-volume series for junior high and high school students. This series, the Young Oxford History of Women in the United States, treats young readers, according to Elaine

Tyler May, "with the respect they deserve and does not avoid controversial issues."

Cott is the recipient of numerous honors, awards, and fellowships. She has been a fellow with Harvard University Law School, the National Endowment for the Humanities, the Charles Warren Center at Harvard University, the Guggenheim Foundation, the Whitney Humanities Center at Yale University, and the Rockefeller Foundation. She has served on the editorial boards for many publications, including *American Quarterly, Feminist Studies, Journal of Social History, Reviews in American History, Gender and History,* and *American National Biography.* She has provided professional service to the American Studies Association, the Berkshire Conference of Women Historians, and the Organization of American Historians. Cott currently serves on advisory boards for Northeastern University Press, the University of North Carolina Press, and the Princeton University Program in Women's Studies. She has been a consultant on many film projects and regularly serves on national prize and fellowship selection committees.

Nancy Cott married Leland D. Cott in 1969. They have two children, Joshua Michael Cott, born in 1974, and Emma Janet Cott, born in 1979. Cott's hobbies include reading, bicycling, skiing, and tennis.

BOOKS BY NANCY COTT

A Woman Making History: Mary Ritter Beard Through Her Letters. New Haven: Yale University Press, 1991.

The Grounding of Modern Feminism. New Haven: Yale University Press, 1987.

Editor, with E. H. Pleck. *A Heritage of Her Own: Towards a New Social History of American Women.* New York: Simon and Schuster, 1979.

The Bonds of Womanhood: "Woman's Sphere" in New England, 1780–1835. New Haven: Yale University Press, 1977.

Root of Bitterness: Documents of the Social History of American Women. New York: E. P. Dutton, 1972; Northeastern University Press, 1986.

ADDITIONAL SOURCES

May, Elaine Tyler. "The Past as Prologue." *Ms.* 5 (Mar./Apr. 1995): 71.

Questionnaire completed by the subject for *American Women Historians, 1700s–1990s: A Biographical Dictionary.*

CRARY, CATHERINE SNELL
(1909–1974)
U.S. History

Catherine Snell Crary, who found a missing original Federalist Paper written in longhand by John Jay, was born in Rochester, New York, on February 12, 1909. She was the daughter of Albert Conrad, an ophthalmologist, and Cora (Nell) Snell. She attended private schools and received a B.A. in 1930 from Mount Holyoke College. She married Calvert Horton Crary, an investment management executive, in 1932 and received a Ph.D. in history in 1933 from Radcliffe College. She taught history at Brearley School in New York City before becoming a history lecturer at Barnard College. In 1957 she became an adjunct professor of history at Finch College in New York City, where she remained until 1959.

In 1965 Catherine Crary wrote *Dear Belle: Letters from a Cadet and Officer to His Sweetheart, 1858–1865. The Price of Loyalty: Tory Writings from the Revolutionary Era* was published in 1973, and the next year she received the American Revolution Bicentennial Roundtable Award. Among her publications in historical and scholarly journals was "The Tory and the Spy" in *William and Mary Quarterly* in 1959. This article revealed that James Rivington, a New York City editor during the British occupation, supplied intelligence information to an agent of George Washington, general of the Colonial Army. Catherine Crary died in New York City on March 11, 1974.

ADDITIONAL SOURCES

BiIn 10, 12; NewYTBS 74; ConAu P-1; NatCAB 58; *Bio-Base.*

CRAWFORD, MARY CAROLINE
(1874–1932)
Popular History

Mary Caroline Crawford, known as "Boston's social historian," was born in Boston, Massachusetts, on May 5, 1874, to James and Mary Coburn Crawford. She attended the Girls' Latin School of Boston and while there heard a newspaperwoman speak. She was determined to become a writer and began her historical career by describing Boston's Old North Church in the school newspaper. She attended Radcliffe College, where she wrote a column for the *Boston Budget,* a society weekly, on activities at Radcliffe, and wrote a similar column for the *Boston Transcript* after graduation. She eventually became an editor and invented her own syndicate by selling her column to New York and Philadelphia papers. These columns grew into *The Romance of Old New England Rooftrees* (1902), a work on old houses in New England which was still selling twenty-five years later. In 1910 she wrote *Romantic Days in Old Boston.*

Crawford departed from local history when she went to Germany to research *Goethe and His Women Friends* (1911). This was followed by *Romantic Days in the Early Republic* (1912) and *The Romance of the American Theatre* (1913), called the first popular book on the history of the theatre. *Social Life in Old New England* was written in 1915. *In the Days of the Pilgrim Fathers* (1921) and two volumes on *Famous Families of Old New England* followed. The latter included rare family portraits of Copleys, Stuarts, Malbones, and other famous New England families. During this time, Crawford also became active in social issues and became known for the Social Service Publicity Bureau she conducted, her Ford Hall meetings, Sunday evening gatherings for workers and their families, and a similar organization at the Old South Meeting House. Mary Crawford died on November 15, 1932.

ADDITIONAL SOURCES

AmAu&B; AmLY; BiCAW; BiD&SB; DcAmAu; DcNAA; REnAL; WhAm 1; WhNAA; WomWWA 14; *Bio-Base.*

CURTIS, EDITH ROELKER
(1893–1977)
Popular History

Edith Roelker Curtis, a *Mayflower* descendant with Benjamin Franklin and Roger Williams among her ancestors, was born on July 29, 1893, in East Greenwich, Rhode Island, to William Greene Roelker, a lawyer, and Eleanor (Jenckes) Roelker. She attended Miss Porter's School in Farmington, Connecticut, from 1909 to 1912. She was married in 1914 to Charles Pelham Curtis, Jr., a member of a 300-year-old "proper Boston family." Curtis attended Radcliffe College from 1919 to 1921. In 1930 she published *Anne Hutchinson: A Biography,* which was translated into many languages, including Portuguese. This was followed by *Lady Sarah Lennox: An Irrepressible Stuart* in 1946. For the next fourteen years, she wrote articles, poetry, book reviews, novels, and magazine stories and lectured on writing. In 1961 she returned to history, publishing *A Season in Utopia: The Story of Brook Farm,* for which she received the National League of American Pen Women Award the next year. Curtis was instrumental in saving Brook Farm in West Roxbury, Massachusetts, site of the experimental communal association during 1844–1848. In 1973 the house and grounds were designated a historical landmark.

Edith Curtis died in Dublin, New Hampshire, on February 1, 1977.

ADDITIONAL SOURCES

Papers in the Women's History Archive of the Sophia Smith Collection at Smith College; BiIn 5, 12; NatCAB 60: ConAu 1R; ForWC 70; IntAu&W 76, 77; WhoAmW 58, 61, 64, 66, 68, 70, 72, 74, 75, 77; WhoE 74, 75, 77; WrDr 76; ConAu 103; *Bio-Base.*

D

DALL, CAROLINE WELLS HEALEY
(1822–1912)
Popular History

Caroline Wells Healey Dall was born in Boston, Massachusetts, on June 22, 1822, to Mark Healey, a well-to-do merchant and banker, and Caroline (Foster) Healey. She was educated by tutors and at private schools. While still a teenager, she contributed essays on religious and moral topics to periodicals, taught Sunday school, worked with the poor, and conducted a nursery school for children of working mothers. At nineteen she was participating in Margaret Fuller's public "conversations." When Mark Healey suffered a reversal of fortunes, Caroline began teaching and from 1840 to 1842 was vice-principal of Miss English's School for Young Ladies in Georgetown, D.C.; from 1842 to 1844 she was principal.

In 1844 Caroline Healey married the Rev. Charles Henry Appleton Dall, a Unitarian clergyman. The Dalls traveled throughout the East and Canada until he went to India as a missionary in 1855. Caroline stayed in the United States and continued her work for women's rights, including holding a position as corresponding editor for Paula Wright Davis's monthly, *Una.* She published a collection of early writings as *Essays and Sketches* in 1849 and began a series of lectures on women's history, which was published as *Historical Pictures Retouched* (1860). That same year she wrote *Women's Right to Labor* and *Life of Dr. Marie Zakrzewska.* In 1861 she wrote *Woman's Rights Under the Law.* In 1865 she founded the American Social Science Association, of which she was director from 1865 to 1880 and vice-president from 1880 to 1905. During that time she wrote *The College, the Market, and the Court; Or Woman's Relations to Education, Labor and Law* (1867). In 1868 she wrote *Egypt's Place in History,* followed by a three-volume children's book, *Patty Gray's Journey to the Cotton Islands* (1869–1870). Five years later she wrote *The Romance of the Association; Or, One Last Glimpse of Charlotte Temple and Eliza Wharton. My First Holiday, Or, Letters Home from Colorado, Utah, and California* was published in 1881, *What We Really Know About Shakespeare* in 1886, *Sordello—A History and A Poem* in 1886, and *Dr. Anadabai Joshee* in 1888. She wrote *Barbara Fritchie—A Study* in 1892, *Transcendentalism in New England* in 1897, a privately printed memoir of her childhood titled *Alongside* in 1900, *Nazareth* in 1903, and *Fog Bells* in 1905.

Caroline Dall died in Washington, D.C., on December 17, 1912.

ADDITIONAL SOURCES

WhoAm, 1908–9; *Evening Star* (Washington, DC), Dec. 18, 1912; F. C. Pierce, *Foster Genealogy* (1899); Alli Supp.; AmAu&B; BiD&SB; BiIn 3, 6, 8, 11; ChPO S1; Dc-AmAu; DcLB; DcNAA; AmBi; AmWom; AmWomWr; ApCAB; DcAmB; LibW; NatCAB 9; NotAW; TwCBDA; WhAm 4; InWom; Lillian O'Connor, *Pioneer Women Orators* (Columbia University Press, 1954), p. 85; Robert Edgar Riegel, *American Feminists* (University of Kansas Press, 1963), pp. 156–63; B. Welter, "Merchant's Daughter: A Tale From Life," *New England Quarterly* 42: 3–22, Mar. 1969; Susan Phinney Conrad, *Perish the Thought* (Citadel, 1978), pp. 162–182; *Bio-Base.*

DAVIS, NATALIE ZEMON
(1928–)
History of France and Early Modern Europe

Natalie Zemon Davis was born on November 8, 1928, in Detroit, Michigan, of Polish-Jewish and Russian-Jewish ancestry. Her father was a successful businessman in the Detroit textile industry and an amateur playwright; her mother was a homemaker and businesswoman. In her intellectual pursuits, Davis was influenced by her father, an avid reader and writer. Davis was also influenced by growing up a Jew in a neighborhood where only two Jewish families had homes. "The ability to identify anti-semitism," she later recalled in an interview with Roger Adelson, "became a part of my life without anyone sitting down and giving me a lesson in it."

After attending elementary school at the Hampton School in Detroit, Davis went to Kingswood, a private girls' school in suburban Detroit. As one of only two Jewish girls in her class, Davis was an outsider. She turned her attention to her studies, earning excellent grades, and to leadership, serving as president of the student council. "I loved history," she remembers, "especially the Enlightenment and the American Revolution."

Davis attended Smith College, participating as a student activist and applying questions offered by her political work to her honors program in history. She was tremendously influenced by Leona Gabel, who supervised Davis's honors thesis on Pomponazzi, an Aristotelian. Davis earned her bachelor's degree in 1949, a year after she eloped, much to the consternation of her parents and professors, with Chandler Davis, a graduate student in mathematics at Harvard University. Natalie and Chandler remained active in political work, protesting the Korean War and the work of the House Un-American Activities Committee (HUAC).

Davis pursued her intellectual work, completing a master's degree at Radcliffe and finding her interests turning more toward the history not of elites but of merchants, artisans, laborers, and peasants. She continued her political work as she pursued a Ph.D. at the University of Michigan. Between 1953, when she passed her general exams, and 1959, when she completed her dissertation, Davis had three children, Aaron Bancroft Davis, Hannah Penrose Davis, and Simone Weil Davis. As she told Adelson, she did not follow an ordinary academic path, "owing to my marriage and children, my husband's and my political activities, my independent style of thinking and writing, and because I have always been deeply concerned with and wanted to reach an audience wider than the narrow circles of scholarship."

In 1959 Davis received her first academic appointment, at Brown University. During that time, Chandler Davis served six months in Danbury Prison for charges brought against him by the House Un-American Activities Committee. Since Chandler was blacklisted in U.S. universities after that, both Davises took jobs at the University of Toronto, he in 1962 and she in 1963. Natalie Zemon Davis also taught at the University of California at Berkeley and at Princeton University, where she was named Henry Charles Lea Professor of History in 1978 and where she continues to teach today.

Natalie Zemon Davis's early work focused on class dimensions in early modern Europe, particularly in France. While at Toronto, she began to explore both literary and anthropological materials and approaches, and her work exemplifies what she calls a multidimensional view of society. Her first book, a collection of essays entitled *Society and Culture in Early Modern France,* has received tremendous scholarly acclaim and has gone through many editions and translations. "I think that people simply want to know more about the common people of the past," Davis argues. And because she wrote about women in this book, Davis was recognized early as a historian of women and of gender. Over the course of her career, Davis has helped to transform our understandings of both the common people and the elite, arguing that "lower- and upper-class worlds were reacting and reflecting on each other and even sometimes sharing rules and readers." In doing this work, Davis has developed an international reputation as a brilliant and challenging scholar. She has published, in addition to six books, over seventy scholarly essays.

Davis is also well known for her participation in the making of the film *Le retour de Martin Guerre.* As a historian consulting on a historical film, Davis struggled with some of the filmmakers' decisions. There were points about the story she felt needed to be made, so she wrote a short book, *The Return of Martin Guerre,* which, as Davis herself puts it, "has generated lively debates in several languages." The book has more than 78,000 copies in print.

Davis is currently one of two co-editors for the Bedford Series in History and Culture, published by St. Martin's Press. The series, which currently has seventeen volumes in print, is expected to grow to twenty-eight volumes by 1996, and many other volumes are in the planning stages or under contract. She is also editor of a recent series volume, *A History of Women in the West: Renaissance and Enlightenment Paradoxes.* According to reviewer Lindsay Wilson, Davis and co-editor Arlette Farge "have succeeded admirably" in creating a history of women from various points of view, summarizing recent research and raising new questions, and bringing the pleasures of reading history to new readers. Like all of her books, her most recent, *Women on the Margins: Three Seventeenth-Century Lives,* will be translated into several languages, including Italian, German, and Finnish.

The recipient of many awards and fellowships, including twenty honorary degrees, Natalie Zemon Davis also served as president of the American Historical Association in 1987. She has been named a fellow of the American Academy of Arts and Sciences and of the British Academy. In 1984 she received the American Historical Association's Eugene Asher Distinguished Teaching Award.

In July 1996, Davis took early retirement from Princeton and moved to Toronto, where her husband lives, and where she is a research associate in the comparative literature department at the University of Toronto. She looks forward to having more free time for writing history books and history film scenarios. Davis also has three grandchildren, Sofia, Max, and Gabriel.

BOOKS BY NATALIE ZEMON DAVIS

Women on the Margins: Three Seventeenth-Century Lives. Cambridge, MA: Harvard University Press, 1995. Forthcoming in French, Italian, German, Portuguese, and Finnish.

Editor, with Arlette Farge. *A History of Women in the West.* Volume 3, *Renaissance and Enlightenment Paradoxes.* Cambridge, MA: Belknap Press of Harvard University Press, 1993. Translated into Italian, French, Dutch, Spanish, and German. Forthcoming in Portuguese and Japanese.

Fiction in the Archives: Pardon Tales and Their Tellers in Sixteenth Century France. Stanford, CA: Stanford University Press, 1987. Translated into French, German, Japanese, and Italian. Forthcoming in Spanish.

Frauen und Gesellschaft am Beginn der Neuzeit. Translated by Wolfgang Kaiser. Berlin: Wagenbach, 1986.

The Return of Martin Guerre. Cambridge, MA: Harvard University Press, 1983. Translated into French, Italian, German, Spanish, Dutch, Japanese, Swedish, Portuguese, and Russian. Forthcoming in Hungarian and Greek.

Society and Culture in Early Modern France: Eight Essays. Stanford, CA: Stanford University Press, 1975. Translated into French, Italian, Japanese, German, Portuguese, and Spanish.

ADDITIONAL SOURCES

Adelson, Roger. "Interview with Natalie Zemon Davis." *The Historian* 53 (Spring 1991): 405–422.

Questionnaire completed by the subject for *American Women Historians, 1700s–1990s: A Biographical Dictionary.*

Wilson, Lindsay. Rev. of *A History of Women in the West.* Volume 3, *Renaissance and*

Enlightenment Paradoxes, ed. Natalie Zemon Davis and Arlette Farge. *American Historical Review* 99 (Dec. 1994): 1678–1679.

DAWIDOWICZ, LUCY
(1915–1990)
Jewish History

Lucy Dawidowicz was born in New York City on June 16, 1915, to Max and Dora (Ofnaem) Schildkret, working-class immigrants from eastern Europe. She received a B.A. degree from Hunter College in 1936 and two years later was a research fellow at the Yivo Institute for Jewish Research in Vilna, Poland. Just before World War II, she returned to New York and the YIVO was reorganized. She became assistant to the research director from 1940 to 1946 and met her husband, Szymon Dawidowicz, an escapee from Poland. After the war, Lucy returned to Europe to work for the American Jewish Joint Distribution Committee, where she aided Jewish survivors in re-creating schools and libraries; she also recovered a large number of collections of books seized by the Nazis.

Upon her return to New York in 1947, Dawidowicz began a lectureship at Yeshiva University in New York and began extensive research into the history of European Jews in the 1930s and 1940s. She researched the information needed for John Hersey to write *The Wall,* a novel of the Warsaw Ghetto. She received an M.A. from Columbia in 1961. Dawidowicz became a research analyst and eventually research director for the American Jewish Committee until 1969, when she joined the faculty of Yeshiva University as Paul and Leah Lewis Professor of Holocaust Studies from 1970 to 1975 and Eli and Diana Zborowski Professor of Interdisciplinary Holocaust Studies from 1976 to 1978.

During this time, Dawidowicz edited *The Golden Tradition: Jewish Life and Thought in Eastern Europe* (1967). In 1975 she wrote *The War Against the Jews 1933–1945,* regarded as a pioneering study of Nazi genocide; it won the Anisfield-Wolf Prize. In 1976 she edited *The Holocaust Reader* and the next year wrote *The Jewish Presence.* In 1981 *The Holocaust and the Historians,* a survey of scholarship on the Holocaust, was published. In 1989 she wrote a memoir, *From That Place and Time,* which included her experiences of European anti-Semitism during her time in Poland from 1938 to 1939.

Dawidowicz lectured at Stanford University, Bowdoin College, and Syracuse University. In 1981 she was visiting professor of Jewish civilization at Stanford. She was a Guggenheim Fellow in 1976, and from 1978 to 1979 she was a member of the President's Commission on the Holocaust. Lucy Dawidowicz died on December 5, 1990.

ADDITIONAL SOURCES
ConAu 25R; DrAS 74H, 78H; WhoA 80; WrDr 80; WhoAm 78; WhoAmW 77; *Facts on File of the 20th Century;* NewYTBS v. 21, pp. 1–12; obituary in NewYT, D-21, Dec. 6, 1990; obituary in NewYTBS 21: 1150, Dec. 1990; obituary in *Time* 136: 113, Dec. 17, 1990; Steven J. Rubin, ed., *Writing Our Lives: Autobiographies of American*

Jews, 1890–1990 (Jewish Publ. Soc., 1991), pp. 218–232; Diane Cole, "Lucy Dawidow-icz," *Jewish Profiles* (J. Aronson, 1991), pp. 57–64; *Bio-Base.*

DEBO, ANGIE
(1890–1988)
Western History

Angie Debo, who fought political pressure and threats of libel to reveal con-spiracies carried out to cheat Native Americans out of their land, was born January 30, 1890, in Beattie, Kansas, to Edward Peter Debo, a farmer, and Lina Elbertha (Cooper) Debo. Nine years later the family arrived in Marshall, Oklahoma Territory, in a covered wagon. Debo attended and eventually taught at rural schools in Kansas and Oklahoma. She seldom had access to libraries or magazines and often had only one book to read, that given to each child in her family at Christmas. She had to wait eight years to go to high school because none existed where she lived; she graduated in the first graduating class of 1913 at the age of twenty-three. Despite her lack of urban education, Angie Debo received an A.B. from the University of Oklahoma in 1918, where she studied under important western historian Edward Everett Dale, who in turn had studied under Frederick Jackson Turner.

Debo continued to teach until 1924, when she received a master's degree from the University of Chicago. Her master's thesis, *The Historical Background of the American Policy of Isolation,* was published with J. Fred Rippy that year. While earning her doctorate, Debo taught at West Texas State Teachers College (now West Texas State University) in Canyon as an assistant professor of history from 1924 to 1933; she received a Ph.D. from the University of Oklahoma, and the next year the University of Oklahoma Press published her doctoral disser-tation, *The Rise and Fall of the Choctaw Republic,* which received the John H. Dunning Prize of the American Historical Association in 1935.

Debo never served for any length of time on the faculty of a university, preferring instead to write freelance; however, she was a curator at the Panhan-dle-Plains Historical Museum in Canyon, Texas, for one year (1933) and was a member of the faculty at Stephen F. Austin State Teachers College in the sum-mer of 1935. In 1940 the controversial book *And Still the Waters Run: The Betrayal of the Five Civilized Tribes* was published by Princeton University Press after being deemed too controversial by the University of Oklahoma Press. In 1941 Debo published *The Road to Disappearance: A History of the Creek Indians* and edited, with John M. Oskison, *Oklahoma: A Guide to the Sooner State.* She was also state director of the Federal Writers Program for Oklahoma in 1940–41.

In 1942 Angie Debo received the Alfred A. Knopf History Fellowship, and in 1943 she wrote *Tulsa: From Creek Town to Oil Capital,* followed the next year by *Prairie City: The Story of an American Community.* She was a fellow of the University of Oklahoma in 1946, and a member of the history faculty at

Oklahoma State University in 1945, 1946, and 1957–58. In 1949 she wrote
Oklahoma: Foot-Loose and Fancy-Free. The next year she was inducted into
the Oklahoma Hall of Fame. From 1947 to 1955 she was curator of maps and
a member of the library staff at the university. She edited *The Cowman's Southwest: Being the Reminiscences of Oliver Nelson* in 1953 and was a member of
the board of directors of the Association of American Indian Affairs from 1956
to 1966. She wrote *The Five Civilized Tribes of Oklahoma: A Report on Social
and Economic Conditions* for the association in 1961. She was editor of H. B.
Cushman's *History of the Choctaw, Chickasaw, and Natchez Indians* in 1962.
In 1970 she wrote *A History of the Indians of the United States,* and in 1976
published *Geronimo: The Man, His Time, His Place.* From 1973 to 1977 she
was a member of the board of directors of the American Civil Liberties Union
in Oklahoma. In 1983 the University of Oklahoma awarded her their highest
award, the Distinguished Service Citation. In 1985 the state of Oklahoma placed
her portrait in the rotunda of its capitol. Two weeks before her death in 1988,
Debo received the Award for Scholarly Distinction from the American Historical
Association and was called "the first lady of Oklahoma history" by Governor
Henry Bellmon (*Oklahoma City Daily Oklahoman*). After her death, the University of Oklahoma Press initiated an award of $5,000 each year for the best
book about the American Southwest published by the press. The award is named
in honor of Angie Debo and was planned to be presented for the first time in
the autumn of 1995.

ADDITIONAL SOURCES

Barbara Abrash, Glenna Matthews, and Anita R. May, "Angie Debo," *Organization of
American Historians Newsletter* 17 (Feb. 1989): 3; *Angie Debo: A Biographical Sketch
and a Bibliography of Her Published Works* (Stillwater, Ok, 1980); Glenna Matthews
and Gloria Valencia-Weber, *Indians, Outlaws and Angie Debo,* documentary film, 1988,
PBS Video, 1320 Braddock Place, Alexandria, VA 22314; obituary, NewYT, Feb. 23,
1988, p. D-30; Helen J. Poulton, "Angie Debo: A Check-List," *Index Bulletin of Bibliography and Magazine Notes* 22 (Sept. 1956–Dec. 1959); Suzanne H. Schrems and
Cynthia J. Wolff, "Politics and the Publication of *And Still the Waters Run,*" *Western
Historical Quarterly* 22: 185–203, May 1991; TexWr; BioIn 4; ConAu 69; WhoAm 74,
78; *Oklahoma City Daily Oklahoman,* Apr. 4, 1985; *Oklahoma City Daily Oklahoman,*
Feb. 4, 1988; interviews with Angie Debo by Glenna Matthews, Gloria Valencia-Weber
and Aletha Rogers, 1981–1985, Angie Debo Collection, Special Collections, Oklahoma
State University Library, Stillwater, Ok; Kenneth McIntosh, "Geronimo's Friend: Angie
Debo and the New History," *Chronicles of Oklahoma* 66 (Summer 1988): 164–177;
correspondence with Joseph A. Brandt in the University of Oklahoma Press Collection,
Western History Archives, University of Oklahoma, Norman; *Bio-Base.*

de ZAVALA, ADINA
(1861–1955)
Local History

Adina de Zavala, called the "Angel of the Alamo," was born on November 18,
1861, at Zavala Point on Buffalo Bayou near San Jacinto battleground in Texas.

Her father was Augustine de Zavala and her mother was Irish-born Julia (Tyrell) de Zavala. Adina was educated by private tutors and could read at age four. When the family relocated to Galveston, she attended the Ursuline Academy, then Sam Houston Normal Institute in Huntsville (now Sam Houston Academy). By 1879 she had obtained a teaching certificate and went to Chillicothe, Missouri, to study music. She then returned to Texas to teach, and, in 1889 was one of the founding members of the Texas Historical and Landmarks Association. De Zavala began efforts to obtain commercial property which adjoined the Alamo and to retain the original Spanish names for streets in the downtown San Antonio area. She lobbied for the public schools in the Alamo City area to be named for Texas heroes and for schoolrooms to display Texas flags. She also lobbied to have March 6 set aside as "Texas Heroes Day." She located the burial place of Ben Milam, shot by Mexicans as he led the attack into San Antonio during the siege of Bexar, and had a gray granite memorial erected to mark Milam Square. In 1892 the Daughters of the Republic of Texas established a de Zavala chapter.

In 1903 de Zavala found that out-of-state developers intended to purchase the Alamo property when her option expired. She worked tirelessly to raise the $75,000 needed to purchase the land. In the end, a friend, Clara Driscoll, purchased the property. In 1905 de Zavala encouraged legislators to pass a bill to fund the Alamo purchase. The bill passed, and the site was to be administered by the Daughters of the Republic of Texas. Unfortunately, groups began fighting among themselves, de Zavala's teaching suffered, and she resigned in January 1907. In February, more commercial development threatened, and de Zavala went on a hunger strike inside the building. It was agreed that title to the Alamo property would pass to the state and that the building would be under its jurisdiction.

Meanwhile, de Zavala was intent on writing the history of the Alamo. In 1911 she wrote *Story of the Siege and Fall of the Alamo: A Resume,* followed by *History of the Alamo and Other Missions in San Antonio* (1917). She also sponsored work done by the Texas Historical and Landmarks Association and the San Antonio Conservation Society. In 1919 de Zavala located the site of the first Spanish mission in Texas and had markers placed there. She also secured an option on the historical Spanish Governor's Palace on San Antonio's Military Plaza, the only remaining example of an aristocratic Spanish residence in the state. In 1929 the city acquired the property, and the San Antonio Conservation Society restored it. In the next few years, Adina de Zavala saved the eighteenth-century home of Francisco Ruiz, one of the original signers of the Texas Declaration of Independence, and worked to save the home of Jose Antonio Navarro; it was restored after her death, which occurred on March 1, 1955, the eve of Texas Independence Day. On the way to the family burial plot in St. Mary's Cemetery, her casket, draped with the Texas flag, passed by the Alamo.

ADDITIONAL SOURCES
DcMAH.

DINER, HASIA R.
(1946–   )
History of Jewish and Irish Peoples in the United States

Born October 7, 1946, in Wisconsin of Jewish ancestry, Hasia Diner attended public elementary and high schools in Milwaukee. Her mother died when Hasia was only two years old, and her father remarried a Holocaust survivor who, like Diner's mother, came from a religious family and was unusually highly educated. Diner has her mother's diploma, which she earned in 1919 as one of the first Jewish women to graduate from the Kharkov (Russia) Women's Gymnasium. Diner's father, a Hebrew teacher and rabbi, was an important influence on her early life, as was her participation in Habonim, a Zionist youth movement.

Diner attended the University of Wisconsin at Madison, graduating with a bachelor's degree in 1968. Because of a long-standing interest in her parents' experiences as immigrants, a love for history, and an intense family commitment to Judaism and progressive politics, she decided to become a historian. She was also influenced in that direction by the civil rights movement and her own activism while a college student.

Following her graduation from college, Diner attended the University of Chicago, where she earned a master's degree in 1970. In 1975 she completed the Ph.D. at the University of Illinois. Diner taught as a lecturer at the University of the District of Columbia and at the University of Maryland, then obtained two one-year visiting assistant professor positions at George Washington University and Goucher College. From 1978 to 1980 Diner was a research associate at the Bunting Institute at Radcliffe College. After a year at Georgetown University and a year at the American University, Diner took a position as assistant professor of American studies at the University of Maryland at College Park. There from 1984 to 1996, Diner was promoted to associate professor in 1987 and professor in 1990. She also served as department chair. In the fall of 1996 Hasia Diner accepted a position as the Paul S. and Sylvia Steinberg Chair in American Jewish History at New York University. This is a joint appointment in History and Hebrew and Judaic Studies.

Author or editor of four books, eleven book chapters, and five articles, Diner is best known for her work on Jewish and Irish immigrants to the United States in the nineteenth and early twentieth centuries. *In the Almost Promised Land,* issued in paperback in 1995, explores the positive relationships that developed between blacks and Jews in the early twentieth century. The book, according to a review in *Labor History,* "should be a model for others writing ethnic history." Diner has also written the second volume of a five-volume history of Jews in the United States from the colonial period to the 1980s. "Her argument will undoubtedly encourage debate," wrote one reviewer, "and perhaps even alter the direction of American-Jewish historiography." Diner is currently working on another book, *Not by Bread Alone: Immigrant Adaptation to America and Creation of Ethnic Cuisine.*

Diner has been the recipient of grants from the National Endowment for the Humanities, the Maryland Humanities Council, the American Philosophical Society, and the Ford Foundation. She has been a Fulbright Lecturer in Haifa, Israel, and was awarded a Distinguished Faculty Research Fellowship from the University of Maryland. She has served as a consultant for three films about Jewish and Irish immigrants in the United States and has been a scholar in residence for the Michigan State University Jewish Studies Program and a consultant for the National Geographic Society and the Smithsonian Institution. Diner is currently an invited member of the Working Group on Black-Jewish Relations at Harvard University, book review editor for *American Jewish History,* consultant for three films about Jews and Irish in the United States, and an invited member of the Library of Congress's Advisory Committee on Copyright, Registration and Deposit.

Hasia Diner is married to Steve Diner, and they have three children. When asked about her significant accomplishments aside from her professional publications, Diner refers immediately to her family. She is also interested in reading, politics, travel, and participation in the Jewish community.

BOOKS BY HASIA DINER

A Time for Gathering: The Second Migration, 1820–1880. Baltimore: Johns Hopkins University Press, 1992. Vol. 2 in The Jewish People in America Series.

Erin's Daughters in America: Irish Immigrant Women in the Nineteenth Century. Baltimore: Johns Hopkins University Press, 1984.

Editor. *Women in Urban Society.* New York: Gale Research, 1979. *In the Almost Promised Land: American Jews and Blacks, 1915–1935.* Westport, CT: Greenwood Press, 1977. Reprint. Johns Hopkins University Press, 1995.

ADDITIONAL SOURCES

Feldman, Egal. Rev. of *A Time for Gathering: The Second Migration, 1820–1880,* by Hasia Diner. *American Historical Review* 99 (Feb. 1994): 286–288.

Questionnaire completed by the subject for *American Women Historians, 1700s–1990s: A Biographical Dictionary.*

DOBIE, EDITH
(1887–1975)
British History

Edith Dobie, an expert on the British Empire and British colonial affairs from 1830 to 1841, was born in Bradford, Pennsylvania, on February 10, 1887 (year of birth sometimes listed as 1894). She was the daughter of William and Phoebe Ann (Derry) Dobie. She graduated from high school in 1903 and taught for two years in a small country school, then in the Bradford public school. She received an A.B. from Syracuse University in 1914, then taught as a history instructor at Cortland Teachers College (later State University of New York College at

Cortland). In 1918 she became a history instructor at Westfield (Massachusetts) Teachers College (later Westfield State College), and in 1920 she was a history instructor at Trenton (New Jersey) Teachers College (later Trenton State College).

In 1922 Dobie received an M.A. from the University of Chicago and became an associate professor of history at Wesleyan College in Macon, Georgia. Four years later, she earned her Ph.D. from Leland Stanford Junior University (later Stanford University) and became an instructor in the problems of citizenship. That same year, she became an instructor in history at the University of Washington in Seattle, where she remained until 1957, when she retired as a full professor and research consultant to the university. During that time, Dobie received a Phi Beta Kappa grant-in-aid to do research in London for the Social Research Council of New York City, and in 1953 she was a Fulbright scholar in Malta. From 1961 to 1962 she was visiting professor of history at Elmira (New York) College and the University of Alberta, and in the summer of 1961 she was visiting professor at the University of Atlanta. In 1975 Edith Dobie established a Syracuse University scholarship for women graduate students in the department of history. She died in Seattle, Washington, on April 24 of that same year.

Dobie's publications include *The Political Career of Stephen Malloroy White: A Study of Party Activities Under the Convention System* (1927; reprinted by Stanford University Press in 1971); *Problems in International Understanding* (1928); *If Men Want Peace* (a contributer; 1946); *The Historiography of the British Empire-Commonwealth* (1966); and *Malta's Road to Independence* (1967).

ADDITIONAL SOURCES
DrAS 76H; WhoAmW 58; ConAu 57; ConAu P-2; obituary in NewYT, Apr. 25, 1975; *Bio-Base*.

DONNAN, ELIZABETH
(1883?–1955)
U.S. History

Elizabeth Donnan was born around 1883 in Morrow County, Ohio, to John W. and Annie Grisell Donnan. She received an A.B. from Cornell University in 1907 and became a member of John Franklin Jameson's staff at the Department of Historical Research of the Carnegie Institution of Washington; until 1909 she was editorial assistant at the *American Historical Review*. In 1920 she became professor of economics at Wellesley College; she remained there until 1949. In 1915 she was editor of *Papers of James A. Bayard* and published *An Historian's World: Selection from Correspondence of John Franklin Jameson* with Leo F. Stock. She wrote *Documents Illustrative of the Slave Trade*, Volumes 1–4, for the Carnegie Institution from 1930 to 1935. She also wrote *Economic Principles and Modern Practice* with H. R. Mussey in 1942. At the time of her death on

March 15, 1955, she was arranging the papers of Jameson, which included large portions of the files of the Department of Historical Research at Carnegie Institution from 1903 to 1928, for transfer to the Manuscripts Division of the Library of Congress.

ADDITIONAL SOURCES

Obituary in NewYT, Mar. 17, 1955, p. 45; obituary *American Historical Review* 60: 1035–1036, July 1955; WhAm 3; BiIn 3, 4.

DURANT, ARIEL
(1898–1981)
World History

Ariel Durant, who collaborated with her husband, Will Durant, in the eleven-volume series *The Story of Civilization,* was born Chaya Kaufman in Proskurov (now Khmelnitski), Russia. Her father was Joseph Kaufman, a newspaper vendor, and her mother was Ethel (Appel) Kaufman. The family immigrated to New York in 1901. Ariel, with the rest of the family, hawked newspapers on New York street corners, although she did attend Ferrer Modern School around 1912, before she met and married historian/philosopher Will Durant in 1913. She began helping him with the organization of his historical research. Her contributions were unofficial in the first six volumes of *The Story of Civilization,* written between 1935 and 1957, but she was credited as co-author beginning with the publication in 1961 of the seventh volume, *The Age of Reason Begins,* and continuing until the publication of the final volume, *The Age of Napoleon,* in 1975. The two wrote a dual biography in 1977 and that same year received the Presidential Medal of Freedom. In addition, Ariel (a name given her by her husband) received the Woman of the Year Award from the *Los Angeles Times* in 1965, and the *Rousseau and Revolution* volume of the series won the 1968 Pulitzer Prize for general nonfiction. Ariel Durant died in Los Angeles on October 25, 1981.

ADDITIONAL SOURCES

NewYTBS 75; BiIn 6, 7, 8, 9, 10, 11; WhoAm 74, 76, 78, 80; WhoAmW 66, 68, 70, 72, 74, 75, 77; WhoWest 74, 76; obituary in NewYT, Oct. 28, 1981, p. B-4; NewYTBS 12: 1338, Oct. 1981; obituary in *Newsweek* 98: 101, Nov. 9, 1981; obituary in *Publishers Weekly* 220: 20, Nov. 6, 1981; obituary in *Time* 118: 110, Nov. 9, 1981.

E

EARLE, ALICE MORSE
(1851–1911)
Popular History

Alice Morse Earle was born in Worcester, Massachusetts, to Edwin Morse, a machinist partner in a tool company and eventually director of the First National Bank, and Abby Mason Clary Morse. She attended Worcester High School and Dr. Gannett's boarding school in Boston. On April 15, 1874, she married Henry Earle, a New York broker, and moved to Brooklyn Heights.

Earle began her historical career by writing magazine articles on Colonial American churches. Her first book was *The Sabbath in Puritan New England,* published in 1891. Over the next twelve years, she published seventeen books and over thirty articles on Colonial American lives, manners, and customs. In her home were fifty subject files filled with notes. *The Sabbath in Puritan New England* was followed by *China Collecting in America* (1892). She wrote several books on Colonial clothing, including *Customs and Fashions of Old New England* (1893), *Costume of Colonial Times* (1894), and *Two Centuries of Costume in America 1620–1820,* a two-volume work published in 1903. The latter was preceded by two books on gardens, *Old Time Gardens* (1901) and *Sun Dials and Roses of Yesterday* (1902). In between were books on almost any subject imaginable for the period—*Colonial Dames and Good Wives* (1895); *Colonial Days in Old New York* (1896); *Home Life in Colonial Days* (1898); *In Old Narragansett: Romances and Realities* (1898); *Child Life in Colonial Days* (1899); and *Stage-coach and Tavern Days* (1900). She took time out to edit the *Diary of Anna Green Winslow, a Boston School Girl of 1771* in 1894 and to write a biography of Margaret Winthrop in 1895.

Alice Earle was very active socially. She belonged to several organizations including Daughters of the American Revolution and the Society of Colonial Dames and often took time out from her writing to travel. In January 1909, on a trip from Boston to Egypt with her sister Frances, their steamer, the *Republic,* struck another steamer off the Nantucket Lightship and was cut in half. The two women almost drowned. Her health suffered, and she died on February 16, 1911, of nephritis.

ADDITIONAL SOURCES

DcAmAu; DcAmB; InWom; NatCAB v. 13; NotAW; TwCBDA; *Bio-Base.*

EASTMAN, MARY HENDERSON
(1818–1887)
Sioux History

Mary Henderson Eastman was born in Warrenton, Fauquier County, Virginia, on February 24, 1818, to Thomas Henderson, a physician and assistant surgeon general of the United States Army, and Anna Maria (Truxtun) Henderson. The family moved to Washington, D.C., and Mary lived there until her marriage in 1835 to Seth Eastman, a graduate of the United States Military Academy and a drawing teacher at West Point. In 1841 the Eastmans were transferred to a new command on the upper Mississippi River at Fort Snelling. Mary learned the Sioux language in order to study Sioux customs and lore. The result was *Dahcotah; Or, Life and Legends of the Sioux Around Fort Snelling,* illustrated by her husband, in 1849. That same year the Eastmans returned to Washington and Mary wrote an "anti-Uncle Tom" book called *Aunt Phillis's Cabin; Or Southern Life as It Is.* This was followed by another joint venture, *The Romance of Indian Life* and *The American Aboriginal Portfolios,* both published in 1853. The next year she wrote *Chicora and Other Regions of the Conquerors and the Conquered,* followed by *American Annual: Illustrative of the Early History of North America.* In the following years, perhaps because her husband was stationed in other areas, Mary Eastman began writing romantic novels. She died in Washington of apoplexy on February 24, 1887.

ADDITIONAL SOURCES

John S. Hart, *The Female Prose Writers of America,* rev. ed. (1855); Mrs. Mary T. Tardy, *The Living Female Writers of the South* (1872); ApCAB; Alli; AmAu&B; BiD&SB; BiDSA; ChPo; DcAmAu; DcEnL; DcNAA; OxAm; REnAL; TwCBDA; AmWomWr; LibW; NotAW; *Bio-Base.*

EATON, RACHEL CAROLINE
(1869–1938)
Western U.S. History

Rachel Caroline Eaton was born in 1869, in Indian Territory, to George W. Eaton, a white man, and Nancy Elizabeth (Williams) Eaton, of Cherokee and Caucasian descent. She attended Cherokee public schools and graduated from Cherokee Female Seminary in 1887. She received a B.A. in 1895 from Drury College (cum laude) and returned to the Cherokee Nation to teach in the public school and at the Female Seminary. In 1911 she entered Chicago University and majored in history, receiving an M.A. in 1911 and a Ph.D. in 1919.

During Eaton's professional career, she was head of the history department at State College for Women in Columbus, Missouri, professor of history at Lake Erie College in Paineville, Ohio, dean of women and the history department head at Trinity University in Waxahachie, Texas, and superintendent of schools in Rogers County, Oklahoma. During this time she wrote extensively on western history, including *Domestic Science Among The Primitive Cherokees; Historic Fort Gibson; John Ross and the Cherokee Indians; Oklahoma Pioneer Life; The Battle of Claremore Mound;* and *History of Pioneer Churches in Oklahoma.* In 1932 the Tulsa Historical Society founded the Rachel Caroline Eaton Chapter, and in 1936 she was inducted into the Oklahoma Hall of Fame. Eaton died in 1938.

ADDITIONAL SOURCES

Emmett Starr, *History of the Cherokee Indians and Their Legends and Folklore; Who's Who Among Oklahoma Indians;* Muriel Wright, "Rachel Caroline Eaton," *Chronicles of Oklahoma,* Dec. 1938, pp. 509–510; *Native American Women: A Biographical Dictionary,* p. 85; *Bio-Base.*

EBREY, PATRICIA BUCKLEY
(1947–   )
Chinese Cultural History

Patricia Buckley Ebrey was born on March 7, 1947, in New Jersey. Her parents, both of European ancestry, were employed by newspapers. Patricia Buckley attended public schools in Hasbrouck Heights, New Jersey, then the University of Chicago, where she earned a bachelor's degree in 1968. While at the University of Chicago she took a course on Western civilization and was motivated to become a historian. She then attended Columbia University, earning a master's degree in 1970 and a Ph.D. in 1975. Ebrey has also studied classical Chinese, modern Chinese, Japanese, and French.

Ebrey's first academic appointment, as visiting assistant professor of East Asian studies and history, was at the University of Illinois at Urbana-Champaign, in 1975. She was promoted to associate professor in 1982 and to professor in 1985. She has also served as visiting assistant director of international programs and studies and department head of East Asian languages and cultures, both at the University of Illinois. Ebrey was visiting fellow of East Asian studies at Princeton University from 1983 to 1984, and visiting scholar for the Institute for Humanistic Research at Kyoto University from 1990 to 1991.

Ebrey's main area of scholarly interest is the social and cultural history of China's Sung dynasty, which ruled from 960 to 1279. She has written four books, edited or co-edited four books, and translated and annotated another two books. She has also written sixteen scholarly articles, twenty-three book chapters, and two teaching aids about Chinese civilization. Her most recent book, *The Cambridge Illustrated History of China,* was published in 1996, and her next most recent, *The Inner Quarters: Marriage and the Lives of Chinese Women in the Sung Period,* was the winner of the Levenson Prize of the Association for Asian Studies. As one reviewer argued, the book "should lay to rest forever the one-dimensional image of the pathetic, downtrodden, and historically immutable 'traditional Chinese woman'—an image that has prevailed too long both within and outside the field of Chinese studies." Ebrey is also said to have written, in this work, "the most thorough discussion of the spread of footbinding available in English."

Ebrey's list of honors and awards includes fellowships with the Whiting Foundation, Columbia University, the Woodrow Wilson Foundation, the Fulbright-Hayes Foundation, the Joint Committee on Chinese Studies, and the National Endowment for the Humanities. She was a University Scholar for the University of Illinois from 1985 to 1988. Ebrey has received seven grants from the National Endowment for the Humanities, including three translation grants and a conference grant.

Patricia Buckley Ebrey has served on the editorial board of *China Review International,* as editor for China to 1644 for the American Historical Association's *Guide to Historical Literature,* and as editor for a symposium in *Modern China* on family life in late traditional China. Ebrey was president of the Tang Studies Society from 1987 to 1989, an elected member of the China and Inner Asia Council of the Association for Asian Studies from 1982 to 1985, and on the Executive Committee of the Association for Asian Studies from 1982 to 1984. She also serves on and will chair the 1988 Program Committee for the Association for Asian Studies annual conference. Ebrey has served as co-organizer for several conferences, including the 1989 Conference on Religion and Society in China, the 1988 Conference on Marriage and Inequality in China, and the 1983 Conference on Family and Kinship in Chinese History.

She has also served on professional committees of the American Council of Learned Societies, the Levenson Prize Selection Committee, the National Endowment for the Humanities, and the Committee on Scholarly Communication with the People's Republic of China. She has given lectures or seminars at nearly two dozen universities across the United States and has traveled for study and research in China, Taiwan, and Japan.

Patricia Buckley Ebrey's interests include Chinese art, especially paintings. She is married to Thomas G. Ebrey, and they have two sons, David and Stephen.

BOOKS BY PATRICIA BUCKLEY EBREY

The Cambridge Illustrated History of China. Cambridge: Cambridge University Press, 1996.

The Inner Quarters: Marriage and the Lives of Chinese Women in the Sung Period. Berkeley: University of California Press, 1993.

Editor, with Peter Gregory. *Religion and Society in T'ang and Sung China.* Honolulu:

University of Hawaii Press, 1993. *Confucianism and Family Rituals in Imperial China: A Social History of Writing About Rites.* Princeton, NJ: Princeton University Press, 1991.

Editor, with Rubie S. Watson. *Marriage and Inequality in Chinese Society.* Berkeley: University of California Press, 1991.

Translator. *Chu Hsi's Family Rituals: A Twelfth-Century Chinese Manual for the Performance of Cappings, Weddings, Funerals, and Ancestral Rites.* Princeton, NJ: Princeton University Press, 1991.

Editor, with James L. Watson. *Kinship Organization in Late Imperial China, 1000–1940.* Berkeley: University of California Press, 1986.

Translator. *Family and Property in Sung China: Yuan Ta'ai's Precepts for Social Life.* Princeton, NJ: Princeton University Press, 1984.

Editor. *Chinese Civilization: A Sourcebook.* New York: The Free Press, 1981. 2nd ed., 1993.

The Aristocratic Families of Early Imperial China: A Case Study of the Poling Ts'ui Family. Cambridge: Cambridge University Press, 1978.

ADDITIONAL SOURCES

Bossler, Beverly. Rev. of *The Inner Quarters: Marriage and the Lives of Chinese Women in the Sung Period,* by Patricia Buckley Ebrey. *Journal of Asian Studies* 53 (May 1994): 529–530.

Questionnaire completed by the subject for *American Women Historians, 1700s–1990s: A Biographical Dictionary.*

ECKSTORM, FANNIE HARDY
(1865–1946)
Native American History

Fannie Hardy Eckstorm, a leading authority on the Penobscot Indians as well as mammals and ornithology, was born on June 18, 1865, to Manley and Emeline Freeman (Wheeler) Hardy. Her ancestors had come from England in 1630, and her father was the largest fur trader in Maine. Fannie was his close companion, often accompanying him on his trips, and his relationship with the Penobscot Indians provided Eckstorm with much of her material in later years.

Eckstorm attended high school in Bangor, Maine, and Abbott Academy in Andover, Massachusetts. She entered Smith College in 1885 with advanced standing. During her time at Smith, she founded the college Audubon Society and discovered Charles G. Leland's *The Algonquin Legends of New England* (1884), which resulted in her own studies of Native Americans. She received an A.B. in 1888, and after graduation she went with her father on the first of many canoe trips through the wilderness; she was often the first white woman to enter the area and probably one of the few to speak the local Indian dialects. She was an expert taxidermist and from 1889 to 1891 served as one of the first women superintendents of schools in Maine. She also joined her father in the fight for fish and game protection laws to control out-of-state hunters by writing a series of articles for *Forest and Stream.*

On October 24, 1893, she married Rev. Jacob A. Eckstorm in Portland,

Oregon. A daughter, Katherine Hardy, was born in 1894, but died in 1901; a son, Paul Frederick, was born in 1896. The two lived in Portland, Oregon City, Eastport, Maine, and Providence, Rhode Island, before his death in 1899. Eckstorm returned to Brewer, Maine, took up taxidermy, became an expert on ornithology, and was one of the first women to be elected to the American Ornithologists' Union (1887). She began writing professionally, and in 1901 published two books: *The Bird Book,* a children's book, and *The Woodpeckers.* In 1904 she wrote about the Penobscot inhabitants in *The Penobscot Man,* which extolled the virtues of river drivers and woodsmen. In 1904 she wrote *David Libbey: Penobscot Woodsman and River Driver.* In 1908 she wrote a critique of Thoreau's *Maine Woods* and founded the public library in Brewer. She contributed a historical survey of lumbering in Louis C. Hatch's *Maine: A History* in 1919.

Eckstorm began collecting and analyzing folk songs, and in 1927 she wrote *Minstrelsy of Maine: Folk Songs and Ballads of the Woods and Coast* with Mary Winslow Smyth of Elmira College. Two years later, she wrote *British Ballads from Maine: The Development of Popular Songs, with Text and Airs* with Smyth and Phillips Barry of Cambridge. That same year, she received an honorary M.A. from the University of Maine, and in 1930 she was co-founder of the Folk Song Society of the Northeast.

At this point in her career, Eckstorm began concentrating on the Indian tribes that she knew so well from travels with her father. In 1932 Eckstorm wrote *The Handicrafts of the Modern Indians of Maine.* Two years later she wrote *Indian Brother* with Hubert Vansant Coryell, and in 1936 they wrote *The Scalphunters.* She wrote *Indian Place-Names of the Penobscot Valley and the Maine Coast* in 1941. In 1942 she fell and was housebound with a broken hip; her son died the next year. In 1945 she wrote her last book, *Old John Neptune and Other Maine Indian Shamans.* Fannie Eckstorm died of angina pectoris on December 31, 1946.

ADDITIONAL SOURCES
BiIn 2, 3, 11; AmAu&B; AmWomWr; ChPO S2; DcNAA; DcAmB S4; LibW; NatCAB 36; NotAW; WhAm 2; WomWWA 14; WhNAA; "Hardy Eckstorm: Maine Woods Historian," *New England Quarterly* 26 (Mar. 1953): 45–64; *Fannie Hardy Eckstorm: A Descriptive Bibliography of Her Writings, Published and Unpublished* (Northwest Folklore Society, 1976); *Bio-Base.*

EDMONDS, HELEN GRAY
(1911–1995)
History of African Americans, the U.S. South, and Modern Europe

Helen Gray Edmonds was born on December 3, 1911, in Lawrenceville, Virginia, the daughter of John Edward Edmonds, a building trades contractor, and Ann Williams, a full-time homemaker. She went to St. Paul's school in Lawrenceville and then Morgan State College. Her parents provided the early influences in her life, particularly as they encouraged her to pursue an education.

"There was never a moment in our family," she later recalled, "that higher education wasn't stressed." Edmonds received a bachelor's degree in history from Morgan State in 1933, then attended Ohio State University, earning a master's degree in 1938 and a Ph.D. in 1946. She was the first African-American woman to earn a Ph.D. in history in Ohio State University's history.

Edmonds accepted a teaching position at Virginia Theological Seminary and College in Lynchburg, Virginia, and then at Saint Paul's College in Lawrenceville. In 1940 she joined the faculty at North Carolina Central University, where she taught until her retirement in 1971 and where she reached the rank of distinguished professor of history. Edmonds also served North Carolina Central University as chair of the history department and dean of the Graduate School of Arts and Sciences. Inspired by W.E.B. DuBois's study at the University of Berlin, she spent a year at the University of Heidelberg, from 1954 to 1955. As professor emeritus, Edmonds has been visiting scholar at the University of Rochester, Harvard University, Massachusetts Institute of Technology, and Radcliffe College.

Author of two books and numerous scholarly articles, Edmonds has also earned several awards, including the American Historical Association's Award of Scholarly Distinction. She was the first recipient of the Candace Award of the Coalition of 100 Black Women, was named Distinguished Woman of North Carolina, and won the Oliver Max Gardner Award of the University of North Carolina, for the "greatest contribution to the human race."

In her service outside the academy, Edmonds served as president of Links, a women's service organization, in a period during which they raised $1 million in support of the United Negro College Fund. She has also held civic positions with the Southern Fellowships Fund, the NAACP Legal Defense Fund, and the Association for the Study of Negro Life and History. She has had a lifelong affiliation with the Republican Party and seconded President Dwight D. Eisenhower's nomination for reelection in 1956. She then served as the President's Special Emissary in Liberia and as an alternate delegate to the United Nations. She was later appointed by President Richard Nixon to the National Advisory Council of the Peace Corps. Helen Gray Edmonds died on May 9, 1995, in Durham, North Carolina.

BOOKS BY HELEN GRAY EDMONDS

Black Faces in High Places. New York: Harcourt Brace Jovanovich, 1971.

The Negro and Fusion Politics in North Carolina, 1894–1901. Chapel Hill: University of North Carolina Press, 1951.

ADDITIONAL SOURCES

Hornsby, Alton, Jr. "Helen G. Edmonds." *Notable Black American Women.* Ed. Jessie Carney Smith. Detroit: Gale Research, 1992, 312–314.

Jones, Beverly. "Edmonds, Helen Gray." *Black Women in America: An Historical Encyclopedia.* Ed. Darlene Clark Hine. New York: Carlson, 1993, Vol. 1, 379–380.

ELBERT, SARAH
(1936–   )
U.S. Cultural History

Sarah Elbert was born on January 5, 1936, in New York State, of mixed race. Her father worked in farming and in restaurant work; her mother worked in retail and as a farm wife. Elbert was influenced to become a historian not by any particular person but instead by the times through which she has lived. She grew up during World War II and what she calls the "not-so-silent fifties," the era of sit-ins, the Stockholm Peace Pact, Julius and Ethel Rosenberg, and Senator Joseph McCarthy. In the 1960s Elbert became an activist, participating in the civil rights and anti–Vietnam War movements.

Elbert attended Cornell University, earning a bachelor's degree magna cum laude with honors in history in 1965. She did her graduate work at Cornell as well, earning a master of arts in teaching in 1966, a master's degree in history in 1968, and a Ph.D. in history in 1974. While in graduate school Elbert participated in Students for a Democratic Society (SDS) and the Union for Radical Political Economics (URPE). She was also a member of the Congress of Racial Equality (CORE) and testified for the defense in the trial of the Chicago Eight in 1969. She made a documentary history of the week of the 1968 Democratic Convention, "The Streets Belong to the People," which was sponsored by the Cornell University Oral History Program and released by American Documentary Films.

Elbert chose to work in state-supported higher education after what she calls "a previous lifetime of elite education," and took a job as assistant professor of history at Binghamton University, State University of New York. She has always remained an activist as well as an academic. Elbert was a single parent from the time her children were, respectively, nine and four years old. As she recalls, that was in 1964, when there were no daycare centers and no child support laws. With the help of many friends, cooperatives she participated in, and the free school movement, Sarah Elbert raised her children. As part of the student movement of the 1960s and 1970s, she helped start alternative schools, communes, and cooperatives, and belonged to Circle Pines Center in Delton, Michigan, a cooperative work camp started in the 1930s. She also helped build, and still maintains, a family homestead and garden in upstate New York.

Sarah Elbert has been on the faculty of Binghamton University since 1973, when she was visiting assistant professor of history. From 1974 to 1981 she was assistant professor; since 1981 she has been associate professor. She has also been visiting assistant professor in Women's studies at Cornell University, visiting professor of American studies at Aarhus University in Denmark, visiting associate professor of rural sociology at Cornell, visiting professor of history at California Polytechnic State University, and Fulbright Professor of American Studies at the University of Tromso in Norway.

The author or editor of six books, Elbert is best known for her work on Louisa

May Alcott, which originated with her dissertation. When graduate student Elbert reread *Little Women,* which she had read as a child, she realized that it contained a subtext that ''dealt with issues of women's rights, of slavery and other social reforms.'' She pursued that interest with the help of her favorite contemporary novelist, Alison Lurie, who encouraged Elbert to work on Alcott by giving her old hardcover Alcott novels and mentoring her at a time when noncanonical works were disdained. Elbert completed her dissertation and later edited collections of Alcott's re-released work and published a critical examination of Alcott, *A Hunger for Home: Louisa May Alcott's Place in American Culture* in 1987.

Sarah Elbert has since renewed scholarly interest in Alcott, whose *Little Women,* an international best-seller, has been read by five generations of girls. When Hollywood filmmakers decided to remake *Little Women,* producer Denise DiNovi purchased Elbert's book, *A Hunger for Home,* for the cast. And when a BBC crew came to New England to work on the Alcott segment of a series on women writers, Elbert spent two days on camera discussing the writer's work and times. As Elbert argues, and as generations of readers seem to agree, *Little Women* ''depicts a remarkably democratic family, one that doesn't exploit girls just to farm them out for labor, a safe haven from which to take flight. It's quite remarkable for a novel about women in the middle of the 19th century.''

Elbert has also written seventeen scholarly articles or book chapters on Alcott and other nineteenth-century writers, contemporary rural women's lives, and the history of women's education. She has also written two television scripts, one on Louisa May Alcott and the other on Elizabeth Cady Stanton. Since 1976 she has been a consultant to Arno Press and to the Women's Studies Archives at Cornell University. She has also been a consultant to the Elizabeth Cady Stanton Papers at Radcliffe College, the National Women's Studies Association, the Kellogg Foundation, and the National Endowment for the Humanities. Elbert has received grants from the U.S. Department of Health, Education and Welfare, the Organization of American Historians, and the U.S. Department of Agriculture.

Sarah Elbert continues to be an active member of her community. She has served on the Social Action Committee of her local Unitarian Church, as a staff writer for *Bookpress,* an Ithaca, New York, publication, as an oral history consultant to the New York State Conference of Organic Farmers, and as a board member of the Tompkins County Friends of the Library and Tompkins County Displaced Homemakers.

Sarah Elbert's son, Adam Kartman, is a family physician in Bellingham, Washington. Her daughter, Carrie Kartman, is a playwright, actress, and graduate student in creative writing in San Francisco. Along with her children and three grandchildren, Elbert's interests include her vegetable garden, a produce marketing cooperative, and swimming and working out with a friendly, diverse group of ''townies'' in Ithaca, New York, where she lives.

BOOKS BY SARAH ELBERT

Editor. *Moods,* by Louisa May Alcott. New Brunswick, NJ: Rutgers University Press, 1991.

A Hunger for Home: Louisa May Alcott's Place in American Culture. New Brunswick, NJ: Rutgers University Press, 1987.

A Hunger for Home: Louisa May Alcott and "Little Women." Philadelphia: Temple University Press, 1986.

Editor. *Diana and Persis,* by Louisa May Alcott. New York: Arno Press, 1978.

Editor. *The Little Colonel,* by Annie Fellows Johnson. New York: Garland, 1976.

Editor. *Two Little Confederates,* by Thomas Nelson Page. New York: Garland, 1976.

Editor. *Work: A Study of Experience,* by Louisa May Alcott. New York: Schocken Books, 1971.

ADDITIONAL SOURCES

Questionnaire completed by the subject for *American Women Historians, 1700s–1990s: A Biographical Dictionary.*

Quindlen, Anna. "She Was Jo, and That Was That." Rev. of *Moods,* edited by Sarah Elbert. *New York Times Book Review,* March 3, 1991.

Shepherd, Lee. "Alcott's Message as Good Today as 126 Years Ago." *Press and Sun-Bulletin,* Feb. 26, 1995, p. 13.

ELLET, ELIZABETH FRIES (LUMMIS)
(1812 or 1818–1877)
U.S. Women's History

Elizabeth Fries Ellet, said to be the first historian of women, was born in Sodus, Lake Ontario, New York, to William Nixon Lummis, a physician, and Sarah (Maxwell), his second wife. (Throughout her lifetime, Ellet gave 1818 as her birthdate, but her birth certificate says 1812.) She attended the Female Seminary in Aurora, New York, and married Dr. William H. Ellet, professor of chemistry at Columbia College, New York City, in 1835. The two lived in Columbia, South Carolina, until 1849, when they returned to New York City. During this time, Ellet began writing poetry and tragedies based on historical events.

In 1848 Ellet's interests turned to women's history. She wrote two volumes of *Women of the American Revolution* and finished a third volume in 1850. The book covered the lives of 160 women who played a part in or commented on history. This work was considered to be the first of its type. That same year, *Domestic History of the American Revolution* was published. In 1852 she wrote *Pioneer Women of the West,* and in 1859, the year of her husband's death, *Women Artists in All Ages and Countries* was published. In 1867 she wrote *The Queens of American Society,* a history of "manners, fashions, prominent hostesses in Washington and other social centers, famous balls, visiting foreign celebrities, and socially dominant families." In 1869 she and Mrs. R. E. Mack wrote *Court Circles of the Republic; or, The Beauties and Celebrities of the Nation,* a book on statesmen and their "leading Ladies" under eighteen presidents from Washington to Grant. Elizabeth Ellet died in New York City on June 3, 1877.

ADDITIONAL SOURCES

NatCAB; DcAmAu; DcAmB; InWom; NatCAB v. 11; NotAW; TwCBDA; Arthur and Elizabeth Schlesinger Library on the History of Women in America, *The Manuscript Inventories of and the Catalogs of the Manuscripts, Books and Pictures,* Vol. 3 (Boston: G. K. Hall, 1973); *Bio-Base.*

ENGEL, BARBARA ALPERN
(1943–   )
Russian History

Barbara Alpern Engel was born on June 28, 1943, in New York City, of eastern European ancestry. Her father was a lawyer, her mother a full-time homemaker. She attended public elementary school in Brooklyn and graduated from Valley Stream Central High School, on Long Island, in 1961. Among her early influences she counts her parents', especially her father's, love of reading, and their "wonderfully diverse, if small, family library." Her high school social studies teacher, Harry Feigenbaum, sparked her interest in the Russian language. Engel then enrolled in his Russian language course, the first of its kind at the school. She was "not a brilliant high school student," she reports, "but I read voraciously."

Engel attended the City University of New York, where she earned a bachelor's degree in Russian area studies in 1965. As an undergraduate, from 1963 to 1964, she was one of five women students accepted into Princeton University's Cooperative Program in Critical Languages. They were the first female undergraduates at Princeton. Although Engel returned to her home institution to graduate, the Princeton experience, as she puts it, "really stimulated me and gave me a push to go on." Engel then attended Harvard University, receiving a master's degree in Russian area studies in 1967.

After completing her Harvard degree, Engel worked for two years as a bilingual secretary and part-time translator for the Smithsonian Astrophysical Observatory in Cambridge, Massachusetts. She enjoyed her work but found that it did not offer her opportunities for advancement, even though men with the same training were moving ahead. Engel felt she should pursue the Ph.D., and she gravitated toward history more than other fields. In 1975 she completed her Ph.D., in Russian history, from Columbia University.

Barbara Alpern Engel's first full-time academic position was as assistant professor at Sarah Lawrence College, where she taught from 1974 to 1976. She then accepted a position at the University of Colorado, where she has worked since, as assistant professor from 1976 to 1982, associate professor from 1982 to 1992, and professor since 1992. From 1993 to 1995 Engel was the director of the Central and Eastern European Studies Program, and she currently serves as chair of the department of history.

Engel has written two single-authored works, the most recent of which is *Between the Fields and the City: Women, Work and Family in Russia, 1861–*

1914. In this work she examines the effects of industrialization and urbanization on Russian peasant women. "Her perceptive and sensitive use of disparate sources," writes a reviewer, "including comparative works on women in Europe and fascinating archival evidence for the experiences of individual female peasants, is particularly noteworthy." Engel also co-edited, with Clifford Rosenthal, *Five Sisters: Women Against the Tsar,* and with Barbara Clements and Christine Worobec, *Russia's Women: Accommodation, Resistance, Transformation.* Engel has also written nearly twenty-five scholarly pieces and numerous book reviews.

A fellow of the Rutgers Center for Historical Analysis, the John D. and Catherine T. MacArthur Foundation, the Woodrow Wilson Center, and the A. Harriman Institute, Engel also served several times on an International Research and Exchange Board, (IREX) with the Soviet Union. She has provided professional service to the American Historical Association, the Western Association of Women Historians, and the International Federation of Societies for Research in Women's History. She has been on the editorial board of *Frontiers,* a consulting editor for *Feminist Studies,* and a manuscript reader for several publishers, including W. W. Norton, Harvard University Press, and Cambridge University Press.

Engel has been honored for her work in a number of ways. She is the recipient of the Chancellor's Writing Award from the University of Colorado, a winner of the Elizabeth Gee Award for Excellence, a Boulder Faculty Assembly Award Winner for Excellence in Research and Creative Work, and the recipient of a Mortar Board Senior Honor Society Excellence in Teaching Award.

Divorced, Barbara Alpern Engel lives with her partner of thirteen years, a political activist, who has a thirteen-year-old son. Her hobbies include gardening, hiking, cross-country skiing, reading novels, yoga, and, most recently, mushroom hunting.

BOOKS BY BARBARA ALPERN ENGEL

Between the Fields and the City: Women, Work and Family in Russia, 1861–1914. New York: Cambridge University Press, 1994.

Editor, with Barbara Clements and Christine Worobec. *Russia's Women: Accommodation, Resistance, Transformation.* Berkeley: University of California Press, 1991.

Mothers and Daughters: Women of the Intelligentsia in Nineteenth Century Russia. New York: Cambridge University Press, 1983.

Five Sisters: Women Against the Tsar. New York: Knopf, 1975. New edition, Routledge, 1992.

ADDITIONAL SOURCES

Bernstein, Laurie. Rev. of *Between the Fields and the City: Women, Work and Family in Russia, 1861–1914,* by Barbara Alpern Engel. *Labor History* 35 (Fall 1994): 612–614.

Questionnaire completed by the subject for *American Women Historians, 1700s–1990s: A Biographical Dictionary.*

F

FADERMAN, LILLIAN
(1940–   )
Lesbian and Gay History

Lillian Faderman was born on July 18, 1940, in the Bronx, New York, of Jewish ancestry. Her mother, a single parent, worked in a garment factory. Faderman began school in the Bronx, then finished elementary school and junior high school in East Los Angeles. She attended Hollywood High School. She participated in the Theater Arts Workshop in East Los Angeles from 1952 to 1955 and counts an interest in the theater as one of her important early influences.

Faderman attended the University of California at Berkeley, earning a bachelor's degree in 1962. As a graduate student in literature, she attended the University of California at Los Angeles, earning a master's degree in 1964 and a Ph.D. in 1967. Faderman also attended Harvard University, earning a certificate from the Institute of Educational Management in 1974.

Lillian Faderman was motivated to become a historian because she wanted to "discover for myself what no sources would tell me about women's intimate relationships in other centuries." Her work reaches both scholarly and popular audiences as she deftly, as one critic puts it, "brings lesbian life out of the archives and onto the streets."

From 1967 to the present, Faderman has taught at the University of California at Fresno, where she is professor of English. From 1989 to 1991, she was visiting professor of English and women's studies at UCLA. While at Fresno, Faderman has chaired the English department, designed and co-founded the Women's Studies Program, and served as acting dean for the School of Humanities.

The author or editor of seven books, fifteen articles, and numerous commentaries and reviews, Faderman is known as an award-winning interdisciplinary scholar, bridging the fields of literature, history, and ethnic studies. Her most recent work, *Chloe plus Olivia: Lesbian Literature from the Seventeenth Century to the Present*, received the Lambda Literary Award for Best Anthology and was named a finalist for the Best Lesbian Studies Book. A previous work, *Odd Girls and Twilight Lovers: A History of Lesbian Life in Twentieth Century America*, was nominated for the Pulitzer Prize and the National Book Award and received great acclaim, including being named "Editor's Choice" and a "Notable Book of 1992" by the *New York Times Book Review*, Best Book of the Year Dealing with Lesbian Subject Matter by the American Library Association's Social Responsibility Task Force, and Bestseller Among University Press Books by *Library Journal*. Faderman's books have been translated into German, Japanese, and Spanish.

An award-winning teacher, Faderman has lectured to thirty-five university groups in and outside the United States. She serves as general co-editor of the Between Men/Between Women Series for Columbia University Press and on the advisory boards for the journals *Thamyris, Women's History Review, Journal of Homosexuality,* and *Signs*. She has served the Modern Language Association by serving on and chairing the Executive Committee of the Women's Studies in Language and Literature Division and by serving on the editorial board of the Gay Caucus of the Modern Language Association (MLA) Lesbian and Gay Newsletter. She was also associate editor of the *Journal of the History of Sexuality* from 1989 to 1993.

Lillian Faderman's partner is Phyllis Irwin, whom she has been with since 1971. Faderman is the mother of a son, Avrom, born in 1975.

BOOKS BY LILLIAN FADERMAN

Editor. *Chloe plus Olivia: Lesbian Literature from the Seventeenth Century to the Present*. New York: Viking Press, 1994.

Odd Girls and Twilight Lovers: A History of Lesbian Life in Twentieth Century America. New York: Columbia University Press, 1991; paperback, 1992; Japanese and Spanish editions forthcoming.

Scotch Verdict. New York: William Morrow, 1983; Columbia University Press, 1993.

Surpassing the Love of Men: Romantic Friendship and Love Between Women from the Sixteenth Century to the Present. New York: William Morrow, 1981; Book of the Month Club Paperback 1994; German edition, Eco Verlag, 1988.

Editor, with Brigitte Eriksson. *Lesbian Feminism in Turn-of-the-Century Germany*. Talahassee, FL: Naiad Press, 1980; *Lesbians in Germany,* Talahassee, FL: Naiad, 1990.

Editor, with Omar Salinas. *From the Barrio: A Chicano Anthology*. San Francisco: Harper and Row, 1973.

Editor, with Barbara Bradshaw. *Speaking for Ourselves: American Ethnic Writing*. New York: Scott, Foresman, 1969; 2nd edition 1975.

ADDITIONAL SOURCES

Questionnaire completed by the subject for *American Women Historians, 1700s–1990s: A Biographical Dictionary*.

Winterson, Jeannette. Quoted on cover of *Odd Girls and Twilight Lovers*.

FEUERLICHT, ROBERTA STRAUSS
(1931–1991)
Biography

Roberta Strauss Feuerlicht was born November 23, 1931, in New York City to Isaac and Lena (Wesler) Strauss. She received a B.A. from Hunter College in 1952 and married Herbert Alan Feuerlicht, a sculptor, in 1958. She worked as an editor for the *Glen Oaks News* and *This Month* magazine in New York before becoming a freelance writer. In 1963 she published her first historical work, *Andrews' Raiders.* In 1965 she began a series on revolutions and biographies called American R.D.M. This resulted in a number of books: *Oliver Wendell Holmes, Gandhi, Madame Curie* (all 1965), *Theodore Roosevelt* and *Martin Luther King, Jr.* (1966). The series led to several more books by commercial publishers such as *The Desperate Act* (1968), *A Free People* (1969), *Henry VIII* (1970), *In Search of Peace* (1971), *America's Reign of Terror* (1971), *Zhivko of Yugoslavia* (1971), and *Joe McCarthy and McCarthyism* (1972). In 1977 she wrote a history of the trial and executions of Nicolas Sacco and Bartolomeo Vanzetti. Roberta Feuerlicht died on October 4, 1991, of congestive heart failure.
ADDITIONAL SOURCES
ConAu 17R; obituary in NewYT, Oct. 5, 1991, p. 10; obituary in NYTBS 22: 1048, Oct. 1991; *Bio-Base.*

FIGUEROA MERCADO, LOIDA
(1917–   )
History of Puerto Rico

Loida Figueroa Mercado was born on October 6, 1917, in Yauco, Puerto Rico, the daughter of Agustin and Emeteria Mercado Figueroa. Her father was a cane seed cutter, her mother a domestic worker. Neither of her parents had any formal education, but they urged their children to study. Her father had a good knowledge of Puerto Rico and other nations despite his lack of schooling. Her mother gained an understanding of the history of Puerto Rico while working as a servant in well-to-do homes. In her childhood, Loida was greatly influenced by the Baptist Church, which her family attended regularly.

Loida Figueroa Mercado attended the Interamerican University of Puerto Rico's San German campus, where she majored in French and history, earning a bachelor's degree, magna cum laude, in 1941. After a career as an elementary and high school teacher, and then an acting school principal, she did graduate work at Columbia University, earning a master's degree in history in 1948. Figueroa Mercado then attended the Universidad Central de Madrid, focusing on Puerto Rican studies and earning the Ph.D. in 1963. Both her master's degree and her Ph.D. were made possible by funding, first from the Puerto Rican government and then from the University of Puerto Rico.

Figueroa Mercado taught at the Mayaguez campus of the University of Puerto Rico, at the City University of New York's Lehmann College and Brooklyn

College, and at the Interamerican University of Puerto Rico. She taught courses on the history of Puerto Rico, Spain, Latin America, and the West Indies. She taught at the University of Puerto Rico until 1974, then taught at Brooklyn College from 1974 until her retirement in 1977. She came out of retirement a second time in 1992 to teach at the San German campus of the Interamerican University.

Figueroa Mercado was at Brooklyn College during a very difficult time, politically, for the Puerto Rican studies program, which was founded in 1971. The college administration imposed a new, and largely unwelcome, administration on the program. After a two-year battle for autonomy, the Puerto Rican studies program won its case. Loida Figueroa Mercado, who was by then a full professor, joined with the students and took to the streets to protest unfair administrative practices. She is still remembered warmly for her unfailing commitment for Puerto Rican people, as she put it in the introduction to *Brief History of Puerto Rico,* to have "the opportunity of studying their own history in an adequate fashion." Her political involvement did not begin in New York, however. Loida Figueroa Mercado had a marked interest in Puerto Rican politics since age seven, and as an adult she became a militant of the pro-independence movement in Puerto Rico.

Figueroa Mercado published the first two volumes of her planned three-volume work, *Brief History of Puerto Rico,* in 1968 and 1969. In 1972 they were translated into English and published as one volume. She dedicated that work "To the generation of Puerto Ricans who are absent from their native soil, lest they become a lost generation." She published the third volume in 1976. She also served as editor of *Atenea.* Figueroa Mercado has been a member of Ateneo Puertorriqueno, Sociedad de Autores Puertorriquenos, Latin American Studies Association, and Phi Alpha Theta. She was also initiated, in 1993, into a Masonic lodge in Puerto Rico, as the first Puerto Rican woman to be admitted into a male lodge.

In the invitation to the reader at the beginning of *Brief History of Puerto Rico,* Maria Teresa Babin states that Loida Figueroa Mercado has been valued by many for "her human warmth, her faith in youth, her uplifting political ideology and her deep love for Puerto Rico."

Loida Figueroa Mercado was married and divorced three times. Since 1956 she has remained single. She is the mother of four daughters, Eunice, Maria Antonia, Rebeca, and Avaris. She also has twelve grandchildren and four great-grandchildren. She currently lives in Puerto Rico, where she plans to write the fourth volume of her work, focusing on the twentieth century in Puerto Rico. She is resident historian at the American University of Puerto Rico's Bayamon campus.

BOOKS BY LOIDA FIGUEROA MERCADO

Brief History of Puerto Rico from the Beginning to 1892. New York: Anaya Book Co., 1972.

Tres puntos claves: Lares, idioma, soberania. Puerto Rico: Editorial Edil, 1972.

Breva Historia de Puerto Rico: Desde 1800 a 1892. Puerto Rico: Editorial Edil, 1969.
Breva Historia de Puerto Rico: Desde sus comienzos hasta 1800. Puerto Rico: Editorial
   Edil, 1968. The two volumes were published in one volume in 1971 by Rio
   Piedras.
Arenales. Puerto Rico: Ediciones Rumbos, 1961.
Aridulces. Puerto Rico: Rodriquez Lugo, 1947.
ADDITIONAL SOURCES
Berry, Pam. "Loida Figueroa." *Notable Hispanic American Women.* Ed. Diane Telgen
   and Jim Kamp. Detroit: Gale Research, 1993, 159–160.

FITZPATRICK, SHEILA
(1941–   )
Russian History

Sheila Fitzpatrick was born June 4, 1941, in Melbourne, Australia, of Scottish,
Irish, and English ancestry. Her father was a historian, her mother a teacher.
Sheila attended the Lauriston Girls' School and then the University of Melbourne. She received a bachelor's degree in 1961 and a doctorate in 1969.

Fitzpatrick's first academic position was at the University of Birmingham,
England, where she was visiting lecturer in Soviet history from 1971 to 1972.
She then spent a year at the University of Texas at Austin, as lecturer in Slavic
languages and literature. Fitzpatrick was appointed associate professor of history
at St. John's University in 1974, and in 1975 she took a job as assistant professor
of history at Columbia University. She was promoted to associate professor
before leaving Columbia, in 1980, to take a job as professor of history at the
University of Texas at Austin. In 1987 Fitzpatrick was named Oliver H. Radkey
Regents' Professor of History at the University of Texas at Austin. In 1990 she
made her most recent move, to the University of Chicago, where she was named
Bernadotte E. Schmitt Professor of History in 1994.

The author or editor of nine books and over forty articles, Fitzpatrick has
explored the cultural, social, and political history of the former Soviet Union.
Her first book, *The Commissariat of Enlightenment,* was translated into both
Italian and Spanish, and her most recent book, *Stalin's Peasants: Resistance
and Survival in the Russian Village After Collectivization,* won the Heldt Prize
in 1994. Reviewer Orlando Figes, writing in the *Times Literary Supplement,*
says of *Stalin's Peasants* that "no other work comes close to it in recounting
the tragedy of collectivization from the peasant's point of view."

Fitzpatrick is currently working on several other books as well. *Everyday
Stalinism* is under contract with Oxford University Press, and *Popular Opposition in the Soviet Union Under Kruschev and Brezhnev,* which she edits with
Vladimir A. Kozlov, is under contract with Yale University Press. Fitzpatrick
is also the editor for a special issue of the journal *Russian History,* which will
be issued in 1996. Among her other current projects is a collection of essays,
which she has titled *Tear Off the Masks! Identity and Imposture in Stalinist
Society.*

Fitzpatrick currently serves on the editorial boards of several publications, including *Annals of Communism, Russian Review,* and the *Journal of Modern History.* She has served in a professional capacity for the American Historical Association, the Council for the Advancement of Slavic and East European Studies, the Joint Committee on Soviet Studies, and the National Council for Soviet and East European Research. She has been the recipient of a Faculty Award for Excellence in Teaching from the University of Chicago and of fellowships from the Guggenheim and Fulbright Foundations, the London School of Economics and Political Science, and the Woodrow Wilson International Center for Scholars.

Sheila Fitzpatrick is married to physicist Michael Danos. Her principal interest outside of work is music, especially violin and piano.

BOOKS BY SHEILA FITZPATRICK

Stalin's Peasants: Resistance and Survival in the Russian Village After Collectivization. New York: Oxford University Press, 1994.

The Commissariat of Enlightenment: Soviet Organization of Education and the Arts Under Lunarcharsky, 1917–1921. London and New York: Cambridge University Press, 1970–71.

The Cultural Front: Power and Culture in Revolutionary Russia. Ithaca, NY: Cornell University Press, 1992.

Editor, with Alexander Rabinowitch and Richard Staites. *Russia in the Era of NEP: Explorations in Soviet Society and Culture.* Bloomington: Indiana University Press, 1991.

Editor, with Lynne Viola. *A Researcher's Guide to Sources on Soviet Social History in the 1930s.* Armonk, NY: M. E. Sharpe, 1990; paperback, 1992.

Editor, with Marc Ferro. *Culture et révolution.* Paris: Editions de l'Ecole des Hautes Etudes en Sciences Sociales, 1989.

The Russian Revolution. New York: Oxford University Press, 1982–83; paperback 1984; Braille 1986; 2nd ed., 1994.

Education and Social Mobility in the Soviet Union, 1921–1932. New York: Cambridge University Press, 1979.

Editor. *Cultural Revolution in Russia, 1928–1931.* Bloomington: Indiana University Press, 1978; paperback, 1984.

ADDITIONAL SOURCES

Figes, Orlando. Rev. of *Stalin's Peasants,* by Sheila Fitzpatrick. *Times Literary Supplement,* Jan. 13, 1995, 26.

Questionnaire completed by the subject for *American Women Historians, 1700s–1990s: A Biographical Dictionary.*

FOX-GENOVESE, ELIZABETH ANN
(1941–   )
U.S. Intellectual, Southern, and Women's History; French History

Elizabeth Ann Fox-Genovese was born May 28, 1941, in Boston, Massachusetts, of Anglo-Saxon Protestant, Scotch-Irish, and German-Jewish ancestry. Her father, Edward Whiting Fox, was a professor of history, and her mother, Elizabeth

Mary Simon Fox, was a researcher and homemaker. Elizabeth attended elementary schools in Ithaca and Lake Placid, New York, and in Princeton, New Jersey. She attended high school in Le Chambon sur Lignon, France, and in Concord, Massachusetts. Among her early influences were her parents and her paternal grandmother. She loved reading, especially Laura Ingalls Wilder and Jane Austen. Several of her teachers and an opportunity to travel in Europe also influenced her thinking as a child.

Elizabeth Fox-Genovese spent a year at Cornell before going to Bryn Mawr College, where she had deferred her admission. She earned a bachelor's degree in history and French in 1963. Since her father was a historian and her mother had a master's degree in history, Elizabeth was drawn to the field. Her grandmother's stories of growing up, combined with her own reading and travel, further influenced her. "Mainly, it came naturally," she states. "I had grown up thinking historically. It seemed more familiar and comfortable than anything else." Fox-Genovese then attended Harvard University, where she earned a master's degree and a Ph.D. in history, in 1966 and 1974.

Fox-Genovese's first academic position was at the University of Rochester, where she worked as assistant and then associate professor of history from 1973 to 1980. From 1980 to 1986 she was professor of history at Binghamton University, State University of New York. She left Binghamton to take a position as professor of history and founding director of Women's Studies at Emory University. In 1988 Fox-Genovese was named Eleonore Raoul Professor of the Humanities at Emory University.

Author or co-author of seven books, editor of another seven books, and author of nearly seventy articles, Fox-Genovese has gained both a national and an international reputation. Her most recent books, *Feminism Is Not the Story of My Life* and *Feminism Without Illusions: A Critique of Individualism,* establish her as one of the most controversial critics of contemporary feminist thought. Another of her books, *Within the Plantation Household: Black and White Women of the Old South,* received the C. Hugh Holman Prize from the Society of Southern Literature and the Julia Cherry Spruill Prize from the Southern Association of Women Historians, and was named Outstanding Book of the Year by the Gustavus Myer Center for the Study of Human Rights. In addition, she is the editor of *Feminist Issues* and has served on the editorial boards of several other journals, including *Southern Cultures, Women's History Journal,* and *Partisan Review.*

The scope of Fox-Genovese's writing is broad, reaching academic and popular audiences and addressing a variety of topics and periods, including contemporary literary criticism, multicultural education, women and religious practice, southern women novelists, African-American women's experiences of slavery, feminist and postmodern theory, and autobiographies of black and white women in the U.S. South. Because of her national and international reputation as both a serious and a controversial scholar, Fox-Genovese has been invited to give lectures and keynote addresses at over eighty colleges and universities in the United States and abroad during the past five years.

Fox-Genovese has been the recipient of many fellowships, including those from the National Humanities Center, the American Council for Learned Societies and Ford Foundation, the Rockefeller Foundation, the Newberry Library, the New York Institute for the Humanities, and the National Endowment for the Humanities. She has performed professional service by serving as a jury member for the Pulitzer Prize in History, on the Harvard Graduate Society Council, on the Steering Committee of the National Council for History Standards, and on the executive council of the Society for the Study of Southern Literature and the Social Science History Association. She currently serves on the advisory boards of the Institute for American Values, the Independent Women's Forum, the American Academy for Liberal Education, the Black Periodical Literature Project, and the American Comparative Literature Association.

Fox-Genovese also has several works in progress, including *Ghosts and Memories: History in the Fictions of African-American Women Writers,* under contract with the University of Virginia Press, and, with Eugene D. Genovese, *The Mind of the Master Class,* a cultural, intellectual, and "psychohistorical" study of the antebellum planter class, under contract with W. W. Norton.

Elizabeth Fox-Genovese married historian Eugene Dominick Genovese in 1969. Her hobbies include needlepoint, professional baseball and football, contemporary women writers, politics, her pets, and friends and family. She also provides community service, currently serving on the boards of directors of the Atlanta Historical Association and the Sheridan Walk Homeowners Association.

BOOKS BY ELIZABETH FOX-GENOVESE

Feminism Is Not the Story of My Life. New York: Doubleday, 1995.

Editor. *Hidden Histories of Women in the New South.* Columbia: University of Missouri Press, 1994.

Editor, with Virginia Bernhard. *Southern Women: Histories and Identities.* Columbia: University of Missouri Press, 1992.

Feminism Without Illusions: A Critique of Individualism. Chapel Hill: University of North Carolina Press, 1991.

With Virginia Bernhard and David Burner. *Firsthand America: A History of the United States.* St. James, NY: Brandywine Press, 1991. Revised and expanded version of *An American Portrait.*

Within the Plantation Household: Black and White Women of the Old South. Chapel Hill: University of North Carolina Press, 1988.

With David Burner, Eugene D. Genovese, and Forrest McDonald. *An American Portrait: A History of the United States.* New York: Macmillan, 1985.

Editor and translator. *The Autobiography of Pierre Samuel DuPont de Nemours.* Wilmington, DE: Scholarly Resources, 1984.

With Eugene D. Genovese. *Fruits of Merchant Capital: Slavery and Bourgeois Property in the Rise and Expansion of Capitalism.* New York: Oxford University Press, 1983.

The Origins of Physiocracy: Economic Revolution and Social Order in Eighteenth-Century France. Ithaca, NY: Cornell University Press, 1976.
ADDITIONAL SOURCES
Questionnaire completed by the subject for *American Women Historians, 1700s–1990s: A Biographical Dictionary.*

FREEDMAN, ESTELLE
(1947–   )
History of Sexuality

Estelle Freedman was born on July 2, 1947, in Harrisburg, Pennsylvania, of Jewish ancestry. Her father was in sales and her mother was a freelance writer. She attended Herbert Hoover Elementary School and Hebrew School as a child, and her early influences included her grandparents and summer camp. Freedman attended Barnard College, earning a bachelor's degree in history, cum laude, in 1969. A combination of concern about the origins of contemporary social issues of the 1960s and a love of historical research motivated her to become a historian. In graduate school Freedman was influenced by concerns about women's issues and the challenge of resisting the obvious discrimination against women scholars.

Freedman pursued graduate work at Columbia University, earning a master's degree in 1972 and a Ph.D. in 1976. She taught at Princeton University as a lecturer while she completed her dissertation, then took an appointment at Stanford University, where she has been since, as assistant professor from 1976 to 1983, associate professor from 1983 to 1989, and professor since 1989. She has also been visiting professor or scholar at California State University at Chico, Oberlin College, and the University of California at Davis. In 1978 Freedman received the Dean's Award for Distinguished Teaching, and in 1981 she received the Lloyd W. Dinkelspiel Award for Outstanding Service to Undergraduate Education, both at Stanford University.

Freedman has held numerous fellowships, including those from the National Endowment for the Humanities, the American Council of Learned Societies, the American Association of University Women, and the Newberry Library. She was named a fellow of the Society of American Historians in 1990. Freedman has also received research grants from the Pew Foundation, the Radcliffe Research Support Program, Stanford University's Institute for Research on Women and Gender, and the National Endowment for the Humanities.

Estelle Freedman's most recent publication, *Intimate Matters: A History of Sexuality in America,* which she wrote with John D'Emilio, describes the evolution of American sexuality during the last three and a half centuries, examining in particular the ways in which sexual practices are influenced by contemporary economic, social, and ideological forces. *Intimate Matters* was a main or alternate selection of the History, Quality Paperback, Psychology Today, and Book-of-the-Month Clubs; it was also a "Notable Book" of 1989 in the *New York*

Times Book Review. Two of Freedman's other works were award winners: *Their Sisters' Keepers: Women's Prison Reform in America, 1830–1930* won the Alice and Edith Hamilton Prize for best scholarly manuscript on women, and *Victorian Women: A Documentary Account,* for which Freedman was an associate editor, won the Sierra Award for the finest multiple-author book from the Western Association of Women Historians. Freedman has also written twenty-seven articles and essays and edited a special issue of the journal *Signs: Journal of Women in Culture and Society.*

In terms of professional service, Freedman has served as consulting editor to *Feminist Studies;* as associate editor of *Signs* and *Journal of the History of Sexuality;* and on the editorial boards of *Journal of Women's History,* the *Journal of Sex Research,* the *Journal of Homosexuality,* and *Women and Criminal Justice.* She has served on the nominating committee for the Organization of American Historians and on the program committee of the Pacific Coast Branch of the American Historical Association. She has also served on the advisory board of the Northern California Lesbian and Gay Historical Society. Estelle Freedman has served as consultant on numerous film productions, including the Academy Award–winning "Common Threads: Stories from the Quilt," about the AIDS quilt, and "The Celluloid Closet," a Public Broadcasting System documentary. She produced a historical documentary video, "She Even Chewed Tobacco," and provided expert testimony for the Federation of Women Teachers of Ontario, Canada.

Estelle Freedman's partner is Susan Kroeger. Her hobbies include playing folk guitar.

BOOKS BY ESTELLE FREEDMAN

Maternal Justice: Miriam Van Waters and the Female Reform Tradition in America, 1887–1974. Chicago: University of Chicago Press, 1996.

With John D'Emilio. *Intimate Matters: A History of Sexuality in America.* New York: Harper and Row, 1988.

Their Sisters' Keepers: Women's Prison Reform in America, 1830–1930. Ann Arbor: University of Michigan Press, 1981.

Associate Editor, with Erna Olafron Hellerstein, Leslie Parker Hume, Karen M. Offen, Barbara Charlesworth Gelpi, and Marilyn Yalom. *Victorian Women: A Documentary Account of Women's Lives in Nineteenth-Century England, France and the United States.* Stanford: Stanford University Press, 1981.

ADDITIONAL SOURCE

Questionnaire completed by the subject for *American Women Historians, 1700s–1990s: A Biographical Dictionary.*

G

GILBERT, AMY MARGARET
(1895–1980)
U.S. History

Amy Margaret Gilbert was born on February 23, 1895, in Chambersburg, Pennsylvania, to Daniel and Mary Margaret (Ott) Gilbert. She attended Cornell University in the summer of 1914 and received an A.B. from Wilson College in 1915. She taught high school until 1916, when she became an instructor in history at Elmira College in Elmira, New York. She received an M.A. in 1919 from the University of Pennsylvania and a Ph.D. in 1922, when she became a professor of history and head of the department. She was a contributor that year to *The Work of Lord Brougham for Education in England* (Alexander C. Flick, editor). She did postdoctoral study at Columbia in 1931 and 1940–41 and attended summer semesters at Geneva Institute of International Relations and Geneva School of International Studies from 1926 to 1932, the University of Michigan in 1933, and the University of Chicago in 1940. She received an LL.D. from Wilson College in 1939. In 1935 she wrote a chapter on the history of the woman's movement for *History of the State of New York*, Volume 8 (A. C. Flick, editor).

Gilbert became academic dean at Milwaukee-Downer College in Milwaukee, Wisconsin, from 1936 to 1941; dean at Rhode Island State College in Kingston from 1941 to 1945; visiting professor of history in 1945 at Temple University in Philadelphia, and head of the history and political science departments of the four units of Associated College of Upper New York (Champlain College, Mohawk College, Sampson College, and Middletown Collegiate Center) from 1946 to 1950. In 1950 Gilbert published *ACUNY—The Associated Colleges of Upper New York: A Unique Response to an Emergency in Higher Education in the State of New York*, an official history of higher education. She was dean of academic administration at State University of New York, Champlain College,

Plattsburgh, from 1950 to 1952 and head of the college from 1952 to 1953. She was professor of history at State University of New York at Binghamton, Harpur College from 1953 to 1965 and professor emeritus until her death in 1980. After her retirement in 1965 she wrote *Executive Agreements and Treaties, 1946–1973* (1973).

Gilbert was official historian of the Associated Colleges of Upper New York and director of Broome County, New York Historical Society from 1956 to 1971. She represented Gannett Newspapers at sessions of the League of Nations in Geneva, Switzerland, in 1927, 1931, and 1932. She also attended the Geneva Disarmament Conference and the Lausanne Conference in 1932. She represented the *Milwaukee Journal* at the Second Meeting of the Ministers of Foreign Affairs of the American Republics at Havana, Cuba, in 1940.

Gilbert died in Endicott, New York, on February 27, 1980, after a long illness. After her death, the Amy M. Gilbert Scholarship fund was established at State University of New York at Binghamton.

ADDITIONAL SOURCES
ConAu 49; DrAS 74H, 78H; WhoAmW 58, 61; obituary in *American Historical Review* 85: 1051–1052, Oct. 1980; *Bio-Base.*

GLUCK, CAROL
(1941–)
Japanese History

Carol Gluck was born on November 12, 1941, in Chicago, Illinois. She grew up in Chicago and then attended Wellesley College, earning a bachelor's degree in philosophy in 1962. While at Wellesley she spent a year at the University of Munich, in Germany. Gluck completed her graduate work at Columbia University, earning the master's degree and the Ph.D., both in Japanese history, in 1970 and 1977. While at Columbia she also earned a certificate from the East Asian Institute at Columbia University, and from 1973 to 1974 she was a Foreign Research Fellow at the Faculty of Law at Tokyo University.

In 1975 Gluck was appointed assistant professor at Columbia University's department of history, department of East Asian languages and cultures, and East Asian Institute. She was promoted to associate professor in 1983 and professor in 1986. In 1988 Gluck was named George Sansom Professor of History at Columbia University; she still holds that position and rank. She also served as chair of the undergraduate program in East Asian studies from 1977 to 1987. While at Columbia Gluck held several visiting professor appointments, at the Tokyo University Faculty of Law, at Harvard University, at the Tokyo University Institute of Social Science, and at l'Ecole des Hautes Etudes en Sciences Sociales in Paris.

Gluck has been the recipient of many awards and fellowships, including those from the Ford Foundation, the Fulbright Foundation, and the Japan Foundation. She was named fellow of the American Academy of Arts and Letters; received the Mark van Doren Award and the Great Teacher Award for teaching, from Columbia University; was awarded the Alumnae Achievement Award from Wellesley College; and was a Distinguished Lecturer for Asian Studies and the Japan Society for the Promotion of Science.

Her special field is the history of modern Japan from the mid-nineteenth century to the present, with writings in modern intellectual history, international relations, postwar Japanese history, historiography, and public memory in Japan and the West. She is the author or co-editor of three books and the author of eighteen scholarly articles. Her best-known work is *Japan's Modern Myths: Ideology in the Late Meiji Period,* which won the John King Fairbank Prize of the American Historical Association and the Lionel Trilling Award of Columbia University. In this work, according to one reviewer, Gluck "set new standards, both methodologically and stylistically, for those working on the interrelation of politics and culture in imperial Japan." Gluck is currently completing two books: *Versions of the Past: The Japanese and Their Modern History,* an examination of historical consciousness in twentieth-century Japan; and *Varieties of Japanese History,* an edited volume of translations of Japanese writings on history-writing.

Gluck has also provided a great deal of service to the profession. She is currently president-elect of the Association for Asian Studies; chair of the American Advisory Committee of the Japan Foundation; government-appointed member of the Japan U.S. Friendship Commission; and member of the board of directors of the Japan Society, the board of trustees of the Asia Society, and the Committee on Research Libraries of the New York Public Library. She is a member of the Council on Foreign Relations, of the National Council for History Standards, of the Publications Committee of Columbia University Press, and of the editorial board of the *Journal of Japanese Studies.*

Carol Gluck is married to Peter L. Gluck; they have two sons, Thomas and William.

BOOKS BY CAROL GLUCK

Editor, with Ainslee Embree. *Asia in Western and World History.* Armonk, NY: M. E. Sharpe, 1995.

Editor, with Stephen Graubard. *Showa: The Japan of Hirohito.* New York: W. W. Norton, 1992.

Japan's Modern Myths: Ideology in the Late Meiji Period. Princeton, NJ: Princeton University Press, 1985.

ADDITIONAL SOURCES

Garon, Sheldon M. Rev. of *Japan's Modern Myths: Ideology in the Late Meiji Period,* by Carol Gluck. *American Historical Review* 92 (Apr. 1987): 472–473.

Questionnaire completed by the subject for *American Women Historians, 1700s–1990s: A Biographical Dictionary.*

GNUDI, MARTHA TEACH
(1908–1976)
History of Medicine, Technology

Martha Teach Gnudi was born in Sycamore, Illinois, on October 26, 1908, to Charles L. and Rosa M. (Tischhouser) Teach. She received a B.A. (cum laude) at the University of Southern California in 1929 and a doctor of letters from the University of Bologna in 1931 (the first woman to receive a degree from this university). She married Dante Gnudi, who was in the hotel business, in 1933. In 1935 she wrote, with Jerome P. Webster at Columbia University Medical Center, *Documenti Inediti Intorse All Vita de Gaspare Tagliacozzi.* From 1942 to 1963 she was librarian of the Webster Library of Plastic Surgery in the Columbia-Presbyterian Medical Center in New York, then was placed in charge of the historical and special collections of the Biomedical Library, University of California. In 1942, with Cyril Stanley Smith, she translated the *Pirotechnia* by Vannoccio Biringuccio (1540), the first book on metallurgy, published in Venice. She then wrote, with Jerome Pierce Webster, a famous plastic surgeon, *The Life and Times of Gaspare Tagliacozzi (1545–1599),* a pioneer in plastic surgery. She was awarded the Welch Medal of the American Association for the History of Medicine in 1954.

From 1967 almost until her death, Martha Gnudi translated Agostino Ramelli's *Le Diverse et Artificiose Machine* (1588). (Ramelli was an engineer for the king of France.) She completed the translation, but died on April 30, 1976, without seeing the final copy.

ADDITIONAL SOURCES

BiDrLUS 70; DrAS 74H; BiIn ll; obituary in *Medical Library Association Bulletin* 64: 453–454, Oct. 1976; obituary in *Technology and Culture* 17: 52L-2, July 1976.

GOEBEL, DOROTHY BURNE
(1898–1976)
U.S. History

Dorothy Burne Goebel, a specialist in American history, was born in Huntington, Long Island, on August 24, 1898. She received an A.B. in 1920 from Barnard College and was Phi Beta Kappa. She received an M.A. in 1922 and a Ph.D. in 1926 from Columbia University. From 1920 to 1926 she was an assistant and lecturer in the history department at Barnard; in 1926 she joined the faculty at Hunter as a history instructor. She became professor and served as chairman of the department from 1942 to 1948 and from 1961 to 1962. She retired as professor emerita in 1963. Goebel wrote *William Henry Harrison* in 1926 and *American Foreign Policy: The Documentary Record, 1776–1960* in 1961. She contributed to the *Dictionary of American Biography* and the *Dictionary of American History* and had articles published in the *American Historical Review, Journal of Economic History,* and *Annals of the American Academy of Political and Social Science.* Her husband, Julius Goebel, Jr., was a legal historian and a professor on the law faculty at Columbia, and in 1925 she assisted in the survey of colonial court records in the state of New York that became his book, *Some Legal and Political Aspects of the Manors of New York* (1928). In 1945 the two wrote *General in the White House*. In 1963 Dorothy Goebel became associate editor of *Law Practice of Alexander Hamilton: Documents and Commentary*, edited by her husband.

Dorothy Goebel was a member of the American Historical Association from 1933. She was on the Albert J. Beveridge Award Committee from 1947 to 1953 and chaired the committee from 1951 to 1953. She received a Guggenheim Fellowship in 1947 to study the free ports of the West Indies; the results of this research appeared in the *William and Mary Quarterly* in July 1963 as "The New England Trade and the French West Indies, 1763–1774: A Study of Trade Policies." Dorothy Goebel died on March 12, 1976, in Huntington, New York.

ADDITIONAL SOURCES

ConAu 65, 69; DrAS 74H; WhoAmW 61, 64; BiIn 10, 11; obituary in *American Historical Review* 81: 1017–1018, Oct. 1976; obituary in NewYT, Mar. 14, 1976, p. 51; obituary in *AB Bookman's Weekly*, Apr. 5, 1976; *Bio-Base*.

GOFF, EUGENIA WHEELER
(1844–?)
Historical Geography

Eugenia Wheeler Goff was born in North Clarkson, Monroe County, New York, on January 17, 1844, to Joseph Lacy and Sarah Ann (Peck) Wheeler. The family moved to Winona, Minnesota, and she graduated from State Normal School in 1869. She taught there for eight years and for nine years in state institutes and teachers' training schools in the state. In 1876 she wrote a textbook, *Minnesota, Its Geography, History and Resources*. It was adopted for use in all common and graded schools in the state. The textbook was the first to combine history, resources, and geography, and leading textbook publishers adopted her ideas for other states.

Eugenia Goff also originated a set of historical wall maps which located leading historical events of the countries. When she married Henry Slade Goff in 1882, they continued this work together. In 1887 they organized the National Historical Publishing Company. For twenty-five years, Eugenia did the historical research and designed historical maps and charts, which eventually numbered over 100 and ranged from book size to large wall maps. In 1893 the Goffs published a historical atlas entitled *The United States and Her Neighbors*. The date of Goff's death is unknown.

ADDITIONAL SOURCES

NatCAB, v. 17; *Bio-Base*.

GOLDMAN, MERLE
(1931–   )
Chinese History

Merle Goldman was born on March 12, 1931. She attended Sarah Lawrence College and then Harvard University, earning a bachelor's degree in 1953, a master's degree in 1957, and a Ph.D. in 1964. She was influenced both by her undergraduate advisor at Sarah Lawrence and by her mentor at Harvard. John Fairbank, her mentor, never lost interest in her work, even though Goldman had four children while in graduate school, and he encouraged her to follow her particular area of interest even though it differed from his own.

Goldman's first academic appointment was at Wellesley College, where she was instructor in Far Eastern history from 1963 to 1964. She was a lecturer for Radcliffe Seminars from 1968 to 1970, and in 1972 she took an appointment as professor at Boston University.

The two most recent of Goldman's three single-authored books were selected as Notable Books by the *New York Times.* The most recent, *Sowing the Seeds of Democracy in China: Political Reform in the Deng Xiaoping Decade,* also won Best Book on Government Award from the American Association of Publishers, Professional and Scholarly Publishing Division. Goldman is also editor or co-editor of five additional books and the author of over forty scholarly articles and numerous newspaper and magazine articles.

Goldman has been the recipient of numerous awards, including the Radcliffe Graduate Medal for Distinguished Achievement. She served as a fellow at the Bunting Institute and for the Guggenheim Foundation, and she received grants from the Social Science Research Council, the State Department, the American Council of Learned Societies, and the Wang Institute. In addition to her work at Boston University, Goldman has been a research associate of the Fairbank Center for East Asian Research at Harvard University.

Goldman's professional service includes committee memberships for the American Historical Association, the Association of Asian Studies, the Council on Foreign Relations, and the Social Science Research Council. She served as vice president and president of the New England Council of the Association of Asian Studies. Goldman is currently a board member of Asia Watch, a division of Human Rights Watch, a Phi Beta Kappa Lecturer, and the chairperson of the New England China Seminar.

Aside from her many academic accomplishments, Goldman takes pride in the work she has done on behalf of human rights. Her work on China's intellectuals in the Chinese Communist Party led her to activism on their behalf when a number of them were persecuted. Goldman served on the Presidential Commission on Radio Free Asia and as a member of the United States delegation to the Commission on Human Rights in Geneva.

Merle Goldman is married to Marshall Goldman. They have four children and nine grandchildren. She credits her family for their continuous support of her work. "Without their support," she states, "I could not have become an historian."

BOOKS BY MERLE GOLDMAN

Sowing the Seeds of Democracy in China: Political Reform in the Deng Xiaoping Decade. Cambridge, MA: Harvard University Press, 1994; paperback, 1995.

Editor, with Paul Cohen. *Fairbank Remembered.* Cambridge, MA: Harvard University Press, 1992.

Editor, with Paul Cohen. *Ideas Across Cultures: Essays on Chinese Thought in Honor of Benjamin Schwartz.* Cambridge, MA: Harvard University Press, 1990.

Co-editor. *Science and Technology in Post-Mao China.* Cambridge, MA: Harvard University Press, 1989.

Editor. *China's Intellectuals and the State: In Search of a New Relationship in the People's Republic of China.* Cambridge, MA: Harvard University Press, 1987.

China's Intellectuals: Advise and Dissent. Cambridge, MA: Harvard University Press, 1981; paperback, 1987.

Editor. *Modern Chinese Literature in the May Fourth Era.* Cambridge, MA: Harvard University Press, 1977; paperback, 1985.

Literary Dissent in Communist China. Cambridge, MA: Harvard University Press, 1967; Atheneum, 1970.

ADDITIONAL SOURCES

Questionnaire completed by the subject for *American Women Historians, 1700s–1990s: A Biographical Dictionary.*

GORDON, LINDA
(1940–   )
U.S. Women's and Family History; Modern Russian History

Linda Gordon was born on January 19, 1940, in Chicago, Illinois, of Russian Jewish and Polish Jewish ancestry. Gordon attended public schools in Chicago; Denver, Colorado; and Portland, Oregon. Her father was a social worker and her mother a nursery school teacher; along with her high school teacher Marcia Freeman, they provided the most significant influences on Linda's early life.

Linda Gordon attended Swarthmore College, earning a bachelor's degree in history, magna cum laude, in 1961. One of her college teachers, Paul Beik, inspired her to become a historian. Gordon then went to Yale University, where she received a master's degree in history and Russian studies in 1963 and a Ph.D. in history in 1970.

Gordon's first academic position was at the University of Massachusetts at Boston, where she taught from 1968 until 1984, attaining the rank of professor of history. In the spring of 1994, Gordon was visiting professor at the University of Amsterdam. From 1984 to 1990 she was professor of history at the University of Wisconsin at Madison. Still at Madison, Gordon was named Florence Kelley Professor of History in 1990 and Vilas Distinguished Research Professor in 1993.

Gordon is best known for her research on birth control, gender and the state, and domestic violence, but her training in Russian studies also produced a book.

She has published over fifty scholarly articles and nearly twenty articles for nonacademic publications, and is the author or editor of seven books. Each of Gordon's four single-author books has been the recipient of or runner-up for one or more awards. *Woman's Body, Woman's Right,* her first book, was the runner-up for the National Book Award in History in 1976. *Cossack Rebellions* won the Antonovych Prize for 1983. *Heroes of Their Own Lives,* Gordon's exploration of domestic violence in the lives of women and children in Boston from 1880 to 1960, won the American Historical Association's Joan Kelly Prize for best book in women's history or theory as well as the Wisconsin Library Association Award, and received nominations for the National Book Award in History, the Robert F. Kennedy Book Award, and the American Historical Association's Merle Curti Award for the best book in social history. Her most recent book, *Pitied but Not Entitled: Single Mothers and the Origins of Welfare,* won the Berkshire Prize for the best book in women's history. A history of what is commonly referred to as welfare in the United States, this book is, as Ruth Crocker writes, "analytically sophisticated, densely footnoted, and informed by the passion that comes from writing about issues that are as urgent now as they were sixty years ago, perhaps more so."

Among the grants and fellowships Gordon has received are a National Institute of Mental Health grant, an American Council of Learned Societies grant, a Guggenheim fellowship, and a Bunting Institute fellowship. She has spent invited residencies at the Bellagio Center, Dickinson College, and Stanford University. She has served on the editorial boards of *American Historical Review, Signs, Feminist Studies, Journal of Women's History, Contention,* and *Gender and History,* and currently serves on the editorial boards of *Journal of American History, Journal of Policy History,* and *Contemporary Society.* She has acted as a consultant for four public television series and four films, and has served on the executive board of the Organization of American Historians. Gordon has lectured at over forty colleges and universities in the United States, Canada, Sweden, France, Poland, the Netherlands, and South Africa. She also regularly talks to nonacademic groups as well, providing historical reflections on family violence, sexuality, and reproductive choice.

Linda Gordon's spouse is Allen Hunter; they have one child, Rosa Gordon Hunter.

BOOKS BY LINDA GORDON

Pitied but Not Entitled: Single Mothers and the Origins of Welfare, 1880–1935. New York: The Free Press, 1994; paperback, Harvard University Press, 1995.

Editor. *Women, the State, and Welfare: Historical and Theoretical Essays.* Madison: University of Wisconsin Press, 1990.

Heroes of Their Own Lives: The Politics and History of Family Violence, Boston 1880–1960. New York: Viking, 1988; paperback, 1989; British edition, Virago, 1989.

Cossack Rebellions: Social Turmoil in the Sixteenth-Century Ukraine. Albany, NY: SUNY Press, 1983.

Editor. *Maternity: Letters from Working Women.* New York: W. W. Norton, 1979.

Woman's Body, Woman's Right: A Social History of Birth Control in America. New
    York: Viking, 1976; Penguin, 1977. 2nd ed., 1990.
Editor, with Rosalyn Baxandall and Susan Reverby. *America's Working Women: A Doc-
    umentary History.* New York: Random House and Vintage, 1976; 2nd ed., W.
    W. Norton, 1995.
ADDITIONAL SOURCES
Crocker, Ruth. Rev. of *Pitied but Not Entitled: Single Mothers and the History of Wel-
    fare, 1880–1935,* by Linda Gordon.
Questionnaire completed by the subject for *American Women Historians, 1700s–1990s:
    A Biographical Dictionary.*

GOULD, ALICE BACHE
(1868–1953)
History of Columbus

Alice Bache Gould was born on January 5, 1868, in Cambridge, Massachusetts,
to Benjamin Apthorp Gould, a well-known astronomer, and Mary (Quincy)
Gould, related to Josiah Quincy of Quincy, Massachusetts, his son, known as
"the patriot," and Alice's great-grandfather, the third Josiah Quincy, president
of Harvard for sixteen years. Alice spent her childhood between the family home
in Quincy, owned by her great-aunts, and Cordoba, Argentina, where Alice's
father had been invited to establish the Argentine Observatory. The family eventually returned to Cambridge, and Alice entered Bryn Mawr, obtaining a bachelor's degree in mathematics in 1889. She did graduate work at the
Massachusetts Institute of Technology and the University of Chicago and wrote
her only book, the biography of naturalist Louis Agassiz, for the *Beacon Biographies Collection.* In 1903 she was sent to Puerto Rico to recover from the
flu, and while perusing the archives there became interested in Barbados. In
1911 she went to Seville on her way to Italy, but as was her custom, stopped
to visit the Archive of the Indies there to research the route Columbus had
traveled to Barbados. She stayed the rest of her life.

Using a variety of documents, Gould identified the crew members on the
Columbus voyages and disputed many errors in history. She found the name of
Pedro de Lepe on one of the receipts and proved that he, whose existence had
long been disputed, had sailed with Columbus on the *Santa Maria.* She went
to municipal, parish, and private archives to research the lives and identities of
each of the crew members. She entered each man's rank, duties, psychological
profile, family history, qualifications, and pay. She found a document in which
Their Majesties granted Columbus and his heirs in perpetuity the titles of Admiral of the Ocean Sea and Viceroy and Governor General of the lands he might
discover. She also found a document outlining the payments the king and queen
of Spain gave to Columbus before the first agreements were signed.

Gould became a legend for her habit of saving documents from destruction.
It was said that the documents on payments had been stuffed into files containing
the remnants of papers in the Simancas castle after its destruction by Napoleon's

troops; the papers had been used in place of straw in the stables. Old documents from the town archives of Mogueer were being used in the local jail for sanitary purposes; in order to go through the pile Gould was locked into the jail each day and let out for lunch. The prisoners helped her catalogue the papers, and the information was added to her research.

Alice Gould published the results of her research in the bulletins of the Spanish Royal Academy of History from 1924 to 1966. In 1924 she was awarded the Cross of Alfonso the Wise, and in 1942 she was the only woman corresponding member of the Spanish Royal Academy of History. In 1952 she received the highest honors of the Order of Isabella the Catholic. On July 25, 1953, Alice Gould was found lying on the bridge to the Simancas castle. She died of a cerebral hemorrhage, and the book she hoped to write on Columbus was never published. A commemorative plaque was placed at the site of her death, and a square in Simancas bears her name.

ADDITIONAL SOURCES

Mercedes Junquera, "In Quest of Columbus . . . ," *Americas,* Oct. 1980, pp. 49–53; BiIn 1, 2, 3, 12; WomWWA 14; obituary in NewYT, July 28, 1953, p. 19; obituary in *Wilson Library Bulletin* 28: 30, Sept. 1953; "Alice in Seville," *Time,* July 7, 1952, 57; *BioBase.*

GREEN, CONSTANCE (WINSOR) McLAUGHLIN
(1897–1975)
U.S. Urban History

Constance Green, a pioneer in urban history, was born August 21, 1897, in Ann Arbor, Michigan, to Andrew Cunningham and Lois Thompson (Angell) McLaughlin. Her grandfather on her mother's side was University of Michigan president James B. Angell; her father taught history at the university, organized the Bureau of Historical Research for the Carnegie Institute, and then became chairman of the history department of the University of Chicago. Constance attended the laboratory school at the university and spent one term at Fraulein von Heidenaber's Hohere Tochter Schule in Munich, Germany, before entering the University of Chicago in 1914 and Smith College in 1916.

In 1919 Constance McLaughlin received an A.B. in history and taught English at the University of Chicago. In 1921 she married Donald Ross Green, a textile manufacturer, and taught at Smith College. In 1925 she received an M.A. in history from Mount Holyoke College. Her thesis, "The New England Confederation of 1643," was published in 1927 in the first volume of *Commonwealth History of Massachusetts,* edited by Albert Bushnell Hart. From 1925 to 1932 she taught part time at Mount Holyoke. In 1937 she received a Ph.D. from Yale; her thesis, *Holyoke, Massachusetts: A Case History of the Industrial Revolution in America,* was published in 1939. It was recognized as one of the earliest scholarly works in urban history and received Yale's Eggleston Prize in history.

From 1939 to 1946 Constance Green was director of research at the Smith

College Council of Industrial Relations and during the war was official historian to the United States Army Ordnance Department in Springfield, Massachusetts. In 1940 she contributed "The Value of Local History" to *The Cultural Approach to History*, edited by Caroline Ware, and in 1944 she contributed chapters to *The Growth of American Economy*, edited by Harold Williamson. In 1946 her husband died, and she moved to Washington, D.C., to become consulting historian for the American National Red Cross. She wrote *The Role of Women as Production Workers in War Plants of the Connecticut Valley*, which appeared as Volume 28 of Smith College Studies in History in 1946.

From 1948 to 1951 Green was chief historian for the Army Ordnance Corps and headed a team of researchers writing a volume on the technical services. Titled *The Ordnance Department*, it was part of the series *The United States Army in World War II* and was published in 1955. During this time, Green also published *History of Naugatuck, Connecticut* (1949).

In 1951 Green left the Pentagon and became a Commonwealth Fund Lecturer at University College, the University of London. In 1952 she became a historian at the research and development board, Office of the Secretary of Defense. Under a six-year grant from the Rockefeller Foundation, Green was named head of a Washington history project. While working on the project, she published *Eli Whitney and the Birth of American Technology* in 1956 and *American Cities in the Growth of the Nation* in 1957. Aided by a second grant from the Chapelbrook Foundation of Boston, she published the first volume of *Washington: Village and Capital, 1800–1878*. The book won the 1963 Pulitzer Prize, twenty-seven years after her father had won the same award for *The Constitutional History of the United States*. The second volume, *Washington, Capital City, 1879–1950*, was published in 1964. In 1965 she wrote *The Rise of Urban America*, and in 1967, *The Secret City: A History of Race Relations in the Nation's Capital*. *The Church on Lafayette Square: A History of St. John's Church, Washington, D.C. 1810–1970* (1970) was followed by *Vanguard: A History* in 1971, with Milton Lomask. Constance Green died December 5, 1975, of generalized arteriosclerosis in Annapolis, Maryland.

ADDITIONAL SOURCES

NewYT, May 3, 1963, p. 35; *Washington Post*, May 8, 1963, Sec. D, p. 5; *Washington Sunday Star*, May 20, 1962, Sec. C, p. 3; the Smith College Archives contain Green's letters, photographs, and clippings and an oral history tape; Bruce M. Stave, "A Conversation with Constance McLaughlin Green," in *The Making of Urban History* (1977); ConAu v. 9–12, pp. 343–344; DcAmB Supp. 4 on Andrew Cunningham McLaughlin; obituary in *Holyoke Transcript & Telegraph*, Dec. 8, 1975; NewYT, Dec. 8, 1975; *Washington Post*, Dec. 7, 1975; *Bio-Base*.

GRIDLEY, MARION E.
(1906–1974)
Native American History

Marion Eleanor Gridley, a prolific writer of popular Native American history, was born in White Plains, New York, to William Thomson Gridley, a transportation engineer, and Ada Antoinette (Robertson) Gridley on November 16, 1906. She married Robinson Johnson on May 15, 1932, and was divorced in 1947 or 1948. During that time, she began to write history and published *Indians of Today* in 1936. In 1939 she was editor of *Indian Legends of American Scenes* and in 1940 wrote *Indians of Yesterday. The Story of Pocahontas* was published in 1948. In 1950 she wrote *Hiawatha.* She attended Northwestern University from 1954 to 1955, then became involved in public relations while freelance writing. She wrote *Indian Legends of American Scenes* in 1959 and compiled *America's Indian Statues* in 1966.

For the Indian Nations Series published by Putnam, Marion Gridley wrote *The Story of the Iroquois* (1969); *The Story of the Pontiac* (1970); *The Story of the Osceola* and *The Story of the Navajo* (1971); *The Story of the Haida* (1972); *The Story of the Sioux* and *The Story of the Seminoles* (1973). In 1972 she also wrote *Contemporary American Indian Leaders,* and in 1973 she finished a biography of Maria Tallchief and *American Indian Women.* She was adopted by the Omaha and Winnebago tribes and was a member of the Daughters of the American Revolution. Marion Gridley died on October 31, 1974.

ADDITIONAL SOURCES

AuBYP; ConAu 45; ForWC 70; WhoAmW 68, 70, 75; WhAm 6; BiIn 2; ConAu 103; SmATA 26N; *Bio-Base.*

H

HALL, GWENDOLYN MIDLO
(1929–   )
Slave Societies in Colonial American History

Gwendolyn Midlo Hall was born on June 27, 1929, in New Orleans, Louisiana, of Russian- and Polish-Jewish ancestry. Her father was a tailor, then an attorney; his role as a civil rights and labor lawyer during the 1930s and 1940s had a tremendous influence on her life. She attended public schools in New Orleans as a child, then the Newman High School, a private school. She attended New-combe College of Tulane University, completing majors in both European and American history. Hall earned her bachelor's degree, however, from the University of the Americas in Mexico City, in 1962. She also studied music theory and classical piano privately in Paris from 1949 to 1953.

After completing her bachelor's degree, Hall stayed on at the University of the Americas, earning a master's degree in Latin American history in 1963. She completed her Ph.D., also in Latin American history, at the University of Michigan in 1970. She then accepted a position as assistant professor of history at Rutgers University. In 1973 she became associate professor, and in 1993 she was promoted to professor of history. She has also served Rutgers as acting chair of Puerto Rican and Hispanic Caribbean studies, acting chair of Puerto Rican studies, and acting chair of the department of history.

Hall was active in the civil rights movement in New Orleans during the 1940s and later did political work with her husband during the 1950s and 1960s. She also initiated medical treatment for heroin addicts in Detroit and Ann Arbor. Hall worked as a temporary legal secretary during the McCarthy era to avoid being fired due to FBI harassment.

Gwendolyn Midlo Hall is the author of three books, two books in preparation, and fifteen articles. Her 1992 publication, *Africans in Colonial Louisiana: The Development of Afro-Creole Culture in the Eighteenth Century,* won several national awards, including the Elliott Rudwick Award of the Organization of American Historians, the John Hope Franklin Prize of the American Studies Association, and the Willie Lee Rose Prize of the Southern Association of Women Historians. It is a "pathbreaking" work, according to reviewer Sylvia Frey, who argues that "no other historian has done such prodigious research in the voluminous records of French and Spanish colonial Louisiana."

Hall has received many awards and fellowships, including those from the Guggenheim Foundation, the National Endowment for the Humanities, the Spanish Ministry of Culture, and the Louisiana Endowment for the Humanities. She has been granted a merit award from the City of New Orleans and a Louisiana Humanist of the Year Award. She has also been active in creating databases and archives for future research on slavery in the early Gulf South, which includes Louisiana, Mississippi, Alabama, and Florida.

Gwendolyn Midlo Hall was married to Harry Haywood Hall, a radical black theoretician and the son of slaves, who is now deceased. She raised their three children alone. One child is now an emergency room physician, the second is a lawyer, and the third has suffered from chronic paranoid schizophrenia for the past thirty years. Hall also has one granddaughter. Her interests include classical music, piano, nature, and dogs.

BOOKS BY GWENDOLYN MIDLO HALL

Editor. *Love, War, and the 96th Engineers (Colored): The New Guinea Diaries of Captain Hyman Samuelson During World War II.* Champaign-Urbana: University of Illinois Press, 1995.

Africans in Colonial Louisiana: The Formation of Afro-Creole Culture in the Eighteenth Century. Baton Rouge: Louisiana State University Press, 1992; paperback, 1995.

Social Control in Slave Plantation Societies: A Comparison of St. Dominique and Cuba. Baltimore: Johns Hopkins University Press, 1971; paperback, Louisiana State University Press, 1996.

ADDITIONAL SOURCES

Frey, Sylvia R. Rev. of *Africans in Colonial Louisiana: The Development of Afro-Creole Culture in the Eighteenth Century,* by Gwendolyn Midlo Hall. *American Historical Review* 98 (Apr. 1993): 454–456.

Questionnaire completed by the subject for *American Women Historians, 1700s–1990s: A Biographical Dictionary.*

HALL, SHARLOT
(1870–1942)
Local History

Sharlot Hall, purported to be the only woman to hold a livestock slaughtering license, was born on October 27, 1870, in Prosser Creek in Kansas Territory to James Hall, a rancher, and Adeline Hall. In 1881 the family moved to Arizona; on the journey, Sharlot suffered a fall from a horse and injured her spine, which would plague her the rest of her life. (She called it "the Mexican Revolution in my spine.") Each time the pain resurfaced, she was forced to lie flat on her stomach on the floor for release. She began writing to keep her mind off the pain and to pass time. In between, she began exploring Arizona when not milking the cows, watering the stock, regulating the windmill, and feeding the pigs on her father's ranch. In 1886, despite her father's fear that she would "git high toned" and think she was above the rest of the family, Sharlot Hall went to school in nearby Prescott during the week, returning to the ranch on weekends. This arrangement ended the next year, when she had to quit to help on the ranch.

Hall began writing and publishing essays on Arizona's history, and in 1901 she was asked to become a temporary editor of *Land and Sunshine* magazine (later *Out West*). She was so successful that she was asked to become a staff member. Hall also began preserving Arizona history by recording the experiences of the Territory's pioneers.

In 1909 a bill established the office of Territorial Historian. Sharlot Hall was named to the post, becoming the first woman to hold a territorial office. Although it was a controversial appointment, Governor Richard E. Sloan stood behind her, and she remained historian as long as he was in office.

Hall made many trips throughout Arizona, gathering historical background on the Territory. In 1906, for instance, she retraced the route by which pioneers entered Arizona from California in 1863. She joined J. Walter Fewke's study and exploration of an area of the Little Colorado River in 1910 and covered the Snake Ceremony at Oraibi, the dedication of Tonto (now Roosevelt) Dam by Theodore Roosevelt, and the Mexican Revolution in Douglas, Arizona. In 1912 a trip from Ganada to Chinle with Navajo Indian guide Grover Cleveland was cut short by her mother's illness and subsequent death.

Despite the fact that her mother's death meant more responsibilities on the ranch, Hall continued to write essays and publish in the *Prescott Courier*. In 1921 she also received an honorary master of arts degree from the University of Arizona. In 1925 she traveled to Washington, D.C., as one of the electors for the presidential election and represented Arizona by wearing a copper dress.

In 1927 the city of Prescott, the first capital of Arizona, presented Sharlot Hall with a life lease on the governor's mansion there. In return, she presented the town with her historical collection, valued at $10,000. She spent the remainder of her life renovating the governor's mansion (now Sharlot Hall Museum) with her own money. She was also one of eight founders of the Historical Society of Prescott. Sharlot Hall died on April 9, 1942.

ADDITIONAL SOURCES

Papers and manuscripts at the Sharlot Hall Museum in Prescott, Arizona; Margaret F. Maxwell, *A Passion for Freedom: The Life of Sharlot Hall* (Tucson: University of Arizona Press, 1982); AmLY: ArizL; ChPo S2; BiIn 7, 10; WhAm 3; WomWWA 14; InWom; Dorothy Daniels Anderson, *Arizona Legends and Lore: Tales of Southwestern Pioneers* (Golden West Publications, 1991); Dale Pierce, *Wild West Characters* (Golden West Publications, 1991); Sharlot M. Hall, *Sharlot Hall on the Arizona Strip: A Diary of a Journey Through Northern Arizona in 1911,* ed. C. Gregory Crampton (Flagstaff,

AZ: Northland Press, 1975); James J. Weston. "Sharlot Hall: Arizona Pioneer Lady of Literature," *Journal of the West* 4: 539–552, Oct. 1965.

HANAWALT, BARBARA A.
(1941–   )
History of Medieval England

Barbara Ann Hanawalt was born on March 4, 1941, in New Brunswick, New Jersey, the daughter of Nelson G. and Pearl Basset Hanawalt. Her parents, of Pennsylvania Dutch/German and English ancestry, raised Barbara in Highland Park, where she attended public elementary and high schools. Her father was a professor of psychology at Douglass College, Rutgers University, and her mother was an elementary school teacher and then a full-time homemaker. Barbara's early influences were many. Her parents encouraged her to read and read books aloud to her that were beyond her reading abilities. She remembers them reading Sir Walter Scott, Charles Dickens, and Mark Twain. One of her uncles, a humorist and specialist on Chaucer and Shakespeare, also encouraged her to read and learn. Her childhood summers, in the Pennsylvania village where her father grew up and on the eastern Pennsylvania farms where her mother's sisters lived, taught her a great deal about village social dynamics and agricultural practices. Hanawalt is sure that her later writings on crime and conflict in English communities and on peasantry were influenced greatly by these childhood adventures. Her family also went on camping trips throughout the United States and Canada, and Barbara found the history of places and of people, particularly Native Americans, very interesting.

Because Hanawalt had "grown up in the academic life and liked it," had long enjoyed history, and had truly inspirational college teachers, she was motivated to become a historian. She completed a bachelor's degree from Douglass College in 1963, a master's degree from the University of Michigan in 1964, and a Ph.D., also from the University of Michigan, in 1970. She did not find her first full-time teaching position for four years, however, partly because she was told by many schools that they did not hire women. Hanawalt remembers her struggles and has longed worked to pave the way for women following her. "Having faced discrimination during my entire career from graduate school through my professional life," she states, "I have devoted a good amount of my energies toward protecting women's careers on the campuses at which I have taught."

Hanawalt resisted discrimination and got teaching positions at San Fernando Valley Community College, the University of Southern California, the University of Oregon, and Indiana University, where she achieved the rank of full professor before leaving for the University of Minnesota, where she now serves as director of the Center for Medieval Studies. Of her many impressive achievements, Hanawalt says that one of the things she is most proud of is the success of the Center for Medieval Studies. "I have blended the interests of medievalists on campus towards an intersection of history and literature that has led to a series of publications and the training of graduate students.'' In fact, mentoring graduate students and junior faculty is a significant part of her service to the university.

Hanawalt has been the recipient of many fellowships and distinctions, including being named fellow of the Royal Historical Society and of the Wissenschaftskollege zu Berlin, receiving several National Endowment for the Humanities grants, a British Academy grant, and a fellowship at the Center for Advanced Studies at Princeton University. Her three books, *Crime and Conflict in English Communities, 1300–1348, The Ties that Bound: Peasant Families in Medieval England,* and *Growing Up in Medieval London: The Experience of Childhood in History,* have gained her an international reputation. Her five edited collections and her twenty-five scholarly articles also demonstrate the breadth of her scholarship, from the study of adolescence in Europe to criminal activity among the nobility of fourteenth-century England.

Hanawalt's professional service includes acting as associate editor of *American Historical Review* and of *Signs,* and work on the editorial board of the *Journal of Women's History.* She served both as president and vice-president of the Social Science History Association and has held council member positions in the Medieval Academy of America and the American Historical Association. Hanawalt has served on external review committees for several universities and for the National Humanities Center. She has also served on the program committees for conferences sponsored by the Social Science History Association, the Midwest British Studies Association, and the Medieval Academy of America.

Divorced from her first husband, Barbara Hanawalt is married to Ronald Giere, professor of philosophy at the University of Minnesota. She has a dog and a cat and enjoys gourmet cooking, eating and entertaining, travel in Europe, and gardening.

BOOKS BY BARBARA A. HANAWALT

Editor, with David Wallace. *Representing Fifteenth-Century England: The Intersection of History and Literature.* Minneapolis: University of Minnesota Press, 1995.

Editor, with Kathryn Reyerson. *City and Spectacle in Medieval Europe.* Minneapolis: University of Minnesota Press, 1994.

Growing Up in Medieval London: The Experience of Childhood in History. New York: Oxford University Press, 1993.

Editor. *Chaucer's England: Literature in Historical Context.* Minneapolis: University of Minnesota Press, 1992.

The Ties that Bound: Peasant Families in Medieval England. New York: Oxford University Press, 1986.

Editor. *Women and Work in Preindustrial Europe.* Bloomington: University of Indiana Press, 1986.

Crime and Conflict in English Communities, 1300–1348. Cambridge, MA: Harvard University Press, 1979.

ADDITIONAL SOURCE
Questionnaire completed by the subject for *American Women Historians, 1700s–1990s: A Biographical Dictionary.*

HANDLIN, MARY FLUG
(1913–1976)
U.S. History

Mary Flug Handlin was born in New York City on September 14, 1913, to Harry and Fanny (Schuck) Flug. She received a B.A. in 1933 at Brooklyn College and an M.A. the next year from Columbia University. She married Oscar Handlin, a professor at Harvard, in 1937, and from 1935 to 1942 she was an analyst for various government agencies. In 1942 she became research historian of the Social Science Research Council, where she worked until 1946. From 1950 to 1954 she was assistant editor of the *Harvard Guide to American History,* and from 1958 to 1976 she was editor for the Center for the Study of the History of Liberty in America at Harvard University. During that time Handlin wrote a number of books with her husband, including *The Dimensions of Liberty* in 1961; *Popular Sources of Political Authority* in 1966; *The American College and the American Culture* (1970); *Facing Life: Youth and the Family in American History* (1971); *Commonwealth: A Study of the Role of Government in American Economy* (1974) and *The Wealth of the American People: A History of American Affluence* (1975). Mary Handlin died in Cambridge, Massachusetts, May 24, 1976.

ADDITIONAL SOURCES:
BiIn 10; ConAu 65; ConAu P-2; NewYTBS 76; LEduc 74; *Bio-Base;* obituary in NewYT, May 25, 1976, p. 38; obituary in *Time,* 107: 78, June 7, 1976.

HAREVEN, TAMARA K.
(1937–   )
U.S. Social History

Tamara K. Hareven was born on May 10, 1937, in Czernautz, Rumania. Her father was an attorney, her mother a mathematics professor. Between the ages of four and seven, she was in a German concentration camp in the Ukraine. She remembers the influence of her maternal grandmother, who narrated folk tales and who taught her to read from scraps of newspaper. In 1946 Hareven's family returned to Rumania, and she attended school there until 1948, when they immigrated to Israel. As a student at Reali High School in Israel, Hareven was influenced by her history teachers. Wanting to understand the response and adaptation of individuals and groups to the larger forces of social change, she decided to pursue history as a course of study. She cites Jacob Talmon at Hebrew University and Robert Bremner at Ohio State University as important influences on her thinking.

Hareven attended Hebrew University in Jerusalem, earning a bachelor's degree in 1961. She then moved to the United States for graduate school, earning a master's degree from the University of Cincinnati in 1962 and a Ph.D. from Ohio State University in 1965. Once she completed her doctorate, Hareven accepted a position as assistant professor at Dalhousie University. She was promoted to associate professor in 1967 and stayed at Dalhousie until 1969, when she accepted a position as associate professor of American history at Clark University. In 1976 she was promoted to professor of history at Clark. In 1988 Hareven left Clark for the University of Delaware, where she was named Unidel Professor of Family Studies and History. She has held many visiting professor positions as well, at Boston University, Harvard University, Doshisha University in Japan, Ecole des Hautes Etudes en Sciences Sociales in Paris, and the University of Paris-Sorbonne.

The author or editor of thirteen books and over fifty scholarly articles, Hareven has been a central figure in the new social history of the family. She has helped to launch interdisciplinary explorations of the family that include historical, sociological, anthropological, and economic perspectives on such issues as urbanization, ethnicity, work, aging, and leisure time. She is currently working on two additional books: *The Silk Weavers of Kyoto: Family Work and Community in a Changing Traditional Industry* and *Generations in Historical Time: The Family, Life Course and Aging in an American Community;* the latter is a sequel volume to her earlier work, *Family Time and Industrial Time.*

Hareven has been the recipient of numerous awards and fellowships, including Fulbright appointments to India and Japan, fellowships at Harvard University, the Bunting Institute at Radcliffe College, the Cambridge Group for the History of Population and Social Structure, and Stanford University's Center for Advanced Study in the Behavioral Sciences. She has served as the president and vice president of the Social Science History Association, has been named an elected fellow of the Gerontological Society of America, and has been awarded a Graduate Society Medal from Radcliffe College. She has received grants from the National Science Foundation, the National Endowment for the Humanities, the Japan Foundation, and the Ford Foundation, among others.

Hareven has served on the editorial boards of many journals, including *American Journal of Sociology, Journal of Youth and Society, Journal of Crosscultural Studies of Aging,* and *Continuity and Change.* She has served on professional committees for the Social Science History Association, the American Historical Association, the National Endowment for the Humanities, the Eleanor Roosevelt Institute, and the National Research Council. In addition, Hareven has worked with several government agencies, including the U.S. State Department, the U.S. Children's Bureau, and the National Institute on Aging. She has testified before Congress on historical changes in the life course and the family and on policy implications for the aged. She has organized over a dozen conferences and presented papers at conferences across the United States and in nearly twenty other countries.

BOOKS BY TAMARA K. HAREVEN

Editor. *Aging and Generational Relations over the Life Course: A Historical and Cross Cultural Perspective.* Berlin: Walter de Gruyter, 1996.

Editor, with Andrejs Plakans. *Family History at the Crossroads.* Princeton, NJ: Princeton University Press, 1988.

Family Time and Industrial Time: The Relationship Between the Family and Work in a New England Industrial Community. New York: Cambridge University Press, 1982. Japanese translation, Waseda University Press, 1990.

Editor, with Kathleen Adams. *Aging and the Life Course in Interdisciplinary and Cross-Cultural Perspective.* New York: Guilford Press, 1982.

Associate editor. *History of the Family and Kinship: A Select Bibliography.* New York: Krauss Thompson, 1980.

Amoskeag: Life and Work in an American Factory City. New York: Pantheon Books, 1978.

Editor. *Transitions: The Family and the Life Course in Historical Perspective.* New York: Academic Press, 1978.

Editor, with Alice Rossi and Jerome Kagan. *The Family.* New York: W. W. Norton, 1978.

Editor, with Maris Vinovskis. *Family and Population in Nineteenth Century America.* Princeton, NJ: Princeton University Press, 1978.

Editor. *Family and Kin in Urban Communities, 1780–1940.* New York: Franklin Watts, 1977.

Editor. *Anonymous Americans: Explorations in American Social History.* Englewood, NJ: Prentice-Hall, 1971.

Associate editor, with Robert H. Bremner. *Children and Youth in America.* Cambridge, MA: Harvard University Press, Vol. 1 (1970), Vol. 2 (1971), Vol. 11 (1974).

Eleanor Roosevelt: An American Conscience. Chicago: Quadrangle Books, 1968.

ADDITIONAL SOURCE

Questionnaire completed by the subject for *American Women Historians, 1700s–1990s: A Biographical Dictionary.*

HARRIS, CHRISTINA PHELPS
(1902–1972)
Middle Eastern History

Christina Phelps Harris was born in New York City on February 9, 1902, to Luis James Phelps, a lawyer, and Marie Christina (Nichols) Phelps. She attended the Sorbonne in Paris from 1919 to 1920 and Wellesley College from 1920 to 1922. She received an A.B. in 1925 and an A.M. from Barnard College in 1927. Harris became an instructor in English history at Vassar College and received a Ph.D. in modern European history from Columbia University in 1930. Her dissertation was published as *The Anglo-American Peace Movement in the Mid-Nineteenth Century.* She traveled for some years in the Middle East, and this resulted in *The Syrian Desert: Caravans, Travels and Explorations,* published in 1937.

Harris became known as an authority on Middle Eastern affairs and in 1938 became an instructor in Middle Eastern history at the extension division of

McGill University, Montreal, Canada. In 1939 she became an associate in history and assistant to the dean at Barnard College. From 1942 to 1946 she was associate professor of history and college dean at Bryn Mawr College in Pennsylvania. During that time she co-authored *This Age of Conflict: A Contemporary World History 1914–1943*. In 1946–47 she was a specialist in the Arab World Division of Near Eastern Affairs for the U.S. Department of State in Washington, D.C., and went on a special mission to London for intensive study of British policy in the Middle East. Upon her return, Harris moved to California and worked on the Middle East Collection at the Hoover Institution on War, Revolution and Peace at Stanford University as a senior research fellow. In 1948, when the collection was formally established, she was appointed the first curator. In 1951 she also became a professor at Stanford on Middle East area studies and professor of political science from 1959 to 1967. Harris continued with the Institute until 1957 and as an advisor until 1967. From 1957 to 1967 she was also departmental editor for Near Eastern history for *Encyclopaedia Britannica*. In 1964 she published *Nationalism and Revolution in Egypt*. After her retirement, she continued to research the explorations and surveys that preceded the connection by telegraph of England and India via the Persian Gulf at the Indian Office Library and Records of the Royal Geographic Society of Great Britain. Christina Harris died in 1972.

ADDITIONAL SOURCES
Biln 10, 11; WhoAmW 68A, 70; NatCAB 57, 210–211, 1977; obituary in *Geographical Journal* 39: 389–90, June 1973; *Bio-Base*.

HASTINGS, MARGARET
(1910–1979)
Medieval English Legal History

Margaret Hastings was born in Springfield, Massachusetts, on May 23, 1910, to William Walter Hastings, a teacher and clergyman, and Elizabeth (Fairbank) Hastings. She graduated from Mount Holyoke College in 1931 and received an M.A. in English medieval history in 1932 and a Ph.D. degree from Bryn Mawr in 1939. She taught in private schools in Waterbury, Connecticut, and Boston, Massachusetts, from 1935 to 1944, and was a research analyst with the army during the war. She was a lecturer in history at Douglass College, New Brunswick, New Jersey, in 1946. The next year she wrote a book that became an instant classic, *The Court of Common Pleas in Fifteenth Century England*. She became an instructor from 1946 to 1949; assistant professor, 1949–1952; associate professor, 1952–1960; and professor of history, 1960–1975. She was a contributer to *Changing Views on British History*, edited by Elizabeth C. Furber (1966), and wrote *Medieval European Society* in 1971. Hastings was a fellow of the Royal Historical Society, and held Guggenheim and Fulbright fellowships. When the Helen Maud Cam visiting fellowship was established at Girton College, Cambridge, Hastings was the first recipient. She was also the first Douglass

College faculty member to receive a Lindback Award for distinguished research, and in 1976 Mount Holyoke gave her an honorary degree.

Hastings died in an automobile accident on October 20, 1979, while on a visit to England.

ADDITIONAL SOURCES

InWom; ConAu 41R; DrAS 74H, 78H; IntAu&W 77; obituary in *American Historical Review* 85: 279, Feb. 1980; *Bio-Base.*

HEBARD, GRACE RAYMOND
(1861–1936)
Local History

Grace Raymond Hebard was born in Clinton, Iowa, to the Rev. George Diah Alonzo and Margaret E. Dominick (Marven) Hebard. Grace attended the State University of Iowa and received a B.S. in civil engineering in 1882. She then became a draftsman in the land office of the United States Surveyor General at Cheyenne, Wyoming, for nine years. While working, she earned an M.A. from Iowa in 1885. In 1891 Hebard became secretary of the board of trustees of the University of Wyoming at Laramie and was appointed a trustee. She served until 1903 and continued as secretary until 1908. In 1906 she had been appointed associate professor of political economy after teaching the subject "informally" since 1891, having earned a doctorate by correspondence from Illinois Wesleyan University. She eventually became head of the department. Hebard also served as the university librarian from 1894 to 1919, and gathered and organized an extensive collection of manuscripts and books related to western history. She was the first woman admitted to the Wyoming bar (1898). She was a state officer of the Daughters of the American Revolution and a Wyoming state tennis champion. She was also active in the suffrage movement.

Despite her very busy schedule, Grace Hebard had a lifelong devotion to Wyoming history, and while her books were considered to be highly romanticized, they were very widely read. She wrote *The History and Government of Wyoming* in 1904, and it went through eleven editions. *Pathbreakers from River to Ocean* was published in 1911, *The Bozeman Trail,* with E. A. Brininstool, in 1922, *Washakie* in 1930, and *Sacajawea, Guide and Interpreter of the Lewis and Clark Expedition* in 1932. In order to obtain information for the books, she spent a number of summers among the Shoshoni Indians. As a member and officer of the state historical society, she also worked to preserve and identify historic trails and points of interest in Wyoming.

Grace Hebard died at the age of seventy-five in Laramie. Her extensive library and manuscript collection was left to the University of Wyoming Library. A plaque inscribed "In memory of Dr. Grace Raymond Hebard, 1861–1936, Wyoming historian, author, educator" was placed on Independence Rock, State 220, near Alcova, Wyoming.

ADDITIONAL SOURCES

The Hebard MS. file in the Western History Research Center of the University of Wyoming Library (30,000 letters, notes, and interviews); President's Letterbooks, 1891–1909, in the University of Wyoming Archives; Janell M. Wenzell, "Dr. Grace Raymond Hebard as Western Historian," Master's thesis, University of Wyoming, 1960; Wilson O. Clough, *A History of the University of Wyoming, 1887–1937* (1937); WomWWA, *1914–1915;* biographical questionnaire in the files of the University of Iowa alumni office; Larene Pearson, "Woman Pathfinder of the West," *Independent Woman,* June 1935; *Woman's Journal,* March 7, 1903; *In Memoriam, Grace Raymond Hebard, 1861–1936* (1937).

HEMENWAY, ABBY MARIA
(1828–1890)
Local History

Abby Maria Hemenway was born in 1828 at Ludlow, Vermont, to Abigail (Barton) and Daniel Sheffield Ludlow, a farmer. She taught at a district school when she was fourteen and in 1847 enrolled in the Black River Academy in Ludlow. In 1852 she taught school and was involved in a local Ladies' Association for Mental and Other Improvement. After three years in Michigan, she returned to Ludlow and began a history of Vermont that would become her life obsession.

Hemenway began a series of treatises on all the towns of the state, each written by a leading citizen. It was to be published in fourteen quarterlies, one for every county. She began with Addison County, the only county in Vermont with a historical society. The faculty of Middlebury College, located in Addison County, declared the plan impractical and especially not suited for a woman. They asked how one woman could accomplish what forty men had been trying to do for sixteen years. Hemenway continued her work, touring the county by stagecoach and wagon and selling copies of *Poets and Poetry of Vermont,* an anthology she had written, to support her research. Back home, she worked in one room of her family's house, refusing to socialize. Six issues of the *Vermont Quarterly Gazetteer* appeared after the first issue on July 4, 1860, until the war interrupted Hemenway's work. In 1867 she published the town histories of five counties in *The Vermont Historical Gazetteer: A Magazine Embracing a History of Each Town, Civil, Ecclesiastical, Biographical, and Military.* A second volume, featuring four counties, appeared in 1871, and a third in 1877. In 1878 the Vermont State Legislature agreed to buy copies of Volumes 1, 4, and 5 if the price did not exceed four dollars a volume and set aside $1,500 for subscriptions for town libraries. In 1882 the fourth volume was published, but the proceeds from the book were attached by the printer, Joseph Poland, as surety for unpaid bills. Hemenway had no credit and was ruined financially. In 1884 she returned to Ludlow to work on the fifth volume but had to leave to escape judgment on the unpaid debt. Hemenway fled to Chicago with her manuscripts and a few pieces of furniture. She installed type cases in her room to try to set the fifth volume by herself. She was run over by a sleigh and suffered a broken collarbone, and in May 1886 three-quarters of her work was destroyed by a fire. She began Volume 5 again and started on Windsor, which would be Volume 6. She became known as an eccentric, living in poverty to work on her histories. When Abby Hemenway died of apoplexy in Chicago on February 24, 1890, she was alone and insolvent, but 6,000 pages had been published. The fifth volume was eventually finished by her sister, Carrie E.H. Page. The sixth volume was acquired by a private collector in 1911 and destroyed by another Chicago fire. ADDITIONAL SOURCES

Alli Supp.; ChPo; DcAmAu; DcNAA; NotAW; TwCBDA; *Bio-Base.*

HIMMELFARB, GERTRUDE
(1922–   )
History of Victorian England

Gertrude Himmelfarb was born August 8, 1922, in Brooklyn, New York, the daughter of Max and Bertha (Lerner) Himmelfarb. She graduated from Utrecht High School in Brooklyn and then Brooklyn College, where she earned a bachelor's degree in 1942. She then attended the University of Chicago, earning a master's degree in 1944 and a Ph.D. in 1950. Her dissertation, later published as *Lord Acton: A Study in Conscience and Politics,* established her reputation as a scholar and as a conservative thinker.

During the 1950s, Himmelfarb worked as an independent scholar, with funding from the American Association of University Women, the American Philosophical Society, and the Guggenheim Foundation. She took a position as professor of history at Brooklyn College, City University of New York, in 1959. She is currently professor emerita of history at the City University of New York.

Himmelfarb's work on poverty in the nineteenth century has drawn a great deal of interest. *The Idea of Poverty,* published in 1984 and widely praised by reviewers, explores the Victorians' evolving perceptions of poverty as a social problem. More recently she wrote *Poverty and Compassion: The Moral Imagination of the Late Victorians,* in which she argues that the late Victorian theorists of poverty need to be reread and listened to for insights relevant to our day.

Himmelfarb has been critical of modernist and postmodern ideas about the past and the present, in particular the notion that there is not one solid truth. One of her most recent publications, a collection of essays entitled *On Looking into the Abyss: Untimely Thoughts on Culture and Society,* is dedicated to the idea, as she puts it, that "there are such things as truth and reality." Himmelfarb has long been engaged in a philosophical battle with those who deconstruct literary and historical canons and write works that explore multiple truths. She argued in an early article that a strong military defense, a strong economy, and strong family ties make for a healthy society, and much of her work is written in defense of the Victorians who practiced such behavior and in support of contemporary writers and politicians who promote the same. Himmelfarb has participated in and generated a great deal of debate in the profession, with an address at an annual meeting of the American Historical Association as well as in her many writings and public presentations.

Himmelfarb received many honors and awards, among them a senior fellowship from the National Endowment for the Humanities, a Phi Beta Kappa visiting scholarship, a Woodrow Wilson International Center fellowship, and an American Council for Learned Societies fellowship. She also served as an overseer to the Hoover Institution on War, Revolution, and Peace.

Gertrude Himmelfarb married Irving Kristol, also a noted neoconservative speaker and scholar, in 1942. They have two children, a daughter, Elizabeth, and a son, William, who served as chief of staff to Vice President Dan Quayle during the Bush administration.

BOOKS BY GERTRUDE HIMMELFARB

The De-moralization of Society: From Victorian Virtues to Modern Values. New York: Alfred A. Knopf, 1995.

On Looking into the Abyss: Untimely Thoughts on Culture and Society. New York: Alfred A. Knopf, 1994.

Poverty and Compassion: The Moral Imagination of the Late Victorians. New York: Alfred A. Knopf, 1991.

The New History and the Old Left. Cambridge, MA: Belknap Press of Harvard University Press, 1987.

Marriage and Morals Among the Victorians: Essays. New York: Alfred A. Knopf, 1986.

The Idea of Poverty: England in the Early Industrial Age. New York: Alfred A. Knopf, 1984.

On Liberty and Liberalism: The Case of John Stuart Mill. New York: Alfred A. Knopf, 1974.

Victorian Minds. New York: Alfred A. Knopf, 1968.

Editor. *On Population,* by Thomas Robert Malthus. New York: Modern Library, 1960.

Darwin and the Darwinian Revolution. Garden City, NY: Doubleday, 1959; reprint W. W. Norton, 1962, 1968.

Lord Acton: A Study in Conscience and Politics. Chicago: University of Chicago Press, 1952.

Editor. *Essays on Freedom and Power,* by John Emerich Edward Dalberg-Acton. Boston: Beacon Press, 1948.

ADDITIONAL SOURCES

Moritz, Charles, ed. "Himmelfarb, Gertrude." *Current Biography.* New York: H. W. Wilson, 1985, 184–187.

HINE, DARLENE CLARK
(1947–   )
History of African Americans, African-American Women, Medicine

Darlene Clark Hine, born February 7, 1947, in Morely, Missouri, of African-American ancestry, is the daughter of Levester Clark and Lottie May Thompson Clark. She attended an all-black two-room school from first through third grade, then public schools in Chicago. She graduated from Crane High School as class valedictorian. Among her early influences she counts her parents and her grand-mother, Fannie Venerable Thompson. They taught her manners, the Lord's Prayer, the need above all to be kind to children, and the value of humor. They and other members of her family helped Darlene, she later recalled, by "providing the essential lessons and ideas that I needed to become the Black woman, scholar, mother, aunt, sister, daughter, companion, and friend that I now imagine myself to be."

Hine attended Roosevelt University, earning a bachelor's degree in 1968. Attracted to the study of the past during the civil rights era as a way to understand present racial strife, Hine decided to pursue a career as a historian. She imagined that a knowledge of the past would also help her live more effectively in the present. Hine received the master's degree and the Ph.D. from Kent State University, in 1970 and 1975.

Hine began her teaching career as assistant professor of history and coordinator of black studies at South Carolina State College in Orangeburg, in 1972. She left there in 1974 to take a position as assistant professor at Purdue University, where she served as interim director of the Africana Studies and Research Center, associate and full professor of history, and vice provost. Since 1987 she has been John A. Hannah Professor of History at Michigan State University, although she spent one year as visiting distinguished professor of women's studies at the University of Delaware.

Editor of forty volumes, author of three award-winning books, and author of over forty articles and essays, Hine has been a pathbreaker in the field of African-American women's history. Her two-volume encyclopedia, the award-winning *Black Women in America,* has been called "the greatest reference book on women in this century." She has also written about black nurses in the early twentieth century, rape and the lives of southern black women, and the politics of black studies. Historian John Hope Franklin, in the introduction to Hine's collection of essays, *Hine Sight,* wrote, "The history of African-American women has become an important topic in the intellectual life of this country in the past fifteen years; and Darlene Clark Hine has been one of those most responsible for bringing that subject to its current level of importance." Hine's most recent book is *Speak Truth to Power: Black Professional Class in United States History,* published in 1996. Hine, Evelyn Brooks Higginbotham, and Leon Litwack also have an edited collection, *The Harvard Guide to African-American History,* forthcoming from Harvard University Press.

Aside from professional publications, Hine has had many special achievements. A project to create a historical archive of black women in the Middle West, funded by the National Endowment for the Humanities, attests to her dedication to expanding the field of history. "I knew that the surest way to change the writing of history was to make accessible abundant archival sources," she later wrote. Hine also created and takes great pride in the comparative black history Ph.D. program at Michigan State University.

Hine has received grants and awards from the Rockefeller Foundation, the

Eleanor Roosevelt Institute, the National Endowment for the Humanities, the American Council of Learned Societies, the National Humanities Center, and the Ford Foundation. She has been a consultant to or reviewed grant proposals for the Ford Foundation, the MacArthur Foundation, the National Endowment for the Humanities, and the American Historical Association. Hine currently serves on many editorial advisory boards, including those for the Martin Luther King, Jr. Papers Project, the Frederick Douglass Papers Project, the *Journal of Women's History,* and *Nursing History Review.*

Darlene Clark Hine has a daughter, Robbie Davine Clark, who lives and works in Chicago. Her hobbies include reading mystery novels, walking, and biking. She is also interested in antiques, collecting books by black American writers, and traveling.

BOOKS BY DARLENE CLARK HINE

Speak Truth to Power: Black Professional Class in United States History. Brooklyn, NY: Carlson Publishers, 1996.

Editor, with D. Barry Gaspar. *More Than Chattel: Black Women and Slavery in the Americas.* Bloomington: University of Indiana Press, 1996.

Editor, with Wilma King and Linda Reed. *"We Specialize in the Wholly Impossible": A Reader in Black Women's History.* Brooklyn, NY: Carlson Publishing, 1995.

Hine Sight: Black Women and the Re-Construction of American History. Brooklyn, NY: Carlson Publishing, 1994.

Editor. *Black Women in America: An Historical Encyclopedia.* 2 Vol. Brooklyn, NY: Carlson Publishing, 1993.

Editor, with Clayborne Carson. *Milestones in African American History.* 16 vol. New York: Chelsea House, 1993.

Editor. *Black Women in the United States, 1619–1989.* 16 vol. Brooklyn, NY: Carlson Publishing, 1990.

Black Women in White: Racial Conflict and Cooperation in the Nursing Profession, 1890–1950. Bloomington, IN: Indiana University Press, 1989.

Editor, with Clayborne Carson, David Garrow, Vincent Harding, and Gerald Gill. *Eyes on the Prize: History of the Civil Rights Era. A Reader.* New York: Viking Press, 1987; revised and expanded 1991.

Editor. *The State of Afro-American History, Past, Present, and Future.* Baton Rouge: Louisiana State University Press, 1986.

Editor. *Black Women in the Nursing Profession: An Anthology of Historical Sources.* New York: Garland, 1985.

Editor, with Patrick K. Bidelman. *Black Women in the Middle West Project: Comprehensive Resource Guide, Illinois and Indiana.* Indianapolis: Indiana Historical Bureau, 1985.

When the Truth Is Told: A History of Black Women's Culture and Community in Indiana, 1875–1950. Indianapolis: National Council of Negro Women, 1981.

Black Victory: The Rise and Fall of the White Primary in Texas. New York: Krauss-Thompson Organization, 1979.

ADDITIONAL SOURCES

Adelson, Roger. "Interview with Darlene Clark Hine." *The Historian* 57 (Winter 1995): 258–274.

Hine, Darlene Clark. "Editor's Preface." *Black Women in America: An Historical Encyclopedia.* Vol. 1. New York: Carlson Publishing, 1993.

Questionnaire completed by the subject for *American Women Historians, 1700s–1990s: A Biographical Dictionary.*

White, Christopher. "Darlene Clark Hine." *African American Women: A Biographical Dictionary.* Ed. Dorothy Salem. New York: Garland, 1993, 248–249.

HU-DEHART, EVELYN
(1947–   )

Latin American/Caribbean History; History of the Asian Diaspora; Ethnic Studies

Evelyn Hu-DeHart was born March 12, 1947, in Chungking, China, of Chinese ancestry. Her father was a banker, and her mother, one of the first generation of women to receive a university education in China, was a high school principal. Her family fled China for Hong Kong in 1949, then came to the United States in 1959 under a special Cold War refugee act. Evelyn attended a British Anglican missionary school in Hong Kong and then junior high school and high school in Palo Alto, California. By the time she was twelve, Evelyn had been twice a refugee. At age seventeen, she attended Stanford University on a full scholarship, one of the first Asians on the Stanford campus in the 1960s. Hu-DeHart notes the sharp contrast between then and now, since the Stanford campus is now about one-third Asian and Asian-American.

The civil rights movement, which Hu-DeHart encountered as a teenager, left a deep impression on her. She joined the forensics team in high school and chose Martin Luther King's "I Have a Dream" speech for her presentation; it took her to the state finals. She was selected for a Good Citizenship Award by her teachers, but was denied the award by the Daughters of the American Revolution because she was an "alien." She quickly took what she learned about citizenship to the streets, picketing local banks for their redlining practices. This happened "much to the horror of my immigrant parents," she recalls, "who thought my pending citizenship application would surely be jeopardized."

While at Stanford, Hu-DeHart encountered and eagerly participated in the antiwar, free speech, women's, and ethnic pride movements. Upon graduation in 1968, she was awarded the coveted Dinkelspiel Award for her academic achievements and her leadership in the Asian community on campus. Hu-DeHart's involvement in these efforts, particularly in the antiwar movement, gave her the motivation to become a historian. "Like many others of my generation who became extremely critical of U.S. intervention in the Third World," she states, "I turned my academic attention to area studies." She chose to focus on Latin America and the Caribbean, partly because she had spent time in Brazil, where she met and was inspired by Dom Helder Camara, archbishop of northeast Brazil, who helped articulate the practice of liberation theology. Hu-DeHart felt compelled to tell the story of "people without a history," or those whom written history had marginalized, distorted, or ignored. She wanted to see these "others'' on center stage, ''as actors and agents in their own history as much as victims of others more powerful.''

Hu-DeHart earned the Ph.D. in history at the University of Texas at Austin in 1976. She worked her way up the academic ranks at Washington University in St. Louis, leaving to take a job as associate professor at Lehman College of the City University of New York. After three years there, she left in 1986 to take a position as professor of history and director of the Center for Studies of Ethnicity and Race in America at the University of Colorado at Boulder, where she continues to teach.

The author of three books and more than twenty-five articles, Hu-DeHart has published in English, Spanish, Chinese, French, and Zoque Mayan, in Great Britain, China, Taiwan, and Canada. She has written about the Chinese in Latin America and in the United States, and about the philosophy and importance of her field, ethnic studies. Among her many and varied contributions to the academy, Hu-DeHart has made it her priority to demonstrate the intellectual and structural viability of ethnic studies and, as she puts it, to ''transcend the conventional boundaries of 'American' to include diasporas in the Americas.'' She has also developed a high profile as a national speaker and consultant on multicultural affairs and race relations, appearing on the McNeil-Lehrer News Hour, on C-SPAN, and before the U.S. Civil Rights Commission. She also performs a great deal of community service, serving on the advisory boards of the Hmong Women's Education Association of Colorado and the Community Mediation Services of Boulder, and as a member of the Finance Task Force for the City of Boulder.

Evelyn Hu-DeHart has been married for twenty-seven years to Dean DeHart, and they have three of what she calls ''hybrid'' children, two daughters and a son. Because they wanted to avoid the situation of being unconnected to the real world, which Hu-DeHart feels is common to dual career couples in academia, Dean quit his job as a historian to become a community organizer and labor activist. This arrangement, she feels, keeps their family connected to the ''real world'' and to the struggles of real people, ''a powerful antidote,'' she argues, ''to the sometimes insulated and fantasy world of the academy.''

Hu-DeHart is an avid reader, a ''news junkie'' as well as a reader of novels by women and scholarship in fields outside her own. She likes to knit and cook, but travel is her favorite activity. Her current research on the Asian diaspora has taken her all over the United States, Latin America and the Caribbean, England, China, Taiwan, Hong Kong, Vietnam, Singapore, Malaysia, Thailand, and Mauritius. She still has plans to visit and complete research in Australia, Fiji, and other locations in the Pacific. Hu-DeHart speaks and/or reads eight languages, and lectures in English, Spanish, and Chinese.

BOOKS BY EVELYN HU-DEHART

Yaqui Resistance and Survival: Struggle for Land and Autonomy, 1821–1910. Madison: University of Wisconsin Press, 1984.

Missionaries, Miners, and Indians: History of Spanish Contact with the Yaqui Indians of Northwestern New Spain, 1533–1830. Tucson: University of Arizona Press, 1981.

ADDITIONAL SOURCE

Questionnaire completed by the subject for *American Women Historians, 1700s–1990s: A Biographical Dictionary.*

HYMAN, PAULA E.
(1946–   )
Jewish History

Paula E. Hyman was born in 1946 in Boston, Massachusetts, the daughter of Sydney Max and Ida Frances (Tatelman) Hyman. As a youth she was involved in New York Havurah, a group of young Jews celebrating and studying Judaism. She also helped found Ezrat Nashim, the first feminist organization actively pressing for the improvement of the status of women within the Jewish community. She attended Hebrew College in Brookline, Massachusetts, and then Radcliffe College, earning a bachelor's degree in 1968. She then attended Columbia University as a student of Judaic studies, earning a master's degree in 1970 and a Ph.D. in 1975.

From 1974 to 1981 Hyman was assistant professor at Columbia University. She was at Jewish Theological Seminary from 1981 through 1986, as associate professor of history and dean of the College of Jewish Studies. In 1986 Hyman was Lady Davis Visiting Associate Professor at Hebrew University of Jerusalem. She returned to the United States to accept a position as Lucy Moses Professor of History at Yale University, where she continues to teach.

The author, editor, or co-editor of five books and numerous scholarly articles, Hyman is also one of the series editors for The Modern Jewish Experience, which includes sixteen volumes thus far and is published by Indiana University Press. Hyman's 1991 publication, *The Emancipation of the Jews of Alsace,* explores how the ideals of acculturation and assimilation were problematic for Alsatian Jews, the first traditional Jewish community in Europe to gain civil equality. Her most recent publication, *Gender and Assimilation in Modern Jewish History: The Roles and Representation of Women,* comes from a series of lectures she delivered at the University of Washington. In this work Hyman continues her interest in women's and gender history. "Although my own professional training was conspicuously silent on the subject of women," she writes, "and gender was a concept only of interest to anthropologists, . . . my involvement with feminism at the university and in the Jewish community sparked my curiosity about women in the past and the role of gender in human experience." In her scholarly work, as Beverly Golemba states, Hyman examines the role of Jewish women in history and argues that the myth of the Jewish woman as the keeper of the Jewish community has perpetuated her servile role in the family.

Hyman has served as contributing editor to *Sh'ma* magazine in New York

City since 1977 and has provided professional service to the American Historical Association, the Association of Jewish Studies, the Leo Baeck Institute, and the Yivo Institute for Jewish Research. She has received grants and fellowships from the National Endowment for the Humanities, the American Council of Learned Societies, and the New York Council for the Humanities.

Paula Hyman is married to Stanley Rosenbaum, and they have two children, Judith Hyman Rosenbaum and Adina Hyman Rosenbaum.

BOOKS BY PAULA E. HYMAN

Gender and Assimilation in Modern Jewish History: The Roles and Representation of Women. Seattle: University of Washington Press, 1995.

The Emancipation of the Jews of Alsace: Acculturation and Tradition in the Nineteenth Century. New Haven: Yale University Press, 1991.

Co-editor, with Steven M. Cohen. *The Jewish Family: Myths and Realities.* New York: Holmes and Meier, 1986.

From Dreyfus to Vichy: The Remaking of French Jewry, 1906–1939. New York: Columbia University Press, 1979.

With Charlotte Baum and Sonia Michel. *The Jewish Woman in America.* New York: Dial Press, 1976.

ADDITIONAL SOURCE

Golemba, Beverly E. "Paula Hyman." In her *Lesser-Known Women: A Biographical Dictionary.* Boulder: Lynne Rienner, 1972, pp. 286–287.

HYSLOP, BEATRICE FRY
(1899–1973)
French History

Beatrice Fry Hyslop was born on April 10, 1899, in New York to James Hervey Hyslop, professor of philosophy and ethics at Columbia College and founder of the American Society for Psychical Research, and Mary Fry (Hall) Hyslop, who died when Beatrice was eighteen months old. She attended Barnard School for Girls from 1912 to 1915 before matriculating at Mount Holyoke College, where she was a Phi Beta Kappa majoring in history and art. She graduated with honors in 1919 and taught two years at Mrs. Day's School in New Haven, Connecticut, before attending graduate school at Columbia University, where she studied the French Revolutionary era. Hyslop was awarded an A.M. in 1924 with a thesis on French guilds. She taught at Rosemary Hall and Mount Holyoke until 1928, when she resumed her studies at Columbia.

In 1931 the French government commissioned Beatrice Hyslop to verify and catalogue the *cahiers de doléances* of 1789 (a list of grievances drawn up during the election of the Estates-General), and she spent three years in France on the project. She was made a Chevalier des Palmes académiques (elevated to Officer in 1952). In 1933 she published "Répertoire critique des cahiers de doléances pour les Etats-généreaux de 1789" as her doctoral thesis. The next year she received her Ph.D. and published *French Nationalism in 1789 According to the General Cahiers.* She also returned to the United States and, because of the

Depression, taught at Kingswood School for Girls in Bloomfield, Michigan. She then secured an appointment as history instructor at Hunter College in 1936. That same year she published *A Guide to the General Cahiers.*

Hyslop became an assistant professor in 1941 and in 1947–1948 edited the "France" section of "Recently Published Articles" for the *American Historical Review.* She became an associate professor in 1949 and full professor in 1954. In 1955 Hyslop founded the Society for French Historical Studies and later served as its third president. In 1959 she received an honorary degree from Mount Holyoke and in 1961 became a Chevalier de la Légion d'Honneur. From 1964 to 1969 she served as a member of the graduate faculty of City University of New York and during that time published *L'Apanage de Philippe-Egalité, duc d'Orléans, 1785–1791.* She retired in 1969 and became a visiting scholar at the University of Kentucky that year and at Winthrop College the next year. In 1970, with Jacques Godechot and David Dowd, she published *The Napoleonic Era in Europe.* Beatrice Hyslop died on July 23, 1973, of a heart attack at her sister's home in Rochester, New York.

ADDITIONAL SOURCES

ConAu 45; WhoAmW 61, 64, 66, 68; WhoE 74; BiIn 10; obituary in *American Historical Review* 80: 208–209, Feb. 1975; obituary in NewYT, July 27, 1973, p. 34; *Bio-Base.*

J

JACOB, MARGARET C.
(1943–   )
History of Science

Margaret Jacob was born on June 9, 1943, and raised in New York City. Her mother, of Irish ancestry, was a domestic worker; her father, of German ancestry, was a mechanic. Among her early influences Jacob counts her Irish ancestry, the political interests of her parents, her participation in church, her school experience studying science, and her aunt, who was a teacher. Jacob was motivated to become a historian because of an interest in Irish-English conflict and a fascination with the past as it shaped the present.

Jacob attended St. Joseph's College in Brooklyn, graduating with a bachelor's degree in 1964. She then attended Cornell University, where she received a master's degree in 1966 and a Ph.D. in 1968. She started her academic career as assistant professor at the University of South Florida, in Tampa, in 1968. From 1969 to 1971 Jacob was lecturer in European history at the University of East Anglia. From 1971 to 1985 she was at Baruch College, the City University of New York, where she received tenure in 1975. Jacob then joined the faculty of the New School for Social Research, where she currently teaches, as professor of history. She served as dean of the Eugene Lange College from 1985 to 1988 and as acting chair of the Committee on Historical Studies from 1994 to 1995.

Margaret Jacob has been the author, editor, or co-editor of eleven books. She has also written twenty-five scholarly articles and several major review essays; co-authored a textbook, *Western Civilization: A Concise History,* now in its fifth edition; and prepared a microfiche collection of European sources on freemasonry. Best known for her studies of Isaac Newton and the development of Western scientific thought, Jacob has also written about the politics of writing history. In *Telling the Truth About History,* which Jacob wrote with Joyce Appleby and Lynn Hunt, the authors survey historiographical approaches and argue, in the face of current debates, that a genuinely diverse community of historians can write accurate and adequate history.

Jacob has received fellowships from Harvard University, the Institute for Advanced Study at Princeton, the Fulbright Foundation, the National Science Foundation, and the Guggenheim Foundation. She has been invited to give lectures at colleges and universities throughout the United States and Europe. Jacob is a fellow of the Royal Historical Society and was a candidate for president of the American Society for Eighteenth Century Studies. She has served on the editorial boards of *Journal of Modern History, Restoration, Journal of British Studies, Isis,* and *Eighteenth Century Studies.*

Margaret Jacob is an excellent cook and an avid home keeper. She enjoys water coloring and reading.

BOOKS BY MARGARET C. JACOB

From Science to Industry: Culture, Mentality, and the Entrepreneurial Spirit. New York: Oxford University Press, forthcoming.

With Betty Jo Teeter Dobbs. *Newton and the Culture of Newtonianism.* New York: Humanities Press, 1995.

With Lynn Hunt and Joyce Appleby. *Telling the Truth About History.* New York: W. W. Norton, 1994.

Editor. *The Politics of Western Science, 1640–1990.* New York: Humanities Press, 1994.

Editor, with W. W. Mijnhardt. *The Dutch Republic in the Eighteenth Century: Decline, Enlightenment and Revolution.* Ithaca, NY: Cornell University Press, 1992.

Living the Enlightenment: Freemasonry and Politics in Eighteenth Century Europe. New York: Oxford University Press, 1991.

The Cultural Meaning of the Scientific Revolution. New York: Alfred A. Knopf, 1988.

Editor, with Phyllis Mack. *Politics and Culture in Early Modern Europe.* Cambridge: Cambridge University Press, 1986.

Editor, with J. R. Jacob. *The Origins of Anglo-American Radicalism.* Boston: Unwin and Hyman, 1983; paperback, Humanities Press, 1991.

The Radical Enlightenment: Pantheists, Freemasons and Republicans. Boston: Allen and Unwin, 1981; Italian translation, *L'Illuminismo Radicale,* 1983.

The Newtonians and the English Revolution, 1689–1720. Ithaca, NY: Cornell University Press, 1976, reprint 1983; Italian translation, *I Newtoniani e las rivoluzione inglese, 1689–1720,* 1980; Japanese translation, 1990.

ADDITIONAL SOURCES

Hollinger, David. Rev. of *Telling the Truth About History,* by Joyce Appleby, Lynn Hunt, and Margaret Jacob. *New York Times Book Review,* March 27, 1994, 16.

Questionnaire completed by the subject for *American Women Historians, 1700s–1990s: A Biographical Dictionary.*

JENSEN, JOAN M.
(1934–)
U.S. Western, Women's, and Rural History

Joan M. Jensen was born on December 9, 1934, in St. Paul, Minnesota, the daughter of an Italian immigrant father and a German first-generation American mother. Her father, who served in the military, also worked as a landscape engineer and a salesman. Her mother worked full time as a homemaker. Joan was raised in California, without much influence from her father's urban Italian Roman Catholic family or her mother's rural German one. As a historian, however, she would later go back to her rural roots. "One of the things I'm trying to do in my writing now," she told Roger Adelson in an interview for *The Historian,* "is to talk more about myself, because it's important for historians and other scholars to let people know how their background might influence what they write."

When Jensen was in high school, she did not know a single person who had graduated from college. Her mother had only finished the seventh grade, her father the eighth, although he later completed high school through a correspondence course. Jensen never went inside a public library until she got to college. Her mother encouraged her to follow the college track in school, though, and Jensen attended Pasadena Community College and then the University of California at Los Angeles. She studied history because she was interested in comparative literature and philosophy, and felt that history encompassed both. Jensen also earned a master's degree and a Ph.D. in history at UCLA, facing discrimination as one of few women pursuing graduate work in history at the time.

Jensen's first academic appointment was at U.S. International University, in San Diego, California, from 1962 to 1971. Events outside the university, however, especially the war in Vietnam, had an impact on Jensen, and she left her job to join a farming commune in southern Colorado. Unlike many other communes, she recalls, this one attempted to practice gender equality. The group of five split up after two years and Jensen returned to the city. "I didn't necessarily plan to remain a historian," she states, "but there were few alternatives and I still really liked history." From 1974 to 1975 Jensen was visiting assistant professor at Arizona State University at Tempe, and from 1975 to 1976 she taught at the University of California at Los Angeles as a visiting lecturer in history. From 1976 until 1992, Jensen was at New Mexico State University, where she was assistant professor, associate professor, and professor. She also directed the women's studies program from 1989 to 1992, and since 1992 has been professor emerita at New Mexico State University.

Joan Jensen combined her interests in feminism and history and began to write women's history, focusing, as she later put it, on those people who were "the least literate, those who had written the least, and those who had contributed the least to high culture." She has been a leader in her field and in encouraging others to write more inclusive, multicultural history. Jensen's most famous essay is "The Gentle Tamers Revisited: New Approaches to the History of Women in the American West," published in *Pacific Historical Review* in 1980. This prize-winning article called for a revised approach, a multicultural approach, to studying women in the West. The essay was the focus of a panel ten years later at the 1990 Western Historical Association Conference and then of a special issue of *Pacific Historical Review.* While some have criticized Jensen for centering white women in her analysis in this article and for not looking at power relations among women, she has also been praised for asking the initial questions and opening up the field to the study of women. Jensen, argues Lois Scharf, has mapped out the path that "will enable us to create an exquisitely detailed, inclusive women's history."

Joan Jensen has written, edited, or co-edited eleven books, among them two award-winners. *Loosening the Bonds: Mid-Atlantic Farm Women, 1750–1850,* won the Western Association of Women Historians Sierra Prize and the Old Sturbridge Village Research Library Society–E. Harold Hugo Memorial Book Prize. *New Mexico Women: Intercultural Perspectives* won the New Mexico Presswomen's Zia Award and the Governor's Award for Historic Preservation. Her most recent work, *One Foot on the Rockies,* explores how women of diverse backgrounds have found a voice in the modern West. Jensen has also written over forty articles addressing theoretical issues about writing western and women's history, sexuality in rural America, rural women and economic development, and East Indians in the West.

Jensen has secured a number of awards, including a United States Information Agency lecture tour in India, a Rockefeller fellowship, a Senior Fulbright in Germany, and a Newberry Library fellowship. She has also served as president and vice president of the Agricultural History Society, on the Board of Editors of the *Pacific Historical Review,* and on the History Committee of the Statue of Liberty–Ellis Island Foundation.

Although Jensen has retired from her academic position, she continues to write. "Writing history is hard work and very labor intensive," she tells Roger Adelson. "My study of rural women has helped me when I am tired because then I think how hard they worked and for such long hours. Remembering those women and saying to myself 'Come on Jensen,' I can continue at the task before me." Jensen lives in Las Cruces, New Mexico.

BOOKS BY JOAN M. JENSEN

One Foot on the Rockies: Women and Creativity in the Modern American West. Albuquerque: University of New Mexico Press, 1995.

Army Surveillance in America, 1775–1980. New Haven, CT: Yale University Press, 1991.

Promise to the Land: Essays on Rural Women. Albuquerque: University of New Mexico Press, 1991.

Passage from India: Asian Indian Immigrants in North America. New Haven, CT: Yale University Press, 1988.

Loosening the Bonds: Mid-Atlantic Farm Women, 1750–1850. New Haven, CT: Yale University Press, 1987; paperback, 1988.

With Gloria Ricci Lothrop. *California Women: A History.* San Francisco: Boyd and Fraser, 1987.

Editor, with Darlis A. Miller. *New Mexico Women: Intercultural Perspectives.* Albuquerque: University of New Mexico Press, 1986.

Editor, with Sue Davidson. *A Needle, a Bobbin, a Strike: Women Needleworkers in America.* Philadelphia: Temple University Press, 1984; paperback, 1985.

Editor, with Lois Scharf. *Decades of Discontent: The Women's Movement, 1920–1940.*

Westport, CT: Greenwood Press, 1983; paperback, Northeastern University Press, 1987.

With These Hands: Women Working on the Land. Old Westbury, NY: Feminist Press, 1981.

The Price of Vigilance. Chicago: Rand McNally, 1968.

ADDITIONAL SOURCES

Adelson, Roger. "Interview with Joan Jensen." *The Historian* 56 (Winter 1994): 245–258.

Questionnaire completed by the subject for *American Women Historians, 1700s–1990s: A Biographical Dictionary.*

JOHANSEN, DOROTHY O.
(1904–   )
Pacific Northwest History

Dorothy O. Johansen was born on May 19, 1904, to John H. Johansen of Germany and Sophie (Binder) Johansen in Seaside, Oregon. She attended Reed College and received her B.A. in 1933, an M.A. from the University of Washington in 1935, and a Ph.D. in 1941. Before that, she taught school from 1922 to 1927 in Oregon and from 1927 to 1930 in Yakima, Washington. After receiving her M.A., Johansen was an instructor in history at Reed College from 1938 to 1943, assistant professor of history from 1943 to 1949, and professor of history and humanities from 1958 until her retirement in 1969. She was also a visiting professor at the University of Washington, the University of Montana, and the University of Oregon in the summers.

Johansen was a director of the Oregon Historical Society and a member of the advisory boards of the *Pacific Northwest Quarterly* and *America: History and Life.* In 1941 she received an award for Pacific history from the Pacific Coast branch of the American Historical Association. She also received a Ford Fellowship in 1954 and the Oregon Historical Society Award in 1958. In 1957 she wrote *Empire of the Columbia: A History of The Pacific Northwest,* with Charles M. Gates. Two years later Johansen wrote *Robert Newell's Memoranda* and *Voyage of the Columbia: Around the World with John Boit, 1790–1793.* The latter was part of the Beaver Book series, of which Johansen was general editor. In 1966 she was president of the Pacific Coast branch of the American Historical Association. Dorothy Johansen lives in a rest home in Milwaukie, Oregon.

ADDITIONAL SOURCES

Capitol's Who's Who for Oregon, 1948–49; (Portland) *Oregonian,* Feb. 16, 1958; Apr. 13, 1958, port.; Apr. 17, 1958, p. 1; (Portland) *Oregon Journal,* Oct. 26, 1957; ConAu P-1; DrAS 74H, 78H; WhoAmW 58, 61, 64; WhoPNW; *Bio-Base.*

JOSEPHSON, HANNAH
(1900–1976)
U.S. History

Hannah Josephson was born on June 6, 1900, in New York, New York, to Abraham David and Anna (Levinson) Geffen. She studied at Hunter College (now Hunter College of the City University of New York) from 1916 to 1918 and at Columbia Graduate School of Journalism from 1918 to 1919. She married Matthew Josephson, a writer, on May 6, 1920. She began working as a newspaper reporter and magazine editor. She was librarian, editor of publications, publicity director, and director of manuscript exhibition for the American Academy of Arts and Letters in New York from 1949 to 1965.

Her first published work was *Aragon: Poet of the Resistance,* with Malcolm Cowley (1945). Josephson published *The Golden Threads,* a book on women who worked in the textile mills of Massachusetts between 1822 and 1850 (1949), and with her husband wrote *Al Smith, Hero of the Cities: A Political Portrait Drawing on the Papers of Frances Perkins* in 1969. Her last book was *Jeanette Rankin: First Lady in Congress* in 1974. In between she translated several books including Louis Aragon's *The Century Was Young* (1941), Philippe Soupault's *Age of Assassins* (1946), and Gabrielle Roy's *The Tin Flute* (1948). She received the Van Wyck Brooks Award of the University of Bridgeport in 1969 for *Al Smith, Hero of the Cities.* Hannah Josephson died on October 29, 1976, in New Milford, Connecticut.

ADDITIONAL SOURCES

BiIn 11; ConAu 69; ConAu P-2; WhoAmW 68; obituary in NewYT, Oct. 31, 1976, p. 40; NewYTBS, 1976; *Bio-Base.*

JUDSON, MARGARET ATWOOD
(1899–1991)
U.S. History

Margaret Atwood Judson was born in Winsted, Connecticut, on November 5, 1899, to George W. and Minnie (Atwood) Judson. She obtained a B.A. from Mt. Holyoke College in 1922 and an M.A. and a Ph.D. from Radcliffe College (1923 and 1933, respectively). She was also awarded an LL.D. from Rutgers University in 1968 and a Litt.D. from Mt. Holyoke in 1972. Judson was an instructor of history at Douglass College, Rutgers University, from 1928 to 1933, assistant professor from 1933 to 1942, associate professor from 1942 to 1948, and full professor in 1948. She chaired the history and political science department from 1955 to 1963 and served as acting dean of Douglass College from 1966 to 1967. She was Alice F. Palmer Visiting Professor at the University of Michigan in 1959 and a Guggenheim fellow from 1954 to 1955. Judson was president of the Berkshire History Conference from 1948 to 1950.

In 1949 Judson wrote *The Crisis of the Constitution.* Twenty years later she wrote *The Political Thought of Sir Henry Vane the Younger.* in 1980 she wrote *From Tradition to Political Reality,* and in 1984 she wrote *Breaking the Barrier: A Professional Autobiography by a Woman Educator and Historian Before the Women's Movement.* In December 1990 Judson won the American Historical Association's Award for Scholarly Distinction. A chair at Rutgers, the Margaret Atwood Judson Professor of History, was established in her name. Margaret

Atwood Judson died in a nursing home in Piscataway, New Jersey, in March 1991.

ADDITIONAL SOURCES

DrAS 74H, 78H; WhoAmW 58, 66, 68, 72, 74, 75; WhoAm 70; *Bio-Base;* obituary in NewYT, March 26, 1991, p. B-8; obituary in NewYTBS 22: 287.

K

KEDDIE, NIKKI R.
(1930–   )
Middle Eastern History

Nikki Keddie was born on August 30, 1930, in New York City, where she attended the City and Country School through grade eight and then Horace Mann-Lincoln High School. Her father, a business manager, and her mother, a translator, were both of Russian ancestry.

As an undergraduate Keddie attended Radcliffe College, where she received a bachelor's degree in history and literature in 1951. She earned a master's degree from Stanford University, also in 1951, and then a Ph.D. at the University of California at Berkeley in 1955. She taught at the University of Arizona at Tucson and Scripps College before joining the faculty of the University of California at Los Angeles, where she has taught since 1961. Since 1967 she has taught as visiting professor at Harvard University, the University of Rochester, the School of Advanced International Studies, and the University of Paris.

Keddie was motivated to become a historian out of her desire to understand how human societies worked without having to follow what she calls the "seeming rigidities of approach of the other social sciences." Her accomplishments in Middle Eastern history make her a true leader in the field. She has written or edited eighteen books and nearly one hundred articles. Her most recent books include *Iran and the Middle East: Resistance and Revolution* (1995); *Debates on Gender and Sexuality* (1995), an edited collection; and *Debating Revolutions* (1995), an edited collection. Keddie has written about Iran, Nepal, Pakistan, Azerbaijan, Turkey, Egypt, Senegal, Sumatra, Tunisia, and Yemen. With Lois Beck, Keddie co-edited *Women in the Muslim World* (1978), a book that has had a significant impact on the study of women in the Middle East. Thirteen years later, in 1991, she co-edited, this time with Beth Baron, *Women in Middle Eastern History: Shifting Boundaries in Sex and Gender,* another groundbreaking work in the field.

Keddie has been named a fellow of the American Academy of Arts and
Sciences and has received fellowships from the Guggenheim and Rockefeller
Foundations and the American Association of University Women. She has
served as president and on the board of directors of the Middle East Studies
Association, on the board of directors of the Society for Iranian Studies, on the
Iran Working Group for the Woodrow Wilson Center, on the editorial board of
International Journal of Middle East Studies, as a consultant on Middle East
educational material for the National Geographic Society, and as the founding
editor of the journal *Contention: Debates in Society, Culture, and Science.*

Primary among Keddie's hobbies is photography. She has held photographic
exhibits on Morocco and Iran, and her work has been part of an exhibit on
Yemen that began at the Smithsonian and traveled throughout the United States.
She also enjoys painting and drawing, mainly in watercolors. She is interested
in politics and current affairs and has particular concerns about the effects of
economic globalization as income gaps and unemployment increase and the
needs of children and their mothers are neglected.

BOOKS BY NIKKI KEDDIE

Iran and the Middle East: Resistance and Revolution. London: Macmillan, 1995.

Editor. *Debates on Gender and Sexuality.* New York: New York University Press, 1995.

Editor. *Debating Revolutions.* New York: New York University Press, 1995.

Editor, with Beth Baron. *Women in Middle Eastern History: Shifting Boundaries in Sex
and Gender.* New Haven: Yale University Press, 1992; paperback, 1993.

Editor, with Mark Gasiorowski. *Neither East nor West: Iran, the Soviet Union, and the
United States.* New Haven: Yale University Press, 1990.

The Iranian Revolution and the Islamic Republic. Completely revised and updated edition. Syracuse, NY: Syracuse University Press, 1986.

Editor, with Juan R. I. Cole. *Shi'ism and Social Protest.* New Haven: Yale University
Press, 1986.

Editor. *Religion and Politics in Iran: Shi'ism from Quietism to Revolution.* New Haven:
Yale University Press, 1983.

Editor, with Eric Hooglund. *The Iranian Revolution and the Islamic Republic: Conference
Proceedings.* Washington, DC: Middle East Institute, 1982.

Roots of Revolution: An Interpretive History of Modern Iran. New Haven: Yale University Press, 1981. Persian translation, Tehran, 1991.

Editor, with Michael E. Bonine. *Modern Iran: The Dialectics of Continuity and Change.*
Albany: State University of New York Press, 1981.

Iran: Religion, Politics and Society. London: Frank Cass, 1980.

Editor, with Lois Beck. *Women in the Muslim World.* Cambridge, MA: Harvard University Press, 1978; paperback, 1980.

Sayyid Jamal ad-Din ''al-Afghani'': A Political Biography. Berkeley: University of California Press, 1972.

Editor. *Scholars, Saints and Sufis.* Berkeley: University of California Press, 1972; paperback, 1978.

*An Islamic Response to Imperialism: Political and Religious Writings of Sayyid Jamal
ad-Din ''al-Afghani''.* Berkeley: University of California Press, 1968; paperback,
1983.

Religion and Rebellion in Iran: The Tobacco Protest of 1891–1892. London: Frank Cass, 1966. Persian translation, Tehran. Amir Kabir, 1976.
ADDITIONAL SOURCE
Questionnaire completed by the subject for *American Women Historians, 1700s–1990s: A Biographical Dictionary.*

KELLOGG, LOUISE PHELPS
(1862–1942)
U.S. Frontier History

Louise Phelps Kellogg, once described as ''the best-known woman historian in the West'' by the American Historical Association, was born to Mary Isabella (Belle) Phelps and Amherst Willoughby Kellogg, an insurance executive, on May 12, 1862, in Milwaukee. She attended school in Evanston, Illinois, and Dearborn Seminary in Chicago. She graduated from Milwaukee College in 1882 and taught at a Milwaukee girls school afterwards.

In 1895 Kellogg approached Frederick Jackson Turner about becoming a historian, and he accepted her as his student at the University of Wisconsin. She graduated with honors in 1897 and received one of the university's few graduate scholarships, serving as Turner's assistant. She also won the Women's Education Association of Boston fellowship for second year graduate work at the London School of History and Economics and the Sorbonne in Paris. Her first article, ''Sur la translation des Restes de Voltaire au Panthéon, le ll Juillet 1791,'' was published in *La Révolution Française* while she was in Paris.

In 1899 Kellogg returned to the University of Wisconsin, where she became an assistant in ancient and medieval history and worked on her dissertation. *The American Colonial Charter: A Study of English Administration in Relation Thereto, Chiefly After 1688* was published by the American Historical Association in 1899 and was awarded the Justin Winsor Prize. Kellogg became a university fellow the next year and was awarded a Ph.D. in 1901. She was appointed to a research post in the State Historical Society of Wisconsin. She began working with Reuben Gold Thwaites on the fifteen-volume *Original Journals of the Lewis and Clark Expedition* (1904–1905) and the thirty-volume *Early Western Travels, 1748–1846* (1904–1907). She also worked on five volumes of the State Historical Society's *Collections* (1902–1911). During the course of this work, Kellogg and Thwaites became partners in 1905 and edited the first volume of the series on the American Revolution in the Ohio valley, *Documentary History of Dunmore's War, 1774.* They published the second volume, *Revolution on the Upper Ohio, 1775–1777,* in 1908, and *Frontier Defense on the Upper Ohio, 1777–1778* in 1912. In 1913 Thwaites died unexpectedly, and Kellogg continued with their work. In 1915 she prepared *Index to Volumes I–XX of the Wisconsin Historical Collections,* published as a separate volume in the series. In 1916 *Frontier Advance on the Upper Ohio, 1778–1779* was published, followed by *Frontier Retreat on the Upper Ohio, 1779–1781* in 1917. In 1925 *The*

French Regime in Wisconsin and the Northwest was published, and in 1935 *The British Regime in Wisconsin and the Northwest* came out.

In addition to her prolific work on the series, Louise Kellogg became a master indexer, often indexing works of other scholars. She was the first woman to be president of the Mississippi Valley Historical Association (now Organization of American Historians), in 1930; was active in the Daughters of the American Revolution, the League of Women Voters, and the National Conference of Christians and Jews; and was a fellow of the Royal Historical Society of Britain. She contributed forty-five short subject entries to the *Dictionary of American History* and seventy-three biographical sketches to the *Dictionary of American Biography.* She wrote *Early Narratives of the Northwest, 1634–1699* as part of the American Historical Association nineteen-volume project *Original Narratives of Early American History,* and in 1923 edited a two-volume Caxton Club edition of *Charlevoix's Journal of a Voyage to North America.* In 1935 the Wisconsin Archaeological Society awarded her the Lapham Medal, and in 1937 Marquette University awarded her an honorary degree.

During her phenomenal career, Louise Kellogg suffered from continuing hearing loss and eventually was forced to carry a bulky hearing machine with her. In 1941, at age seventy-nine, Kellogg drove to historic Vincennes, Indiana, then to the meeting of the Mississippi Valley Historical Association in Lexington, Kentucky. She died the next year on July 11.

ADDITIONAL SOURCES

AmWomWr; BiIn 5; LibW; NotAW; WhAm 3; WomWWA 14; AmAu&B; DcNAA; OxCan; WhNAA; WisWr; *Bio-Base.*

KELLY, JOAN
(1928–1982)
European, Women's History

Joan Kelly Gadol was born on March 29, 1928, in Brooklyn, New York, to George V. and Ruth (Jacobsen) Kelly. She attended St. John's University College and received a B.A. (summa cum laude) in 1953. She received an M.A. in 1954 from Columbia University and a Ph.D. in 1963. She was a lecturer for City College of the City University of New York from 1956 to 1963. She was assistant professor from 1963 to 1968 and associate professor from 1968 to 1972. During this time she published *Leon Battista Alberti* (1969). She was a professor of history from 1972 until her death. During that time she was also visiting assistant professor at Columbia University (1963–1964) and, with Gerda Lerner, founded and co-directed in 1972–1974 the first master of arts program in women's history at Sarah Lawrence College; she was acting director of the women's studies program at City University of New York (CUNY) in 1976–1977. Kelly was the chair of the American Historical Association's Committee on Women Historians from 1975 to 1977. She was also co-chair of the New York City chapter of the Coordinating Committee for Women in the Historical

Profession from 1973 to 1974. She won a Woodrow Wilson fellowship for 1953–1954, a Danforth fellowship for 1960–1961 and a junior fellowship from the National Foundation for the Arts and Humanities for 1967–1968.

By the 1970s Kelly had become well known for her publications on feminist history. Her article "Did Women Have a Renaissance?" in *Becoming Visible: Women in European History,* edited by Renate Bridenthal and Claudia Koonz, was considered ground-breaking in the area of historical scholarship. With Amy Swerdlow, Renate Bridenthal, and Phyllis Vine she co-authored *Household and Kin* in 1980. *Women, History, and Theory,* a collection of essays, was published posthumously by the University of Chicago. Joan Kelly died of cancer in 1982.

ADDITIONAL SOURCES

ConAu 61, 107; DrAS 74H, 78H; WhoAmW 75; *Bio-Base;* obituary in FemStud 9: 174–177, Spring 1983; *Ms.* 11: 18, Dec. 1982; NewYT, Aug. 18, 1982, p. B-5; NewYTBS 13: 1025, Aug. 1982.

KESSLER-HARRIS, ALICE
(1941–   )
U.S. Labor and Women's History

Born in Leicester, England, on June 2, 1941, of Hungarian and Czech ancestry, Alice Kessler-Harris attended school in Cardiff, Wales, at the Birchgrove School and then Cardiff High School for Girls. She completed her secondary schooling in Trenton, New Jersey. Her father was a shoe designer; her mother died when she was only forty years old. Kessler-Harris counts as her earliest and most significant childhood influences her refugee status and "foreign" parentage.

Alice Kessler-Harris attended Goucher College, receiving a bachelor's degree cum laude in 1961. Rhoda Dorsey, one of her professors at Goucher, played a significant role in encouraging Kessler-Harris to become a historian, but as she puts it, "my own search for a past participated mightily." Kessler-Harris then attended Rutgers University, earning a master's degree in history in 1963 and a Ph.D. in 1968. She has been awarded honorary degrees from Goucher College and the Uppsala University in Sweden.

Kessler-Harris's first academic appointment was at Hofstra University, where she was assistant professor from 1968 to 1974, associate professor from 1974 to 1981, and professor from 1981 to 1988. While at Hofstra, Kessler-Harris was co-director of the Center for the Study of Work and Leisure from 1976 to 1988, and she held visiting faculty positions at Sarah Lawrence College, the University of Warwick, and Binghamton University, the State University of New York. In 1988 she accepted a position as professor of history at Temple University, and in 1990 she left Temple for her current position as professor of history at Rutgers University. From 1990 to 1995 she was also director of women's studies at Rutgers.

Alice Kessler-Harris is the author or editor of ten books, author of twenty-five scholarly articles, and author of another twenty-five essays and miscellaneous pieces. She also holds contracts for two additional books, *Gender Ideology in Social Policy,* which will be published by Oxford University Press, and *Gender and Culture: Re-viewing the Historical Paradigm,* which will be published by the University of North Carolina Press. *Out to Work: A History of Wage-Earning Women in the United States,* was awarded the Philip Taft Prize for the Best Book in Labor History in 1982 and has been excerpted in three subsequent texts. One of her most recent works is a collection of essays in honor of Gerda Lerner that she edited with Linda Kerber and Kathryn Kish Sklar. Several reviewers have argued that this collection defines the state of the art of women's history in the United States today.

Kessler-Harris is the first historian in the United States effectively to merge the fields of labor history and women's history. She has been instrumental in changing both fields, looking forward to and helping to create a time in which "we would, for the first time," she writes, "have to write books in which 'workers' meant women as well as men." She regularly publishes in labor history and women's history publications, bridging what has too often been an enormous gap in scholarship.

When asked about her accomplishments aside from teaching and publishing, Kessler-Harris cites developing the women's studies program at Rutgers University and co-founding the Labor College for District 65 of the United Auto Workers, officially called the Institute of Applied Social Science. She has been the recipient of fellowships from the Guggenheim, Rockefeller, and Ford Foundations, a research associate at the New School for Social Research, and a winner of the John B. Commerford Award for Labor Education. She has been an invited lecturer at universities throughout the United States as well as in Tokyo, Berlin, Amsterdam, Vancouver, Stockholm, and Oslo. She also served as an expert witness and historian for the *Equal Opportunity Employment Commission v. Sears Roebuck and Company* case before the U.S. District Court.

A member of both the American Historical Association (AHA) and the Organization of American Historians (OAH) since 1968, Kessler-Harris has served these professional organizations in several capacities, including chair of the Committee on Women Historians of the AHA and chair of the advisory board for the OAH newsletter. She has served on the editorial boards of many journals, including *Journal of American History, Labor History, Gender and History,* and *Signs.* A member of the nominating jury for the Pulitzer Prize in History in 1987, Kessler-Harris has also served as consultant to the Woodrow Wilson Foundation and on the evaluation teams for history and American studies programs at the University of Massachusetts, Bryn Mawr and Haverford Colleges, and the University of Minnesota.

Alice Kessler-Harris has been married to Bert Silverman since 1982. She is the mother of a daughter, Ilona, from her first marriage, and the grandmother of Emma. She also has two stepdaughters, Julie and Devorah. Her hobbies include cooking, tennis, theater, and gardening.

BOOKS BY ALICE KESSLER-HARRIS

Editor, with Linda Kerber and Kathryn Kish Sklar. *U.S. History as Women's History: New Feminist Essays*. Chapel Hill: University of North Carolina Press, 1995.

Editor, with Ulla Wikander and Jane Lewis. *Protecting Women: Labor Legislation in Europe, the United States, and Australia*. Chicago: University of Illinois Press, 1995.

A Woman's Wage: Historical Meanings and Social Consequences. Lexington: University Press of Kentucky, 1990.

Editor, with Carroll Moody. *Perspectives on American Labor History: The Problem of Synthesis*. DeKalb: Northern Illinois University Press, 1990.

Editor, with William McBrien. *Faith of a Woman Writer*. Westport, CT: Greenwood Press, 1988.

Editor, with Judith Friedlander, Blanche Cook, and Carroll Smith-Rosenberg. *Women in Culture and Politics: A Century of Change*. Bloomington: Indiana University Press, 1986.

Out to Work: A History of Wage-Earning Women in the United States. New York: Oxford University Press, 1982.

Women Have Always Worked: An Historical Overview. New York: Feminist Press and McGraw-Hill, 1981.

Selected, with an Introduction. *The Open Cage: An Anzia Yezierska Collection*. New York: Persea, 1979.

Editor, with Blanche Cook and Ronald Radosh. *Past Imperfect: Alternative Essays in American History*. New York: Alfred A. Knopf, 1973.

ADDITIONAL SOURCES

Kessler-Harris, Alice. "Equal Opportunity Employment Commission v. Sears Roebuck and Co.: A Personal Account." *Radical History Review* 35 (1986): 57–79.

Questionnaire completed by the subject for *American Women Historians, 1700s–1990s: A Biographical Dictionary*.

KIBRE, PEARL
(1900–1985)
Medieval History

Pearl Kibre was born in Philadelphia on September 2, 1900, to Kenneth and Jane (du Pione) Kibre. The family moved to California, and Pearl attended the Manual Arts High School in Los Angeles. She obtained a B.A. and an M.A. from Berkeley, studying under Louis J. Paetow. In 1937 she received a Ph.D. from Columbia University. She taught mainly at Hunter College in New York until her retirement in 1970. She was elected a fellow of the Medieval Academy of America in 1964. In 1976 she was honored with a commemorative volume, *Science, Medicine and the University, 1200–1500*, published in *Manuscripta*. Her specialties were the organization of medieval universities, codicology, and the problems of medieval science and medicine.

Pearl Kibre was a member of the United States Subcommission for the History of Universities within the International Committee of Historical Sciences and a member of the editorial board of *Medieval and Renaissance Latin Translations and Commentaries.* In 1936 she published *The Library of Pico della Mirandola,* followed by *A Catalogue of Incipits of Mediaeval Scientific Writings in Latin* in 1937. In 1948 she published *The Nations in the Mediaeval Universities,* and in 1962 *Scholarly Privileges in the Middle Ages. Hippocrates Latinus* was published in eight installments in *Traditio* from 1975 to 1982 and eventually published in book form by Fordham University Press. Kibre died in New York City on July 15, 1985.

ADDITIONAL SOURCES
DrAS 74H, 78H; WhoAm 74, 76, 78, 80; WhoAmW 66, 68, 70, 72, 75, 77, 79; WhoE 74, 75, 77, 79; obituary in *Speculum* 61: 761–763, July 86; *Bio-Base.*

KIDWELL, CLARA SUE
(1941–   )
Native American History, History of Science

Clara Sue Kidwell, historian of science, of Native American cultural practices, and of Native American women, was born on July 8, 1941, in Tahlequah, Oklahoma, of Choctaw/Chippewa/French/English/Scotch-Irish ancestry. Her parents, Hardin Milton Kidwell and Martha Evelyn St. Clair, were both clerks with the Bureau of Indian Affairs. Clara Sue grew up in Muskogee, Oklahoma, raised by her grandmother, Susie Kidwell, while her parents worked. Kidwell graduated from Central High School in 1959, then attended the University of Oklahoma at Norman, where she received a bachelor's degree in 1963, a master's degree in 1966, and a Ph.D. in 1970.

Kidwell remembers three early influences on her life. Her grandmother counseled her, "If you want something done right, don't depend on other people to do it for you." Her mother, who worked for the Bureau of Indian Affairs for thirty-one years, told her to "make a carbon copy of everything." And Gladys Nunn, Clara's high school teacher, in emphasizing that quotation marks at the beginning of a quote are right side up commas, and those at the end are upside down commas, taught Clara attention to details.

Kidwell attributes her early interest in history to her grandmother, who, she says, "took the *Reader's Digest* religiously." From the *Digest,* Kidwell learned an impressive amount of trivial information, which she used to qualify for the College Bowl Team at the University of Oklahoma. Two historians of science happened to be on the selection committee for the team, and they offered her a fellowship in the history of science when she finished her bachelor's degree. She continued her studies in the history of science through the doctorate.

Kidwell's first teaching job was at the Haskell Institute in Lawrence, Kansas, her parents' alma mater. After two-year stays at Haskell and then at the University of Minnesota, Kidwell accepted a position as associate professor in the Native American studies program at the University of California at Berkeley. She left Berkeley in 1993 to serve as the assistant director for cultural resources at the National Museum of the American Indian, where she tried to "infuse a sense of history'' into the planning of exhibits for the current facility in New York and the new facility in Washington, D.C., which is scheduled to open in 2001. In 1995 Kidwell became director of the Native American studies program and tenured professor of history at the University of Oklahoma, where she plans to pursue her interest in the history of the Choctaws in Mississippi.

The recipient of numerous fellowships, including those from the Rockefeller Foundation, Newberry Library, and the Smithsonian Institution, Kidwell has produced two books and many articles on American Indian technologies, women in Native American cultures, Choctaw land claims in Mississippi, and educational issues for Native Americans. Her most recent works include her book *Choctaws and Missionaries in Mississippi, 1818–1918* and "Choctaw Women and Cultural Persistence in Mississippi," in Nancy Shoemaker's edited collection, *Keepers of Tradition, Advocates of Change: Historical Perspectives on Women and Gender in Native American Societies* (New York: Routledge, 1994). Her article "Systems of Knowledge," summarizing the complexities of Native American science in comparison to European scientific thought and practice during the era of Columbus, is included in Alvin M. Josephy's edited collection, *America in 1492: The World of the Indian Peoples Before the Arrival of Columbus,* a collection reviewer Michael D. Green claims probably comes closer than any other to being the "official" history of the period.

Kidwell's professional responsibilities have included serving as director of Berkeley's Consortium for Graduate Opportunities for American Indians and as director of two National Endowment for the Humanities Summer Institutes for College Teachers: "Great Traditions in American Indian Thought" and "Myth, Memory and History: Alternative Sources for Writing American Indian History." In 1995 Kidwell also accepted the role of contributing editor for the Museums and Interpretive Programs column in the newsletter of the American Historical Association.

Clara Sue Kidwell has a brother and sister, and her parents, both in good health, are "happy as bed bugs," according to Kidwell's mother. Kidwell also has two cats, Betsy and Bertrand Russell. Her hobbies include gardening and cooking, especially with Hugo, the sourdough starter Kidwell has been nurturing and using for seven years.

BOOKS BY CLARA SUE KIDWELL

Choctaws and Missionaries in Mississippi, 1818–1918. Norman: University of Oklahoma Press, 1995.

With Charles Roberts. *The Choctaws: A Critical Biography.* Bloomington: University of Indiana Press, 1980.

ADDITIONAL SOURCES

Green, Michael D. Rev. of *America in 1492: The World of the Indian Peoples Before the Arrival of Columbus.* Ed. Alvin M. Josephy, Jr. *Journal of American History* 79 (Mar. 1993): 1572–1573.

Noah, Phyllis. "Picturestone." "Clara Sue Kidwell." In *Notable Native Americans.* Ed. Sharon Malinowski. Detroit: Gale Research, 1995, 233–234.

Questionnaire completed by the subject for *American Women Historians, 1700s–1990s: A Biographical Dictionary.*

KING, GRACE ELIZABETH
(1853?–1932)
Local History

Grace Elizabeth King is thought to have been born on November 29, 1853, in New Orleans, Louisiana. Her father, William Woodson King, was a lawyer and state legislator; her mother, Sarah Ann Miller, was his second wife. Grace was taught mostly at home and in Creole schools in Louisiana before attending the Institut St. Louis, graduating at age sixteen. She then attended a school established by Madame Cenas and made her intellectual debut with an essay, "The Heroines of Fiction," for the Pan-Gnostic Society, a literary group headed by Julia Ward Howe. She began writing fiction based on Creole society and enjoyed minimal success.

In 1892 King turned to writing history. She began with a biography written for the Makers of America series on the founder of New Orleans, Jean Baptiste Le Moyne, Sieur de Bienville. The next year, she collaborated with John R. Ficklen, a Tulane professor, on a high school textbook, *A History of Louisiana.* In 1895 she published *New Orleans: The Place and the People,* and in 1898 she wrote *De Soto and His Men in the Land of Florida.*

In addition to her writing, Grace King was at one time recording secretary for the Louisiana Historical Society and was on the advisory board of the society's *Quarterly* after its foundation in 1917. Her mother and two sisters, with whom she lived, took on the household work so that King could write and hold Friday afternoon receptions. She summered in Hartford with a friend, Charles Dudly Warner, and became friends with Mark Twain and his family. She was a fellow of the Royal Society of Arts and Science in England and an Officier de l'Instruction Publique in France. King received a doctor of letters degree from Tulane University. She sporadically returned to fiction, with little success, and in 1921 finished *Creole Families of New Orleans.* Grace King died of nephritis on January 14, 1932. Her *Memories of a Southern Woman of Letters* was published posthumously the same year.

ADDITIONAL SOURCES:

DcAmAu; DcAmB; InWom; NatCAB 2; NotAW; TwCBDA; Alli Supp.; AmAu&B; AmWomWr; BiD&SB; BiDSA; BiIn 1, 3, 8, 9, 10, 11, 12; ChPo; ChPo S2; DcLeL; DcNAA; OxAm; WhAm 1; WomWWA 14; AmBi; Robert Bush, "Charles Gayarre and Grace King: Letters of a Louisiana Friendship," *Southern Literary Journal* 7: 100–131, Fall 1974; Robert Bush, "Grace King: The Emergence of a Southern Intellectual Woman," *Southern Review* 13: 272–288, Spring 1977; Theodora R. Graham, "Grace King," in *American Women Writers,* v. 2 (Ungar, 1980), pp. 456–458; Robert Bush, *Grace King: A Southern Destiny* (Baton Rouge: Louisiana State University Press, 1983); David Kirby, *Grace King* (Boston: Twayne, 1980); Gregory Lansing Paine, ed., *Southern Prose Writers* (American Book Company, 1947), pp. 207–208; Clayton Rand, *Stars in*

Their Eyes (Dixie Press, 1953), pp. 202–203; A. Turner, "Grace Elizabeth King," in Louis D. Rubin, Jr., ed., *Bibliographical Guide to the Study of Southern Literature* (Baton Rouge: Louisiana State University Press, 1969), pp. 234–235; *Bio-Base;* Robert Bush, "Grace King and Mark Twain," American Literature 44: 31–51, March 1972.

KINZIE, JULIETTE AUGUSTA MAGILL
(1806–1870)
Local History

Juliette Augusta Magill Kinzie was born in Middletown, Connecticut, on September 11, 1806. She was descended from one of Connecticut's oldest families, dating back to 1636 and the founding of Windsor. Her mother was Frances (Wolcott) Magill, daughter of Alexander Wolcott, a leader of the Republican party in Connecticut and grandson of Roger Wolcott, colonial governor, judge, and major general in the Louisberg Expedition of 1745. Her father was Arthur William Magill, her mother's second husband, of whom little is known. He left the family in 1820.

Kinzie was tutored at home by her mother and uncle except for a short stint at a New Haven boarding school. She attended the Troy (New York) Female Seminary of Emma Willard, but was forced to leave before the end of the first year because of family financial problems. On August 9, 1830, she married John Harris Kinzie, an Indian agent at Fort Winnebago, Wisconsin. Her experiences in Wisconsin resulted in a book published in 1856, *Wau-Bun: The "Early Day" in the North-West*. It was reprinted seven times in the nineteenth century and four in the twentieth century. Besides a description of her travels, it included an account of the Black Hawk War and sympathetically told stories of Indian legends and Indian captivities, including that of her mother-in-law, the elder Mrs. John Kinzie. This work chronicled early Chicago history, including the massacre of the garrison at Fort Dearborn during the War of 1812 (first published separately and anonymously in 1844 as *Narrative of the Massacre at Chicago*). It became a primary source for future histories and perpetuated the legend that her father-in-law was the "Father of Chicago."

The Kinzies moved to Chicago in 1834, and Juliette entertained many official and distinguished visitors. She was active in founding St. Luke's Hospital and working with St. James Church. She had seven children, one of whom died in the Civil War and two of whom were captured by the Confederates. One daughter, Eleanor Little, was the mother of Juliette Gordon Low, founder of the Girl Scouts of America. On September 15, 1878, while vacationing at Amagansett, New York, Juliette Kinzie died after taking morphine tablets accidentally delivered instead of quinine. The old Indian Agency House where she lived in Portage, Wisconsin, was restored and refurnished in 1932, a centennial project of the National Society of Colonial Dames of America in the State of Wisconsin.

ADDITIONAL SOURCES
Alli Supp.; BiIn 5; DcAmAu; DcNAA; AmWomWr; ApCAB; LibW; NotAW; *Bio-Base.*

KITE, ELIZABETH SARAH
(1864–1954)
French-American History

Elizabeth Sarah Kite, a Quaker, was born in Philadelphia, Pennsylvania, in 1864. Her parents are not mentioned in references, but it is known she attended a Quaker boarding school in Westchester, Chester County, Pennsylvania, before studying in England, France, Germany, and Switzerland for six years. While studying in England in 1906, Kite was baptized a Catholic. Upon her return, she taught in a number of private schools in Pennsylvania, California, and Massachusetts. From 1912 to 1918 she participated in psychological research at Vineyard, New Jersey, at the Training School for Mental Defectives. She also contributed research to *The Kallikak Family: A Social Security Survey of the People of the Pines* by Henry H. Goddard and translated Binet-Simon's *Development of Intelligence in Children* and *Intelligence of the Feeble-minded.*

During this time, Kite also began researching French topics and began publishing her own historical volumes, starting with *Beaumarchais and the War of American Independence* in 1917. In 1929 she wrote *L'Enfant and Washington,* and in 1931 *Correspondence of General Washington and Compte de Grasse* was published. In 1933 she wrote *Lebegre Duportail, Comdt. of Engineers, 1777–1783* and became the first laywoman to receive the degree of doctor of literature at Villanova. The next year, she wrote *Lafayette and His Companions in the Victorie,* followed by *The Catholic Part in the Making of America* in 1936, which dealt with the policy of Louis XVI and his minister of foreign affairs in aiding America's fight for independence.

Kite, who had a study room in the Library of Congress for years, was instrumental in placing photostats of documents from the French Revolution in the library. For this she was awarded the Cross of Chevalier de la Légion d'honneur. She was also archivist for the American Catholic Historical Society of Philadelphia. Elizabeth Kite died on January 6, 1954, in Wilmington, Delaware.
ADDITIONAL SOURCES
CathA, 1930; WomWWA 14; BiIn 1, 3; *Bio-Base.*

KUPPERMAN, KAREN ORDAHL
(1939–   )
Colonial English American History

Karen Ordahl Kupperman was born on April 23, 1939, in Devils Lake, North Dakota, of Swedish and Norwegian ancestry. Her mother was principally a homemaker; her father was a colonel in the United States Army. Kupperman attended elementary school in Fort Benning, Georgia, and then in Fargo, North Dakota. She attended junior high school in Fargo and then in U.S. Army schools in Japan, and high school in Springfield, Missouri. Her favorite childhood books were a boxed set of Grimm's and Andersen's fairy tales, and she loved them because of the distant worlds they recreated. Karen's most important early influence, though, was the experience of living in different parts of the country during World War II and again in her teenage years. When she was twelve, her father's national guard regiment was called up and sent to the southeast corner of Alabama, a place, she recalls, "that was about as different culturally from North Dakota as possible within the United States." Much shocked and surprised her, and the young Karen became interested in different historical experiences of regions of the United States. The year she spent in Japan when she was fourteen also gave her firsthand experience in cultural difference and insights into the ways culture is constructed.

Karen Kupperman attended the University of Missouri, earning a bachelor's degree in history in 1961. History has always been her favorite subject. After college she went to Harvard on a Woodrow Wilson fellowship, but like many women she felt stifled by the academic atmosphere and left after earning a master's degree there in 1962. "When my children were young," she writes, "I began teaching as an adjunct at the University of Connecticut, and realized that my real interest lay in teaching and writing history. Therefore my husband and children and I went to Cambridge for two years, which is the required residency for the Ph.D." Kupperman completed the Ph.D. at Cambridge in 1978.

Following her completion of the doctorate, Kupperman accepted a position at the University of Connecticut. From 1980 to 1981, she was a Mellon Faculty Fellow at Harvard University. She stayed at the University of Connecticut until 1995, when she was named professor of history at New York University. For the academic year 1995–96, however, she is the Times-Mirror Foundation Professor at the Huntington Library in San Marino, California.

The author of four monographs, editor of four books, and co-author of an American history textbook, Kupperman is perhaps best known for her award-winning work, *Providence Island, 1630–1641: The Other Puritan Colony,* winner of the 1995 Albert J. Beveridge Award of the American Historical Association for the best book in American history, including Canada and Latin America, published in 1993. Hilary Beckles writes that this work, an examination of Puritan efforts in the West Indies, "makes a seminal contribution to early West Indian economic and social history." One of Kupperman's nearly twenty scholarly articles, "Apathy and Death in Early Jamestown," won the Binkley-Stephenson Award of the Organization of American Historians for the best article in the *Journal of American History* in 1979. Her most recent project, under contract with Cornell University Press, is a new edition of *Settling with the Indians,* a 1990 publication rewritten in the light of the literature on encounters generated by the Columbian Quincentennial.

Kupperman's first fellowship was a dissertation fellowship from the American Association of University Women, and she has since been a fellow of the American Philosophical Society, the National Humanities Center, the American Council of Learned Societies, the Rockefeller Foundation, and the National Endowment for the Humanities. She was elected to membership in the American

Antiquarian Society and the Colonial Society of Massachusetts. Kupperman has also been named Distinguished Alumna for the University of Missouri.

Karen Kupperman has provided a great deal of service to the profession. She currently serves on the nominating committee for the American Historical Association and has served as chair and council member for the Council of the Institute of Early American History and Culture, as the chair of the board of editors and member of the editorial board of *William and Mary Quarterly,* as co-chair of the New England Seminar in American History, on the board of editors of *Virginia Magazine of History and Biography,* and on the committee of publications for the American Antiquarian Society.

Karen Ordahl Kupperman is married to Joel Kupperman, professor of philosophy at the University of Connecticut. They have two sons, Michael Joel and Charles Anders Kupperman. Her interests outside of work include walking and hiking.

BOOKS BY KAREN ORDAHL KUPPERMAN

Editor. *America in European Consciousness.* Chapel Hill: University of North Carolina Press for the Institute of Early American History and Culture, 1995.

Providence Island, 1630–1641: The Other Puritan Colony. New York: Cambridge University Press, 1993.

North America and the Beginnings of European Colonization. Washington, DC: American Historical Association, 1992.

Editor. *Major Problems in American Colonial History.* Lexington, MA: D. C. Heath, 1992.

Co-author, with Wilson Gilbert. *The Pursuit of Liberty.* 3rd ed. New York: HarperCollins, 1995.

Editor. *The Providence Island Venture, 1630–1641.* In the British Association for American Studies series, *British Records Relating to American in Microform,* under the general editorship of W. E. Minchinton by Microform Academic Publishers, 1990.

Editor. *Captain John Smith: A Selected Edition of His Writings.* Chapel Hill: University of North Carolina Press for the Institute of Early American History and Culture, 1988.

Roanoke: The Abandoned Colony. Totowa, NJ: Rowman and Littlefield, 1984; reissued 1991.

Settling with the Indians: The Meeting of English and Indian Cultures in America, 1580–1640. Totowa, NJ: Rowman and Littlefield and J. M. Dent, 1980.

ADDITIONAL SOURCES

Beckles, Hilary McD. Rev. of *Providence Island, 1630–1641: The Other Puritan Colony,* by Karen Kupperman. *William and Mary Quarterly* 52 (Jan. 1995): 178–179.

Questionnaire completed by the subject for *American Women Historians, 1700s–1990s: A Biographical Dictionary.*

L

LAMB, MARTHA JOANNA READE NASH
(ca. 1826–1893)
Local History

Martha Joanna Reade Nash Lamb was born in Plainfield, Massachusetts, on August 13, 1826 or 1829, to Arvin Nash and Lucinda Vinton. Her paternal ancestors were *Mayflower* settlers in 1620; her mother's relatives were French Huguenots who settled in the 1640s. Martha attended school in Goshen, Massachusetts, before entering Williston Seminary in Easthampton in 1844 and attending Northampton High School thereafter. In 1847 she published "A Visit to My Mother's Birthplace" in the *Hampshire Gazette*. She then taught mathematics in schools in Newark, New Jersey, and Maumee, Ohio, during the next few years. On September 8, 1852, she married Charles A. Lamb, a mechanic, and lived in Ohio until 1857, when they moved to Chicago. The next year she founded, with Jane C. Hoge, the Home for the Friendless and the Half-Orphan Asylum.

During the Civil War, Martha Lamb was secretary for Chicago's first Sanitary Fair and helped raise money for soldiers' relief. In 1866 she moved to New York City, probably as a divorcée, as records show that Charles Lamb eventually remarried. She began writing to support herself, producing a variety of children's books, short stories, a romantic novel, and magazine articles. She also began working on a history of New York City, researching old volumes, records, and manuscripts and interviewing survivors of old New York families. In 1877 the first volume of *History of the City of New York: The Origins, Rise, and Progress* was published in a subscription edition by A. S. Barnes. It covered the Colonial period in 786 pages. The second volume appeared in 1880 and was praised by historian George Bancroft, *Nation* magazine, and the *Edinburgh Review*.

In 1883 Lamb published *Historical Sketch of New York for the Tenth Census* and purchased and edited *Magazine of American History*, which had been founded in 1877. She wrote over fifty signed articles and many unsigned pieces for the magazine. (Some of these were later published in book form as *Wall Street History* in 1883, and "Washington Portraits," compiled in 1888 but unpublished.) In addition, Lamb belonged to over twenty-five historical and patriotic societies including the New-York Historical Society. She was honored at a White House dinner by President Grover Cleveland in 1886 and by President Benjamin Harrison in 1889. In 1891 she was invited to a meeting of the Royal Society of Canada, an honor never before offered to women not having royal blood. In January 2, 1893, Martha Lamb died of pneumonia. The *Magazine of American History* was sold and ceased publication in September of that same year.

ADDITIONAL SOURCES

InWom; Alli Supp.; AmAu; AmAu&B; BbD; BiD&SB; DcAmAu; DcNAA; AmWomWr; LibW; NotAW; AmBi; ApCAB; DcAmB; NatCAB; TwCBDA; WhAmHS; *Bio-Base;* BiIn 12.

LARSON, AGNES MATILDA
(1892–1957)
Local History

Agnes Matilda Larson, who became known as an expert on the history of lumbering in Minnesota, was born to Hans Olaf Larson, a farmer/businessman, and Karen Marie Nordgaarden on March 15, 1892, in Preston, Minnesota. That same year the family moved back to Bloomfield until 1911, when they moved to Northfield. From 1912 to 1913 Agnes and her sisters, Henrietta and Nora, attended St. Olaf College. Agnes and Henrietta both became historians. Agnes graduated with a B.A. in history and English. She studied social work at the University of Chicago in the summer and taught high school in Walcott, North Dakota, and Northfield, Minnesota. She attended graduate school at Columbia University in 1921 and received her M.A. in 1922. She began teaching college at the State Teachers College in Mankato, Minnesota. In 1926 she began teaching at Northfield and St. Olaf's. In 1929 she received a second M.A., from Radcliffe College, and she was given a $1,500 regional fellowship in 1931 by the American Association of University Women. She worked with Frederick Merk at Harvard University, studying the white pine industry in Minnesota. In 1932 she returned to Northfield to teach, research her thesis, and catalogue for the Norwegian-American Historical Association. In 1933 Larson tramped the northern woods interviewing lumberjacks and influential lumber families such as the Weyerhaeusers and Lairds. She received her doctorate in 1938 and spent her summers in Washington, D.C., studying economics at the Brookings Institution and researching land titles at the Department of the Interior. She was department chair of history at St. Olaf's from 1942 to 1960. During that time she completed *History of the White Pine Industry in Minnesota.* Just before her death on January 24, 1957, Agnes Larson published *John A. Johnson: An Uncommon American,* a biography of a pioneer Wisconsin businessman.

ADDITIONAL SOURCES
WhoAmW 58; WhAm 5; BiIn ll; C. Jenson, "Larson Sisters: Three Careers in Contrast,"
in *Women in Minnesota* (Minnesota Historical Society Press, 1977), pp. 301–324; *Bio-Base.*

LARSON, HENRIETTA MELIA
(1894–1983)
Business History

Henrietta Melia Larson was born on September 24, 1894, in Ostrander, Minnesota, to Hans Olaf Larson, a businessman, and Karen Marie (Nordgaarden) Larson. She graduated with a B.A. in 1918, taught high school for one year at Wheaton, Minnesota, then became an instructor from 1921 to 1922 at Augustana College in Sioux Falls, South Dakota. From 1922 to 1924 she pursued graduate study at the University of Minnesota. She taught from 1925 to 1926 at Bethany College, in Lindsborg, Kansas, and from 1926 to 1928 at Southern Illinois University in Carbondale. In 1926 she received a Ph.D. from Columbia University and published *The Wheat Market and the Farmer in Minnesota, 1858–1900.* She was an associate in research at Harvard University Graduate School of Business Administration from 1928 to 1939; assistant professor from 1939 to 1942; associate professor from 1942 to 1960 (the first woman to be so named), and professor of business history from 1960 to 1961.

In 1936 Larson wrote *Jay Cooke, Private Banker* with N.S.B. Gras as part of the Harvard Studies in Business History; it became a classic in its field. The two compiled *Casebook in American Business History* in 1939, which consisted of forty-three studies of individual men and companies from the Colonial period to the twentieth century. In 1938 she was editor of the *Bulletin of the Business Historical Society.* In 1943 she was given an honorary doctorate by St. Olaf, and in 1947 she and Gras were on the original board of directors of the Business History Foundation. Their first major project was a multivolume history of Standard Oil of New Jersey and a book on Humble Oil. Meanwhile, in 1948, she wrote *Guide to Business History* with Kenneth Wiggins Porter, a monumental work of annotated references to some 5,000 works. That same year she became associate editor of the Harvard Studies in Business History and became editor in 1950. In 1955 Gras died; Larson continued as director and senior author of *History of Humble Oil and Refining Company* with Evelyn H. Knowlton and Charles S. Popple (1959) and *History of Standard Oil Company (New Jersey), Vol. 3: New Horizons, 1927–1950* (1971), also with Knowlton and Popple. From 1965 to 1966 Henrietta Larson spent several months in Ahmedabad, India, as a Ford Foundation consultant of the Indian Institute of Management on a program in business history. She died on August 25, 1983.

ADDITIONAL SOURCES
ConAu P-2; ConAu 110; BiIn 5, 6, 11; DrAS 74H; WhoAm 74, 76, 78, 80; WhoAmW 58, 61, 64, 74; *Bio-Base;* obituary in NewYT, Sept. 1, 1983; obituary in *Chicago Tribune,* Aug. 29, 1983; "Lady of Harvard," *Newsweek* 57: 45, Jan. 2, 1961; "Henrietta M.

Larson: An Appreciation," *Business History Review* 36: 3–10, Spring 1962; C. Jenson, "Larson Sisters: Three Careers in Contrast," in *Women of Minnesota* (Minnesota Historical Society Press, 1977), pp. 301–324.

LATIMER, MARY ELIZABETH WORMELEY
(1822–1904)
Popular History

Mary Elizabeth Wormeley Latimer was born on July 26, 1822, to Rear Admiral Ralph Randolph Wormeley of the British Navy and Caroline (Preble) Wormeley in London, England. Her father was descended from Ralphe Wormeley, who received a grant of land in Virginia in 1649, and from Ralphe Wormeley of Middlesex County, Virginia, one of the first trustees of the College of William and Mary.

The Wormeley family traveled extensively, and Mary was educated by tutors or "parlor boarded" in the school of Mrs. Cockle of Ipswich, Massachusetts. She attended the funeral of William IV, saw Victoria enter Westminster for her coronation, witnessed the funeral of Napoleon, and counted among her family's friends William Makepeace Thackeray and Julia Ward Howe. In the 1840s the family moved permanently to Boston and Newport, Rhode Island, where Mary wrote poetry and fiction and nursed soldiers during the Civil War. She married Randolph Brandt Latimer of Baltimore in 1856.

In the 1890s Mary Latimer began writing popular history. In 1892 she wrote *France in the Nineteenth Century* and followed it with books in the same mode on Russia and Turkey in 1893. She wrote one on England in 1894, on Europe in Africa in 1895, and on Spain in 1897. In between, in 1896, she wrote *Italy in the Nineteenth Century and the Making of Austro-Hungary and Germany.* She dropped the series after 1897, and in 1898 wrote *My Scrap Book of the French Revolution,* followed by *Judea from Cyrus to Titus: 1537 B.C.–70 A.D.* the next year. Her last book, *The Last Year of the Nineteenth Century,* was published in 1900. She was writing a history of Germany in the nineteenth century when ill health and the death of her husband brought a halt to her writing.

During her productive years, Mary Latimer also translated a wide variety of books: *A History of the People of Israel* (1888–1896) with J. H. Allen; *The Steel Hammer* (1888); *Nanon* (1890); *The Italian Republic* (1901); *The Love Letters of Victor Hugo, 1820–22* (1901); and *Talks of Napoleon at St. Helena with General Baron Gourgaud* (1903). Latimer died on January 4, 1904, in Baltimore.

ADDITIONAL SOURCES

Alli Supp.; AmAu; AmAu&B; DcAmAu; DcAmB; LibW; NatCAB 9; *Bio-Base;* InWom; NatCAB; Phoebe Hannaford, *Daughters of America: Women of the Century* (Augusta, ME: True and Co., 1883).

LEBRA, JOYCE CHAPMAN
(1925–   )
History of Japan, India

Joyce Chapman Lebra, born in Minneapolis, spent her childhood in Honolulu, where she attended the Punahou School. The multiethnic society and the tropical setting of Hawaii were early influences and stimulated her interest in other areas of the world. Lebra attended the University of Minnesota, where she received a bachelor's and then a master's degree. She completed her work for the doctorate at Radcliffe College/Harvard University.

Believing that an understanding of the present world is predicated on an understanding of the past, Lebra pursued the study of history. She went on to write or edit ten books on Japanese history and Indian history, the first of which, *Chandora Bosu to Nihon,* she published in Japanese. Her more recent books include *Women's Voices in Hawaii, The Rani of Jhansi: A Study in Female Heroism in India,* and *Women and Work in India,* an edited collection. Her most recent publication demonstrates Chapman's new direction: *The Sword of Durga* is a work of historical fiction. She has also written two screenplays and produced a play based on *Women's Voices in Hawaii.*

Professor emerita of Japanese history and Indian history at the University of Colorado, Chapman is currently writing a second historical novel. Her hobbies include photography, swimming, whale watching, and ceramics. And she is, she reports, ''developing new interests.''

BOOKS BY JOYCE C. LEBRA

The Sword of Durga. Delhi: Harper Collins, 1995.

Women's Voices in Hawaii. Boulder: University Press of Colorado, 1991.

The Rani of Jhansi: A Study in Female Heroism in India. Honolulu: University of Hawaii Press, 1986.

Editor. *Women and Work in India.* New Delhi: Promilla, 1984.

Editor. *Chinese Women in Southeast Asia.* Singapore: Times Books International, 1980.

Japanese-Trained Armies in Southeast Asia: Independence and Volunteer Forces in World War II. Hong Kong: Columbia University Press and Heinemann Educational Books, 1977. In Japanese, Shuei Shobo, 1981.

Editor. *Women in Changing Japan.* Boulder, CO: Praeger/Westview, 1976; paperback, Stanford University Press, 1978.

Japan's Greater East Asia Co-prosperity Sphere: Selected Readings and Documents. Kuala Lumpur: Oxford University Press, 1975.

Okuma Shigenobu, Statesman of Meiji Japan. Canberra: Australian National University Press, 1973. In Japanese, Waseda University Press, 1980.

Jungle Alliance: Japan and the Indian National Army. Singapore: Asia/Pacific Press, 1971.

Chandora Bosu to Nihon. In Japanese. Tokyo: Hara Shobo, 1968.

ADDITIONAL SOURCES

Questionnaire completed by the subject for *American Women Historians, 1700s–1990s: A Biographical Dictionary.*

LERNER, GERDA
(1920–   )
U.S. Women's History

One of the founders of the field of women's history, Gerda Lerner was born in Vienna, Austria, on April 30, 1920. As a child she attended the Red Gymnasium. Her father, Robert Kronstein, was a pharmacist, and her mother, Ilona Neumann Kronstein, was an artist. Six weeks before her college entrance exams, Lerner was put in jail. Her father, fearing the Nazi executioners, had fled the country, and Gerda now feared her own death because of her participation in the resistance movement. Lerner was released from prison, however, and took her college entrance exams the very next day.

Lerner worked before attending college, as a governess in Europe and then as an office worker, waitress, sales clerk, and x-ray technician in the United States. She attended the New School for Social Research, earning a bachelor's degree in 1963. While a college student, she realized that the history of Western civilization had largely ignored the lives and stories of women. She decided to pursue graduate work in this largely unexplored area, she later recalled, "to make women's history respectable." Lerner then attended Columbia University, where she completed a master's degree in 1965 and a Ph.D. in 1966. Women's history, a field she helped define and promote as well as make respectable, is, as she argued, "an absolute lifeline to self-recognition and to giving our life meaning."

From 1963 to 1965 Lerner was lecturer at the New School for Social Research. She taught at Long Island University from 1965 to 1968, first as assistant and then as associate professor. Lerner accepted a position as associate professor at Sarah Lawrence College in 1968, and she stayed there until 1980, serving as the director of the master's program in women's history from 1972 to 1976 and again from 1978 to 1979. She left Sarah Lawrence to join the faculty at the University of Wisconsin at Madison, retiring from there as Robinson-Edwards Professor of History and Wisconsin Alumni Research Foundation Senior Distinguished Research Professor. She also directed the graduate program in women's history at the University of Wisconsin from 1981 to 1990. As professor emerita Lerner continues her work, lecturing, writing, and editing, among other things, an eleven-volume work titled *Scholarship in Women's History, Rediscovered and New,* for Carlson Publishing Company.

Lerner's first work of history, *The Grimké Sisters of South Carolina: Rebels Against Slavery,* was originally a novel based on historical events. However, when she enrolled in the graduate program at Columbia University, Lerner decided to make it a historical biography. As an immigrant, she often felt outside the mainstream experience in the United States; this feeling manifests itself in Lerner's explorations of others outside the mainstream, both black and white women. Her *Black Women in White America,* published in 1972, paved the way for the study of black women's history in the United States. Several of her books have won significant awards. *The Creation of Patriarchy* won the Joan Kelly Prize of the American Historical Association, and Judith Bennett has called the second volume of her overview of women and history, *The Creation of Feminist Consciousness,* an "invaluable contribution to the development of women's history." In another review, Ellen DuBois writes, "More of our careers should culminate in such learned and ambitious efforts."

Since her graduate school days, Gerda Lerner has been dedicated to the development of women's history as a field. She was determined, with that goal in mind, to making accessible the documents about women's lives that were "disorganized, uncatalogued, and not infrequently rotting in file boxes in basement storage rooms." Lerner, along with fellow pathbreaker in women's history Anne Firor Scott and several others, initiated a project to conduct a survey of historical archives in every state to identify holdings pertaining to women. After a mail survey to which they received responses from 7,000 repositories, they compiled a two-volume reference tool, *Women's History Sources: A Guide to Archives and Manuscript Collections in the United States.*

Lerner has served as president of the Organization of American Historians. She has received grants and fellowships from the National Endowment for the Humanities, the Ford Foundation, the Guggenheim Foundation, and the American Association of University Women. She is also the recipient of eight honorary degrees. She has been honored most recently by the publication of *U.S. History as Women's History: New Feminist Essays,* edited by Linda Kerber, Alice Kessler-Harris, and Kathryn Kish Sklar. A tribute to Lerner and her influence on succeeding generations of historians of women, the collection highlights the work of those who have learned from Lerner and then taken the field in new directions.

Gerda Lerner is a widow. She has two children and four grandchildren. Her hobbies include gardening and other outdoor activities. Aside from her scholarly publications, she has published two literary books and written a screenplay.

BOOKS BY GERDA LERNER

Women and History: Volume 1: The Creation of Patriarchy. Volume 2: The Creation of Feminist Consciousness: From the Middle Ages to 1870. New York: Oxford University Press, 1986.

A Death of One's Own. Madison: University of Wisconsin Press, 1985.

Teaching Women's History. Washington, DC: American Historical Association, 1981.

Black Women in White America: A Documentary History. New York: Pantheon, 1979.

The Majority Finds Its Past: Placing Women in History. New York: Oxford University Press, 1979.

The Female Experience: Documents in U.S. Social History. Indianapolis: Bobbs-Merrill, 1976; published as *The Female Experience: An American Documentary,* Macmillan, 1979.

The Woman in American History. Menlo Park, CA: Addison-Wesley, 1971.

The Grimké Sisters from South Carolina: Rebels Against Slavery. Boston: Houghton Mifflin, 1967; new edition published as *The Grimké Sisters from South Carolina: Pioneers for Women's Rights and Abolition.* New York: Schocken Books, 1967.

Black Like Me (screenplay). Walter Reade Distributors, 1964.
No Farewell (novel). New York: Associated Authors, 1955.
ADDITIONAL SOURCES
Bennett, Judith M. Review of *The Creation of Feminist Consciousness,* by Gerda Lerner.
   American Historical Review 98 (Oct. 1993); 1193–95.
Du Bois, Ellen. Review of *The Creation of Feminist Consciousness,* by Gerda Lerner.
   Journal of American History 80 (Mar. 1994): 1422–23.
Lerner, Gerda. "Editor's Introduction." *Scholarship in Women's History: Rediscovered
   and New.* 11-volume series. New York: Carlson Publishing, 1994.
Questionnaire completed by the subject for *American Women Historians, 1700s–1990s:
   A Biographical Dictionary.*

LEWIS, SAMELLA SANDERS
(1924–   )
Art History

Samella Sanders Lewis was born on February 27, 1924, in New Orleans, Louisiana, of African-American ancestry. Her father was a farmer, her mother a
seamstress. She attended Thomy Lafon Elementary School, J. W. Hoffman Junior High School, and McDonogh #35 Senior High School, all in New Orleans.
Among her early influences Lewis counts historian Benjamin Quarles and her
art professor, Elizabeth Catlett. After meeting and getting to know people from
different cultures, studying anthropology, and feeling a desire to include people
from neglected cultures, Lewis decided to pursue a career as a historian.

She attended Hampton University, earning a bachelor's degree in art in 1945.
Lewis then pursued graduate work at Ohio State University, earning the master's
degree in art in 1948 and the Ph.D. in art history in 1951. She taught at Hampton
University as an instructor from 1946 to 1947, then accepted a position as associate professor at Morgan State University, where she stayed until 1953, when
she was appointed professor and chair of fine arts at Florida A & M University.
While she lived in the Southeast, Lewis played an active role in the National
Association for the Advancement of Colored People (NAACP). When she designed a greeting card for the NAACP that emphasized "Peace on Earth, Good
Will to All Men," the state of Florida accused her of having communist sym-
pathies. Lewis was pursued, as were many others during the McCarthy era, by
the government and then by the Ku Klux Klan, who shot out the rear windows
of her home.

In 1958 Lewis left the South and took a position at the State University of
New York College at Plattsburgh, as professor of art history. She remained
politically active, founding the Plattsburgh chapter of the NAACP. Before she
officially left the State University of New York, in 1968, Lewis taught at California State University at Long Beach as associate professor of art from 1966
to 1967. From 1970 to 1984 she was professor of art history at Scripps College,
one of the Claremont Colleges. During the early 1970s she and artist Bernie
Casey established the Contemporary Crafts Gallery, which served primarily as

a showcase for young black artists. "The Gallery," as it came to be known, was headed by Lewis until 1979. In 1984 Lewis was named Professor of the Year and Professor Emerita at Scripps College.

Lewis has written five books and five scholarly articles, and she has written catalogues for or curated nine shows, including her most recent, Caribbean Visions: Contemporary Paintings and Drawings, a national and international traveling exhibition. She has written extensively on African-American art and artists, focusing in particular on the work of internationally renowned sculptor and printmaker Elizabeth Catlett, with whom Lewis studied. Lewis is known for bringing the work of African-American women artists to the foreground of discussion of visual art in the United States. Because she has studied Asian art as well, particularly Chinese and Japanese art, she also brings cross-cultural perspectives to her writings and curated shows.

Lewis has been the recipient of several postdoctoral fellowships, including those from the Fulbright Foundation, the National Research Council, and the Ford Foundation. She has received over a dozen honors and awards, including a UNICEF Award for the Visual Arts, a Women's Caucus for the Arts Honor Award for Outstanding Achievement in Visual Arts, and honorary doctorates from the University of Cincinnati, Hampton University, and Chapman College. She has provided service to the profession through her leadership as project director for the National Endowment for the Arts, as editor of the *International Review of African American Art,* as founder of the Museum of African American Art, and as director of the Scripps College Clark Humanities Museum.

Samella Lewis is an accomplished artist as well as an accomplished art historian. Her own work is primarily figurative and concerns her African-American heritage. She has had solo exhibitions at many colleges and museums, including the Robert Joseph Gallery in Cincinnati, the University of California at San Diego, and the Junior Black Academy of Arts and Letters in Dallas. She has also been in twenty group exhibitions over the past fifteen years, including traveling exhibitions for the Smithsonian Institution and the Studio Museum of Harlem. Her work is represented in ten permanent collections, including those of the Baltimore Museum of Fine Arts, the High Museum of Atlanta, the Oakland Museum, and the museums of Hampton, Howard, and Ohio State universities. She has also produced five films on black artists in the United States. Samella Lewis has lived out the words she has written for others: "The Black artist should also establish a direct relationship with Black people at all socioeconomic and educational levels. In this role the artist is an interpreter, a voice that makes intelligible the deepest, most meaningful aspirations of the people."

Lewis remains active professionally, and her current research focuses on lasting African influences on the contemporary world. Samella Lewis's spouse is Paul Lewis. She is the mother of two sons, Alan and Claude Lewis, and the grandmother of Gabriella Giancarlo and Unity Lewis. Her main interest outside of her work and family is photography.

BOOKS BY SAMELLA S. LEWIS
African American Art and Artists. Berkeley: University of California Press, 1994.
African American Art for Young People. Los Angeles: Handcraft Studios, 1991.
The Art of Elizabeth Catlett. Los Angeles: Museum of African American Art and Hand-
    craft Studios, 1984.
Art: African American. New York: Harcourt Brace Jovanovich, 1978; revised, Handcraft
    Studios, 1990.
With Elizabeth Waddy. *Black Artists on Art.* 2 vols. Los Angeles: Contemporary Crafts,
    Handcraft Studios, 1969.
ADDITIONAL SOURCE
Questionnaire completed by the subject for *American Women Historians, 1700s–1990s:
    A Biographical Dictionary.*

LOGAN, DEBORAH NORRIS
(1761–1839)
Local History

Deborah Norris Logan, called a "collector of historical records," was born
October 19, 1761, to Charles Norris, a Quaker merchant, and Mary Parker, his
second wife. They lived in Philadelphia, two doors away from the State House,
and on July 8, 1776, when Deborah was fourteen, she stood on the garden fence
to hear the first public reading of the Declaration of Independence. She attended
the Friends Girls School in Philadelphia but was mostly self-taught. On September 6, 1781, she married George Logan, a Quaker physician, and two years later
they moved to Stenton, north of Philadelphia, to the family farm. Her husband
entered politics and became a United States Senator.

In 1814 Logan found a series of old letters in the family attic that turned out
to be the correspondence of William Penn and James Logan, her husband's
grandfather. She got up at daybreak each day afterwards to copy the letters,
which she presented to the American Philosophical Society. They were published in *Memoirs* of the Historical Society of Pennsylvania (vols. 9–10, 1870–
1872). The next year Logan began keeping a diary and included the reminiscences of Charles Thomson, secretary of the Continental Congress. In 1821
her husband died; she began a memoir of his life, published in 1899 as *Memoir
of Dr. George Logan of Stenton.* It contained letters and anecdotes of Washington, Jefferson, Citizen Genet, and Randoph of Roanoke, all guests of the Logans.
In 1827 Logan became the first woman member of the Historical Society of
Philadelphia (an honorary member), and in 1830 John F. Watson's *Annals of
Philadelphia* included her memoirs and some of the manuscripts she rescued.
Deborah Logan died on February 2, 1839. The Historical Society of Philadelphia
issued a tribute to her as a Pennsylvania historian.
ADDITIONAL SOURCES
DcAmB; InWom; NatCAB 25; NotAW; *Bio-Base.*

Frances Acomb. Photograph courtesy of the Duke University Archives.

Mary Barnes. Photograph courtesy of Special Collections, Penfield Library, State University of New York at Oswego.

Delilah L. Beasley. Photograph from *Humbugs
and Heroes* by Richard H. Dillon.

Fawn Brodie. Photograph © Utah State Historical Society. All rights reserved. Used by permission.

Sucheng Chan. Photograph courtesy of Sucheng Chan.

Bettye Collier-Thomas. Photograph courtesy of Bettye Collier-Thomas.

Natalie Zemon Davis. Photograph by Denise Applewhite, Communications Department, Princeton University.

Hasia Diner. Photograph by Zweig Photography, Inc. Copyright 1995.

Fannie Hardy Eckstorm. Photograph courtesy of the Northeast Archives of Folklore and Oral History, a part of the Maine Folklife Center.

Lillian Faderman. Photograph courtesy of Lillian Faderman.

Loida Figueroa Mercado. Photograph courtesy of Loida Figueroa Mercado.

Gwendolyn Midlo Hall. Photograph courtesy of LSU Press.

Sharlot Hall. Sharlot Hall at the Grand Canyon,
c.1913. Photograph courtesy of the Sharlot Hall
Museum Library/Archives, Prescott, Arizona,
photo no. Po 160p B.

(Above) Darlene Clark Hine. Photograph
courtesy of Darlene Clark Hine.

(Top Right) Evelyn Hu-DeHart. Photograph
courtesy of Evelyn Hu-DeHart.

(Right) Nikki Keddie. Photograph courtesy of
Nikki Keddie.

Alice Kessler-Harris. Photograph by Andrew Kessler.

Clara Sue Kidwell. Photograph courtesy of Clara Sue Kidwell, OU photo # 95438.

Samella Sanders Lewis. Photograph by Armando Solis.

Florencia Mallon. Photograph by Jeff Miller.

Mary Elizabeth Massey. Photograph from Southern Historical Collection/Southern Folklife Collection/University Archives, Wilson Library, CB#3926, The University of North Carolina at Chapel Hill.

Nell Irvin Painter. Photograph courtesy of Halford H. Fairchild.

Dorothy Porter. Photograph courtesy of Dorothy Porter.

Trudy Huskamp Peterson. Photograph courtesy of Trudy Huskamp Peterson.

Bernice Johnson Reagon. Photograph by Sharon Farmer.

Vicki Ruiz. Photograph courtesy of Vicki Ruiz.

Virginia Sanchez Korrol. Photograph courtesy of Virginia Sanchez Korrol.

Ann Firor Scott. Photograph by Les Todd, Duke Photo Department, File # 0338-94B, #50.

Rosemary Stevens. Photograph courtesy of Rosemary Stevens.

Merze Tate. Photograph courtesy of Moorland-Spingarn Research Center, Howard University Archives.

M

MALLON, FLORENCIA E.
(1951–   )
Latin American History

Florencia Elizabeth Mallon was born on October 28, 1951, in Santiago, Chile, of South American ancestry. Her mother was an educator; her father was an economist. She was an international student as a child, attending elementary school in the United States, Pakistan, Chile, and Argentina, and high school in Argentina, Colombia, and the United States. Her early influences included her paternal grandfather, after whom she was named. This grandfather, an amateur historian, spent a lot of time with Florencia, his first grandchild. She was also influenced by her family's travels, especially by the poverty she witnessed in Pakistan when she was between seven and nine years old.

Mallon attended Harvard University, earning a bachelor's degree, magna cum laude in history and literature, in 1973. When she entered college she wanted to be a writer and to work on issues related to Latin America. As a junior, though, she took a graduate research seminar with John Womack, who asked the students to study the influence of one of a number of intellectuals on the development of the Mexican Revolution. He sparked her interest in history, and Mallon went on to complete a master of arts degree, a master of philosophy degree, and a Ph.D. in Latin American history from Yale University, in 1975, 1976, and 1980.

Mallon began her teaching career at the Universidad Nacional Agraria La Molina in Lima, Peru, where she co-taught a mini-seminar on Latin American history with Steve J. Stern, her husband. She also taught as instructor and then assistant professor at Marquette University from 1979 to 1982, in the Latin American and Third World history program. Mallon shared a visiting position at Yale University with Steve Stern during the spring semester of 1982. She then accepted a position as assistant professor of modern Latin American history at the University of Wisconsin at Madison, where she continues to teach. Mallon was promoted to associate professor in 1984 and professor in 1988. During the summer of 1990 she taught a graduate seminar, "The Nation-State in the Andes," at the Latin American Faculty of Social Sciences in Quito, Ecuador.

Mallon is the author or co-author of three books, the most recent of which, *Lucha campesina y transicion capitalista, 1860–1940: En defensa de la comunidad en la sierra central,* is in progress. Her previous books both received critical acclaim. *Peasant and Nation: The Making of Postcolonial Mexico and Peru,* published in 1995, was designated a Centennial Book by the University of California Press and received the Bryce Wood Award from the Latin American Studies Association. Her 1983 publication, *The Defense of Community in Peru's Central Highlands: Peasant Struggle and Capitalist Transition, 1860– 1940,* is in its fourth paperback printing and received an honorable mention for the Bolton Prize. Mallon has also written over thirty scholarly articles and edited a special issue of *Latin American Perspectives.*

Florencia Mallon has received grants and fellowships from the Fulbright Foundation, the National Endowment for the Humanities, the Center for Advanced Study in the Behavioral Sciences at Stanford University, the Tinker Foundation, and the Joint Committee on Latin American Studies of the American Council on Learned Societies and the Social Science Research Council. She has also provided a great deal of service to the profession, chairing the selection subcommittee for the Fulbright Scholars Program in Latin America, serving on the board of the Council on the International Exchange of Scholars, and acting as president, in 1994, of the Conference on Latin American History. Mallon currently serves on the board of directors of *Latin American Research Review,* on the board of editors of *Political Power and Social Theory,* and as participating editor for *Latin American Perspectives.* She has also provided professional service to the American Historical Association, the Conference on Latin American History, and the Latin American Studies Association.

Mallon is passionately dedicated to teaching. "If you are excited about what you do," she states, "it is possible to communicate that excitement to students." In 1995 she received the University of Wisconsin's Emil H. Steiger Distinguished Teaching Award as well as the history department's Karen Fredrikka Falk Johnson Distinguished Teaching Award. She has also been involved in a pilot project in the history department whereby faculty would conduct peer reviews of teaching and has lectured on the practice and rewards of research and teaching.

Florencia Mallon has been married to Steve J. Stern since 1978. They have two children, Ramon Joseph, born in 1982, and Ralph Isaiah, born in 1986. Her interests include playing guitar and singing, swimming, and writing. Her writing projects include fiction, including a completed novel and, occasionally, poetry.

BOOKS BY FLORENCIA E. MALLON

Peasant and Nation: The Making of Postcolonial Mexico and Peru. Berkeley: University of California Press, 1995.

With Frederick Cooper, Steve J. Stern, Allen F. Isaacman, and William Rosenberry. *Confronting Historical Paradigms: Peasants, Labor and the Capitalist World System in Africa and Latin America.* Madison: University of Wisconsin Press, 1993.

The Defense of Community in Peru's Central Highlands: Peasant Struggle and Capitalist Transition, 1860–1940. Princeton, NJ: Princeton University Press, 1983.

ADDITIONAL SOURCE

Questionnaire completed by the subject for *American Women Historians, 1700s–1990s: A Biographical Dictionary.*

MARRIOTT, ALICE LEE
(1910–   )
Western U.S. History

Alice Lee Marriott was born on January 8, 1910, in Wilmette, Illinois, to Richard Goulding and Sydney (Cunningham) Marriott. She received a B.A. in English and French from Oklahoma City University in 1930 and a B.A. in anthropology from the University of Oklahoma in 1935. From 1938 to 1942 she was a field representative with the U.S. Department of Interior Indian Arts and Craft Board, and from 1942 to 1945 she worked for the American Red Cross in the Southwest. In 1945 she also began writing *The Ten Grandmothers,* with Carol K. Rachlin, published by the University of Oklahoma Press. In 1947 she wrote *American Indian Mythology* and *Winter-Telling Stories,* followed by *Indians on Horseback* and *Maria, the Potter of San Halefonso* in 1948. In 1949 she wrote *Valley Below,* and the next year she wrote *These Are the People. Indians of the Four Corners* (1952), *Greener Fields: Experiences Among the American Indians* (1952), and *Hell on Horses and Women* (1953) followed. In 1952 she received the University of Oklahoma Achievement Award.

In 1956 Alice Marriott turned to another biography, *Sequoyah: Leader of the Cherokees* and then wrote *Black Stone Knife* in 1957. In 1958 she became a member of the Oklahoma Hall of Fame, and in 1960 she wrote *First Comers: Indians of America's Dawn* and became associate director of Southwest Research Associates. In 1961 *Oklahoma: Its Past and Its Present* was published. In 1962 Marriott became a consultant to the Oklahoma Indian Council and the next year published *Saynday's People,* which included reprints of *Winter-Telling Stories* and *Indians on Horseback.* In 1964 she became associate professor of anthropology at the University of Oklahoma, Norman, a position she held until 1966. In 1965 she wrote *Indian Anne: Kiowa Captive.* In 1968 she wrote *Kiowa Years: A Study in Culture Impact,* became artist-in-residence at Central State University, Edmond, Oklahoma, and won the Oklahoma City University Achievement Award. The Key Award from Theta Sigma Pi was given to her in 1969, and she published *American Epic: The Story of the American Indian* with Carol K. Rachlin; the two also wrote *Peyote* (1971), *Oklahoma: The Forty-Sixth Star* (1972), and *Plains Indian Mythology* (1975). Marriott also became a member of the Literary Hall of Fame in 1972.

ADDITIONAL SOURCES
WhoAmW 58, 61; AmAu&B; AnCL; AuBYP 64, pp. 154–155; BiIn 2, 7, 8; ConAu 57; InWom; H. S. Taylor, "Alice Lee Marriott," *Wilson Library Bulletin* 24: 396, Feb. 1950; Turner S. Kobler, "Alice Marriott," *Southwest Writers* (Steck-Vaughn, 1969); *Bio-Base.*

MARSHALL, HELEN EDITH
(1898–   )
Nursing History

Helen Edith Marshall was born on October 25, 1898, in Braman, Oklahoma, to David Conwell Marshall, a blacksmith, and Laura (Souter) Marshall. She received an A.B. from the College of Emporia in 1923, an M.A. from the University of Chicago in 1929, and a Ph.D. from Duke University in 1934. During some of this time, from 1916 to 1931, she taught school in Kansas, Colorado, and New Mexico. In 1930 Marshall became an instructor in history for the University of New Mexico, and from 1934 to 1935 she was professor of history and head of the social science department at Eastern New Mexico College (now University), Portales. In 1935 she became an instructor in American history at Illinois State University, Normal; she stayed until 1967, eventually reaching the rank of professor.

During her teaching career, Helen Marshall wrote *Dorothea Dix: Forgotten Samaritan,* a Book-of-the-Month Club alternate in 1937. In 1956 Illinois State University Press published *Grandest of Enterprises* and in 1967 *The Eleventh Decade.* In 1972 Marshall wrote *Mary Adelaid Nutting: Pioneer in Modern Nursing* with a U.S. Public Health Grant. The year before her retirement, she was also consultant to the Nurses Historical Committee. Helen Marshall contributed various magazine articles to periodicals such as the *Journal of Illinois Historical Society* and the *New Mexico Quarterly.*

ADDITIONAL SOURCES
ConAu 37R; WhoAmW 58, 61, 64, 68; IntAu&W 77; WrDr 76, 80; *Bio-Base.*

MARSOT, AFAF LUTFI AL-SAYYID
(1933–   )
Middle Eastern History

Afaf Lutfi al-Sayyid Marsot was born on October 29, 1933, in Cairo, Egypt, of Egyptian parents. Her father worked as undersecretary of state for social affairs; her mother was a full-time homemaker. She grew up in Heliopolis, a suburb of Cairo. During her childhood, Afaf was schooled by an English governess at home; from the ages of six to fifteen she lived at an English mission school. At school, she later recalled in an interview, they studied only one semester of Egyptian history but eight years of English history. "When I went home," she remembered, "I got another view of the British, so school did not Anglicize me."

Among Marsot's early influences were her father, to whom she was very close and who taught her history, and her uncle, a famous philosopher, politician, and writer. She grew up in a wealthy and very political family; they received three newspapers daily, each of which took a different stand on contemporary politics in Egypt. Marsot also grew up with three languages: Arabic, spoken at home, and English and French, which she learned from her governess. She was, she later recalled, "a politically precocious child."

Marsot hoped to earn a premed degree in college. "I studied the biological sciences, but my father and I had to keep this a secret from my mother. When she found out that her daughter was studying a field that she believed inappropriate for ladies, she made me stop." Marsot did earn a bachelor's degree, however, from the American University of Cairo, in 1952. She then attended Stanford University, earning a master's degree in political science in 1956. After she taught for a time at the American University of Cairo, Marsot decided to pursue a doctorate. She went to Oxford, studied with Albert Hourani, and wrote her dissertation on the British occupation of Egypt from 1882 to 1907. The first Egyptian woman to obtain a Ph.D. from Oxford, Marsot completed the degree in 1963.

Marsot's work has focused on the roles that gender, class, culture, and religion have played in the history of Egypt since the eighteenth century. She has emphasized comparative studies as well as critical analyses of Western views of the Middle East. The work she is most proud of is her *Egypt in the Reign of Muhammad Ali,* "because his rule of Egypt in the first half of the nineteenth century has not been appreciated in the West."

In 1964 Marsot married Alain Marsot, a Frenchman she met at Oxford. Fearing her parents' disapproval, she married, then wrote them and told them that if they did not accept her husband they would never see her again. She also worked, at that time, on her first book, *Egypt and Cromer,* about Lord Cromer, whom she saw as an example of the arrogant assumptions of British imperialists in relation to Egypt. Marsot taught at St. Anthony's College, Oxford, and then accepted a position in 1968 as associate professor at the University of California, Los Angeles. Promoted to professor in 1977, Marsot remains at UCLA, teaching Near and Middle East history.

Marsot has served as president of the American Research Center in Egypt. She also edited the *International Journal of Middle East Studies* and was the first woman president of the Middle East Studies Association. She also directed the education abroad program in Cairo for the University of California system.

Afaf Lutfi al-Sayyid Marsot is the mother of two daughters, Vanina and Vanessa. Her hobbies include jewelry making, writing, and music, especially opera. She hopes someday to write historical novels.

BOOKS BY AFAF LUTFI AL-SAYYID MARSOT

Women and Men in Late Eighteenth Century Egypt. Austin: University of Texas Press, 1995.

A Short History of Modern Egypt. New York: Cambridge University Press, 1985.

Egypt in the Reign of Muhammad Ali. New York: Cambridge University Press, 1984.

Egypt's Liberal Experiment: 1922–1936. Berkeley: University of California Press, 1977.
Egypt and Cromer. New York: Praeger, 1968.
ADDITIONAL SOURCES
Adelson, Roger. "Interview with Afaf Lutfi al-Sayyid Marsot." *The Historian* 54 (Winter
    1992): 225–242.
Questionnaire completed by the subject for *American Women Historians, 1700s–1990s:
    A Biographical Dictionary.*

MASSEY, MARY ELIZABETH
(1915–1974)
U.S. Civil War History

Mary Elizabeth Massey, the first woman to address the New Orleans Civil War
Round Table, was born on December 25, 1915, in Morrilton, Arkansas, to
Charles Leonidas and Mary (McClung) Massey. She received a B.A. from Hendrix College in 1937 and an M.A. in 1940; she received a Ph.D. from the
University of North Carolina, Chapel Hill in 1947. She taught on the high school
level in Arkansas from 1937 to 1939 and was head of the department of history
at Hendrix College in Conway, Arkansas, from 1940 to 1942. She was professor
of history at Flora Macdonald College in Red Springs, North Carolina, from
1942 to 1944 and a teaching fellow at the University of North Carolina at Chapel
Hill from 1944 to 1946. She was assistant professor at Winthrop College in
Rock Hill, South Carolina, from 1947 to 1950, associate professor from 1950
to 1954, and professor of history beginning in 1954. Massey also acted as chair
of the department from 1960 to 1964.

In 1952 Mary Massey published *Ersatz in the Confederacy* and in 1959 was
a contributor to *Education in the South* (Rinaldod Simenini, editor). From 1961
to 1965 she was on the advisory council of the National Civil War Centennial
Committee and the South Carolina Civil War Centennial Committee. From 1962
to 1963 she was a member of the South Carolina Commission of Archives and
History, and in 1963 she was awarded a Guggenheim fellowship. In 1964 she
published *Refugee Life in the Confederacy,* followed by *Bonnet Brigades: American Women and the Civil War* in 1966. Massey was also the only woman to
contribute to the fifteen-volume Impact Series on the Civil War and in 1967
was the first woman to receive the Distinguished Alumna Award from Hendrix
College. From 1968 to 1971 she was on the South Carolina Tri-Centennial
Commission, and from 1971 to 1972 she served as president of the Southern
Historical Association, the third woman to do so. In 1974 Massey became a
member of the board of advisors of the National Historical Society. Before her
death on December 24, 1974, at Duke University Hospital, Mary Massey com-
pleted a paper on Mary Todd Lincoln that was read for her before the National
Historical Society.
ADDITIONAL SOURCES
AmAu&B; ConAu P-2; WhAm 6; BiIn 10; WhoAmW 58, 61, 64, 68, 70, 72, 74; DrAS
74N, *Bio-Base;* obituary in *American Historical Review* 80: 1087–1088, Oct. 1975.

McALLISTER, ANNA SHANNON
(1888–   )
Catholic Women's History

Anna Shannon McAllister was born in Cincinnati, Ohio, in 1888. She was educated by the Sisters of Notre Dame de Namur and graduated from the Columbus School for Girls. She obtained a B.A. from Ohio State University in 1909 and married Earl Sadler McAllister in 1911. In 1934 she wrote *Ellen Ewing, Wife of General Sherman* after reading Lloyd Lewis's *Sherman—Fighting Prophet*. To research Ellen Ewing's life, McAllister wrote to Ellen Sherman's son as well as P. Tecumseh Sherman and other relatives who gave her family letters, diaries, and scrapbooks. The book was the Catholic Book of the Month Club selection for June 1936 and was awarded third prize in the 1938 nonfiction contest of the National League of American Penwomen.

McAllister's second biography was of Sarah Worthington King Peter, *In Winter We Flourish* (1939). She wrote *Flame in the Wilderness* in 1944, a biography of Mother Angela Gillespie, the American founder of the Sisters of the Holy Cross. (Gillespie was also a cousin and lifelong friend of Ellen Ewing Sherman.)

McAllister was a member of the Daughters of the American Revolution, the American Association of University Women, and the Columbus Chapter of the National League of American Penwomen. No date for her death is given.
ADDITIONAL SOURCES
BkC 1; CathA 1930; OhA&B; *Bio-Base.*

McINTOSH, MARJORIE KENISTON
(1940–   )
British History

Marjorie Keniston McIntosh was born on November 15, 1940, in Ann Arbor, Michigan, of mixed northern European ancestry. She was the daughter of two University of Michigan employees: her father was a professor and dean, her mother a librarian. Marjorie attended public schools in Ann Arbor. Her father and her high school and college teachers influenced her to become a historian.

McIntosh attended Radcliffe College, earning a bachelor's degree in European history, magna cum laude, in 1962. In 1963 she received a master's degree in English history from Harvard University. From 1965 to 1966 she participated in the Tudor/Stuart seminars at the Institute of Historical Research in London, England, and in 1967 she earned a Ph.D. in Tudor/Stuart history from Harvard University.

McIntosh's first regular academic appointment was as assistant professor of history at the University of Colorado at Boulder, where she has been since 1979. In 1986 she was promoted to associate professor, and in 1992 to professor. She was also the founder and first executive director of the Center for British Studies at the University of Colorado at Boulder.

McIntosh has written two single-authored books and nearly twenty scholarly articles. In 1995 she received a Guggenheim Fellowship to complete work on one of two books in progress, *Order, Control, and Regulation of Behavior in English Communities, 1350–1600,* a study of how English villages and towns in the later medieval period tried to control social misbehavior that threatened their stability. Her other book in progress is *Local Responses to the Poor in England, 1350–1600.* McIntosh, in joining the ranks of distinguished historians who have won the Guggenheim Fellowship, was one of 152 artists, scholars, and scientists chosen from among 2,856 applicants.

McIntosh also received two prestigious awards in 1995, a teaching award from her peers at the University of Colorado and a Robert L. Stearns Award for Extraordinary Achievement, also from the University of Colorado. She has also received grants and fellowships from the National Endowment for the Humanities, the American Council of Learned Societies, the Howard Foundation at Brown University, and the American Philosophical Society. She has provided professional service to the North American Conference on British Studies, the American Historical Association, the Social Science and Humanities Research Council of Canada, and the National Endowment for the Humanities.

Marjorie Keniston McIntosh is married to a professor of molecular biology at the University of Colorado; they have three children. Her oldest son is in the real estate business in Hungary. Her daughter is a graduate student in classical archaeology, and her younger son is an African economist. McIntosh's interests include music and Africa. She and her family have hosted several African exchange students, and she has read and traveled widely.

BOOKS BY MARJORIE KENISTON McINTOSH

A Community Transformed: The Manor and Liberty of Havering, 1500–1620. New York: Cambridge University Press, 1991.

Autonomy and Community: The Royal Manor of Havering, 1200–1500. New York: Cambridge University Press, 1986.

ADDITIONAL SOURCE

Questionnaire completed by the subject for *American Women Historians, 1700s–1990s: A Biographical Dictionary.*

MESSENGER, RUTH ELLIS
(1884–1964)
Medieval Hymns

Ruth Ellis Messenger, a famous hymnocologist, was born on February 29, 1884, in New York City to Joseph Ellis Messenger, a physician, and Anne Jane (Dudman) Messenger. She received an A.B. from Normal college (later Hunter College) in New York City in 1905 and was Phi Beta Kappa. In 1907 she became an instructor in the Hunter College high school, teaching history and the classics. In 1911 she received an A.M. from the University of Illinois, and in 1930 she completed her Ph.D. at Columbia University in history; her thesis was "Ethical Teachings in the Latin Hymns of Medieval England." In 1933 Messenger joined the history department at Hunter College as assistant professor; she eventually became a full professor. She remained at Hunter until her retirement in 1950; she then taught hymnology at the Union Theological Seminary in New York City and began writing. In 1953 she completed *The Medieval Hymn* and from 1954 until her death was associate editor and later editor of *The Hymn*, a quarterly published by the Hymn Society of America. Ruth Messenger assisted in editing *A Short Bibliography for the Study of Hymns* which was published after her death on March 3, 1964.

ADDITIONAL SOURCES

BiIn 6, 8; NatCAB 51: 566, 1969; obituary in NewYT, March 4, 1964, p. 37; *Bio-Base.*

MILLER, PAGE PUTNAM
(1940–   )
Public History

Page Putnam Miller was born on December 12, 1940, in Columbia, South Carolina, of Scots ancestry. Her father was a postal worker, her mother a full-time homemaker who had worked on the Works Progress Administration's State Guide for South Carolina before getting married. Page enjoyed music, arts, and sports in school and earned an award as a top high school debater. She was also active in the Presbyterian Church as a youth and took a great interest in current events. She was motivated to become a historian from an interest in history but also because she felt that some other areas of interest, such as law, were closed to her as a southern woman in the 1960s.

Miller attended Mary Baldwin College, earning a bachelor's degree in 1963. She then attended Yale Divinity School, earning thirty credits toward a master's degree in religion. She left Yale and later attended the University of Maryland, earning a master's degree in history in 1974 and a Ph.D. in American history in 1979. After completing her doctorate, Miller worked for a year as instructor at University College, University of Maryland. She then took a job as director of the National Coordinating Committee for the Promotion of History, a post she has held since 1980. In her capacity as director, Miller has been involved in many national projects. She coordinated the Organization of American Historians and the National Park Service's collaborative project to revise the National Park Service's Thematic Framework. She also served as project director for the Women's History Landmark Project, a cooperative project of the National Park Service, the Organization of American Historians, and the National Coordinating Committee for the Promotion of History.

The author or editor of five books, Miller is perhaps best known for her most recent work, *Reclaiming the Past: Landmarks of Women's History,* which brings together public and academic historians to address how the history of women has, or has not, been addressed and interpreted at historic sites. The essays in this collection address issues of economics and preservation, interpretation when no structure remains to commemorate a woman's life, and interpreting women's lives at sites not normally viewed as women's history landmarks. As Miller claims, the ultimate goal of the book is "to stimulate increased efforts to connect women's past to tangible resources." Miller has also written nearly twenty articles on topics ranging from the Freedom of Information Act to the preservation of electronic historical records. In addition, she writes a monthly column for the American Historical Association's *AHA Perspectives* and a bimonthly column, "Washington Beat," for *Archival Outlook,* a publication of the Society of American Archivists.

Page Putnam Miller has been the recipient of several citations and distinguished service awards. She received a Directors Award for Distinguished Service from the Federation of Genealogical Societies, and Outstanding and Dedicated Service Award from the Society for History in the Federal Government, and an Exemplary Service Citation from the Society of American Archivists. She also received a Mellon Research Fellowship for the study of modern archives, and was a project director for an Exxon Education Grant on Strengthening the Teaching of History in Secondary Schools.

Since 1982 Page Putnam Miller has provided testimony to United States House and Senate committees or subcommittees on thirty-five separate occasions. These include the Senate Subcommittee on Treasury, Postal Service, and General Government; the House Subcommittee on National Parks and Public Lands; the Senate Judiciary Subcommittee on the Constitution; and the Senate Committee on Governmental Affairs.

BOOKS BY PAGE PUTNAM MILLER

Editor. *Reclaiming the Past: Landmarks of Women's History.* Bloomington: Indiana University Press, 1991.

Developing a Premier National Institution: A Report from the User Community to the National Archives. Washington, DC: National Coordinating Committee for the Promotion of History, 1989.

A Claim to New Roles. Metuchen, NJ: Scarecrow Press, 1985. Editor. *Resource Guide: Strengthening the Teaching of History in Secondary Schools.* Washington, DC: National Coordinating Council for the Promotion of History, 1985.

Editor. *Directory of Historical Consultants.* Washington, DC: National Coordinating Council for the Promotion of History, 1981.

ADDITIONAL SOURCE

Questionnaire completed by the subject for *American Women Historians, 1700s–1990s: A Biographical Dictionary.*

MINAULT, GAIL
(1939–   )
History of South Asia

Gail Minault was born on March 25, 1939, in Minneapolis, Minnesota, of French and Scots-Irish ancestry. Her parents were both schoolteachers: her mother taught reading and math in primary school, and her father taught French and Latin in secondary school. She attended public schools in Pottstown, Pennsylvania, through ninth grade, then the Northfield School for Girls in East North-field, Massachusetts, for the remainder of high school. Minault grew up bilingual, learning French from her immigrant father. Among her early influences were her paternal grandmother, a war widow from World War I, and her mother's sister, a war widow from World War II. These women's experiences showed her the need for women to be educated and self-sufficient in order to support themselves and raise their children by themselves, if necessary.

Minault attended Smith College, spending her junior year at Ecole Nationale des Sciences Politiques in Paris, and graduating in 1961. After graduation from college and before attending graduate school, Minault worked for three years for the U.S. Foreign Service as a trainee in Washington, D.C., a junior officer trainee in Beirut, Lebanon, and an assistant cultural affairs officer in East Pakistan, now Bangladesh. She studied several languages, traveled extensively, and made a decision to specialize in the history of South Asia. She resigned from the foreign service to do graduate work on a language fellowship at the University of Pennsylvania. She earned a master's degree in South Asia regional studies in 1966 and a Ph.D. in 1972. Her dissertation focused on Indian Muslim political leadership in the early twentieth century.

Minault's first academic appointment was at the University of Texas at Austin, where she still teaches as associate professor of history. She has been visiting professor at the University of California at Berkeley and at Centre d'Etudes de l'Inde et de l'Asie de Sud, Ecoles des Hautes Etudes en Sciences Sociales in Paris. Minault is fluent in French, Hindi, and Urdu, and has speaking and/or reading knowledge of Persian, Italian, and German. She has spent about ten years of her life in South Asia, either in foreign service or on research fellowships. She has also traveled extensively in the Middle East, Southeast Asia, Australia, and Europe.

Gail Minault is the author or editor of five books and more than thirty-five scholarly articles. She has written on women and women's rights in Islamic communities, political poetry, and contemporary politics in India. She has received grants from the National Endowment for the Humanities, the Fulbright Foundation, the American Institute for Indian Studies, and the Joint Committee on South Asia of the Social Science Research Council and the American Council of Learned Societies.

Minault's first marriage, to Thomas Graham, Jr., ended in divorce. They had one son, Mark Emlen Graham, who died at age two following open heart surgery, and have one adopted daughter, Laila Minault, born in 1973 in India. Minault later married Leon W. Ellsworth and now has one stepson, Alex Ellsworth, born in 1979. Her interests include music, singing, swimming, biking, gardening, and historic preservation in her Austin, Texas, neighborhood.

BOOKS BY GAIL MINAULT

Editor, with Christian W. Troll. *Abul Kalam Azad: An Intellectual and Religious Biography.* By the Late Ian H. Douglas. New Delhi: Oxford University Press, 1988.

Translator. *Voices of Silence: Khwaja Altaf Husain Hal'es Majalis un-Nissa (Assemblies of Women) and Chup ki Dad (Homage to the Silent).* Delhi: Chanakya Publications, 1986.

The Khilafat Movement: Religious Symbolism and Political Mobilization in India. New York: Columbia University Press, 1982.

Editor, with Hanna Papanek. *Separate Worlds: Studies of Purdah in South Asia.* Delhi: South Asia Books and Chanakya Publications, 1982.

Editor. *The Extended Family: Women and Political Participation in India and Pakistan.* Columbia, MO: South Asia Books, 1981.

ADDITIONAL SOURCES

Questionnaire completed by the subject for *American Women Historians, 1700s–1990s: A Biographical Dictionary.*

MINER, DOROTHY EUGENIA
(1904–1973)
Art History

Dorothy Eugenia Miner was born on November 4, 1904, in New York City to Roy Waldo Miner, a marine biologist at the American Museum of Natural History (curator of marine life) and former Episcopalian minister, and Anna Elizabeth (Carroll) Miner, a former Catholic nun. Miner attended Graham School in New York City and Horace Mann School for Girls. In 1922 she entered Barnard College, majoring in English and the classics. She graduated from Barnard in 1926 and entered Bedrod College at the University of London as the first Barnard International Fellow. She studied with Meyer Schapiro at Columbia University in the field of medieval manuscript illumination from 1928 to 1929 and began her doctoral dissertation on a Carolingian Apocalypse manuscript. She continued working on the dissertation in Europe from 1929 to 1930 as a president's fellow.

In 1933–34 Miner was hired by the Pierpont Morgan Library in New York City to help prepare an exhibition of illuminated manuscripts. The director of the Morgan Library, Belle Da Costa Greene, recommended her for the position of keeper of manuscripts at the Walters Art Gallery in Baltimore. Miner began working on the over 20,000 objects and became one of the first professionally trained art historians employed in an American museum. She was also curator of Islamic and Near Eastern Art and for several years head of the reference library. In 1937 she wrote, with Grace Frank, *Proverbes et Rimes.* From 1938 to 1969 she edited the *Journal of the Walter Gallery* and many catalogues published by the museum which became standard reference works. Some examples are *Early Christian and Byzantine Art* (1947); *Illuminated Books of the Middle Ages and Renaissance* (1949); *The World Encompassed* (maps and cartography) (1952); *The History of Bookbinding, 525–1950* (1957); *The International Style* (1962); and *2000 Years of Caligraphy* (1965). Miner also wrote a variety of articles on works from the Walters collections. In 1954 she edited *Studies in Art and Literature* for Belle Da Costa Greene. Dorothy Miner was honored with a copy of a festschrift, *Gatherings in Honor of Dorothy Miner,* shortly before her death from cancer in Baltimore in May 1973. A posthumously published lecture, *Anataise and Her Sisters, Women Artists of the Middle Ages* (1974), was also given and has been considered groundbreaking in the field.

ADDITIONAL SOURCES

WhoAmW 74; WhoAmA 73, 76N, 78N, 80N; NotAW Supp. v. 1; *Bio-Base;* professional correspondence in the Walters Gallery, Baltimore; Ursula E. McCracken, Lilian M.C. Randall, and Richard H. Randall, Jr., eds., *Gatherings in Honor of Dorothy Miner* (1974); Richard H. Randall, Jr., "In Memorian: Dorothy Miner," *Journal of the Walters Art Gallery,* 1977, pp. v–vii; "Dorothy E. Miner," *Bulletin of the Walters Art Gallery,* Oct. 1973; Madeleine Hooke Rice, "Dorothy Miner," *Barnard College Alumnae Monthly,* March 1938, pp. 9–10; *Medieval Art 1060–1550: Dorothy Miner Memorial,* a catalog of an exhibition at the University of Notre Dame (1974); obituary in NewYT, May 17, 1973; obituary in *Library of Congress Information Bulletin,* May 25, 1973; obituary in *AB Bookman's Weekly,* June 11, 1973; obituary in *Gesta,* 1974.

MOORE, ELIZABETH FINLEY
(1894–1976)
Local History

Elizabeth Finley Moore was born in York, South Carolina, on January 29, 1894, to David Edward Finley, a congressman, and Elizabeth (Gist) Finley. From 1910 to 1911 she studied at Winthrop College in Rock Hill, South Carolina. In 1914 she obtained an A.B. at the College for Women in Columbia, South Carolina. She married Walter Bedford Moore on July 19, 1916. In 1926 Moore became a charter member of the Daughters of the American Revolution (DAR). From 1934 to 1936 she chaired the History-Graph Committee, and from 1936 to 1938 she chaired the Columbia Sesquicentennial Historical Marker Committee. Moore helped select fifty sites in Columbia and Richland County for marking and wrote inscriptions and the guidebook. From 1940 to 1967 she was on the committee to save Columbia's Hampton-Prestol House. In 1950 she and her husband helped bring historical memorabilia and Renaissance art (her brother David E. Finley was the first director of the National Gallery of Art in Washington, D.C.) to the Columbia Museum of Art. She was also a member of the advisory committee of the state DAR and helped place the *South Carolina* battleship silver in the governor's mansion. In 1952 she chaired the committee to preserve Fort Moultrie.

In 1960 Moore founded and became director of what would later be called the Historical Columbia Foundation. As director she was responsible for preserving historical homes such as the Boylston home, the Horry-Guignard House, "Lace House" (Caldwell Mansion), and the boyhood home of Woodrow Wilson. She was also instrumental in obtaining funds from the state for the acquisition and restoration of Rose Hill in Union County, South Carolina, home of William Henry Gist, the state's Secessionist governor, which became a state historical park. She helped prevent the encroachment of the grounds of the State

Capitol and the conversion of the state Historical library (circa 1850s) into a cafeteria.

In 1960 Moore became founder and member of the executive board of the Confederation of South Carolina Local Histories Societies. It consisted of over thirty societies and a membership exceeding 7,000. From 1960 to 1966 she was also advisor to the South Carolina Confederate War Centennial Commission and in 1964 was a board member of the Palmetto Outdoor Historical Drama Association, which produced plays on the Revolutionary era. In 1968 she received a citation from the National Trust for Historic Preservation. Elizabeth Moore died in Columbia on November 17, 1976.
ADDITIONAL SOURCES
NatCAB v. 60.

MOSSIKER, FRANCES SANGER
(1906–1985)
Popular History

Frances Mossiker, who wrote her first book at age fifty-five, was born April 9, 1906, in Dallas, Texas to Elihu Sanger, a merchant, and Evelyn (Beekman) Sanger. She attended the Hockaday School in Dallas and studied French and Romance languages at Smith College in Massachusetts. She received a B.A. from Barnard College in 1927 before studying on the graduate level at the Sorbonne in Paris. In 1934 she married Jacob Mossiker, who worked in the investment field. Frances Sanger Mossiker worked most of her life in the field of radio. While recovering from a radical mastectomy in the 1950s, she wrote her first book, *The Queen's Necklace* (1961), which won the Carr P. Collins nonfiction award at the Texas Institute of Letters; her second book, *Napoleon and Josephine: Biography of a Marriage,* won the same award for 1964 and was a Literary Guild selection. In 1969 she wrote *The Affair of the Poisons: Louis XIV, Madame du Montespan and One of the World's Great Unsolved Mysteries,* and in 1971 she wrote *More than a Queen: The Life of Josephine Bonaparte.* In 1976 *Pocahontas: The Life and the Legend* was published. She completed *Madame de Sevigne: A Life and Letters* (1983) before her death on May 8, 1985, at Baylor Medical Center of a heart ailment.
ADDITIONAL SOURCES
New York Times Book Review, Oct. 26, 1969; *New Yorker,* Jan. 31, 1970; *Observer Review,* June 7, 1970; *New York Review of Books,* July 23, 1970; *Books and Bookmen,* Aug. 1970; NewYT, May 12, 1985, p. 34; NewYTBS 16: 558, May 1985; ConAu 9R; *Bio-Base.*

MURRAY, LOUISE SHIPMAN WELLES
(1854–1931)
Local History

Louise Shipman Welles was born on January 2, 1854, to Charles Fisher and Elizabeth (LaPorte) Welles in Athens, Pennsylvania. Her father's ancestors included Thomas Welles, a colonial governor of Connecticut, and her mother's ancestors included Bartholomew Laporte, one of the French emigrés who founded Asylum, Pennsylvania. Louise attended Athens Academy, Moravian Seminary at Bethlehem, Pennsylvania, and Brown's School in Auburn, New York. In 1872 she graduated from Wells College in Aurora, New York, and in 1876 she married Millard P. Murray. In 1882 excavations for the Murrays' home in Athens, Pennsylvania, unearthed an unusual Indian burial plot that included portrait pottery and skeletal remains. The Murrays theorized that they were Andastes or Susquehannochs as described in Capt. John Smith's histories. Louise Murray worked on this theory until her death, and the results were published posthumously.

In 1898 Murray founded the Tioga Point Historical Society and the Tioga Point Museum. She was director and archaeologist for three decades, using primary sources and progressive techniques unusual for so small a town. She also carried out independent research on local history and in 1903 published *The Story of Some French Refugees and Their "Azilum," 1793–1800*. In 1908 she wrote *A History of Old Tioga Point and Early Athens, Pennsylvania*, which became the standard authority for the area. In 1921 she wrote an article for *American Anthropologist* on aboriginal sites in and near "Teaga" (Athens), and in 1929 she wrote *Notes... on the Sullivan Expedition of 1799*, a series of documents in the Tioga Point Museum and other archives. In 1931 she became a charter member and second vice-president of the Society for Pennsylvania Archaeology; its first publication, *Selected Manuscripts of General John S. Clark Relating to the Aboriginal History of the Susquehanna*, was written by Murray. She died on April 22, 1931.

ADDITIONAL SOURCES

DcNAA; DcAmB; *Bio-Base*.

MYRES, SANDRA L.
(1933–1991)
Western U.S. History

Sandra L. Myres was born on May 17, 1933, in Columbus, Ohio, to George Y. Swickard, a physician, and Lucille (Stockdale) Swickard. She attended Rice University from 1950 to 1951 and in 1953 married Charles E. Myres, a chemist. (She was divorced in 1973.) Myres received a B.A. in 1957 from Texas Technological College (now Texas Tech University) in biology. She received an M.A. in history from Texas Tech in 1960 and from 1960 to 1961 was an instructor in history at Kerrville, Texas. In 1961 Myres privately published *S.D. Myres: Saddlemaker*. In 1967 she received a Ph.D. from Texas Christian University and in 1968 published *Force Without Fanfare*. She became an assistant professor at the University of Texas at Arlington, and in 1969 published *The Ranch in Spanish Texas: 1690–1800* and edited, with Harold M. Hollingsworth, *Essays on the American West*. In 1970 she was a contributor to *One Man, One*

Vote: Gerrymandering vs. Reapportionment. In 1971 Myres was named associate professor and was a contributor that same year to *Indian Tribes of Texas.* In 1974 she was editor, with Margaret F. Morris, of *Essays on U.S. Foreign Relations.* Two years later she contributed to *Broken Treaties and Forked Tongues* and in 1977 wrote the introduction to *Cavalry Wife: The Diary of Eveline Alexander, 1866–67.* She also contributed to *McGraw-Hill Encyclopedia of World Biography* and *Readers Encyclopedia of American West.*

From 1980 to 1987 Sandra Myres was chair of the Walter Prescott Web Lecture Series, and from 1987 to 1988 she was president of the Western History Association, the second woman to have filled that post. During this time she authored *Westering Women and the Frontier Experience,* a History Book Club selection and winner of recognition from the Western University Press and *Choice* magazine. She died on October 16, 1991. At the time of her death she was writing *Plainswoman: The Canadian and United States Experience* for the University Press of Kansas and *Victoria's Daughters: Nineteenth Century Frontiersmen in Australia, New Zealand, Canada, and the United States West.* During her career, Sandra Myres published over 200 articles, reviews, essays, and book introductions.

ADDITIONAL SOURCES

ConAu 33R; DrAS 74R, 78H; WhoAmW 75, 77; obituary in *Western Historical Quarterly* 23: 136, Feb. 1992; *Bio-Base.*

N

NAKUINA, EMMA KAILI METCALF BECKLEY
(1847–1929)
Hawaiian History

Emma Kaili Metcalf Beckley Nakuina was born on March 5, 1847, at Kauaaia in Honolulu's Manoa Valley to Theophilus Metcalf, a civil engineer and sugar planter, and the nephew of Chief Justice Metcalf of Massachusetts, and Chiefess Kailikapuolono of Kukaniloko, granddaughter of the legendary Kalani-kupaulakea. Emma attended Sacred Hearts Academy and Punahou School, both in Honolulu, and the Mills' Seminary for Young Ladies in Benicia, California. She was also privately tutored by her father in Greek, Latin, Hebrew, French, German, English, and Hawaiian. In 1867 Emma married Frederick William Beckley, a plantation owner and eventually chamberlain to King Kalakaua (1875) and governor of Kauai (1880). Beckley died in 1881 at the age of thirty-six, and Emma married the Reverend Moses Keaea Nakuina in 1887.

While she was attached to the court of Kamehameha IV, the king had Emma trained in laws about water rights, and she was made custodian of the laws. She also became an authority on the workings of all ancient laws. During the 1880s and 1890s, Nakuina was the first curator of the Hawaii National Museum. She wrote many articles on Hawaii; some, like "Ancient Hawaiian Water Rights and Some Customs Pertaining to Them," have been considered primary sources. She also wrote of Hawaiian folklore and published *Hawaii: Its People and Their Legends* in 1904. Emma Nakuina died on April 27, 1929.

ADDITIONAL SOURCES

Margaret M. Lam, "Six Generations of Race Mixture in Hawaii," Master's thesis, University of Hawaii, 1932; *The Friend,* Jan. 1, 1868, Feb. 4, 1881; Thomas Thrum, *Hawaiian Almanac and Annual,* v. 19, 1893, v. 20, 1894, v. 23, 1897.

NEILSON, NELLIE
(1873–1947)
European History

Nellie Neilson was born on April 5, 1873, in Philadelphia, Pennsylvania, to William George Neilson, a metallurgical engineer, and Mary Louise (Cunningham) Neilson. She attended Miss Cooper's School in Philadelphia and received an A.B. in 1893 and an A.M. in 1894, both from Bryn Mawr College. After a year as a resident fellow at Bryn Mawr and additional graduate study, she spent a year of research in England. She received her Ph.D. in 1899 from Bryn Mawr. Neilson was awarded an honorary degree (LHD) from Smith College in 1938 and an honorary Litt.D. degree from Russell Sage in 1940.

From 1897 to 1900 Neilson taught at Miss Irwin's School in Philadelphia. In 1899 she wrote *Economic Conditions on the Manors of Ramsey Abbey*. She returned to Bryn Mawr College from 1900 to 1902 as a reader in English. In 1902 she went to Mount Holyoke College as an instructor in history and two years later was appointed professor of European history. She became a full professor in 1905 and retired from teaching in 1939. In 1943 Neilson became the first woman president of the American Historical Society. She was also a member of the American Political Science Association and the Royal Historical Society. Other publications included *Customary Rents* (1910), *Survey of the Honour of Denbigh* (1914), *The Terrier of Fleet Lincolnshire* (1920), and *The Cartulary of Bilsington Kent* (1927). Nellie Neilson died on May 26, 1947, in South Hadley, Massachusetts.

ADDITIONAL SOURCES

NatCAB v. 36; NotAW; *Bio-Base;* obituary in *American Historical Review* 53: 219–220, Oct. 1947; obituary in NewYT, May 27, 1947, p. 25; obituary in *School & Society* 65: 424, June 7, 1947; Margaret Hastings and Elisabeth G. Kimball, "Two Distinguished Medievalists—Nellie Neilson and Bertha Putnam," *Journal of British Studies,* Spring 1979.

NOCHLIN, LINDA
(1931–   )
Art History

Linda Nochlin was born on January 30, 1931, in Brooklyn, New York, the daughter of a businessman father and a homemaker mother. She attended Brooklyn Ethical Culture School and Midwood High School. Among her early influences were her maternal grandfather, who was interested in art and literature; her mother's brother, who was interested in art; and the general atmosphere of Brooklyn, with its culture and politics.

Nochlin attended Vassar College, earning a bachelor's degree in philosophy in 1951. She began her graduate work at Columbia University, earning a master's degree in English in 1952. Nochlin then attended New York University, where she completed the Ph.D. in art history in 1963. She then accepted a position as assistant professor of art at Vassar College. She stayed at Vassar until 1979, earning the rank of associate professor in 1966, professor in 1969, and Mary Conover Mellon Professor of Art History in 1971. After working as visiting professor at the City University of New York Graduate Center from 1975 to 1976, Nochlin accepted a position there as distinguished professor in 1980. Then, after a year as visiting professor at Yale University, Nochlin accepted a position there as Robert Lehman Professor of the History of Art in 1990. She is currently Lila Acheson Wallace Professor of Modern Art at New York University's Institute of Fine Arts.

Linda Nochlin is the author or editor of thirteen books and over seventy scholarly articles. She is currently working on another book, *Courbet: The Real Allegory: Essays on Painting and Ideas.* One of her books, *Realism,* was nominated for the National Book Award. She has also written extensively on many nineteenth-century artists, including Courbet, the subject of her doctoral dissertation. Well known as a feminist art historian, Nochlin published "Why Have There Been No Great Women Artists?" in 1971. This article, considered the first in the field of feminist art history, was also the first of many such explorations Nochlin would make. *Women, Art, and Power,* a 1988 publication, is the culmination of almost twenty years of Nochlin's own writings in the field.

Nochlin has held fellowships with the Fulbright Foundation, the American Council of Learned Societies, and the Guggenheim Foundation. She was named Woman of the Year by *Mademoiselle* magazine in 1977, is a fellow of the American Academy of Arts and Sciences, and has received honorary doctoral degrees from Colgate University, Massachusetts College of Art, and the Parsons School of Design.

Linda Nochlin has provided service to the academic world and to the arts communities where she has lived. She was on the board of editors of the *Art Bulletin,* a member of the international advisory board of *Art History,* a contributing editor of *Art in America,* and an advisor on the *Art of the Western World* television series. She serves on the Battery Park City Authority Fine Arts Committee and as an advisor to the Metropolitan Museum of Art/John Paul Getty Trust Program for Art on Film and Video, and on the editorial board of the Yale *Journal of Criticism.* She was also a panelist on the 1994 New York Selection Panel for the President's Commission on White House Fellowships.

Linda Nochlin was married to Philip Nochlin, who died in 1960, and Richard Pommer, who died in 1991. She is the mother of two children, Jessica Trotta and Daisy Pommer, and the grandmother of two children, Julia Trotta and Dominic Trotta. Her interests include race walking, music, dance, and theater.

BOOKS BY LINDA NOCHLIN

Editor, with Tamar Garb. *The Jew in the Text: Modernity and the Construction of Identity.* London: Thames, 1995.

The Body in Pieces: The Fragment as Metaphor of Modernity. London: Thames and Hudson, 1994.

The Politics of Vision: Essays on Nineteenth Century Art and Society. New York: Harper and Row, 1989.

Women, Art, and Power and Other Essays. New York: Harper and Row, 1988.

With Sarah Faunce. *Courbet Reconsidered.* Brooklyn, NY: Brooklyn Museum and Yale
    University Press, 1988.
With Henry Millon. *Art and Architecture in the Service of Politics.* Cambridge, MA:
    MIT Press, 1978.
Gustave Courbet: A Study of Style and Society. New York: Garland, 1976.
With Ann Sutherland Harris. *Women Artists, 1550–1950.* New York: Alfred A. Knopf,
    1976.
Editor, with Thomas B. Hess. *Woman as Sex Object: Studies in Erotic Art, 1730–1970.*
    New York: Newsweek Books, 1972.
Realism. New York: Penguin, 1971.
Impressionism and Post-Impressionism, 1874–1904: Sources and Documents. Englewood
    Cliffs, NJ: Prentice-Hall, 1966.
Realism and Tradition in Art, 1848–1900: Sources and Documents. Englewood Cliffs,
    NJ: Prentice-Hall, 1966.
Mathis at Colmar: A Visual Confrontation. New York: Red Dust, 1963.
ADDITIONAL SOURCES
"About the Author." In *Women, Art, and Power,* by Linda Nochlin. New York: Harper
    and Row, 1988.
Questionnaire completed by the subject for *American Women Historians, 1700s–1990s:
    A Biographical Dictionary.*

NORTON, MARY BETH
(1943–)
U.S. Women's History

Mary Beth Norton was born on March 25, 1943, in Ann Arbor, Michigan, of
English and Irish ancestry. Her father's ancestors immigrated to the United
States from England in the seventeenth century; her mother's parents were immigrants from Northern Ireland. Norton's father was a college professor; her
mother was a high school teacher and then later a college professor. She attended
public schools in Greencastle, Indiana, through high school. She was influenced
to pursue history by her parents, both of whom had advanced degrees in history,
although neither taught history. They took many trips around the United States
when she was a child, and the family always visited historic sites. Mary Beth
also read "constantly," as she puts it, both historical fiction for children and
biographies of great women and men. "My parents *always* encouraged my intellectual aspirations," she recalls. "I probably would not have sought a Ph.D.
in 1964 (i.e., so soon) without that, given societal pressures at the time versus
such career choices by women."

Norton attended college at the University of Michigan, earning a bachelor's
degree in history, with high distinction and high honors, in 1964. She pursued
her graduate degrees at Harvard University, earning a master's degree in 1965
and a Ph.D. in 1969. Her dissertation, written under the direction of Bernard
Bailyn, won the Allen Nevins Prize for the best-written dissertation in American
history in 1970.

From 1969 to 1971 Mary Beth Norton was assistant professor of history at the University of Connecticut. In 1971 she joined the faculty of Cornell University as assistant professor. She was promoted up the ranks at Cornell and is currently Mary Donlon Alger Professor of History, a title she has held since 1987.

Mary Beth Norton is the author, editor, or co-editor of six books and the author of thirty scholarly articles. Her third book, *Liberty's Daughters: The Revolutionary Experience of American Women, 1750–1800,* won the Berkshire Conference Prize for best book by a woman historian in 1981 and set Norton in the forefront of the emerging field of U.S. women's history. She recalls that she was motivated to study history because of her parents' encouragement and her own love for piecing together stories. Her participation in the feminist movement, however, and its impact on her life, provided her with a means to do history by looking at women's lives and at gender.

Norton has been the recipient of numerous fellowships, including those from the Guggenheim Foundation, the Rockefeller Foundation, the Charles Warren Center at Harvard University, the Woodrow Wilson Center, and the American Antiquarian Society. She is currently general editor for the *AHA Guide to Historical Literature,* member of the board of trustees for the National Council for History Education, and a member of the Historical Advisory Committee of the Commission on Preservation and Access. She has served as vice president for research for the American Historical Association, as co-organizer of the first meeting of the International Federation for Research in Women's History, chair of the Committee on the Status of Women for the Organization of American Historians, and president of the Berkshire Conference of Women Historians.

Norton has honorary degrees from Siena College, Marymount Manhattan College, DePauw University, and Illinois Wesleyan University. She has always been very active in campus and intercampus politics. She was the University of Michigan's campus delegate to the National Student Association meetings and was an active member of Students for a Democratic Society (SDS) in its early days. She was also head of the all-campus government as an assistant professor at Cornell University. Norton has been elected twice, and currently serves, as faculty trustee at Cornell.

Mary Beth Norton has no current partner. She has never been married and has no children. Her interests include Chinese cooking, guitar playing, reading mystery novels, and swimming and sailing.

BOOKS BY MARY BETH NORTON

Editor. *Major Problems in American Women's History.* Lexington, MA: D. C. Heath, 1989.

Editor, with Carol Groneman. *To Toil the Livelong Day: America's Women at Work, 1790–1980.* Ithaca, NY: Cornell University Press, 1987.

Editor, Norton et al. *A People and a Nation.* Boston: Houghton Mifflin, 1982; 2nd ed. 1986; 3rd ed. 1990; 4th ed. 1994.

Liberty's Daughters: The Revolutionary Experience of American Women, 1750–1800. Boston: Little, Brown, 1980.

Editor, with Carol Berkin. *Women of America: A History.* Boston: Houghton Mifflin, 1979.

The British-Americans: The Loyalist Exiles in England, 1774–1789. Boston: Little, Brown, 1972.

ADDITIONAL SOURCE

Questionnaire completed by the subject for *American Women Historians, 1700s–1990s: A Biographical Dictionary.*

O

ORD, ANGUSTIAS DE LA GUERRA
(1815–1890)
Local History

Angustias de la Guerra Ord was born in San Diego, California, on June 11, 1815, to Jose de la Guerra y Noriega and Maria Antonia Carrillo, who was of noble blood. The family moved to Santa Barbara immediately after Angustias's birth, and her father became commander of the Presidio. Angustias married Manuel Jimeno Casarin in 1833 and moved to Monterey, where her husband served as secretary of state, senior member of the Assembly, and occasionally acting governor. He died of cholera in 1853 during a visit to Mexico, and she later married James L. Ord, a U.S. Army surgeon, grandson of King George IV of England and Maria Fitzherbert. The Ords moved back to Santa Barbara; before dissolving their marriage in 1875, they met President Ulysses S. Grant at the White House and Mexico's President Benito Juarez at the castle of Chapultepec. Meanwhile, California fell under United States military rule and de la Guerra Ord wrote of the power struggles and rebellions that were part of her life. Her reflections on this historical period were published in *Occurrences in California*, dictated to Thomas Savage of the Bancroft Library in Berkeley, California, in 1878. The manuscript was placed in the Hubert Howe Bancroft Collection; it was translated into English and published by the Academy of American Franciscan History in 1956 as *Occurrences in Hispanic California*. It became one of the authoritative works of pre-statehood. Angustias de la Guerra Ord died on June 21, 1890, and was buried in the Santa Barbara Mission cemetery. "I wish to rest with those I loved so well" is written in Spanish on her tombstone, and her home is considered a Santa Barbara architectural landmark.
ADDITIONAL SOURCES
Joseph A. Thompson, *El Gran Capitan* (1961); Walker A. Tompkins, *Santa Barbara History Makers* (1983); *Santa Barbara Daily News,* May 20, 1922; *Santa Barbara News-Press,* Dec. 2, 1956, p. B14; NotHSAW 93; BiIn 16; MexAmB; *Bio-Base.*

P

PAINTER, NELL IRVIN
(1942–   )
U.S. History, Southern

Nell Irvin Painter was born August 2, 1941, in Houston, Texas, of African-American ancestry. The daughter of Frank Edward Irvin, Sr., and Dona Lolita McGruder Irvin, Nell moved with her family to Oakland, California, as an infant. Her parents, who met as students at Houston College for Negroes, both had careers in education. They instilled in her the importance of making connections with the larger community (by taking her to the ballet, opera, and theater) and encouraged her to explore the African cultures of her ancestors.

Painter attended public schools in Oakland and then the University of California at Berkeley. She spent the summer of 1962 in Kano, Nigeria, with her parents, as part of the Project Crossroads Africa. Along with other Nigerian and American students, she constructed a school building for the indigenous people of the area. A a result of this experience Painter chose to study anthropology, graduating with a bachelor of arts degree in 1964.

When Painter returned to Africa, this time to Ghana, she discovered that history, particularly history that discussed imperialism and social change, provided the kinds of intellectual challenges she wanted. She then attended the University of California, earning a master's degree in history in 1967, and Harvard University, earning the Ph.D. in 1974. As Caroline Moseley has written about Painter, her own life taught her to focus upon ''more than one variable at a time—class, race and gender all at once.'' That has been her mark as a historian. Painter was also greatly influenced by two other historians, Frank Fidel, her mentor at Harvard, and John Hope Franklin, with whom she often consulted.

Painter's first academic appointment was at the Ghana Institute of Languages, where she taught from 1964 to 1965. She has also taught at Harvard University, the University of Pennsylvania, the University of North Carolina, Hunter College of the City University of New York, and Princeton University, where she now teaches, and was named Edwards Professor of American History in 1991.

Author of thirty publications, including three books, Painter has written about black Americans during Reconstruction, Sojourner Truth, and multiculturalism on the American university campus. Professor Painter has received numerous awards and fellowships, among them the Candace Award, National Coalition of 100 Black Women; the Coretta Scott King Award from the American Association of University Women; and fellowships from the American Council of Learned Societies, the Guggenheim Foundation, and the National Endowment for the Humanities.

Nell Irvin Painter was married to Colin Painter from 1965 to 1966. In 1989 she married Glenn R. Shafer, who teaches at the University of Kansas. She is the stepmother of Richard and Dennis Shafer. Her hobbies include swimming, jogging, and knitting.

BOOKS BY NELL IRVIN PAINTER

Standing at Armageddon: U.S., 1877–1919. New York: W. W. Norton, 1987; paperback, 1989.

The Narrative of Hosea Hudson: His Life as a Negro Communist in the South. Cambridge: Harvard University Press, 1977; Norton paperback, 1993.

Exodusters: Black Migration to Kansas After Reconstruction. New York: Alfred A. Knopf, 1976; Norton paperback, 1992.

ADDITIONAL SOURCES

Irvin, Dona L. "Nell Irvin Painter." *Notable Black American Women.* Ed. Jessie Carney Smith. Detroit: Gale Research, 1992, 818–820.

Moseley, Caroline. "Painter Presents History of the Souths." *Princeton Today* 4 (Summer 1990): 12.

PETERSON, TRUDY HUSKAMP
(1945–   )
Archivist

Trudy Huskamp Peterson was born on January 25, 1945, in Estherville, Iowa, of German ancestry. Her father was a farmer, her mother a full-time homemaker. As a child Trudy attended a small town school, then entered a junior and senior high school that incorporated three small towns. Her graduating class had thirty-two students. As an only child growing up on a farm, she was influenced by farm life and by the stories her grandmother told her about pioneer life, including tales of breaking the sod, building the barn, and watching the railroad being built.

Peterson attended Iowa State University, earning a bachelor's degree in English and history in 1967. She planned to pursue law but, as she puts it, "after a semester of law school I discovered I was a humanist, that I wanted to know why and to make judgments about the answer to 'why.' " She then attended the University of Iowa, earning a master's degree and a Ph.D. in U.S. history, in 1972 and 1975.

Peterson has worked as an archivist since 1968. From 1968 to 1971 she worked at the National Archives, as historian and archivist at the Herbert Hoover Presidential Library, editor of the John F. Kennedy Oral History Project, and research assistant at the Office of Presidential Libraries. She was back at the National Archives from 1974 to 1993, as archivist in the Office of Presidential Libraries, team leader for the FBI Records Appraisal Task Force, chief of the Legislative and Natural Resources Branch, chief of the Machine-Readable Records Branch, archives specialist, deputy assistant archivist, and acting assistant archivist. As acting assistant archivist for eight years, she was responsible for 600 employees in more than a dozen facilities nationwide with an annual budget of $25 to $30 million.

In 1993 Peterson was appointed acting archivist and deputy archivist of the United States. She was responsible for a budget of nearly $250 million and 3,000 employees in facilities nationwide. In this position, as in her position as acting archivist, she testified before Congress, made policy-setting public speeches, dealt with major media, and worked with a variety of boards. As acting archivist she also initiated the development of a nationwide computer network for the National Archives and served as a forceful advocate of international standards for the description of materials held in archives. Peterson also served, during that time, as commissioner of the U.S.-Russia Joint Commission on Missing in Action/Prisoners of War.

Trudy Huskamp Peterson retired from the U.S. National Archives in 1995 and accepted a position as the first executive director of the Open Society Archives at Central European University in Budapest, Hungary. Her previous international work includes consulting with the Centro Estudios de la Realidad Puertorriquena, in San Juan, Puerto Rico, the International Council on Archives, and the United Nations.

An accomplished writer as well as archivist, Peterson is the author, co-author, or editor of four books and the author of nearly twenty scholarly articles. Her first book, *Agricultural Exports, Farm Income, and the Eisenhower Administration,* was a revision of the dissertation Peterson completed with Ellis Hawley. Peterson retained an interest in agricultural history throughout her career at the National Archives, publishing historical studies of agriculture and serving on the editorial advisory board of *Agricultural History* and as president of the Agricultural History Society.

Peterson has been the recipient of many honors and awards, the most recent of which was the 1995 Order of Arts and Letters from the Republic of France. She also received the Hancher-Finkbine Medallion from the University of Iowa and the University of Iowa Distinguished Alumni Award, both in 1995. In 1994 she received the Federal 100 Award; in 1982 she received the Archivist's Special Citation; and she won Commendable and Outstanding Service awards from the National Archives in 1979, 1981, 1985, and 1986. Her professional service, far too extensive to list here, includes holding the presidency of the International Conference of the Round Table on Archives, vice presidency of the International Council on Archives, and presidency of the Society of American Archivists. Peterson was also co-chair of the East-West Symposium on Access and delegate to the International Council on Archives consultation on privacy.

Trudy Huskamp Peterson is married to Gary M. Peterson. She makes almost all of her clothes, cooks, plays the piano, and enjoys opera, theater, and reading. She also travels both for business and pleasure.

BOOKS BY TRUDY HUSKAMP PETERSON

With Gary M. Peterson. *Archives and Manuscripts: Law.* Chicago: Society of American Archivists, 1985.

Basic Archival Workshop Exercises. Chicago: Society of American Archivists, 1982.

Editor. *Farmers, Bureaucrats, and Middlemen: Historical Perspectives on American Agriculture.* Washington, DC: Howard University Press, 1980.

Agricultural Exports, Farm Income, and the Eisenhower Administration. Lincoln: University of Nebraska Press, 1979.

ADDITIONAL SOURCE

Questionnaire completed by the subject for *American Women Historians, 1700s–1990s: A Biographical Dictionary.*

PIERCE, BESSIE LOUISE
(1888–1974)
Local History

Bessie Louise Pierce was born in Caro, Michigan, on April 20, 1888, to Clifton J. and Minnie Cornelia (Pierson) Pierce. She received a B.A. in 1910 from the University of Iowa, an M.A. from the University of Chicago in 1918, and a Ph.D. in 1923 from the University of Iowa. She was a Phi Beta Kappa and a Guggenheim Fellow twice as well as an American Association of University Women Fellow and a Newberry Fellow. After teaching in public schools in Iowa, Pierce joined the faculty of the University of Iowa in 1916. In 1924 and 1925 she wrote *Courses in the Social Studies,* followed in 1926 by *Public Opinion and the Teaching of History.* That same year, she became president of the National Council for Social Studies.

In 1929 Pierce became a professor of American history at the University of Chicago, where she taught until 1953. During that time, she continued to write on educational concerns, publishing *Civic Attitudes in American School Textbooks* (1930). She also became interested in the history of Chicago and in 1933 published the first volume of *A History of Chicago.* A second volume appeared in 1940 and a third in 1957. Bessie Pierce was editing the fourth volume at the time of her death on October 3, 1974, in Iowa City, Iowa.

ADDITIONAL SOURCES

NewYTBS 74; WhE&EA; WhoAmW 61, 68, 70, 72; AmAu&B; BiIn 10; ConAu 53; WhAm 6; obituary in NewYT, Oct. 5, 1974, p. 34; *Bio-Base.*

PITTS, MARY CAROLYN
(1924–   )
Architectural Historian

Mary Carolyn Pitts, known as Carolyn, was born on November 15, 1924, in Philadelphia. She was raised there as well, and studied at Moore College of Art, where she received a full scholarship for five years, and at the University of Pennsylvania, earning a master's degree in fine arts in 1949. She has taught at several art schools in the Philadelphia area as well as at the Philadelphia Museum of Art. She also taught as a Fulbright lecturer in Istanbul, Turkey, from 1952 to 1953.

An architectural historian for the United States Department of the Interior's National Park Service since 1974, Carolyn Pitts searches for landmark buildings in all fifty of the United States. The National Historic Landmark program, for which she works, assigns landmark status to a select group of buildings. If the buildings meet certain criteria, and the owners are in agreement with the decision, which carries rights as well as responsibilities, Pitts recommends the buildings to the Secretary of the Interior's Advisory Board, which makes the final decision. Since she has been at the National Park Service, Pitts has helped designate more than 200 structures and districts as National Historic Landmarks in the field of architecture.

Carolyn Pitts started her career as a painter, then taught art and architectural history at Culver Stockton College in Missouri, St. Joseph's College, the Fleisher Art Memorial in Philadelphia, the Tyler School of Fine Arts of Temple University, and Beaver College. In 1974 she took a job as the architectural historian within the National Park Service's history division. In 1979 she became the senior architectural historian for the Historic American Buildings Survey, Heritage Conservation and Recreation Service, U.S. Department of the Interior.

Pitts got her start in preservation working as a consultant. She led the fight in Cape May, New Jersey, in the 1960s and early 1970s to protect a group of Victorian summer cottages and boarding houses. Urban renewal funds were earmarked for building demolition, and these houses, designed by leading architects of the day, were scheduled to go. Pitts quickly learned about the contentious politics of the preservation movement. "It got pretty thick for a while," she later recalled. In the end, Pitts was successful, and the entire town of Cape May was placed on the National Register of Historic Places. In 1976 the town became a National Historic Landmark.

Her first series of recommendations to the Secretary of the Interior concerned New York City skyscrapers. Considering skyscrapers the nation's "great contributions to world architecture," Pitts broke the second rule of the agency, that all buildings be at least fifty years old. The Chrysler Building, one of New York's most beautiful, was forty-eight years old at the time and scheduled for receivership. "As far as I'm concerned," she later argued about her successful battle, "regulations don't mean beans if you know something has a place." Pitts has a reputation for being able to recognize a building's historic value almost instantly.

The philosophy of the Landmark program is not simply to list historic places: the larger program, the National Register of Historic Places, does that, with approximately 75,000 registered sites around the country. The Landmark program is smaller, with only 2,470 sites registered, and has different goals. Buildings are not to be restored simply to have them turned into museums. Money is used for restoration, but the ultimate goal is to have the buildings used in new and profitable ways. Among Pitts's success stories are the Boston Public Library, Philadelphia's City Hall, Frank Lloyd Wright's Fallingwater in Pennsylvania, and the Mission Inn in Riverside, California.

Writer Daniel Levy argues that Carolyn Pitts "has done as much as anyone else to transform the field of historic preservation from a grass-roots trend to a mainstream movement." Passionate about her work, Pitts looks for and then fights for what she considers national treasures: "Tearing down a building and paving a parking lot is idiotic," she stated in an interview. "Designation says that there is something important here, that there are properties that tell us where we've been and what we are, and we ought to take care of them."

Pitts has published articles and monographs on her work in Cape May, public sculpture in Philadelphia, and historic monuments in France. She is a stockholder of the Athenaeum of Philadelphia, on the Committee of 100 for the Federal City, and has been a lecturer for state and local organizations as well as many colleges and universities. She has been written about in *Smithsonian, New York Times, Wall Street Journal,* and *Time.*

Carolyn Pitts has a reputation as being tough, cantankerous, impatient, and irreverent. Most of her detractors, however, are also ardent admirers. As one of her co-workers put it, "Maybe we're a little better off with a few—but just a few, mind you—people like her around." Pitts doesn't worry about other people's difficulties with her manner. "I don't regret anything I've done," she stated in an interview. "If we can get people to read a plaque on a building and just take a look, a good look at the building, then we've moved a step past the throwaway society we've become."

ADDITIONAL SOURCES

Boslough, John. "The Landmark Hunter." *Historical Preservation* 38 (Apr. 1986): 46–51.

Levy, Daniel S. "Outracing the Bulldozers." *Time,* Aug. 6, 1990, 80.

Scanlon, Jennifer. Telephone interview with Carolyn Pitts, 1995.

Stewart, Doug. "She Can Size Up Your Old Building in a Heartbeat." *Smithsonian* 24 (Apr. 1993): 127–136.

PLUMMER, BRENDA GAYLE
(1946–   )
Haitian History; U.S. Foreign Policy

Brenda Gayle Plummer was born on October 20, 1946, in Durham, North Carolina, of African-American ancestry. Her mother was a factory worker; her father was a laborer. She attended public and private schools in New York City as a child, then Antioch College, where she earned a bachelor's degree in 1969. An interest, as she puts it, "in how society works so it can be changed" led her to study history, and she completed a master's degree at Teachers College, Columbia University, in 1973, and a Ph.D. in history at Cornell University in 1981. Plummer also participated in graduate study programs at Vanderbilt University and the University of Ibadan in Ibadan, Nigeria.

Plummer's first academic position was as instructor at Fisk University from

1973 to 1975. From 1979 to 1981 she was lecturer and research fellow in the black studies department and Center for Black Studies at the University of California at Santa Barbara. When she completed the Ph.D., in 1981, Plummer accepted a position as assistant professor of history at the University of Minnesota; in 1987 she was promoted to associate professor. While at the University of Minnesota Plummer also taught as adjunct professor in the department of Afro-American and African studies. In 1991 she accepted a position as associate professor of history and Afro-American studies at the University of Wisconsin at Madison, where she was promoted to professor in 1994 and continues to teach.

Plummer has provided a great deal of consulting experience as well. She spent the 1990–1991 academic year working as a Knight Foundation Consultant at Macalester College. She worked on a program to provide resources for the incorporation into the college of faculty of color. She was also a curricular consultant for ''Caribbean Connections: Classroom Resources for Secondary Schools,'' a project of the Ecumenical Program on Central America and the Caribbean, and the Network of Educators' Committees on Central America, in 1989. Earlier in her career, in 1977, Plummer was a member of the Revision Project for the New York State College Proficiency Examination in Afro-American History. She has also provided professional service as an associate editor of the journal *Signs* from 1990 to 1992, as a manuscript reader for *Signs* and for three university presses, and as a member of the advisory board for *Dictionary of Twentieth Century Culture,* Volume 3, an African-American culture project for Greenwood Press.

The author of two published books, one book in press, and eleven book chapters and scholarly articles, Plummer has studied the diplomatic relations between Haiti and the United States. Her most recent work, *Haiti and the United States: The Psychological Moment,* explores the way in which racism has affected the relationship between the United States and Haiti since the late eighteenth century. As Alfred Hunt puts it, Plummer's important work ''offers a well-written and balanced survey of a relationship that is quite odd in its complexity.'' Her next book, which will be published by the University of North Carolina Press, is *Rising Wind: Foreign Affairs and the Afro-American Freedom Struggle, 1935–1960.* Plummer's current research interests include Afro-Americans and the Cold War, and race, gender, and the Cold War.

Brenda Plummer's most recent fellowship was with the Schomburg Center for Research in Black Culture, where she was a National Endowment for the Humanities Fellow from January to June 1994. She has also received a Social Sciences Research Council fellowship in foreign policy studies, a University of California at Los Angeles Institute of American Cultures postdoctoral fellowship, and a Dorothy Danforth Compton Foundation fellowship. Since 1994 she has held a Vilas Associateship from the Vilas Trust at the University of Wisconsin.

Brenda Plummer's partner is Donald Culverson. She is the mother of one child, Robert. Her interests include photography and gardening.

BOOKS BY BRENDA GAYLE PLUMMER
Haiti and the United States. Athens: University of Georgia Press, 1992.
Haiti and the Great Powers, 1902–1915. Baton Rouge: Louisiana State University Press, 1988.
ADDITIONAL SOURCES
Hunt, Alfred. Review of *Haiti and the United States: The Psychological Moment,* by Brenda Gayle Plummer. *Journal of American History* 81 (June 1994): 313–314.
Questionnaire completed by the subject for *American Women Historians, 1700s–1990s: A Biographical Dictionary.*

POMEROY, SARAH B.
(1938–   )
Ancient History

Sarah B. Pomeroy was born on March 13, 1938, in New York City. Her mother, a teacher, and her father, a businessman, were both of Eastern European ancestry. Pomeroy attended the Birch Wathen School. She remembers visiting museums as a child, and these experiences, combined with a gift for investigating and writing, encouraged her to pursue a career as a historian.

Pomeroy attended Barnard College, earning a bachelor's degree in 1957. She then attended Columbia University for graduate school, earning a master's degree in 1959 and a Ph.D. in 1961. Pomeroy also studied Roman law at Columbia University from 1962 to 1963. Her first academic appointment was at the University of Texas at Austin, where she was instructor in classics from 1961 to 1962. From 1964 to 1965 she was lecturer in classics at Hunter College. From 1967 to 1968 she was lecturer in classics at Brooklyn College. Since 1968 Pomeroy has been back at Hunter College and at the Graduate Center at the City University, where she has earned the rank of professor of classics. She has also held visiting positions at Vassar College and Columbia University.

The author or editor of six books and the author of thirty scholarly articles, Pomeroy's areas of interest include the family in classical antiquity, Greek literature, and papyrology. One of her recent publications, the co-authored work *Women in the Classical World: Image and Text,* was a 1995 selection of the History Book Club. Her first book, *Goddesses, Whores, Wives, and Slaves: Women in Classical Antiquity,* was published in 1975, reissued in 1994, and translated into Italian, German, and Spanish. She is currently working on three additional books, two of which, *The Family in Classical and Hellenistic Greece* and *Ancient Greece,* are under contract with Oxford University Press.

A 1995 recipient of a City University President's Award for Excellence in Scholarship, Pomeroy has also received grants, awards, and fellowships from the National Endowment for the Humanities, the Mellon Foundation, the Ford Foundation, the American Council of Learned Societies, and the American Numismatic Society.

Sarah Pomeroy has provided a great deal of service to the profession. She is currently associate editor of the *Journal of Women's History* and has served on the board of advisors for *Women and History* and *American Journal of Philol-*

ogy. She has been an outside reader for over a dozen journals, including *American Historical Review, American Journal of Ancient History,* and *American Journal of Archaeology*. Pomeroy has also served on the boards of directors for the American Philological Association and the American Society of Papyrologists.

Pomeroy's spouse is Lee Harris Pomeroy, an architect. They have three children: Jordana Pomeroy, an art historian; Jeremy Pomeroy, a lawyer; and Alexandra Pomeroy, a documentary film maker. Pomeroy is also a grandmother of two. Among her hobbies are music, cooking, reading, and swimming.

BOOKS BY SARAH B. POMEROY

Xenophon Oeconomicus: A Social and Historical Commentary. Oxford: Oxford University Press, 1994.

With E. Fantham, H. P. Foley, N. Kampen, and H. A. Shapiro. *Women in the Classical World: Image and Text*. New York: Oxford University Press, 1994.

Editor. *Women's History and Ancient History*. Chapel Hill: University of North Carolina Press, 1991.

Women in Hellenistic Egypt from Alexander to Cleopatra. New York: Schocken, 1984; Wayne State Press, 1990.

Editor, with Hunter College Women's Studies Collective. *Women's Realities, Women's Choices: An Introduction to Women's Studies*. New York: Oxford University Press, 1983; reprint, 1995.

Goddesses, Whores, Wives, and Slaves: Women in Classical Antiquity. New York: Schocken, 1975; reprint, 1994. Italian translation, Einaudi, 1978; German translation, Alfred Kroner, 1985; Spanish translation, Editorial Akal, 1987.

ADDITIONAL SOURCE

Questionnaire completed by the subject for *American Women Historians, 1700s–1990s: A Biographical Dictionary*.

PORTER, DOROTHY
(1905–   )
Curator, History of African-American Women

The "doyenne of black bibliography," Dorothy Porter was born Dorothy Louise Burnett on May 25, 1905, in Warrenton, Virginia, of African-American ancestry. Her father, Hayes Joseph Burnett, was a physician; her mother, Bertha Ball Burnett, was a professional tennis player. She was raised in Montclair, New Jersey, where she attended public school. She moved to Washington, D.C., in 1923 to pursue a teaching degree at the Miner Normal School. Porter earned her degree and took a job as a librarian at Miner and then as a cataloguer at the Carnegie Library at Howard University. At Howard, her primary responsibility was to build a collection on African Americans for the Library of Negro Life and History. While at Howard, Porter earned a bachelor's degree in 1928. In 1930 she left Howard to attend Columbia University, where she received a master of library science degree in 1932. She was one of the first black women to be awarded this degree at Columbia.

Porter returned to Howard University, where she continued to work in collection development. The Library of Negro Life and History was renamed the

Moorland-Spingarn Research Center, and Porter worked there until her retirement in 1973. She identified, acquired, and organized over 3,000 items on African Americans into a workable collection and provided the means for countless historians and students of African-American life to complete meaningful research. Porter's collection includes black newspapers, microfilms, prints, photographs, oral histories, manuscripts, and artifacts.

Dorothy Porter is well known for her persistence and skill in acquiring materials and in finding ways to make them accessible. As Esme Bahn writes, "By the time black studies gained acceptance as a recognized discipline in the 1960s, Dorothy Porter was a master of her craft and sought to teach others how to uncover the neglected history." She compiled a series of bibliographies and research aids to help people gain access to the materials, and she wrote several scholarly articles.

Dorothy Porter has received tremendous accolades for her work, including honorary degrees from the University of Susquehanna, Syracuse University, and Radcliffe College. She was also invited as visiting scholar at the DuBois Institute at Harvard University. As the director of the DuBois Institute argued, Porter "has contributed as much as any living individual to the critical analysis . . . of Afro-American source material." Her most recent honor, in 1994, came when President Bill Clinton announced Porter as one of the recipients of the National Medal of Arts.

Dorothy Burnett married James Amos Porter, artist and head of the fine arts department at Howard, in 1930. They had one child, Constance Burnett, in 1939. James Amos Porter died in 1970, and Dorothy Porter married Charles Wesley, educator, historian, minister, and administrator, in 1979. Wesley died in 1987. Some information on Dorothy Porter is available in the vertical files at the Moorland-Spingarn Collection. Dorothy Porter lives in Washington, D.C.

BOOKS BY DOROTHY PORTER

Afro-Braziliana: A Working Bibliography. Boston: G. K. Hall, 1978.

North American Negro Poets: A Bibliographical Checklist of Their Writings, 1760–1944. Hattiesburg, MS: The Book Farm, 1975.

Early Negro Writing, 1760–1837. Boston: Beacon Press, 1971.

The Negro in the U.S.: A Selected Bibliography. Washington, DC: Library of Congress, 1970.

A Working Bibliography on the Negro in the U.S. Ann Arbor, MI: University Microfilms, 1969.

A Catalogue of the African Collection in the Moorland Foundation, Howard University Library. Washington, DC: Howard University Press, 1958.

ADDITIONAL SOURCES

Bhan, Esme. "Porter, Dorothy." *African American Women: A Biographical Dictionary.* Ed. Dorothy C. Salem. New York: Garland, 1993, 402.

Britton, Helen H. "Dorothy Porter Wesley: A Bio-bibliographical Profile." *American Black Women in the Arts and Social Sciences.* Edited by Ora Williams. Metuchen, NJ: Scarecrow Press, 1994, 3–8.

Hersh, Amy. "Julie Harris Among Winners of National Medal of the Arts." *Backstage* 35 (Oct. 14, 1994): 1.

PUTNAM, BERTHA HAVEN
(1872–1960)
Medieval History

Bertha Haven Putnam was born in New York City in 1872 to George Haven Putnam, head of the publishing firm of G. P. Putnam's Sons, and Rebecca (Shepard) Putnam. She attended Miss Audobon's School and Miss Gibbon's School, both in New York City. She received a B.A. from Bryn Mawr College in 1893 and taught Latin there until she returned to New York after her mother's death. After her father remarried in 1899, Putnam taught special classes at the Brearley School while attending graduate school at Columbia University from 1895 to 1897 and from 1900 to 1903. She earned a Ph.D. in 1908 and became an instructor in history at Mount Holyoke College. She advanced to assistant professor in 1912 and full professor in 1924.

In 1908 Putnam's dissertation, *The Enforcement of the Statutes of Labourers During the First Decade After the Black Death, 1349–1359,* was published. Work on her dissertation eventually led her to specialize in medieval English criminology. While completing her research on the restrictive statutes of laborers enacted in 1349 and 1351 in England, Putnam discovered a misclassification in a Record Office entry which led to her first discovery of a record of proceedings before a justice of the peace. She later discovered 100 of these records describing previously unstudied activities of magistrates who dealt with cases ranging from eavesdropping to murder.

In 1924 Putnam wrote *After the Black Death, 1349–1359,* and in 1933 she published *Kent Keepers of the Peace, 1316–17.* In 1938 she edited *Proceedings Before the Justices of the Peace in the Fourteenth and Fifteenth Centuries,* for which she received the first Haskins Medal, awarded by the Medieval Academy of America in 1940. She had retired from teaching at Mount Holyoke College in 1937, and spent 1938 lecturing at Bryn Mawr College. That same year she was the first woman and nonlawyer to become a research fellow at Harvard Law School. In 1939 she published *Yorkshire Sessions of the Peace, 1361–1364.*

In the late 1940s, an attack of shingles left her partially blind, ending her scholarly career. She was awarded His Majesty's Medal for Service in the Cause of Freedom in 1946 by King George VI for her work as chair of the Mount Holyoke Chapter of the British War Relief Society. Her last book, *The Place in Legal History of Sir William Sharehull, Chief Justice of the King's Bench,* was published in England in 1950. Bertha Putnam died of arteriosclerosis in South Hadley, Massachusetts, on February 26, 1960.

ADDITIONAL SOURCES

Margaret Hastings and Elisabeth G. Kilmball, "Two Distinguished Medievalists—Nellie Neilson and Bertha Putnam," *Journal of British Studies,* Spring 1979; BiIn 5, 6; NatCAB 43; WomWWA 14; NotAW; *Bio-Base;* obituary in *American Historical Review* 65: 1048, July 1960; obituary in NewYT, Feb. 27, 1960, p. 19; obituary in *Publishers Weekly* 177: 35, Mar. 21, 1960; obituary in *Speculum* 35: 522–523, July 1969; obituary in *The Times* (London), Mar. 4, 1960; obituary in *Archives* (Journal of British Records Association), v. 4, 1960.

R

RAMIREZ, SUSAN E.
(1946–   )
Colonial Spanish American History

Susan Elizabeth Ramirez was born on October 11, 1946, in Toledo, Ohio, of Mexican, Irish, and German ancestry. Her immigrant father, Eduardo Ramirez, sold and repaired typewriters, and her mother, Helen McCartney Ramirez, was a full-time homemaker. In addition to scouting and the YMCA, her parents provided a great influence on her young life. Susan attended elementary school and high school in Chicago and in Elmhurst, Illinois.

Ramirez's father was opposed to higher education for women but, she argues, he provided her with a thirst for learning about her heritage by taking the family on frequent trips to Mexico. It was her mother, however, who had the greatest influence on Ramirez's future. "The most crucial thing that ever happened to me was that my father wouldn't let me go to college," she later recalled. "But my mother schemed with the high school counselor and she got me accepted at the University of Illinois-Urbana. I was so thrilled to be tapped for college. I was packed before I graduated."

Susan Ramirez attended the University of Illinois at Urbana, earning high honors and distinction in Latin American studies. She then received a master's degree and a Ph.D. in history at the University of Wisconsin at Madison, in 1973 and 1977. She was drawn to history because it "gave me the freedom to do what I want," she stated, but she also pursued a graduate certificate in business administration at the Wharton School of the University of Pennsylvania. In addition, Ramirez studied demography at Cornell University and anthropology at Centro Intercultural de Documentacion in Mexico.

Ramirez's first academic position was as assistant professor of history at Ohio University in Athens, where she worked from 1977 to 1982. She served, while there, as associate director of Latin American studies from 1979 to 1980. In

1982 she accepted a position as assistant professor of history at DePaul University in Chicago, where she still works. Ramirez was promoted to associate professor in 1984 and professor in 1989. She also serves as the co-director of Latin American studies.

Author, editor, or translator of four books and more than twenty-five articles, Ramirez is an award-winning historian. Her article "The Dueno de Indios," published in *Hispanic American Historical Review* in 1987, received an honorable mention for the 1988 James Alexander Memorial Prize for the Conference on Latin American History, and her book *Provincial Patriarchs* received an Outstanding Book Award from *Choice* magazine.

Ramirez has received grants from the Fulbright Foundation, the National Endowment for the Humanities, the Social Science Research Council, and the Rockefeller Foundation. She has served on the editorial board of *The Americas,* as president of the Illinois Congress of Latin Americanists, and on the executive board of the Rocky Mountain Council on Latin American Studies. She is currently editor of South American ethnohistory for *Handbook of Latin American Studies,* to be published by the Library of Congress.

Among her hobbies are Latin American colonial history, Andean ethnohistory, stamp collecting, textile collecting, and music.

BOOKS BY SUSAN RAMIREZ

The World Upside Down: Cross Cultural Contact and Conflict in Colonial Peru. Stanford, CA: Stanford University Press, 1996.

Patriarcas Provincials: La tenencia de la tierra y la economia del poder en el Peru colonial. Madrid: Alianza Editorial, 1991; translation of *Provincial Patriarchs.*

Editor, with Murdo J. MacLeod. *Indian-Religious Relations in Colonial Spanish America.* Syracuse, NY: Syracuse University Press, 1989.

Provincial Patriarchs: Land Tenure and the Economics of Power in Colonial Peru. Albuquerque: University of New Mexico Press, 1986.

ADDITIONAL SOURCES

Paladino, Larry. "Susan Elizabeth Ramirez." *Notable Hispanic American Women.* Ed. Diane Telgen and Jim Kamp. Detroit: Gale Research, 1993, 331–332.

Questionnaire completed by the subject for *American Women Historians, 1700s–1990s: A Biographical Dictionary.*

RAWSKI, EVELYN
(1939–   )
Chinese History

Evelyn Rawski was born on February 2, 1939, in Honolulu, Hawaii, of Japanese-American ancestry. Her mother was a registered nurse, her father an accountant. She attended Kapalama Elementary School, R. L. Stevenson Junior High School, and Roosevelt High School, all in Hawaii. Rawski then attended Cornell University, graduating in 1961 with a bachelor's degree, with high honors, in economics. Inspired by Knight Biggerstaff, a Chinese historian at Cornell, Rawski decided to pursue historical studies in graduate school. She attended Radcliffe

College, earning a master's degree in East Asian regional studies in 1962, then Harvard University for a Ph.D. in history and Far Eastern languages, which she earned in 1968. She is fluent in Chinese, Japanese, French, and Manchu.

Rawski's first academic appointment was in the department of history at the University of Pittsburgh, where she still teaches. From 1967 to 1972 she was assistant professor; from 1973 to 1979 she was associate professor; and since 1980 she has been professor. In 1988 Rawski was also named research professor for the University Center for International Studies.

Rawski has written extensively on Ch'ing dynasty history. Her most recent work is *Harmony and Counterpoint: Ritual Music in Chinese Context* (1996), edited with Bell Yung and Rubie S. Watson. She has written or edited five other books and twenty scholarly articles, publishing in U.S. and Chinese publications. In addition, Rawski has completed another book, *Ritual and Rulership in East Asia,* and is in the process of working on a long-term project on the evolution of the Ch'ing imperial institution and its political, ritual, and social context.

Rawski has received postdoctoral grants and fellowships from the Guggenheim Foundation, the Woodrow Wilson International Center, Harvard University, the University of Pittsburgh, the American Council of Learned Societies, the University of Michigan, the National Endowment for the Humanities, and the Joint Committee on Chinese Studies. She has been a member of the editorial boards of *Ming Studies, Peasant Studies Newsletter,* and *Sinica Leidensia,* and was associate editor of *Encyclopedia of Social History.* She served as an elected member of the board of directors of the Association for Asian Studies and as council member of the Center for Social History at Carnegie-Mellon University. She has served on and chaired the John K. Fairbank Prize of the American Historical Association and as a member of several American Council of Learned Societies committees on Chinese studies. Rawski is currently vice president of the Association of Asian Studies; in 1996 she will assume the presidency of the organization.

Evelyn Rawski is married to Thomas G. Rawski. Her interests include Oriental carpets, cooking, and reading mystery stories.

BOOKS BY EVELYN RAWSKI

Editor, with Bell Yung and Rubie S. Watson. *Harmony and Counterpoint: Ritual Music in Chinese Context.* Stanford, CA: Stanford University Press, 1996.

Editor, with James L. Watson. *Death Ritual in Late Imperial and Modern China.* Berkeley: University of California Press, 1988.

With Susan Naquin. *Chinese Society in the Eighteenth Century.* New Haven, CT: Yale University Press, 1987.

Editor, with David Johnson and Andrew J. Nathan. *Popular Culture in Late Imperial China.* Berkeley: University of California Press, 1985.

Education and Popular Literacy in Ch'ing China. Ann Arbor: University of Michigan Press, 1979.

Agricultural Change and the Peasant Economy of South China. Cambridge, MA: Harvard University Press, 1972.

ADDITIONAL SOURCE

Questionnaire completed by the subject for *American Women Historians, 1700s–1990s: A Biographical Dictionary.*

REAGON, BERNICE JOHNSON
(1942–   )
History of African Americans, Cultural Worker, Curator

Bernice Johnson Reagon, perhaps best known for her work with the performance group Sweet Honey in the Rock, is also a historian, writer, curator emeritus, and civil rights activist. Born on October 4, 1942, outside of Albany, Georgia, of African-American heritage, Reagon is the daughter of the Reverend Jessie Johnson and Beatrice Wise Johnson. At an early age Bernice's church singing brought her attention, and she credits her father for her singing style. In fact, the a cappella style Sweet Honey in the Rock is so famous for originated in the Baptist Church Reagon attended in Albany, Georgia. "Like most of the rural churches in the region," she later remembered, "we did all of our singing unaccompanied except for our hands and our feet; to this day I am an a cappella singer."

Bernice Johnson Reagon attended Blue Springs Elementary School and then was among the first generation of black children in her region to be bused to the county secondary schools. She entered Albany State College in 1959 as a music major. While in college she became interested in the civil rights movement, eventually holding the position of secretary of the local National Association for the Advancement of Colored People (NAACP) Youth Chapter. During her junior year of college, Reagon participated in a Student Nonviolent Coordinating Committee (SNCC) march and was subsequently suspended from school and then arrested. In jail she again learned the power of song, as the forty to fifty incarcerated women sang together to unite in their struggle.

Reagon was the highest-ranking student at Albany State College, but she left there to attend Spelman College as a non-Western history major. She left school again, however, to join the Freedom Singers of SNCC. This group traveled around the country to raise money for the civil rights movement. During this time she wrote her most militant songs, favoring African-American separatism rather than integration into white society. She completed her degree at Spelman in 1970, then took a position in Washington, D.C., as vocal director at the District of Columbia Black Repertory Theater. While there, Reagon organized Sweet Honey in the Rock and began to study for the Ph.D. in history at Howard University. By 1975 she had completed her dissertation, which focused on songs of the civil rights movement. In the field of history, states biographer Ondine Le Blanc, Reagon found work "that could sustain her passion for music and for the African American community."

From 1976 to 1988 Reagon worked as cultural historian and director of the Program in Black American Culture at the Smithsonian Institution. From 1988 to 1993 she served as a curator in the Division of Community Life, and since 1994 she has been curator emeritus of the Smithsonian Institution. Currently Distinguished Professor of History at American University, Reagon continues to contribute to the collection and dissemination of information about the cultural practices, past and present, of African Americans. Douglas Barasch put it well when he wrote, in a *New York Times* article, "Her work, her music and her life have been devoted to the preservation of black oral culture."

Bernice Johnson Reagon has been the recipient of many awards, including a MacArthur Foundation "Genius" fellowship. Among her many contributions to the field is her decade-long project, "Wade in the Water," a series of National Public Radio broadcasts celebrating African-American sacred music of the nineteenth and twentieth centuries.

Sweet Honey in the Rock, of which Reagon is founder and artistic director, regularly performs a cappella music from the African diaspora at churches, concerts, and festivals. Sweet Honey's political and spiritual messages resound with audiences in the United States and on group tours in Africa, Asia, and Australia. Their name, which comes from a gospel song, is based on a parable about a land so rich that its rocks, when cracked, poured out honey. "And over the years," states Reagon, "I have come to believe that black women are like that land. The properties of honey and rock represent the complexities of sweetness and strength that we struggle to offer up in our lives."

Bernice Johnson Reagon was married to Cordell Reagon from 1963 until 1967, when they divorced, and is the mother of two children, Toshi and Kwan.

BOOKS BY BERNICE JOHNSON REAGON

Editor. *We'll Understand It Better By and By: Pioneering African American Gospel Composers.* Washington, DC: Smithsonian Institution Press, 1993.

Editor. *We Who Believe in Freedom: Sweet Honey in the Rock . . . Still on the Journey.* New York: Anchor Books, 1993.

Black American Culture and Scholarship: Contemporary Issues. Washington, DC: Smithsonian Institution Press, 1986.

Compositions One: The Original Compositions of Bernice Johnson Reagon. Washington, DC: Songtalk Publishing, 1986.

The African Diaspora: World Family of Black Culture. Washington, DC: Smithsonian Institution Press, 1980.

ADDITIONAL SOURCES

Le Blanc, Ondine. "Bernice Johnson Reagon." *Contemporary Black Biography.* Ed. Barbara Carlisle Bigelow. Detroit: Gale Research, 1994, 231–236.

Pagan, Margaret. "Bernice J. Reagon." *Notable American Women.* Ed. Jessie Carney Smith. Detroit: Gale Research, 1992, 926–928.

ROBINSON, JANE MARIE BANCROFT
(1847–1932)
European and U.S. History

Jane Marie Bancroft Robinson was born on December 24, 1847, to the Reverend George C. and Caroline J. (Orton) Bancroft in West Stockbridge, Massachusetts.

She graduated from the Emma Willard School in Troy, New York, in 1871 and from the New York State Normal School in 1872. She received a Ph.B. degree from Syracuse University in 1877 and a Ph.M. degree, also from Syracuse, in 1884. She continued her studies at the University of Zurich in 1886–1887. In 1887–1888 Robinson became the first woman to be admitted to the Ecole des Hautes Etudes at the Sorbonne University in Paris. She was dean of women and professor of French at Northwestern University from 1877 to 1886. As dean of women at Northwestern, she was a founder of the Western Association of Collegiate Alumnae, forerunner of the American Association of University Women. In 1886 she was appointed the First Fellow in History at Bryn Mawr College.

Jane Robinson wrote *The Parliament of Paris and the Other Parliaments of France* in 1885, and *Deaconesses in Europe and Their Lessons for America* and *The Early History of Deaconess Work in American Methodism* in 1888. In 1898 she commemorated her future husband's family in *Ebenezer Robinson, a Soldier of the Revolution.* She married George Orville Robinson on May 7, 1891. Robinson founded the National Training School in 1900, and in 1908 she was elected president of the Woman's Home Missionary Society of the Methodist Episcopal Church. She was active in the church for the rest of her life, and her scholarly work ended. Jane Robinson died in 1932.

ADDITIONAL SOURCES

DcNAA; AmWom; BiCAW; InWom; NotAW; WhAm 1; WomWWA; *Bio-Base.*

ROELKER, NANCY LYMAN
(1915–1993)
French History

Nancy Lyman Roelker was born on June 15, 1915, in Warwick, Rhode Island, to William Greene Roelker, a historian, and Anna (Koues) Roelker. She received an A.B. from Radcliffe College in 1936, an A.M. from Harvard University in 1937, and a Ph.D. from Harvard in 1953. She taught European history from 1937 to 1941 at Concord Academy in Concord, Massachusetts, and from 1941 to 1963 at Winsor School in Boston, Massachusetts. She was assistant professor at Tufts University in Medford, Massachusetts, from 1963 to 1965, associate professor from 1965 to 1969, and professor from 1969 to 1971. She then became professor of European history at Boston University. Roelker retired in 1980. In 1960 and 1970 she received research grants from the American Philosophical Society, and in 1965–66 she was a Guggenheim fellow. She received the Distinguished Achievement Medal from the Radcliffe Graduate Society in 1970. In 1985 she was awarded the Gold Medal of Paris for contributions to that city's history.

Roelker translated and edited *The Paris of Henry of Navarre* by Pierre de L'Estoile in 1958, was contributing editor and translator of *In Search of France* in 1963, and was editor and translator of Jean-Batiste Duroselle, *From Wilson to Roosevelt: American Foreign Policy, 1913–1945,* that same year. In 1965 she was editor of Raymond Aron's *The Great Debate: Theories of Nuclear Strategy,* and in 1968 she wrote *Queen of Navarre: Jeanne d'Albret, 1529–1572.* She returned to editing and translating with *Correspondence of Jeanne d'Albret, 1541–1572,* and her last book, *One King, One Faith: The Parliament of Paris and the Reformations of the Sixteenth Century,* was scheduled for publication when she died in December 1993; it was placed on the University of California Press's centennial roster of the 100 most distinguished books published by the press since 1895.

ADDITIONAL SOURCES

ConAu 9R; DrAS 74H, 78H; WhoAmW 75; obituary in NewYTBS, v. 24, p. 1650, Dec. 1993.

ROSS, DOROTHY
(1936–   )
U.S. Intellectual History

Dorothy Ross was born in Milwaukee, Wisconsin, on August 13, 1936, of Russian-Jewish ancestry. Her father worked in sales; her mother was a secretary and homemaker. Ross attended public schools through high school in Milwaukee. Among her early influences Ross counts her parents, who had great respect for education and encouraged her efforts. Their own immigrant status and, ironically, their desire to forget their old-world past whet young Dorothy's appetite for learning about the past. Her parents were also politically conscious and encouraged the same in her. Growing up during World War II and the McCarthy era in the United States also encouraged her knowledge of and attention to political matters. Ross came to history through an interest in journalism and politics. In high school she only studied United States history and found it "virtually incomprehensible."

Ross attended Smith College and discovered an affinity for the study of history through inspirational faculty: Sidney Packard, through a western civilization course, opened the door to her; both Donald Sheehan and Arthur Mann confirmed her growing interest in U.S. history; and Elizabeth Koffka, who taught European intellectual history, taught her that it was possible for a passionate woman to be passionate about ideas. Ross earned the Smith College History Prize and graduated magna cum laude in 1958.

She attended Columbia University, earning a master's degree in 1959 and a Ph.D. in 1965. Ross was a Woodrow Wilson Fellow from 1958 to 1959, a Columbia University President's Fellow from 1960 to 1961, and a Social Science Research Council Pre-doctoral Fellow from 1962 to 1964. Since completing her doctorate she has received several additional grants and fellowships, including those from the National Science Foundation and the Center for Advanced Study in the Behavioral Sciences at Stanford University. In 1993 she was elected to the Society of American Historians.

Professor Ross accepted a position as lecturer at Hunter College in the Fall of 1965, then a position as Fellow in History and Psychiatry at Cornell University Medical College, Payne Whitney Clinic, in New York, where she worked from 1965 through 1967. She was a research associate in the Department of Psychology at George Washington University from 1967 through 1968. In 1971, Ross worked as professorial lecturer in History at George Washington University then accepted a position as special assistant to the Committee on Women Historians of the American Historical Association; she stayed in this position until 1972. Dr. Ross's next appointment was at Princeton University, where she was assistant professor from 1972 to 1978. In the spring of 1977 she also served as special assistant to the Secretary, Department of Health, Education, and Welfare. From 1978 to 1990, she was associate professor and professor of History at the University of Virginia, and since 1990 has been Arthur O. Lovejoy Professor of History at Johns Hopkins University.

Dorothy Ross is the author or editor of three books and more than twenty scholarly articles. Her first book, *G. Stanley Hall: The Psychologist as Prophet* (1972), introduced Ross's work on the history of social thought and the human sciences. Her next work, *The Origins of American Social Science* (1991), surveys the early development of the disciplines of economics, sociology, political science, and history. It is, Robert Westbrook writes, "a marvelously orchestrated story" that raises the stakes on issues concerning historians of the social sciences.

Aside from her children and her publications, according to Ross, her most important accomplishment has been to help open the historical profession to women. As the first assistant to the Committee on the Status of Women of the American Historical Association, she inaugurated the first job roster for women and the first institutional efforts on the part of the AHA to reverse a long history of discrimination. Ross takes pride as well in the undergraduate and graduate students she has taught who are now themselves devotees of history. She also serves as a consultant to the President's Science Advisory Council Panel on Youth and on committees for the Social Science Research Council, the American Historical Association, the National Science Foundation, the Organization of American Historians, and the Carter G. Woodson Institute of Afro-American and African Studies. Her other contributions include serving as editor, with Kenneth J. Cmiel, of the Johns Hopkins University Press series, New Studies in American Intellectual and Cultural History; serving as advisory editor of *Isis;* and serving as a member of the Board of Editors of the *Journal of the History of Ideas.*

Dorothy Ross is married to Stanford G. Ross. They have two children: John Nathan, born in 1965, and Ellen Sarah, born in 1967. Ross has no grandchildren, "yet." She is interested in many areas of history, philosophy, literature, politics, social science, and science. Outside of academic interests, she enjoys reading, tennis, travel, and yoga.

BOOKS BY DOROTHY ROSS

Editor. *Modernist Impulses in the Human Sciences, 1870–1930.* Baltimore, MD: The Johns Hopkins University Press, 1994.

The Origins of American Social Science. New York: Cambridge University Press, 1991.

G. Stanley Hall: The Psychologist as Prophet. Chicago: The University of Chicago Press, 1972.

ADDITIONAL SOURCES

Questionnaire completed by the subject for *American Women Historians, 1700s–1990s: A Biographical Dictionary.*

Westbrook, Robert. Review of *The Origins of American Social Science,* by Dorothy Ross. *Journal of American History,* vol. 79, no. 2 (Sept. 1992): 613–615.

RUIZ, VICKI L.
(1955–   )
Chicana History

Vicki Lynn Ruiz, the daughter of Robert Mercer and Ermina Ruiz, was born May 21, 1955, in Atlanta, Georgia, and grew up in Florida. Her father, a fisherman, took tourists deep sea fishing, and Vicki, her sister, and her mother all worked for the family business. They followed the tourist migration, so Vicki would attend school in Panama City until Thanksgiving, in Marathon from December or January to April, then back in Panama City for the remainder of the year. Her job as a child was to sell tickets for the fishing trips and place flyers in the souvenir racks of local hotels.

Vicki Ruiz's interest in history comes from her family. As a severely asthmatic child, Vicki spent many days at home with her mother, who told her stories of her own Colorado girlhood, during which she became the sole supporter of her mother and two sisters. "At times when I was bogged down with my dissertation or when I'm embroiled in some sort of academic politics," writes Ruiz, "I always think of my mother and I very much admire her."

Ruiz identifies herself as a third generation Chicana, recalling the history of her immigrant grandfather, a coal miner, and her U.S.-born grandmother, who also told young Vicki tales of the past. Although her father's ancestry is part Austrian, Ruiz knows little about and fails to identify with that side of her family. When he married her mother, Ruiz's father was "more or less disowned" by his parents, so her paternal grandparents played hardly any role in her young life.

Life for a Mexican-American girl in small-town Florida was not easy. Some parents did not want their sons dating Mexican-American girls, and Ruiz was denied an academic scholarship sponsored by the United Daughters of the Confederacy, even though she had scored the highest on the standardized test in history, because she could not trace her ancestry to the pre–Civil War South. Ruiz attended Gulf Coast Community College and then Florida State University, hoping that an education would also provide her with an escape. She planned to become a teacher but listened to the advice of one of her professors, Jean Gould-Bryan, who encouraged her to go on to graduate school. "I applied to Stanford on a whim," she writes, but she got accepted and earned both a master's degree and a Ph.D. there.

During a summer research trip to Mexico, Ruiz met another person who was to have a significant impact on her life, union organizer Luisa Moreno. After spending a summer with her, listening to stories about Moreno's work with cannery workers, Ruiz decided to write her dissertation on the Mexican cannery workers and their struggle for unionization. Moreno and others convinced Ruiz that the stories she had heard, of the victimization of Mexican women, told only part of the story. "For instance," she argues, "no one knew that cannery workers in southern California received equal pay for equal work. Some had day care centers on the job site." Ruiz began the work that would define her as someone who helps create and define knowledge more broadly to encompass the life histories and struggles of marginalized peoples. Ruiz's work, published as *Cannery Women, Cannery Lives: Mexican Women, Unionization, and the California Food Processing Industry, 1930–1950,* was reviewed by William Flores as "essential reading for anyone engaged in research on Chicanos and Mexicans, on cannery workers, and more broadly on issues of gender and work." *Unequal Sisters: A Multicultural Reader in U.S. Women's History,* a book Ruiz edited with Ellen Carol DuBois and now a standard text in the field, is the first collection that provides for a more inclusive, multicultural women's history, focusing on the experiences of Latinas, African-American women, Asian American women, and Native American women.

Ruiz's first academic appointment was at the University of Texas at El Paso, where she worked from 1982 to 1985. She was then hired as assistant and later associate professor at the University of California at Davis. She left Davis in 1992 to take a position as Andrew W. Mellon All-Clarement Professor in the Humanities at the Claremont Graduate School. Ruiz's most recent move has taken her to Arizona State University at Tempe, where she is professor of women's studies and history.

The author, editor, or co-editor of seven books and author of over a dozen book chapters and seven articles, Ruiz has won two book awards, from the National Women's Political Caucus and the American Educational Studies Association, and two research awards, from the Chicana/Latina Research Project and the California Council for the Humanities. She has also won a community service award, an Outstanding Faculty Award, and an Honored Faculty Award from the University of California at Davis. Ruiz has worked on public history and oral history projects, served as an advisory board member on ten film projects, and served on the editorial boards of many publications, including *Encyclopedia of the American West, The Latino Encyclopedia, The Reader's Companion to the History of American Women,* and *Frontiers: A Journal of Women's Studies.* Her most recent work is *From Out of the Shadows: A History of Mexican Women in the United States,* in progress.

She takes pride in her work at the University of California at Davis with the MURALS program. A mentorship program, MURALS matches upper division students of color with faculty members to collaborate either on the professor's own research or on an independent student project. Clear about the need to draw students of color into academia, and for senior faculty to mentor junior faculty, Ruiz remembers the words of Luisa Moreno: "One person can't do anything; it's only with others that things are accomplished."

Vicki L. Ruiz took the name Ruiz in 1979 to honor her mother and to signify her marriage to a distant cousin. They had two children, Miguel and Daniel, and divorced in 1989. Ruiz takes great pride in raising her sons. "Raising feminist sons amid the Terminator and MTV is certainly a challenge," she writes. "Miguel and Daniel are intelligent, loving children who care about people and about issues." In 1992 Vicki Ruiz married Victor Becerra, a college administrator. A bachelor at thirty seven, he had never been married or had children. "However," Ruiz notes, "he has become an absolutely terrific parent!" He is also employed at Arizona State University, as academic advisor for the College of Liberal Arts.

BOOKS BY VICKI L. RUIZ

Editor, with Susan Armitage, Helen Bannan, and Katherine Morrissey. *Women in the West: A Guide to Manuscript Sources.* New York: Garland, 1991.

Editor, with Ellen Carol DuBois. *Unequal Sisters: A Multicultural Reader in U.S. Women's History.* New York: Routledge, 1990. 2nd ed., 1994.

Editor, with Lillian Schlissel and Janice Monk. *Western Women: Their Land, Their Lives.* Albuquerque: University of New Mexico Press, 1988.

Cannery Women, Cannery Lives: Mexican Women, Unionization, and the California Food Processing Industry, 1930–1950. Albuquerque: University of New Mexico Press, 1987.

Editor, with Susan Tiano. *Women on the U.S.-Mexico Border: Responses to Change.* Winchester, MA: Allen and Unwin, 1987; reprinted by Westview Press, 1991.

ADDITIONAL SOURCES

Dominguez, Francisco J. "Interview: Dr. Vicki Ruiz on the Chicana Feminist Struggle." *Third World Forum,* April 30, 1990, 6–7, 11.

Pendergast, Tom. "Vicki Ruiz." *Notable Hispanic American Women.* Edited by Diane Telgen and Jim Kamp. Detroit: Gale Research, 1993, 360–361.

Questionnaire completed by the subject for *American Women Historians, 1700s–1990s: A Biographical Dictionary.*

Ruiz, Vicki L. "The Quest for Balance." Presentation at American Historians Association Committee on Women's Historians, 1994, San Francisco, California. Quoted with permission of author.

S

SALMON, LUCY MAYNARD
(1853–1927)
U.S. History

Lucy Maynard Salmon was born on July 27, 1853, in Fulton, New York, to George Salmon, a bank director and owner of a successful tannery, and Maria Clara Maynard Salmon, principal of Fulton Female Seminary from 1836 until her marriage. Lucy's mother died when she was seven, and her father remarried a year later. Lucy attended school in Oswego and at the Falley Seminary (the Fulton Female Seminary, which had become coeducational). She was eventually sent to Michigan to stay with relatives and entered the University of Michigan in 1872, one of about fifty women students studying there. She graduated in 1876. Salmon became assistant principal, then principal, of the high school in McGregor, Iowa, then returned to Ann Arbor in 1882 for graduate work in modern European history and English and American constitutional history. After receiving her A.M. degree, she taught at the Indiana State Normal School at Terre Haute, then received a fellowship at Bryn Mawr College for 1886–87 to study American history.

In 1888 Lucy Maynard Salmon became the first history teacher at Vassar College and was made full professor in 1889. In 1885 she had published a monograph entitled *Education in Michigan During the Territorial Period,* and her master's thesis, *History of the Appointing Power of the President,* was published in 1886 in the first volume of the American Historical Association *Papers.* She published *Domestic Service* in 1897 and *Progress in the Household* in 1906. In 1923 she published *The Newspapers and the Historian* and *The Newspaper and Authority.* Two books were published posthumously, *Why Is History Rewritten?* in 1929 and *Historical Material* in 1933. Salmon was a member of the American Historical Association from its founding in 1884 and served on its executive committee from 1915 to 1919. She helped found the Association of

History Teachers of the Middle States and Maryland and was its first president. When retirement age came around at age seventy, she obtained permission to continue to teach, and in 1926 friends established the Lucy Maynard Salmon Fund for Research, which gave her the funds to continue her scholarly work. In February 1927, Lucy Maynard Salmon suffered a stroke and died in Pough-keepsie.

ADDITIONAL SOURCES

Louise Fargo Brown, *Apostle of Democracy: The Life of Lucy Maynard Salmon* (1943); *Addresses at the Memorial Service for Lucy Maynard Salmon, Held at Vassar College, March 6, 1927* (1927); Elsie M. Rushmore, "In Memory of Lucy Maynard Salmon," *Vassar Quarterly,* July 1932; Rebecca Lowrie, *Lucy Maynard Salmon* (1951); miscellaneous papers on file at the Vassar College Library; AmAu&B; DcAmAu; DcAmB; DcNAA; LibW; NotAW; WhAm 1; WomWWA 14; *Bio-Base.*

SANCHEZ KORROL, VIRGINIA
(1936–   )
Puerto Rican History

Virginia Sanchez Korrol was born on August 27, 1936, in New York City to Antonio Sanchez Feliciano and Elisa Santiago Rodriguez. Her mother was a full-time homemaker and her father a blue-collar worker on the Pennsylvania Railroad; both were from Puerto Rico. She attended St. Anselm's Elementary School in the Bronx and then Walton High School in the Bronx and Bay Ridge High School in Brooklyn. Her early influences included her family, school, sports, and a love of reading, music, movies, and theater.

A leader in multicultural education, Sanchez Korrol writes that her first encounters with multicultural reality occurred when she was raised Irish Catholic. "How does a light-skinned Puerto Rican girl," she jokes, "who could hardly distinguish the SH in shore from the CH in chicken, get raised Irish Catholic?" For Sanchez Korrol, attending an Irish Catholic school in the South Bronx as one of only a "fistful" of Puerto Ricans, the need to survive amid contradictions was paramount. She learned nothing in school about her own rich multicultural and multiracial history, but she learned to admire the tenacity of the Irish as they fought British domination. She learned to negotiate the language and other cultural differences between home and school, celebrating St. Patrick at school, enjoying her mother's bottomless pots of rice and salsa-enhanced beans with her extended family at home. "If you wanted to survive you had to train yourself to see the forest *and* the trees," she writes, "for both were equally important."

Sanchez Korrol attended Brooklyn College as an undergraduate, earning a bachelor's degree in 1960. Her first field was English literature and secondary education. She took graduate classes in literature and pedagogy at Chicago Teachers College and Brooklyn College before changing fields. Since history had always formed the context for her studies of literature, the progression from literature to history was a natural one. "My decision to study history," she states, "coincided with my desire to write about Puerto Ricans in the U.S."

Sanchez Korrol then received a master's degree and a Ph.D. in Latin American history from the State University of New York at Stony Brook. She is professor of Puerto Rican studies at Brooklyn College.

In her tenure at Brooklyn College, Sanchez Korrol served as coordinator of Caribbean studies from 1982 to 1984 and as coordinator of studies in Asia, Africa, and Latin America from 1988 to 1990. She currently serves both as co-director for Latino studies and as chair of the department of Puerto Rican studies. Among her many contributions to the university and the community are her creation of the Hispanic Advisory Council for the Office of the Brooklyn Borough President and her enrichment and outreach programs to connect the college and the city's Hispanic communities.

Virginia Sanchez Korrol's publications include her book *From Colonia to Community: The History of Puerto Ricans in New York City,* reissued in 1994 by the University of California Press. She also has two edited collections and nearly twenty articles, including "In Search of Unconventional Women: Histories of Puerto Rican Women in Religious Vocations Before Mid-Century," in Vicki Ruiz and Ellen DuBois's edited collection *Unequal Sisters: A Multicultural Reader in U.S. Women's History* (1990), and *The Puerto Rican Struggle: Essays on Survival in the U.S.,* edited with Clara E. Rodriguez and Jose Oscar Alers. She is co-author, with Mario Garcia, Gerald Poyo, and Zaragoza Vargas, of *Latino: A Comparative History of Hispanics in the U.S.,* forthcoming.

Aside from her publications, Sanchez Korrol takes pride in her curriculum work for the New York State Education Department, her efforts in establishing Puerto Rican studies as a discipline, and her founding presidency of the Puerto Rican Studies Association. She has received many awards, including a Brooklyn District Attorney's Office Puerto Rican Higher Education Award, a Leadership Citation from the Brooklyn Borough President, and most recently, a March of Dimes Woman of Distinction Award. The March of Dimes recognized her in part for her personal conviction that "each of us is accountable to the communities we represent and shares responsibility for their advancement."

Virginia Sanchez Korrol has also served on an external evaluation team for the Museum of the City of New York, as a consultant on the Brooklyn's Hispanic Communities Oral History Project, and as one of three U.S. scholars on the international program committee of the Fifth International Congress on Hispanic Cultures in the United States, which was held in Madrid, Spain, in 1992.

Virginia Sanchez Korrol is married to Charles R. Korrol and has two daughters, Pamela and Lauren. Her hobbies include reading, swimming, and home decorating. She also enjoys her "professional hobby" of creating conferences and organizations where none existed before.

BOOKS BY VIRGINIA SANCHEZ KORROL

From Colonia to Community: The History of Puerto Ricans in New York City. Berkeley: University of California Press, 1994. (Original version: *From Colonia to Community: The History of Puerto Ricans in New York City, 1917–1948,* Greenwood Press, 1983.)

Editor, with Edna Acosta Belen. *The Way It Was and Other Writings: Historical Vignettes About the New York Puerto Rican Community,* by Jesus Colon. Houston: Arte Publico Press, 1993.

Editor, with Clara E. Rodriguez and Jose Oscar Alers. *The Puerto Rican Struggle: Essays on Survival in the U.S.* New York: Puerto Rican Migration Consortium, 1980. Reissued by Waterfront Press, 1984.

ADDITIONAL SOURCES

Questionnaire completed by the subject for *American Women Historians, 1700s–1990s: A Biographical Dictionary.*

Sanchez Korrol, Virginia. "A Personal Journey Towards a Multicultural Curriculum." Paper prepared for the Multicultural Conference, Brooklyn College, CUNY, April 1995.

SANDOZ, MARI
(1896–1966)
Western U.S. History

Mari Sandoz was born Marie Susette on May 11, 1896, in Sheridan County, Nebraska, to Jules Sandoz and Mary Fehr. She began school at the age of nine; at the age of sixteen, after only four and a half years of formal schooling, she passed the rural teachers' examination. In 1912 she accepted a teaching position in the Sheridan County School and later moved to the Cheyenne County School. In 1922 she entered the University of Nebraska as a special adult student and held a variety of positions including assistant in the university's English department. In 1934 Sandoz accepted the position of researcher at the Nebraska State Historical Society, where she remained until 1943. She also taught creative writing at the University of Colorado (1941), Indiana University (1946), and the Writers' Institute at the University of Wisconsin (1947–1953, 1955–1956).

Sandoz began writing a variety of western histories in 1935, the first of which was *Old Jules,* a serious biography of her father, who had died in 1928. It won the Atlantic Press Nonfiction Prize for 1935 and was the November Book-of-the-Month Club selection. She moved to Denver in 1940 and wrote *Crazy Horse* in 1942, *Cheyenne Autumn* in 1952, *The Buffalo Hunters: The Story of the Hide Men* in 1954, and *The Cattlemen: From the Rio Grande Across the Far Marias* in 1958. In the 1960s she wrote *These Were the Sioux* (1961), *The Beaver Men: Spearheads of Empire* (1964), and *The Christmas of Phonograph Records: A Recollection* and *The Battle of Little Big Horn,* both completed before her death on March 10, 1966, in New York City. A Mari Sandoz Heritage Society and the Mari Sandoz Center for the Study of Man were established at Chadron State College in Nebraska. In 1974 she was elected to the Nebraska Hall of Fame. The Mari Sandoz Museum on State 27 in Gordon, Nebraska, is a recreation of her Greenwich Village apartment in New York City, where she did much of her writing. A nearby historical marker also commemorates her success.

ADDITIONAL SOURCES:

Mari Sandoz's correspondence and manuscripts are at the George Arents Research Library at Syracuse University, Syracuse, New York; other papers are at the University of

Nebraska Library in Lincoln, Nebraska; Helen Winter Stauffer, "Mari Sandoz," *Boise State Western Writers Series* 63 (1948): 20–23; Helen Winter Stauffer, *Mari Sandoz, Story Catcher of the Plains* (Lincoln: University of Nebraska Press, 1982); LinLibL; InWom; AmAu&B; AuBYP 64, p. 221; BiIn 3, 4, 5, 7, 9, 10; CnDAL; ConAu 1R; ConAu 25R; OxAm; REn; REnAL; SmATA v. 5, 1973, pp. 159–161; *Third Book of Junior Authors*, 1972, pp. 248–250; TwCA; TwCA Supp.; WhNAA; *Bio-Base*.

SANFORD, EVA MATTHEWS
(1894–1954)
Medieval History

Eva Matthews Sanford was born in Nebraska City, Nebraska, on July 6, 1894 to Edgar Lewis and Anna Eugenia (Munson) Sanford. She received an A.B. degree summa cum laude in 1916, an M.A. in 1922, and the Ph.D. in 1923, all from Radcliffe College. She also attended the American Academy in Rome and Yale University. She was a member of Phi Beta Kappa and received a Whitney Traveling Fellowship from Radcliffe as well as research grants from the American Council of Learned Societies.

Sanford wrote *Saslvian: On the Government of God* in 1930. She was a member of the faculty of Mather College and of the graduate school of Western Reserve University in Cleveland before being appointed assistant professor of history at Sweet Briar College in 1937. In 1938 she wrote *The Mediterranean World in Ancient Times*. She served as section editor for commentaries on Latin authors, 1300–1600, for the *Bibliographical Guide to Mediaeval and Renaissance Commentaries and Translations of Classical Authors*. She was a consulting editor for the series Corpus of Roman Law, the first volume of which was published in 1952. In 1950, as a Fulbright Scholar, Sanford searched for medieval manuscripts of commentaries on Juvenal in libraries in Italy and France. At the time of her death, Eva Sanford was translating Augustine's *De Civitate Dei* for the Loeb Classical Library. She died on March 26, 1954.

ADDITIONAL SOURCES

AmWom; BiIn 3; obituary in *American Historical Review* 59: 1081, July 1954; obituary in NewYT, March 27, 1954; p. 17; obituary in *Wilson Library Bulletin* 28: 734, May 1954.

SCHLESINGER, ELIZABETH BANCROFT
(1886–1977)
U.S. Women's History

Elizabeth Bancroft Schlesinger was born in Columbus, Ohio, on July 3, 1886, to Arthur Bancroft, a newspaperman, and Clara Weilnman Bancroft. She attended Ohio State University, sometimes teaching in a one-room country school to get money for college. She graduated in 1910 and taught high school in Kalamazoo, Michigan. In 1914 she married Arthur M. Schlesinger, who eventually became a noted Harvard historian. Their son, Arthur M. Schlesinger, Jr., won the Pulitzer Prize in history in 1945 and served in President John F. Kennedy's administration.

After World War II, Schlesinger began pioneering for the study of women's history. She wrote articles on notable nineteenth-century American women such as "Fanny Fern" (Sara Willis Parton), "Jenny June" (Jane Cunningham Croly), Abigail May Alcott, Eliza Farrar, Eliza Follen, and many others for magazines such as the *New England Quarterly, New York History, William and Mary Quarterly, New York Historical Society Quarterly,* and *American Heritage.* In 1965 the Radcliffe College Women's Archives were renamed the Arthur and Elizabeth Schlesinger Library on the History of Women in America. Elizabeth Bancroft Schlesinger died June 3, 1977, in Williamsburg, Virginia.

ADDITIONAL SOURCES

BiIn 11; ConAu 69; NewYTBS 77; obituary in NewYT, June 2, 1977, p. B-12; obituary in *Washington Post,* June 2, 1977.

SCOTT, ANNE FIROR
(1921–   )
U.S. Southern History

Anne Firor Scott was born on April 24, 1921, in Montezuma, Georgia, of German, Scotch-Irish, English, and Polish ancestry. Her father was a college professor, her mother a full-time homemaker. Her parents lost their savings in a bank failure the year she was born, and they had difficulty paying the doctor who delivered her at home. Since she was born nine months after the suffrage amendment was passed, Scott reports that she never has to count on her fingers the number of years women have had the right to vote. Anne was influenced early by reading; her father read aloud to the children, choosing his favorites rather than children's stories. Growing up the only girl among four siblings, Scott did not learn that girls were inferior. In fact, she states, it was not until she was twenty-one and in college that she was told, by a favorite professor, that being female might limit her opportunities in the world.

Scott attended the University of Georgia, graduating summa cum laude and Phi Beta Kappa in 1941. She did not, however, immediately pursue education or employment as a historian. In her autobiographical essay, "A Historian's Odyssey," Scott reads back through her journals, which by 1984 approached twenty volumes, examining her choices and realizing that she began to do history by chance. "If my journal is to be believed," she writes, "I went out into the world in 1940 in search of fame, fortune, and a husband, in no particular order. As to how that search was to be conducted the journal is significantly silent. It was very much a matter of what might turn up."

She held a job at International Business Machines (IBM) and briefly entered a graduate program for personnel managers, but a United States Congressional internship, during which she had the opportunity to write speeches and listen to politicians talking, had the greatest impact on her. These experiences, she later wrote, "made me so painfully aware of my ignorance that I went back to school."

Scott attended Northwestern University, earning a master's degree in political science. After a job with the National League of Women Voters, Scott married and moved to Cambridge, Massachusetts, where she contemplated going to Harvard. "The program in American Civilization seemed to have few requirements but plenty of scope," Scott remembered later. But before she could finish her dissertation, she followed her husband, who had already finished, to Washington, D.C., where he had secured a job. "All our planning was for his career; it did not occur to me to think this odd," Scott later mused. Seven years and three children later, Scott finished her dissertation and took a job teaching history at Haverford College.

"If I came to history by indirection," she writes, "my decision to study the history of women was not, in retrospect, accidental." Her maternal grandmother had worked for the League of Women Voters, and Scott herself had decided at age twenty-three to write a history of women, beginning with Eve. Her interests led her to research the history of southern American women, "a study for which there was almost no historiographical tradition and no network of established scholars. My temerity rested not on courage but on ignorance; if I had known what was involved I might never have begun."

After temporary appointments at Haverford College and the University of North Carolina at Chapel Hill, Scott took a job as assistant professor of history at Duke University. She remains at Duke, having earned in 1980 the distinguished rank of W. K. Boyd Professor of History, and in 1991 W. K. Boyd Professor of History Emerita. She has been the recipient of many fellowships, prizes, and honorary degrees, including a University Medal from Duke in 1994, a Berkshire Conference Prize in 1980, and honorary degrees from Queens College, Northwestern University, Radcliffe College, and the University of the South.

In addition to her ten books and more than twenty-five articles, Scott has written chapters for books and introductions to the work of other scholars. She is best known, though, for her work as one of the first historians of U.S. women. "Dismissed as political or ignored completely by many colleagues," she wrote of her cadre of young women scholars, "we responded by forming a community of scholars that cut across generations, ideologies, race and class." Scott went on to write social histories of white and black women in the South. *The Southern Lady,* her first such work, brought Scott to the attention of southern historians and those who hoped to do women's history, and *Making the Invisible Woman Visible* is considered a classic in the field of women's history. In her most recent book, *Unheard Voices: The First Historians of Southern Women,* Scott looks back to the women who came before her: "It is impossible to measure the cost to the world of scholarship of their marginality (and that of so many others)," she writes in that text, "or the cost to themselves."

Among her most significant contributions outside of teaching and research, her appointment, from President Lyndon Johnson, to the Citizens Advisory Council on the Status of Women, in 1965, surely stands out. She also served as president of the Organization of American Historians and president of the Southern Historical Association, and on the advisory boards of the Schlesinger Library, the Princeton University department of history, and the Woodrow Wilson International Center for Scholars.

Anne Firor Scott married Andrew MacKay Scott in 1947, and they are the parents of a daughter and two sons and the grandparents of four children.

When she writes in "A Historian's Odyssey" that the field of women's history is now so full that "it will require considerable skill to make use of it in our teaching and our textbooks," Scott is wrong only in not attributing to herself significant credit for that development.

BOOKS BY ANNE FIROR SCOTT

Unheard Voices: The First Historians of Southern Women. Charlottesville: University of Virginia Press, 1993.

Natural Allies: Women's Associations in American History. Urbana: University of Illinois Press, 1991.

Co-author, with Suzanne Lebsock. *Virginia Women: The First Hundred Years.* Williamsburg, VA: Colonial Williamsburg Foundation, 1988.

Making the Invisible Woman Visible. Urbana: University of Illinois Press, 1984.

Editor, with Libby Carter. *Women and Men.* New York: Praeger, 1977.

Co-author, with Andrew MacKay Scott. *One Half the People.* New York: J. B. Lippincott, 1975; reprints: New York: Harper and Row, 1979; Urbana: University of Illinois Press, 1983.

Editor. *Women in American Life.* Boston: Houghton Mifflin, 1979.

The American Woman: Who Was She? Englewood Cliffs, NJ: Prentice-Hall, 1970.

The Southern Lady. Chicago: University of Chicago Press, 1970.

Editor. *Democracy and Social Ethics,* by Jane Addams. Cambridge, MA: Harvard University Press, 1964.

ADDITIONAL SOURCES

Questionnaire completed by the subject for *American Women Historians, 1700s–1990s: A Biographical Dictionary.*

Scott, Anne Firor. "A Historian's Odyssey." In her *Making the Invisible Woman Visible.* Urbana: University of Illinois Press, 1984, xi–xxvii.

SCOTT, JOAN WALLACH
(1941–   )
French Social History, History of Gender

Born in Brooklyn, New York, on December 18, 1941, Joan Wallach Scott was the daughter of two high school teachers. She knew early in life that she wanted to be a historian. Scott attended Brandeis University as an undergraduate, earning a bachelor's degree magna cum laude in 1962. She continued her studies at the University of Wisconsin, where she earned a Ph.D. in 1969.

Scott's first academic appointment was as assistant professor at the University of Illinois at Chicago Circle. Following that she was at Northwestern University, where she was the first woman faculty member in the history department. She was appointed assistant and then associate professor at the University of North Carolina at Chapel Hill. In 1980 she was appointed Nancy Duke Lewis Professor at Brown University. Again she was a first, this time the first woman to secure tenure in the history department at Brown University. At Brown she also served as director of the Pembroke Center for Teaching and Research on Women.

Scott was only the second woman to be invited to join the faculty of the Institute for Advanced Studies at Princeton University, where she currently works. She had spent a year at the institute, which was founded by Albert Einstein and others in 1930, from 1978 to 1979. As she stated in an interview with Katherine Hinds, Scott saw her appointment to the institute's faculty as significant to women's studies, a field "which has been struggling to legitimize itself in the scholarly world for the last ten to fifteen years."

Joan Scott's first book, *The Glassworkers of Carmaux: French Craftsmen and Political Action in a Nineteenth-Century City,* published in 1974, won the American Historical Association's prize for the best first book written by an American on European history. In this work she tied together the two primary interests of her early professional career, social history and labor history, and made a major contribution to the new labor history. Scott is also well known for her explorations of gender dynamics in history and in historiography. She moved in that direction, she states, when students began to demand courses on women. In her second book, *Women, Work, and Family,* which she wrote with Louise Tilly, Scott went about addressing the invisibility of gender she readily admitted characterized her first book. "I'm most interested in how women figure—actually and symbolically—in working-class history," she told Katherine Hinds in 1985. "Since labor history is my field, it seems appropriate to take these questions about women and gender and work them into labor history." More recently, Joan Scott has been influential in the consideration of French postmodern theory as it applies to the study of history. She borrows from Michel Foucault in arguing that history is the study of politics, not simply politics narrowly defined in governmental terms but rather as "contests that involve power." Power, as Scott and others continue to debate, is not only "a relationship of repression or domination but also a set of relationships or processes that produce positive effects." There are no set data waiting to be used as history, she maintains; all history is decision making, all history is political.

Scott has also provided a great deal of service to the profession, in and outside of her universities. She chaired the Committee on Women Historians for the American Historical Association and the University of North Carolina Committee on the Status of Women. She helped set up women's studies programs at the University of North Carolina and at Brown University.

Joan Scott is married to Donald Scott; they have a son and a daughter.

BOOKS BY JOAN W. SCOTT

Editor. *Love and Politics in Wartime: Letters to My Wife, 1943–45,* by Benedict S. Alper. Urbana: University of Illinois Press, 1992.

Gender and the Politics of History. New York: Columbia University Press, 1988.
With Louise Tilly. *Women, Work, and Family.* New York: Holt, Rinehart and Winston, 1978.
The Glassworkers of Carmaux: French Craftsmen and Political Action in a Nineteenth-Century City. Cambridge, MA: Harvard University Press, 1974.
ADDITIONAL SOURCE
Hinds, Katherine. "Joan Wallach Scott: Breaking New Ground for Women." *Change* 17 (July/Aug. 1985): 48–53.

SEARS, CLARA ENDICOTT
(1863–1960)
U.S. History

Clara Endicott Sears was born in Boston, Massachusetts, on December 16, 1863, to Knyvet Winthrop and Mary Crowninshield (Peabody) Sears. She went to private schools in Boston and was tutored privately in Europe. She became interested in colonial history and the preservation of houses of historical interest. In 1912–13 she bought and restored "Fruitlands," home of Bronson Alcott in Harvard, Massachusetts, where the New Eden Utopian community was started in 1843. She had the oldest house built by the Shakers moved from an abandoned Shaker village at Harvard to Fruitlands Hill in 1911. In between she wrote *Bronson Alcott's Fruitlands* (1915), *Gleanings from Old Shaker Journals* (1916), and *Peace Anthem* (1919). She wrote *Days of Delusions,* a history of the Millerites (1924); *The Great Powwow* (1934); *Wind from the Hills* (1935); *Some American Primitives* (1941); *Highlights Among the Hudson River Artists* (1947); *Snapshots from Old Registers* (taken from the registers of 1880–1900 of the Hotel Vendome in Boston) (1955); and *Early Personal Reminiscences in the Old George Peabody Mansion in Salem* (1956). She also compiled *Prentice Mulford's Works* in 1913 and *The Power Within,* writings of various New Thought authors, in 1914. Sears was a trustee of the Society for the Preservation of New England Antiquities and was awarded a gold medal by the National Society of New England Women in 1942. She was a member of the Society of Mayflower Descendants, Colonial Dames of America, and the New England Historic Genealogical Society. Clara Sears died in Boston on March 25, 1960.
ADDITIONAL SOURCES
AmAu&B; BiCAW; BiIn 7; NatCAB 47, 293–294, 1965; WhNAA; *Bio-Base.*

SEYMOUR, FLORA WARREN
(1888–1948)
Popular Western U.S. History

Flora Warren Seymour was born in 1888 in Cleveland, Ohio, to Charles Payne and Eleanor De Forest (Potter) Smith. She attended George Washington University and received a B.A. in 1906. She edited *Quest* magazine from 1908 to 1912 and was associate editor of the *Woman Lawyer's Journal* in 1918. She studied law, receiving an LL.B. from the Washington College of Law in 1915 and an LL.M. from the Kent College of Law in Chicago in 1916. She was admitted to the District of Columbia Bar in 1915, to the Illinois Bar in 1916, and to practice before the Supreme Court of the United States in 1919. She married George Steele Seymour in 1915 and worked for the United States Indian Service while getting her degrees. Seymour and her husband organized the Order of Bookfellows, a national society of writers and readers. She became the first woman member of the Board of Indian Commissioners in 1922, and in 1926 began writing about the Native Americans she had studied. Seymour wrote *The Indians Today* in 1926, followed by *Story of the Red Man* in 1929. She wrote *Lords of the Valley* and *Women of Trail and Wigwam* in 1930. Ten years passed before she wrote *We Called Them Indians* and *Indian Agents of the Old Frontier* (1941). During this time, she also wrote a number of popular biographies, some for young readers, including *William De Morgan, a Post-Victorian Realist* (1922), *Boy's Life of Fremont* (1928), *Boy's Life of Kit Carson* (1929), *Sam Houston, Patriot* (1930), *Daniel Boone, Pioneer* (1931), *Meriwether Lewis, Trail-Blazer* (1937), and *La Salle, Explorer of Our Midland Empire* (1939). Seymour was a member of the Daughters of the American Revolution and in 1916 and 1917 was president of the Bureau of Volunteer Social Service. During World War I she was on the Women's Committee of the Illinois State Council of Defense and was delegate to the National Council of Women in 1917 and 1919. She died in 1948.

ADDITIONAL SOURCES

InWom; AmAu&B; BiIn 2; OhA&B; WhNAA; BiCAW; WhAm 2; CurBio 42; *Bio-Base*.

SKINNER, CONSTANCE LINDSAY
(1877–1939)
U.S. History

Constance Lindsay Skinner was born in Quesnel, British Columbia, to Robert James Skinner, an agent for the Hudson's Bay Company, and Annie (Lindsay) Skinner on December 7, 1877. She was reared at a fur-trading post in the Peace River area and educated at home. In 1891 the family moved to Vancouver and Constance attended private school. Two years later, she was sent to live with an aunt in California because of health reasons. There she began writing drama and music criticism for the *Los Angeles Times* and the *San Francisco Examiner*. Skinner eventually moved to Chicago and wrote for the *Chicago American,* then to New York City, where she worked as a freelance writer and wrote book reviews for the *Herald Tribune.* She began writing poetry and plays, then was asked to write two volumes dealing with frontier topics as part of the fifty-volume Yale University Chronicles of America series. *Pioneers of the Old Southwest* was published in 1919 and *Adventurers of Oregon* in 1920. In 1925 *Adventures in the Wilderness* was published as part of the Yale Pageant of America series. In 1933

Skinner wrote *Beaver, Kings and Cabins.* Some of her work was criticized as being imprecise, but historian Frederick Jackson Turner praised her writing and the two corresponded. Skinner eventually returned to poetry and fiction from 1925 to 1934, then began editing a monumental history of American rivers. This became the Rivers of America series published by Farrar and Rinehart. The first volume, *Kennebec: Cradle of America* by Robert P. Tristram Coffin, was published in 1937, and more than forty volumes followed. Constance Skinner was working on her own volume on the Missouri River when she died on March 27, 1939, of arteriosclerosis and a coronary occlusion. In 1940 the Women's National Book Association initiated the Constance Lindsay Skinner Award for women who made "an outstanding contribution to the world of books."

ADDITIONAL SOURCES

Constance Skinner, "History as Literature: And the Individual Definition," *Bookman,* Aug. 1919; Frederick Jackson Turner, letter to Skinner and introduction by her in *Wisconsin Magazine of History,* Sept. 1935, pp. 91–103; Jean West Maury, "From a Fur-Trading Post to N.Y.," in *Boston Transcript,* May 6, 1933; Durwward Howes, ed., *American Women, 1937–38; Horn Book,* July-Aug. 1939; obituary in *Publishers' Weekly,* Apr. 1, 1939; obituary in *Library Journal,* Apr. 15, 1939; obituary in NewYT, March 28, 1939; InWom; NatCAB, csv2 and csv5; NotAW; WhAm 1; AmWomWr; LibW; AmBi; AmAu&B; BiIn 1, 4, 6, 11, 12; CanNov; ChPo; DcLEL; DcNAA; JBA 34; MorJA; OxAm; OxCan; Str&VC; TwCA; TwCA Supp.; WhNAA; YABC 1; *Bio-Base.*

SKLAR, KATHRYN KISH
(1939–   )
U.S. Women's History

Kathryn Kish Sklar was born on December 26, 1939, in Columbus, Ohio, of Scotch-Irish ancestry on her mother's side and Hungarian ancestry on her father's side. Her parents were small business owners who had their start as grocers. Kathryn attended public schools in Columbus, and counts as her most significant early influence her mother, who "held together the diverse ingredients required to run a successful family business."

Sklar attended Radcliffe College, graduating magna cum laude in history and literature in 1965. She decided to pursue graduate work in history, hoping to understand the ways in which things are shaped by what went before, to pursue meaningful work capable of influencing her own time, and to transcend her own time by connecting with the past. Sklar did her graduate work at the University of Michigan, earning a master's degree in 1967 and a Ph.D. in 1969. She also has an honorary doctorate from Eastern Michigan University.

Kathryn (Kitty) Sklar's first academic appointment was at the University of Michigan, where she was lecturer and then assistant professor from 1969 to 1974. From 1974 to 1981 Sklar was associate professor of history at the University of California at Los Angeles. She attained the rank of professor at UCLA in 1981 and stayed there until 1988, when she took a position as Distinguished Professor at Binghamton University, the State University of New York.

The author or editor of ten books and author of ten book chapters and a dozen scholarly articles, Sklar is perhaps best known for her first book, *Catherine Beecher: A Study in American Domesticity,* and her most recent, *Florence Kelley and the Nation's Work: The Rise of Women's Political Culture, 1830–1900.* The first, a biography of Beecher and an exploration of nineteenth-century domestic culture, was a winner of the Berkshire Prize and a finalist for the National Book Award. The study of Florence Kelley represents Sklar's second major attempt at writing biography, and has already earned significant attention. "Sklar has used her extraordinary talent as a biographer to reveal both intensely personal aspects of Florence Kelley's life and the dynamics of social reform in late nineteenth-century America," writes historian David Montgomery. And the collection she co-edited with Linda Kerber and Alice Kessler-Harris, *U.S. History as Women's History,* brings together the work of many of the most eminent senior scholars in the field.

Asked about her most significant achievements, aside from teaching and publications, Sklar cites her work as the founder and coordinator for ten years of the Workshop on Teaching U.S. Women's History. This workshop for college teachers of U.S. women's history continues to thrive nearly twenty years after its inception. Sklar also co-coordinated, with Gerda Lerner, a National Endowment for the Humanities Conference of Graduate Teachers in Women's History, held in 1988 in Wisconsin. She has also chaired the committees of sixteen completed dissertations and is currently chairing the committees of about that many more.

Sklar has been the recipient of many fellowships, including those from the National Humanities Center, the Andrew W. Mellon Foundation, the Woodrow Wilson International Center for Scholars, and the American Association of University Women. She has served the American Historical Association, Organization of American Historians, and Berkshire Conference of Women Historians in several capacities. Most recently, she served as the president of the Society for Historians of the Gilded Age and Progressive Era and as chair of the Upstate New York Women's History Organization. Sklar has served on the editorial boards of over a dozen publications, including *American Quarterly, Journal of American History, Feminist Studies, Ms,* and *American National Biography.*

Kathryn Kish Sklar's partner is historian Thomas Dublin. She is the mother of two children, Leonard Sklar and Susan Sklar Friedman, and the grandmother of Nevona Sklar Friedman. Her hobby is family photography.

BOOKS BY KATHRYN KISH SKLAR

Editor. *Women's Rights and the Anti-Slavery Movement: A Brief Collection of Documents.* New York: Bedford Books, St. Martin's Press, forthcoming.

Editor, with Anja Schuler and Susan Strasser. *A Transatlantic Dialogue: Women and Social Reform in Germany and the United States, 1880–1930.* Washington, DC: German Historical Institute and Cornell University Press, forthcoming.

Florence Kelley and the Nation's Work: The Rise of Women's Political Culture, 1830–1900. Volume 1 of a two-volume study. New Haven, CT: Yale University Press, 1995.

Editor, with Linda Kerber and Alice Kessler-Harris. *U.S. History as Women's History: New Feminist Essays.* Chapel Hill: University of North Carolina Press, 1995.

Editor, with Martin Bulmer and Kevin Bales. *The Social Survey in Historical Perspective, 1880–1940.* Cambridge: Cambridge University Press, 1991.

Editor, with Thomas Dublin. *Women and Power in American History: A Reader.* 2 vols. New Jersey: Prentice-Hall, 1991.

Editor. *The Autobiography of Florence Kelley: Notes of Sixty Years.* Chicago: Charles Kerr, 1986.

Editor. *A Treatise on Domestic Economy,* by Catherine Beecher. New York: Schocken, reprint of 1841 original, 1981.

Editor. *Uncle Tom's Cabin, or Life Among the Lowly; The Minister's Wooing; Oldtown Folks,* by Harriet Beecher Stowe. New York: Literary Classics of the United States, 1981.

Catherine Beecher: A Study in American Domesticity. New Haven, CT: Yale University Press, 1973; paperback, Norton, 1976.

ADDITIONAL SOURCES

Gallagher, Dorothy. Rev. of *Florence Kelley and the Nation's Work,* by Kathryn Kish Sklar. *New York Times Book Review,* July 9, 1995, 9.

Questionnaire completed by the subject for *American Women Historians, 1700s–1990s: A Biographical Dictionary.*

SMITH, BONNIE G.
(1940–)
European History

Bonnie G. Smith was born on June 30, 1940, in Bridgeport, Connecticut. Her father was a clergyman; her mother was a full-time homemaker. Growing up, she was influenced by her parents' political and social activism. A love of history, an interest in culture and society, and her involvement in the women's movement provided the impetus for Smith to become a historian. She attended Smith College, earning a bachelor's degree there in 1962. She went on to graduate school at the University of Rochester, earning a Ph.D. in 1976.

Smith's first academic appointment was at the University of Rochester, where she was a lecturer in history from 1976 to 1977. From 1977 to 1981 she was assistant professor of history at the University of Wisconsin at Parkside. She left Wisconsin to return to the University of Rochester, where she was assistant professor from 1981 to 1984, associate professor from 1984 to 1988, and professor from 1988 to 1990. Since 1990 Smith has been professor of history at Rutgers University. She has also held visiting appointments at the University of California at Irvine, Universitat Bielefeld, and Princeton University. She also spent a year as Directeur d'études associés at the Ecole des Hautes Etudes in France.

Bonnie Smith is the author, co-author, editor, or co-editor of five books. Her first book, *Ladies of the Leisure Class: The Bourgeoises of Northern France in the Nineteenth Century,* published in 1981 and subsequently translated into French and Japanese, explores the domestic life of women in the families that ran the textile industry in the Nord. For that work and her second book, *Confessions of a Concierge,* Smith became known as a historian who drew on the skills of the anthropologist in her research. She is also the author of twenty articles and three books in progress. One of those, *Pages from History: Imperialism,* is forthcoming.

Smith has held fellowships from the Guggenheim Foundation, the Shelby Cullom Davis Center for Historical Studies at Princeton University, the American Council of Learned Societies, the National Humanities Center, and the University of Rochester. In 1979 she received the University of Wisconsin's Distinguished Teaching Award. Smith also designed a project, co-sponsored by the Organization of American Historians, to integrate the study of women into survey courses. She has served as a consultant to the Selection Committee of Brown University's Pembroke Center and as referee and consultant for over twenty publishers and for several journals. She has been on the board of editors of *French Historical Studies,* a consulting editor to *Feminist Studies,* and on the board of associate editors for *Journal of Women's History.*

Smith's professional service also includes serving on several committees for the American Historical Association, the Berkshire Conference of Women Historians, and the Society for French Historical Studies. She has led a faculty development seminar and served on a dissertation fellowship review panel for the National Endowment for the Humanities. She has also been active in planning advanced placement tests in European history, serving on and currently chairing the Educational Testing Service's Advanced Placement European History Test Development Committee.

Bonnie Smith's spouse is Donald R. Kelley. She has two children, Patience H. Smith and Patrick W. Smith, and one stepson, John R. Kelley. Her interests include art, music, and theater.

BOOKS BY BONNIE G. SMITH

With Lynn Hunt et al. *The Challenge of the West: Peoples and Cultures from the Neolithic to the Global Age.* Lexington, MA: D. C. Heath, 1995.

Editor, with Donald R. Kelley, and translator. *What Is Property?,* by P. J. Proudhon. Cambridge: Cambridge University Press, 1994.

Changing Lives: Women in European History Since 1700. Lexington, MA: D. C. Heath, 1989.

Confessions of a Concierge: Madame Lucie's History of Twentieth Century France. New Haven, CT: Yale University Press, 1985. French translation, Librarie Académique Perrin, 1987.

Ladies of the Leisure Class: The Bourgeoises of Northern France in the Nineteenth Century. Princeton, NJ: Princeton University Press, 1981. French translation, Librairie Académique Perrin, 1989; Japanese translation, Hosei University Press, 1995.

Pages from History: Imperialism. New York: Oxford University Press, forthcoming.

ADDITIONAL SOURCE

Questionnaire completed by the subject for *American Women Historians, 1700s–1990s: A Biographical Dictionary.*

STANARD, MARY MANN PAGE NEWTON
(1865–1929)
Local History

Mary Mann Page Newton Stanard was born in Westmoreland County, Virginia, to the Rt. Rev. John Brockenbrough and Roberta Page (Williamson) Newton. She was educated in ordinary schools near her home, then graduated from the Leache-Wood School in Norfolk. She married William Glover Stanard, corresponding secretary of the Virginia Historical Society, on April 17, 1900, and moved to Richmond. She began collaborating with her husband on *The Colonial Virginia Register,* published in 1902, then on her own wrote *The Story of Bacon's Rebellion,* published in 1907. She wrote several biographies including *The Dreamer; A Romantic Rendering of the Life-Story of Edgar Allan Poe* (1909), *John Marshall* (1913), and *John Brockenbrough Newton* (1924). She also wrote a series of social histories of Virginia including *Colonial Virginia, Its People and Customs* (1917) and *Richmond, Its People and Its Story* (1923). She edited *Edgar Allan Poe Letters Till Now Unpublished in the Valentine Museum, Richmond, Va.* in 1925. Her last book, *The Story of Virginia's First Century,* was published in 1928. She was historian of the Association for the Preservation of Virginia Antiquities until her death and was vice-president of the Virginia Society of the Colonial Dames of America. She was also on the executive committee of the Edgar Allan Poe Shrine and the Virginia War History Commission. Mary Stanard died in Richmond on June 5, 1929.

ADDITIONAL SOURCES

Daniel Grinnan, *Virginia Magazine of History and Biography,* July 1929; obituary in *Richmond Times-Dispatch,* June 6, 1929; AmAu&B; BiDSA; ChPo; DcAmB; DcNAA; WhAm 1; WomWWA 14; *Bio-Base.*

STARKEY, MARION LENA
(1901–   )
U.S. History

Marion Lena Starkey was born on April 13, 1901, in Worcester, Massachusetts, to Arthur E. Starkey, a painter and publisher, and Alice T. (Gray) Starkey. She received a B.S. from Boston University in 1922, an M.A. from Boston University in 1935, and did graduate study at Harvard in 1946. She was editor of the *Saugus Herald* in Saugus, Massachusetts, from 1924 to 1929, then became an associate professor of English at Hampton Institute, Hampton, Virginia, from 1930 to 1943. Her first book, *The First Plantation: A History of Hampton and Elizabeth City County, Va., 1607–1887,* was privately printed. She entered the Women's Army Corps in 1943 and remained until 1945 as translator and editor for the Office of Strategic Services in Algiers, Bari, Caserta, and Paris. She returned to the United States and became an assistant professor of English at the University of Connecticut, New London from 1946 to 1950 and the University of Connecticut, Hartford from 1950 to 1961 before becoming a full-time writer.

Marion Starkey wrote *The Cherokee Nation* in 1946; *The Devil in Massachusetts: A Modern Enquiry into the Salem Witch Trials* in 1949; *A Little Rebellion* in 1955; *Land Where Our Fathers Died: The Settling of the Eastern Shores, 1607–1735* in 1962; *Striving To Make It My Home: The Story of Americans from Africa* in 1964; *The Congregational Way: The Role of the Pilgrims and Their Heirs In Shaping America* in 1966; *Lace Cuffs and Leather Aprons: Popular Struggles in the Federalist Era, 1738–1800* in 1972; *The Visionary Girls: Witchcraft in Salem Village* (juvenile) in 1973; and *The Tall Man from Boston* in 1975. It was said that in *The Devil in Massachusetts* she was the first historian to use the unpublished verbatim transcriptions of documents and papers on witchcraft in Salem.

ADDITIONAL SOURCES

ConAu 1R; ConAu 1NR; ForWC 70; SmATA 8, 13; WhoAmW 58, 61, 64; WrDr 76, 80, 82, 84; BiIn 11; *Bio-Base*.

STERN, MADELEINE BETTINA
(1912–   )
U.S. Women's History

Madeleine Bettina Stern was born on July 1, 1912, in New York City to Moses R. and Lillie (Mack) Stern. She received a B.A. from Barnard College in 1932 and an M.A. from Columbia University in 1934. She taught high school English from 1934 to 1943, when she received a Guggenheim fellowship. In 1945 she opened a rare book store with Leona Rostenberg. She also began writing history, beginning with *The Life of Margaret Fuller* in 1942. *Louisa May Alcott* was published in 1950 and *Purple Passage: The Life of Mrs. Frank Leslie* in 1953. *Imprints on History: Book Publishers and American Frontiers* was published in 1956 and *We the Women: Career Firsts of Nineteenth Century America* in 1963. She wrote *So Much in a Lifetime: The Story of Dr. Isabel Barrows* in 1964, *Queen of Publishers' Row: Mrs. Frank Leslie* in 1965, and *The Pantarch: A Biography of Stephen Pearl Andrews* in 1968. *Heads and Headlines: The Phrenological Fowlers* came out in 1971, and in 1972 she edited the four-volume *Women on the Move*. She wrote *Old and Rare: Thirty Years in the Book Business* with her partner Leona Rostenberg in 1974 and edited *The Victoria Woodhull Reader, Louisa's Wonder Book: An Undiscovered Alcott Juvenile,* and *Behind a Mask: The Unknown Thrillers of Louisa May Alcott* in 1975. Stern continued with *Plots and Counterplots: More Unknown Thrillers of Louisa May Alcott* in 1976.

ADDITIONAL SOURCES

ChPo S3; AuBYP; ChPo; ConAu 7NR; ConAu 17R; DrAS 78E; DrAS 82E; IntA&W 77, 82; SmATA 14; WhoWor J 72, 78; WrDr 76, 80, 82, 84; BiIn 8, 10, 12; ForWC 70; WhoAmJ 8; WhoAmW 58, 61, 64, 66, 68, 70, 72, 74, 75, 77, 83; WhoE 7, 77; *Bio-Base*.

STEVENS, ROSEMARY A.
(1935–   )
History of Medicine

Rosemary A. Stevens was born on March 18, 1935, in Great Britain, of Anglo-Saxon and Celtic ancestry. Her father was a bank employee; her mother was a full-time homemaker. Stevens was schooled in British state girls' schools. Her early influences included World War II and the promise of education, which she says was a way of "breaking out." Seeking a way of understanding power relations and explaining the present, Stevens became interested in English and history. She obtained a bachelor's degree from St. Hilda's College, Oxford University, in 1957. In 1959 Stevens earned a diploma in social administration from the University of Manchester. She earned a master's degree from Oxford in 1961, then a master's in public health from Yale University in 1963. Stevens's Ph.D., which she completed at Yale in 1968, was in epidemiology.

Stevens worked as assistant professor of public health at Yale University from 1968 to 1971. She was then promoted to associate professor, and she earned full professor status in 1974. Stevens left Yale in 1976 to work as professor of health systems management and adjunct professor of political science at Tulane University. She served as chair of the department of health systems management from 1977 to 1978. Since 1979 Rosemary Stevens has been at the University of Pennsylvania, as professor of history and sociology of science. She has also served as a senior fellow at the Leonard Davis Institute for Health Economics, as chair of the department of history and sociology of science, as UPS Foundation Professor in the Social Sciences, and, since 1991, as dean and Thomas S. Gates Professor in the School of Arts and Sciences.

Rosemary Stevens has also held many visiting academic appointments, at the London School of Economics and Political Science, at Johns Hopkins University, and at the Brookings Institution. She has worked in administration for the Ministry of Health and the Princess Beatrice Hospital in London, Gaylord Hospital in Wallingford, Connecticut, and for the Government of Tanganyika Commission on Health Services.

Stevens is the author or co-author of six books and the author of over fifty articles. *In Sickness and in Wealth: American Hospitals in the Twentieth Century* earned Stevens the James A. Hamilton Book Award of the American College of Healthcare Executives for the best book of 1990. As Morris Vogel wrote, the book can be read "as a fascinating history of twentieth-century medicine, as a powerful analysis of contemporary social policy, and as an exploration of

American values.'' She has written on the hospital as a social and medical institution, on historical changes in internal medicine, and on licensing and education of medical students.

The list of Rosemary Stevens's professional and consulting appointments is too long to include here. She has served on and chaired many boards and advisory panels, including those for the National Board of Medical Examiners, the American Board of Pediatrics, the Board of Overseers of Dartmouth Medical School, and the Institute of Medicine, National Academy of Sciences. She has served the federal government in this capacity as well, through the Office of Technology Assessment of the U.S. Congress, the U.S. Department of Health and Human Services, the National Institutes of Health, and the U.S. House of Representatives Advisory Panel on National Health Insurance. An international as well as national consultant, Stevens has also served as a consultant to the World Health Organization in Geneva.

The list of Stevens's awards and fellowships is equally long, and includes membership in the American Academy of Arts and Sciences and fellowships from the Rockefeller Foundation and the Guggenheim Foundation. She is an Alpha Omega Alpha honorary member since 1990, and has received honorary doctorates from the Medical College of Pennsylvania, Rutgers University, Hahnemann University, and Northeast Ohio College of Medicine. Stevens received the 1990 Baxter Foundation Prize for distinction in health services research, the 1990 Welch Medal for distinction in the history of medicine from the American Association for the History of Medicine, the 1990 Arthur Viseltear Award from the American Public Health Association, and the 1990 American Board of Medical Specialties Special Award for unusually important contributions to specialist certification. She has also lectured widely, in and outside the United States.

Rosemary Stevens has been a United States citizen since 1968. Her second marriage is to Jack Barchas. She is the mother of a daughter, Carey, an aircraft mechanic, and a son, Richard, a student nurse. Her interests include antiques, piano, and painting.

BOOKS BY ROSEMARY A. STEVENS

In Sickness and in Wealth: American Hospitals in the Twentieth Century. New York: Basic Books, 1989; paperback, 1990.

With Louis Wolf Goodman and Stephen S. Mick. *The Alien Doctors: Foreign Medical Graduates in American Hospitals.* New York: Wiley-Interscience, 1978.

American Medicine and the Public Interest. New Haven, CT: Yale University Press, 1971; paperback, 1974.

With Robert Stevens. *Welfare Medicine in America: A Case Study of Medicaid.* New York: Free Press, 1974.

With Joan Vermeulen. *Foreign-Trained Physicians and American Medicine.* Washington, DC: U.S. Department of Health, Education and Welfare, 1972.

Medical Practice in Modern England: The Impact of Specialization and State Medicine. New Haven, CT: Yale University Press, 1966.

ADDITIONAL SOURCES

Questionnaire completed by the subject for *American Women Historians, 1700s–1990s: A Biographical Dictionary.*

Vogel, Morris J. Review of *In Sickness and in Wealth: American Hospitals in the Twentieth Century,* by Rosemary A. Stevens. *Isis* 82 (June 1991): 410–411.

STROBEL, MARGARET ANN
(1946–)
African Women's History, History of Imperialism

Margaret Ann Strobel was born on February 15, 1946, in Grand Forks, North Dakota, of German, Norwegian, and Swedish ancestry. Her father was an assistant superintendent for a Standard Oil Company warehouse; her mother was a homemaker, then a motel maid and factory worker. Strobel attended Winship Elementary School in Grand Forks, and then Central Junior High, Westwood Junior High, and St. Louis Senior High School in St. Louis Park, Missouri.

Although neither of her parents went to college, they provided Margaret Strobel with the motivation to attain an education. Her father was her biggest early influence. He was basically self-taught, having gone to small two-room schools in rural North Dakota, but he loved to read philosophy, history, and Russian novelists, especially Tolstoy and Dostoyevsky. As a young man he wrote a history of his own family, interviewing his grandfather about the Strobels' migration from southern Germany into the Odessa area under Catherine the Great and their subsequent immigration to the Midwest in the 1880s. Margaret read her father's book and many of the others he regularly purchased from estate sales of people living near the University of North Dakota. The other early influence on her life was her high school humanities teacher, Marjorie Bingham, who modeled for Strobel the life of an intellectual.

Strobel attended Michigan State University on a National Merit Scholarship earmarked for children of Standard Oil employees. As a first-year student, she was challenged by a faculty member to go to Nigeria as part of a university program. That same year she took an anthropology course from a professor who was a Bengal specialist. Strobel initially went to Africa with a strong interest in Indian studies, and she pursued South Asia studies for a time. She then decided to pursue African history, and applied to and was accepted into an African history program at the University of California at Los Angeles.

At UCLA in the late 1960s, Strobel became involved in the feminist movement. Her Ph.D. exams took place the day after four students were killed by national guardsmen at Kent State University, and her exams were stopped before the completion of the agreement of the committee because the police were assaulting students outside the building. At the encouragement of her advisor, Strobel combined her interests in feminism and African history and proposed a dissertation in African women's history, a field with not a single monograph yet published. She received a Fulbright Hayes dissertation fellowship. "I am amazed that the selection committee took the leap of faith and gave me what was by the early 1970s a very scarce resource," she recalls.

After receiving her doctorate in 1975, Strobel accepted a position as interim director of women's studies and lecturer in history at the University of California at Los Angeles. From 1978 to 1979 she was lecturer in women's studies at San Diego State University, and in 1979 she accepted a position as associate professor of women's studies and history at the University of Illinois at Chicago. Strobel was promoted to professor in 1988. She has also served the Women's Studies Program at the University of Illinois, as director from 1979 to 1990 and as acting director from 1990 to 1991.

Margaret Strobel is the author or editor of six books, one of which, *Muslim Women in Mombasa, 1890–1975,* was the co-winner of the Herskovits Award from the African Studies Association. A second, *Three Swahili Women: Life Histories from Mombasa, Kenya,* has been translated into Swahili. She has explored issues related to African women's history, Western women and imperialism, and restoring women to history in studies of Africa, Asia, Latin America and the Caribbean, and the Middle East. Dorothy Helly, in a review of Strobel's *European Women and the Second British Empire,* writes that she "demonstrates that rewriting an imperial history that is sensitive to gender, culture, race, sexuality and power is an exhilarating enterprise." Strobel has also written more than fifteen scholarly articles. Her current research interests have taken her in a somewhat different direction: her book in progress is titled *Feminism in the 1970s: Socialist Feminism and the Women's Liberation Unions.*

Strobel has held many fellowships and received many awards. She has been a fellow with the Fulbright Foundation, the Woodrow Wilson Foundation, the Institute for the Humanities at the University of Illinois, and the National Endowment for the Humanities. She was selected as one of fifteen women for a biennial photo exhibit, "Celebrating Chicago's Women Leaders," in 1992, and was one of ninety women to be honored in "Full Circle," a public art project in 1993. She received the University of Illinois at Chicago's Award for Excellence in Teaching in 1993 and is currently a Great Cities Institute Scholar at the university.

Strobel has provided a great deal of professional service, from co-coordinating the first National Women's Studies Association national conference in 1979, to serving as chair for the American Historical Association's program committee for the 1997 annual conference. She is currently co-planner for a forthcoming conference on women and global history, chair of the elections committee for the National Women's Studies Association, and member and future chair of the selection committee for the Joan Kelly Prize in Women's History and Theory for the American Historical Association.

Margaret Strobel is married to William J. Barclay and has one child, Jessica Barclay-Strobel. Bill gave up his job as an assistant professor of sociology at San Diego State University so that she could take up her job at the University of Illinois at Chicago. Strobel's interests include canoeing, reading feminist murder mysteries, and "overcommitting" herself to activities inside and outside the university. The activist interests that she developed while at UCLA influence her current activities, which include addressing issues of multiculturalism and gender in the schools; running candidates for local office; and, on campus, pushing feminist issues, building alliances with other units, and pushing the university orientation toward service and relevance to the community while it remains a research institution.

BOOKS BY MARGARET ANN STROBEL

Editor, with Nupur Chaudhuri. *Western Women and Imperialism: Complicity and Resistance.* Bloomington: Indiana University Press, 1992.

Editor, with Cheryl Johnson-Odim. *Expanding the Borders of Women's History: Essays on Women in the Third World.* Bloomington: Indiana University Press, 1992.

European Women and the Second British Empire. Bloomington: Indiana University Press, 1991.

Editor, with Sarah Mirza. *Three Swahili Women: Life Histories from Mombasa, Kenya.* Bloomington: Indiana University Press, 1989; Swahili translation, Indiana University Press, 1990.

Editor, with Cheryl Johnson-Odim. *Restoring Women to History: Women in the History of Africa, Asia, Latin America and the Caribbean, and the Middle East.* Bloomington, IN: Organization of American Historians, 1988.

Muslim Women in Mombasa, 1890–1975. New Haven, CT: Yale University Press, 1979.

ADDITIONAL SOURCES

Helly, Dorothy O. Review of *European Women and the Second British Empire,* by Margaret Strobel. *American Historical Review* 97 (Oct. 1992): 1216.

Questionnaire completed by the subject for *American Women Historians, 1700s–1990s: A Biographical Dictionary.*

T

TARBELL, IDA MINERVA
(1857–1944)
Business History

Ida Minerva Tarbell was born on November 5, 1857, on a farm in Erie County, Pennsylvania, to Franklin Summer Tarbell, the first manufacturer of wooden tanks for the oil industry in Pennsylvania, and Esther Ann (McCullough) Tarbell, a former teacher whose ancestors included Sir Walter Raleigh and Samuel Seabury, America's first Anglican bishop. Ida attended local public schools after her family moved from the rowdy settlement of Rouseville near the oil fields of Pennsylvania to Titusville. She received her B.A. from Allegheny College in Meadville, Pennsylvania, as one of only five women enrolled and the only woman in the freshman class. She graduated in 1880 and began teaching at the Poland (Ohio) Union Seminary, then returned to Meadville to write for *Chautauquan* magazine from 1883 to 1891.

In 1891 Tarbell went to Paris to study the role of women in the French Revolution. She enrolled at the Sorbonne and the Collège de France and continued writing freelance, including articles for the newly formed *McClure's* magazine. In 1894 S. S. McClure, the publisher, encouraged her to return to New York to write full time for the magazine and to supply the text for a collection of Napoleon prints he was about to publish. Her articles on Napoleon were printed in book form in 1895 under the title *A Short Life of Napoleon Bonaparte,* which sold 100,000 copies. (It was republished as *McClure's Complete Life of Napoleon* in London, also in 1895, and enlarged as *A Life of Napoleon Bonaparte* in 1901.) In 1896 she published *Madame Roland: A Biographical Study* and *The Early Life of Abraham Lincoln* (assisted by J. McCan Davis). In 1897 she edited *Napoleon's Addresses: Selections from the Proclamations, Speeches and Correspondence of Napoleon Bonaparte.* In 1900 her articles on Abraham Lincoln, aided by J. McCan Davis, were collected into a book entitled *The Life of Abraham Lincoln, Drawn from Original Sources and Containing Many Speeches, Letters and Telegrams Hitherto Unpublished* in two volumes. It became the standard work on Lincoln until 1947, when the Lincoln papers were finally made available to researchers.

In 1900 Tarbell also began her famous series of articles on the development of the Standard Oil Trust, published in book form as *The History of the Standard Oil Company* in 1904. In 1906 Tarbell, Lincoln Steffens, and Ray Stannard Baker purchased the *American Magazine,* which they edited until 1915. Tarbell wrote two more books on Lincoln, *He Knew Lincoln* (1907) and *Father Abraham* (1909), and edited one, *Selections from the Letters, Speeches and State Papers of Abraham Lincoln* (1911), and began another series of articles on the tariff which was published in 1911 in book form as *The Tariff in Our Times.* In 1912 she wrote *The Business of Being a Woman* and in 1915 *The Ways of Woman.* She studied the trends in business and wrote *New Ideals in Business: An Account of Their Practice and Their Effects upon Men and Profits* in 1916. In 1919 she wrote *The Rising Tide: The Story of Sabinsport* (her only novel) before returning to Lincoln for *In Lincoln's Chair* (1920), *Boy Scouts' Life of Lincoln* (1921), *He Knew Lincoln and Other Billy Brown Stories* (1922), and *In the Footsteps of the Lincolns* (1924). In 1922 Tarbell wrote *Peacemakers— Blessed and Otherwise: At an International Conference,* then two biographies of business leaders, *The Life of Elbert H. Gary: The Story of Steel* (1925) and *Owen D. Young: A New Type of Industrial Leader* (1932), followed by *A Reporter for Lincoln: Story of Henry E. Wing, Soldier and Newspaperman* in 1927.

When *American Magazine* was sold in 1915, Tarbell became a lecturer for Chautauqua on business; she continued this career until 1932. She was also on the Woman's Committee of the United States Council of National Defense in World War I and was a delegate to President Wilson's Industrial Conference in 1919 and President Harding's Conference on Unemployment in 1921. Tarbell wrote one last book on business in 1935, *The Nationalizing of Business, 1878– 1898,* as part of the distinguished A History of American Life series edited by Arthur M. Schlesinger, Sr., and Dixon Ryan Fox. She continued to teach courses on the methods of biography into her eighties; she published her autobiography, *All in the Day's Work,* in 1939 at the age of eighty-two. Ida Tarbell died of pneumonia in Bridgeport, Connecticut, on January 6, 1944.

ADDITIONAL SOURCES

Victoria and Robert O. Case, *We Call It Culture* (1948); Benjamin P. Thomas, *Portrait for Posterity: Lincoln and His Biographers* (1947); Louis Filler, *Crusaders for American Liberalism* (1939); Frank L. Mott, *A History of American Magazines,* v. 3 and 4 (1938– 1957); David M. Chalmers, *The Social and Political Ideas of the Muckrakers* (1964); Virginia Hamilton, "The Gentlewoman and the Robber Baron," *American Heritage,* Apr. 1970; papers at Allegheny College in Meadville, Pennsylvania, at the Drake Memorial Museum, Titusville, Pennsylvania, and at Smith College in Northampton, Massachusetts; Kathleen Brady, *Ida Tarbell: Portrait of a Muckraker* (1984); OxAm; REn; REnAL; TwCA; TwCA Supp.; WebAB; WebAB 79; DcAmB S3; DcLEL; DcNAA; EncAB;

GoodHs; InWom; LibW; LinLibS; McGEWB; NatCAB 14; NotAW; HerW; IntDcWB; CurBio 44; LinLibL; HarEnUS; WhLit: AmAu&B; AmWomWr; ApCAB x; BiD&SB; BiIn 1, 2, 3, 4, 5, 6, 8, 9, 10, 11; CnDAL; DcAmAu; WhAm 2; WhNAA; WomWWA 14; *Bio-Base.*

TATE, MERZE
(1905–   )
European and U.S. Diplomatic History

Merze Tate was born February 6, 1905, in central Michigan, the daughter and granddaughter of black pioneers. By the time she was five years old, a one-room schoolhouse had been built less than a quarter mile from her home. After elementary school she attended Blanchard High School, which was four miles from home. Tate walked each way, sometimes wading in snow up to her hips or water up to her ankles. Tate was the only black student and the valedictorian of her tenth grade class, the last class she could complete at the school, which was destroyed by fire. Tate completed high school in Battle Creek, then enrolled at Western Michigan Teachers College, now Western Michigan University. She graduated in 1927, with the highest scholastic record at the college and as the first "colored" American at Western Michigan College to be awarded a bachelor of arts degree.

Despite her excellent academic record, racism kept Merze Tate from securing a job: blacks were prevented from teaching in Michigan's secondary schools. Several administrators at the college loaned Tate money to secure employment outside the state. She took a position at the new Crispus Attucks High School in Indianapolis, where she taught for five years. While there she attended summer sessions at Columbia University, earning a master's degree at Teachers College in 1930. In 1932 she matriculated at Oxford University, the first African-American woman to do so, and she earned a bachelor's degree there in 1935. After a summer session at Harvard, Tate decided to pursue graduate study there. She became the first African-American woman to receive the Harvard University and Radcliffe College Ph.D. degree in government.

Tate's first academic appointment after completing the Ph.D. was as dean of women and associate professor of political science at Morgan State University. After a year at Morgan, she joined the history department at Howard University. She and Caroline Ware, also appointed that year, were the first female members of Howard University's department of history. She retired from the faculty at Howard in 1977 after a very distinguished career.

During the 1940s, Tate published her first two books, *The Disarmament Illusion: The Movement for a Limitation of Armaments to 1907* and *The United States and Armaments,* both of which have been widely consulted for their insights on armaments and on disarmament. Her research through the late 1950s and 1960s focused on the expansion and rivalry of the Great Powers in the Pacific. She received grants from the American Council of Learned Societies, the Rockefeller Foundation, the *Washington Evening Star,* and Howard University. As a result of her research in the United States and in England, France, West Germany, Fiji, New Zealand, and Australia, she completed two books and thirty scholarly articles on diplomatic history. One of these books, *The United States and the Hawaiian Kingdom: A Political History,* was a best-seller for Yale University Press during 1965 and 1966. The second, *Hawaii: Reciprocity or Annexation,* was also considered a major contribution to the field. In 1973 twenty-seven of her articles on Pacific affairs were published in one book, *Diplomacy in the Pacific.* Tate continues to write through her retirement, having now published five books and fifty scholarly articles.

Merze Tate has served as a member of the National Advisory Board of the W.E.B. DuBois Institute at Harvard University and on the Advisory Committee on Black Women's Oral History for the Schlesinger Library on the History of Women at Radcliffe College. She has received dozens of awards, including the National Urban League Achievement Award, the Detroit Mayor's Award of Merit, the American Black Artist's Pioneer Award, and the Radcliffe College Alumnae Achievement Award. She also received the tenth annual national Distinguished Alumnus Award of the American Association of State Colleges and Universities. For this award, Tate was chosen from among nominees from roughly 340 state colleges and universities.

Merze Tate has traveled extensively, for professional and personal reasons. She has traveled around the world twice, has visited eleven countries in Africa, and has traveled to or through Europe eight times. Among her other interests are cooking, photography, and contract bridge. She is also an inventor who holds two patents, one of which is for an ice cream maker. She has also worked to see that others succeed; Tate, who has donated generously to individual students, reports that none of these students has defaulted on their loans or dropped out of school. There is a Merze Tate Fellowship for the Mary Graham Bunting Institute at Radcliffe College, a Merze Tate Scholarship at Western Michigan University, and a Merze Tate Fund at Howard University. She has received honorary degrees from several colleges and universities, including Western Michigan University, Morgan State University, Lincoln University, and Bowie State College.

Although Merze Tate no longer teaches, she is not forgotten at Howard University, especially by the women who have come after her. Mary Frances Berry was among Tate's students. The following quote from Dean Annette Eaton's letter honoring Tate when she was still at Howard continues to resonate:

Rarely do those in the academic world have the opportunity to know as a colleague a truly great, or truly world-renowned scholar. When that precious opportunity is given to the women on a campus by one of their own, it provides the inspiration, the strength, and the courage to continue the fight against the prevailing atmosphere of paternalism. ... This is what you mean to Howard University and especially to its women. You are the model for us to copy, not just to gaze upon. You are the standard to be kept before our eyes as we shape our own careers.

BOOKS BY MERZE TATE

Diplomacy in the Pacific: A Collection of Twenty-Seven Articles on Diplomacy in the Pacific and Influence of the Sandwich (Hawaiian) Islands Missionaries. Washington, DC: Howard University, 1973.

Hawaii: Reciprocity or Annexation. East Lansing: Michigan State University Press, 1968.

The United States and the Hawaiian Kingdom. New Haven, CT: Yale University Press, 1965.

The United States and Armaments. Cambridge, MA: Harvard University Press, 1948; reprinted 1969.

The Disarmament Illusion: The Movement for a Limitation of Armaments to 1907. New York: Macmillan, 1942; reprint, Russell and Russell, 1970.

ADDITIONAL SOURCE

Harris, Joseph E. "Professor Merze Tate (1905–): A Profile." *Profiles* (Howard University Graduate School of Arts and Sciences) (Dec. 1981): 1–24.

TAYLOR, LILY ROSS
(1886–1969)
Roman History

Lily Ross Taylor was born in Auburn, Alabama, to William Dana Taylor, a railway engineer, and Mary (Ross) Taylor. The family moved often, and Lily attended a number of schools before receiving an A.B. from the University of Wisconsin in 1906. She entered Bryn Mawr College in 1906 and attended the American Academy in Rome in 1909–10. She received a Ph.D. from Bryn Mawr in 1912 with the thesis "The Cults of Ostia," which was published as a book in 1912. She became a Latin instructor at Vassar in 1912, remaining until 1927. In 1917 she was the first woman fellow of the American Academy in Rome, but interrupted her studies during World War I to join the American Red Cross and serve in Italy and the Balkans. Her American Academy fellowship was renewed in 1919, and in 1927 she became professor of Latin and chair of the department at Bryn Mawr College.

In 1923 Lily Taylor wrote *Local Cults in Etruria,* and in 1931 she wrote *The Divinity of the Roman Emperor,* which covered the cult of the emperor. In 1942 Taylor became dean of the graduate school at Bryn Mawr, although she continued teaching and was one of the teachers recognized by *Life* magazine with an award in 1952. She was also associate editor of *Classical Philology* and principal social science analyst in the Office of Strategic Services in Washington, D.C., during World War II. She was president of the American Philological Association in 1942 and vice president of the American Institute of Archaeology from 1935 to 1937. She was the first woman to become Sather Professor of Classics at the University of California (1947) and delivered the Sather Lectures, which became *Party Politics in the Age of Caesar* (1949).

Lily Taylor retired in 1942 and became professor in charge of the Classical

School of the American Academy in Rome until 1955. She returned to Bryn Mawr, where she was Phi Beta Kappa Visiting Scholar during 1956–57. She lectured throughout the United States and was visiting professor at several universities for the next decade, including a year spent as a member of the Institute for Advanced Study at Princeton. In 1960 she published *The Voting Districts of the Roman Republic: The Thirty-Five Urban and Rural Tribes.* In 1964 Taylor became Jerome Lecturer at the American Academy in Rome and the University of Michigan. These lectures became *Roman Voting Assemblies* in 1966. She was elected to the American Philosophical Society and became a fellow of the American Arts and Sciences. She received the Achievement Award of the American Association of University Women in 1952 and the Citation for Distinguished Services by Bryn Mawr for its seventy-fifth anniversary in 1960. She earned the Award of Merit of the American Philological Association and received the Cultori di Roma gold medal in 1962. Lily Taylor was working on a book about the Roman Senate at the age of eighty-three when she was killed by a hit-and-run driver in Bryn Mawr on November 18, 1969.

ADDITIONAL SOURCES

Papers at Bryn Mawr College Archives; bibliography of her publications to 1966 published by Bryn Mawr College; bibliography in Elisabeth and Jean-Claude Morin, translation of *Party Politics in the Age of Caesar* (*La Politique et les partis à Rome au temps de César*); Agnes Kirsopp Michels, "Lily Ross Taylor," American Philological Association *Proceedings,* 1969, pp. xviii–xix; T.R.S. Broughton, "Lily Ross Taylor (1886–1969)," *American Philological Society Year Book 1970* (1971), pp. 172–79; T.R.S. Broughton, "Lily Ross Taylor" *Gnomon,* Nov. 1970, pp. 734–735; Agnes Michels, "Lily Ross Taylor," *Bryn Mawr Alumnae Bulletin,* Winter 1970; T.R.S. Broughton, "Roman Studies in the Twentieth Century," convocation in her honor at Bryn Mawr, Feb. 28, 1970; obituary in Philadelphia *Inquirer,* Nov. 19, 1969; obituary in Philadelphia *Evening Bulletin,* Nov. 19, 1969; obituary in NewYT, Nov. 20, 1969; obituary in London *Times,* Nov. 27, 1969; WhoAmW 58, 61, 70; BiIn 2, 3, 8, 12; NotAW: Mod; WhAm 5; *Bio-Base.*

THOMPSON, CLARA MILDRED
(1881–1975)
Franklin Delano Roosevelt/Reconstruction History

Clara Mildred Thompson was born in Atlanta, Georgia, in 1881. She did her undergraduate work at Vassar College and graduated in 1903. She received her Ph.D. from Columbia University. Thompson became dean of Vassar College in 1923 and remained there until 1948. She was also dean of the history department. In 1942 Thompson was the only woman appointed to the United States delegation to the Conference of Allied Ministers of Education. In 1945 she, Senator William J. Fulbright, and retired United States Supreme Court Justice Felix Frankfurter were appointed to the United Nations Education Conference that drafted the charter for the United Nations Educational, Scientific and Cultural Organization (UNESCO), to which she was twice the U.S. delegate.

After she retired from Vassar College, Clara Thompson taught history at the University of Georgia from 1948 to 1952. While there, she conducted a study on the education of women at the university. She then was appointed dean of women at the College of Free Europe in Strasbourg, France. Known as an authority on Franklin Delano Roosevelt, Thompson served as a member of the planning committee for the Franklin Delano Roosevelt Memorial and served on the board of advisors of the Roosevelt Library. She wrote *Reconstruction in Georgia* and *Carpetbaggers in the U.S. Senate.* Clara Thompson died on February 16, 1975, in Atlanta, Georgia.

ADDITIONAL SOURCES

WhoAmW 58; *Bio-Base;* obituary in NewYT, Feb. 17, 1975, p. 24.

THRUPP, SYLVIA L.
(1903–   )
Medieval History

Sylvia Lettice Thrupp was born in 1903 in England. She attended the University of British Columbia, where she earned both a bachelor's degree and a master's degree. She then attended the London School of Economics, where she earned the Ph.D. in 1931. Thrupp stayed on at the London School of Economics, completing a postdoctoral fellowship there in 1933. She then held a fellowship from the Social Science Research Council from 1933 to 1935.

Thrupp's first academic appointment was at the University of British Columbia, where she taught from 1935 to 1944. She then taught for a year at the University of Toronto before accepting a job at the University of Chicago, where she taught from 1945 to 1961. From 1961 to 1977, when she retired, Sylvia Thrupp held the Alice Freeman Palmer Chair at the University of Michigan. The Palmer Chair, offered only to women historians, was established in the name of the first president of Wellesley College, a graduate of the University of Michigan.

Thrupp is perhaps best known and most respected for editing and founding an interdisciplinary journal, *Comparative Studies in Society and History,* published by Cambridge University Press. Founded in 1958 and still one of the preeminent journals in social science in the world, *Comparative Studies* was international as well as interdisciplinary from the start. As Thrupp argued, comparative work was the best defense against the errors that would result in the work of scholars who "snatched at systems based on cursory leaping at apparent similarities." The union of history and the social sciences, in fact, was her lifelong ambition. One of her early arguments along these lines, "What History and Sociology Can Learn from Each Other," published in 1956, provided a discussion of the multiple uses of quantitative methods in research.

In her own research, which includes several major studies of medieval England, Thrupp explored the many coexisting cultures of England as well as the broader context of Europe in the Middle Ages. She wrote two books, edited three others, and wrote over thirty articles. Her influence among scholars of many nations and many disciplines has been widespread. A collection of her essays, entitled *Society and History: Essays by Sylvia Thrupp,* was published in 1977. Four internationally known scholars, from four different countries and disciplines, introduce the sections of the book, which contains twenty-three essays. "Probably few historians of any nation have ranged as widely and expertly over both history and the social sciences as Sylvia Thrupp," argues Thomas Cochran in his introduction.

BOOKS BY SYLVIA L. THRUPP

Society and History: Essays by Sylvia Thrupp. Edited by Raymond Grew and Nicholas H. Steneck. Ann Arbor: University of Michigan Press, 1977.

Editor. *Millennial Dreams in Action: Studies in Revolutionary Religious Movements.* The Hague: Mouton, 1962; reprint, New York: Schocken, 1970.

Editor. *Early Medieval Society.* New York: Appleton-Century-Crofts, 1967.

Editor. *Change in Medieval Society: Europe North of the Alps, 1050–1500.* New York: Appleton-Century-Crofts, 1964; reprint, Toronto: University of Toronto Press, 1988.

The Merchant Class of Medieval London, 1300–1500. Chicago: University of Chicago Press, 1948; reprint, Ann Arbor: University of Michigan Press, 1962, 1976.

A Short History of the Worshipful Company of Bakers. London: Galleon Press, 1933.

ADDITIONAL SOURCE

Grew, Raymond. Interview with Jennifer Scanlon, 1995.

TILLY, LOUISE A.
(1930–)
European History

Louise Audino Tilly was born on December 13, 1930, in Orange, New Jersey, of Italian ancestry. Her father was an engineer, her mother a homemaker who had been trained as an artist. Tilly attended public school at P.S. 12 in Queens, New York, then at Longfellow School and Teaneck Junior and Senior High Schools in Teaneck, New Jersey. Among her early influences, Tilly remembers her fourth grade teacher, Mr. Hopper. An interest in the past and in faraway places, nurtured by early voracious reading, encouraged her to study history. She attended Douglass College, Rutgers University, earning a bachelor's degree in history, with high honors, in 1952. She then earned a master's degree from Boston University in 1955 and a Ph.D. from the University of Toronto in 1974.

Tilly taught at Michigan State University, first as lecturer and then as assistant professor. She then taught at the University of Michigan, as assistant professor from 1975 to 1977, associate professor from 1977 to 1982, and professor from 1982 to 1984. While there she also served as director of women's studies from 1975 to 1977, and in 1980, 1983, and 1984. Tilly is currently Michael E. Gellert Professor of History and Sociology at the Graduate Faculty of the New School for Social Research, and chair of its Committee on Historical Studies. She has also worked as a fellow at the Shelby Cullom Davis Center for Historical Studies

at Princeton University and as Directeur d'Etudes Associés, Ecole des Hautes
Etudes en Sciences Sociales in Paris, in 1979, 1980, 1988, and 1991.

Louise A. Tilly is the author, editor, or co-editor of nine books and fifty
scholarly articles. She is known as an interdisciplinary scholar, one who bridges
history and sociology as she explores the small-scale effects of large-scale social
change on concrete historical settings. In her most recent book, *Politics and
Class in Milan, 1881–1901,* Tilly explores the relationship between the development of the working class and the rise of the socialist movement in Milan,
Italy, at the turn of the century. In her works in progress, Tilly is studying the
ways in which industrialization, class formation, and the development of welfare
states have shaped gender and family relations globally.

Tilly has been the recipient of many grants and fellowships, including those
from the Rockefeller Foundation Population Policy, the Council for European
Studies, the American Council of Learned Societies, the Guggenheim Foundation, the Center for Advanced Study in the Behavioral Sciences, and the Russell
Sage Foundation. She has served as an evaluator of grants and fellowships for
the National Science Foundation, the National Endowment for the Humanities,
the American Philosophical Society, the Canadian Social Science Research
Council, the Russell Sage Foundation, and several other national and interna-
tional bodies. She is currently co-editor of *International Labor and Working
Class History* and a member of the editorial boards of *Gender and History,* the
Journal of Historical Sociology, Passato e Presente, Theory and Society, and
Women and Work.

Louise Tilly has provided a great deal of service to the profession. She has
been president of the American Historical Association and served as chair of
the Higby Prize Committee, member and chair of the Committee on Quantifi-
cation in History, and member of the Council of the Association. She has also
been president of the Social Science History Association and a member of the
board of the Social Science Research Council.

Louise Tilly's former spouse is Charles Tilly. They have four children: Christopher, an economist; Kathryn, a molecular biologist; Laura, a lawyer; and
Sarah, a graduate student in clinical psychology. Tilly also has two grandchildren, Charlotte and Christopher, the children of her daughter Laura. Her interests
include hiking, reading, travel, music, and art.

BOOKS BY LOUISE A. TILLY

Politics and Class in Milan, 1881–1901. New York: Oxford University Press, 1992.
Editor, with John Gillis and David Levine. *The European Experience of Declining Fer-
tility, 1850–1970: A Quiet Revolution.* London: Blackwell, 1992.
Editor, with Patricia Gurin. *Women, Politics, and Change.* New York: Russell Sage
Foundation, 1990.
With Heidi Hartmann and Robert Kraut. *Computer Chips and Paper Clips: Technology
and Women's Employment.* Washington, DC: National Academy Press, 1986.
Translater, with Kathryn L. Tilly. *Meme Santerre, a French Woman of the People.* New
York: Schocken, 1985.

Editor, with Vivian Patraka. *Feminist Re-visions: What Has Been and Might Be.* Ann
      Arbor: University of Michigan Press, 1983.
With Charles Tilly. *Class Conflict and Collective Action.* Beverly Hills: Sage
      Publications, 1981.
With Joan Scott. *Women, Work and Family.* New York: Holt, Rinehart and Winston,
      1978; 2nd ed., Methuen, 1987.
With Charles Tilly and Richard Tilly. *The Rebellious Century.* Cambridge, MA: Harvard
      University Press, 1975.
ADDITIONAL SOURCE
Questionnaire completed by the subject for *American Women Historians, 1700s–1990s:
A Biographical Dictionary.*

TOWNSEND, MARY EVELYN
(1884–1954)
History of European Colonialism

Mary Evelyn Townsend was born in New York City on June 5, 1884, to Charles
and Mary Evelyn (Mulligan) Townsend. She received an A.B. from Wellesley
College in 1905, an A.M. from Columbia University in 1917, and a Ph.D. from
Columbia in 1921. She continued her postgraduate work at the University of
Wisconsin, the University of London, and the University of Berlin. Townsend
taught at St. Mary's School in New York from 1906 to 1912. She was head of
the history department of the Vail-Deane School in Elizabeth, New Jersey, from
1912 to 1917. She became an instructor of history at Teachers College in 1919
and was an exchange lecturer in history at Bedford College at the University of
London in 1921 and 1922. In 1935 Townsend became an associate professor at
Columbia and was named full professor in 1939. During World War II, Townsend worked for the American Red Cross, the Office of Civilian Defense, and
the United States Military Intelligence Service.

   Dr. Townsend was the author of *Origins of German Colonialism* (1921), *The
Rise and Fall of Germany's Colonial Empire* (1930), *Economics and Public
Law* (1932), *European Colonial Expansion Since 1871* (1941), and *Teachers
College Columbia University* (1954). Mary Townsend died on May 9, 1954, in
New York City.
ADDITIONAL SOURCES
WhE&Ea; BiIn 3; WhAm 3; *Bio-Base;* obituary 1n NewYT, May 10, 1954, p. 23; *Wilson
Library Bulletin* 29: 12, Sept. 1954.

TUCHMAN, BARBARA
(1912–1989)
World History

Barbara Tuchman was born in New York City on January 30, 1912, to Maurice
Wertheim, a banker, art collector, and publisher, and Alma (Morgenthau) Wertheim. She attended the Walden School in New York City and received a B.A.
from Radcliffe College in 1933. She became research and editorial assistant for

the Institute of Pacific Relations in 1933 and was a staff writer and foreign correspondent for *Nation* in Tokyo in 1934–35. She was moved to Madrid in 1937 and covered the early stages of the Spanish Civil War. She continued to write on the war in London, where she was staff writer on *The War in Spain.* The next year she became U.S. correspondent for *New Statesman and Nation.* In 1940 she married physician Lester Tuchman and worked from 1943 to 1945 as editor of Far Eastern Affairs for the Office of War Information.

In 1938 Tuchman had written a history book entitled *The Lost British Policy: Britain and Spain Since 1700.* Years later, in 1956, she returned to writing history with *Bible and Sword: England and Palestine from the Bronze Age to Balfour.* The next year *The Zimmerman Telegram* appeared, and in 1962 *The Guns of August* was published; it won the Pulitzer Prize for 1963. In 1966 she wrote *The Proud Tower: A Portrait of the World Before the War, 1890–1914,* followed by *Stilwell and the American Experience in China, 1911–1945,* which came out in 1971 and also won the Pulitzer Prize (1972). In 1972 Tuchman wrote *Notes from China,* and in 1978, *A Distant Mirror: The Calamitous Fourteenth Century;* she was awarded the gold medal for history by the American Academy of Arts and Sciences that same year. This was followed by *Practicing History* in 1981 and *The March of Folly: From Troy to Vietnam* in 1984. Her last book, *The First Salute—A View of the American Revolution,* was published in 1988.

Barbara Tuchman died of a stroke on February 6, 1989. Before her death she had received many honorary degrees, including those from Yale University, Columbia University, New York University, Williams College, the University of Massachusetts, Smith College, Hamilton College, Mount Holyoke College, and Boston University. She was president of the Society of American Historians, council member of the Smithsonian Institution, and the first woman president of the American Academy and Institute of Arts and Letters.

ADDITIONAL SOURCES

CurBio 24: 37–39, Dec. 1963; CurBio Yrbk 1963: 426–428, 1964; AmWorWr; BiIn 6, 10, 11, 12; CelR 73; ConAu 3NR; LinLibL; WrDr 80, 82, 84; DrAS 74H, 78H, 82H; IntAu&W 76, 77; IntWW 74, 75, 76, 77, 78, 79, 80, 81, 82, 83; WhoWorJ 72, 78; WhoAmJ 80; WhoWor 74, 78, 80, 82; AmAu&B; Au&Wr 71; ConAu 1R; InWom; LibW; OxAm; WhoAm 74, 76, 78, 80, 82; WhoAmW 58, 61, 64, 66, 68, 70, 72, 74, 75, 77, 81, 83; WhoE 74; WorAu; WrDr 76; *Newsweek* 103: 78+, Mar. 12, 1984; *Publishers Weekly* 225: 95–96, Mar. 2, 1984; *New Yorker* 60: 39–41, Mar. 26, 1984; CurBio Yrbk 1989; obituary in *AB Bookman's Weekly* 83: 1288–1289, Mar. 20, 1989; obituary in CurBio 50: 64, Mar. 1989; obituary in *NewYT,* Feb. 7, 1989, p. A-1+; obituary in NewYTBS 20: 145–146, Feb. 1989; obituary in *Nation* 248: 292–293, March 6, 1989; obituary in *Newsweek* 113: 71, Feb. 20, 1989; *Time* 133: 94, Feb. 20, 1989; *World Authors 1950-70,* pp. 1449–1451; *Major 20th Century Writers; A Selection of Sketches from Contemporary Authors,* pp. 2987–2990; NewYTBS 9: 1269–1270, Dec. 1978; NewYTBS 10: 261–262, Feb. 1979; *Bio-Base.*

U

ULRICH, LAUREL THATCHER
(1938–   )
Colonial U.S. History, Biography

Laurel Thatcher Ulrich was born on July 11, 1938, in Idaho, the daughter of John Kenneth and Alice (Siddoway) Thatcher. She graduated from the University of Utah in 1960 with a bachelor's degree in English. She married soon after college and had five children, Karl, Melinda, Nathan, Thatcher, and Amy. Then, in the late 1960s, Ulrich discovered the feminist movement and began, as she states, to redefine herself and her work. Along with a group of women friends in Massachusetts, she edited a book and founded a scholarly journal and a newspaper. Her interest then was in the history and thought of Mormon women. At the same time, she earned a master's degree in English from Simmons College.

When Ulrich's husband joined the faculty of the University of New Hampshire, she decided to pursue a Ph.D. in history there. "I had become more interested in context than text," she explains, "and at that time the distinction between the two was more rigidly applied in literary criticism than it is today." She also pursued history hoping to write works that might be widely read.

In pursuing women's history in the colonial period, Ulrich brought together several of her interests. Her first book, *Good Wives: Images and Reality in the Lives of Women in Northern New England, 1650–1750*, explores the many and varied roles that women, "good wives" among them, played in the social, economic, and political life of the New England colonies. Her second examination of women's lives during the period, *A Midwife's Tale: The Life of Martha Ballard, Based on Her Diary, 1785–1812*, earned her, among many other national prizes, the Pulitzer Prize for history. This biography of a Maine midwife provides, as Jan Lewis argues, "perhaps the finest and most richly textured description of colonial women's experience yet written." It also provides a critique of the ways in which colonial history has generally been written and provides, as this same reviewer claims, "feminist history by example."

Laurel Thatcher Ulrich's Pulitzer Prize–winning work was the recipient of many other honors as well, including the Berkshire Conference of Women Historians' annual book award and two awards from the American Historical Association, one for the best book on United States history and the other for the best book on Canada, the United States, or Latin America. It was also one of two titles to win Columbia University's Bancroft Prize in history.

A faculty member of the University of New Hampshire since completing her Ph.D., Ulrich took a position as tenured professor of history and women's studies at Harvard University in 1995.

BOOKS BY LAUREL THATCHER ULRICH

A Midwife's Tale: The Life of Martha Ballard, Based on Her Diary, 1785–1812. New York: Knopf, 1990.

Good Wives: Image and Reality in the Lives of Women in Northern New England, 1650–1750. New York: Knopf, 1982.

ADDITIONAL SOURCES

Heller, Scott. "Getting It Right: Historian Shepherds Her "Midwife's Tale" Through Filming." *Chronicle of Higher Education* 41 (Jan. 13, 1995): A7, A13.

Lewis, Jan. Review of *A Midwife's Tale: The Life of Martha Ballard, Based on Her Diary, 1785–1812,* by Laurel Thatcher Ulrich. *Signs* 17 (Spring 1992): 672–676.

Winkler, Karen J. "A Prize-Winning Historian in Spite of Herself." *Chronicle of Higher Education* 37 (June 26, 1991): A3.

V

VAN RENSSELAER, MARIANA ALLEY GRISWOLD
(1851–1934)
Popular History

Mariana Van Rensselaer was born in New York City to George and Lydia (Alley) Griswold. Her paternal grandfather and uncle founded the shipping firm of N. L. & G. Griswold in order to enter the Canton tea trade. Mariana was educated by tutors and at schools in Dresden, where the family spent several years. She married Schuyler Van Rensselaer, a mining and metallurgical engineer, in Dresden on April 14, 1873. The two resided in New Brunswick, New Jersey, and traveled frequently. Mariana also began writing poetry and articles on art and published *Book of American Figure Painters* in 1886.

Schuyler Van Rensselaer died in 1884, and Mariana subsequently returned to New York City, where she lived with her mother. She began concentrating on architectural criticism and wrote *English Cathedrals* (1892) and *Henry Hobson Richardson and His Works* (1888). In 1889 she began *Garden and Forest,* which studied gardening from earliest times to the Middle Ages. After her son's death in 1894, Van Rensselaer became interested in social problems, especially school reform. She also became interested in New York's colonial past and published a two-volume *History of the City of New York in the Seventeenth Century* (1909); however, she then returned to poetry and put her historical work aside. Columbia University made her an honorary doctor of literature in 1910, and she received a gold medal "for distinction in literature" from the American Academy of Arts and Letters in 1923. Van Rensselaer was an honorary member of the American Institute of Architects (1890) and the Society of Landscape Architects. She died January 20, 1934.

ADDITIONAL SOURCES

Glen E. Griswold, *The Griswold Family: England—America* (1943); Florence Van Rensselaer, *The Van Rensselaers in Holland and in America* (1956); WhAm v. 1 (1942);

obituaries in *New York Herald Tribune* and NewYT, Jan. 21, 1934; DcAmAu; AmAu&B; AmLY; BiD&SB; DcNAA; *Bio-Base*. Sculptor Augustus Saint-Gaudens's relief portrait is in the Fogg Museum at Harvard University.

VICTOR, FRANCES AURETTA FULLER
(1826–1902)
Local History

Frances Victor was born in Rome, New York, to Adonijah and Lucy A. (Williams) Fuller. The family eventually moved to Ohio, and Frances attended a female seminary. She and her sister, Metta, published poems and fiction and, encouraged by several editors and critics, moved to New York City. Before her career could blossom, however, Frances's father died and she was forced to rejoin her family when they relocated in St. Clair, Michigan. She married Jackson Barritt on June 16, 1853, and although the marriage was short-lived she did not officially obtain a divorce until 1862. She returned to New York, where her sister's husband, Orville James Victor, was editor of Beadle's Dime Novels. Frances wrote a number of dime novels and in May 1862, married Orville's brother, Henry Clay Victor, a navy engineer. The two moved to San Francisco, and Frances resumed her writing under the name "Florence Fane." When her husband's health forced him to resign from the navy, the Victors moved to Oregon, where Frances became interested in local history. She wrote a history of mountain man Joe Meek in *The River of the West* in 1870 as well as a travel book, a temperance book, and some fiction. After her husband's death by drowning, in the wreck of the *Pacific* in 1875, Frances was offered a position by historical promoter Huber Howe Bancroft in 1878. She would help prepare his *History of the Pacific States*. She worked on the project until the twenty-eighth volume was published in 1890; although Bancroft was cited as author of the entire series, it was eventually learned that Victor had written the two volumes on Oregon, the volumes on Washington, Idaho, Montana, Nevada, Colorado, and Wyoming, as well as large portions of other volumes on California, the Northwest Coast, and British Columbia.

Frances Victor returned to Oregon in 1890 and was commissioned by the legislature to write a history of the native Indians. This resulted in *The Early Indian Wars of Oregon* in 1894. She died in Portland on November 14, 1902. In 1947 the Portland chapter of the Daughters of the American Revolution and the Board of the Oregon Historical Society erected a marker at her grave at Riverview Cemetery, Portland, Oregon.

ADDITIONAL SOURCES

Hazel E. Mills, *Pacific Northwest Quarterly,* Oct. 1954; William A. Morris, "The Origin and Authorship of the Bancroft Pacific States Publications," *Oregon Historical Society Quarterly,* Dec. 1903; William T. Coggeshall, *The Poets and Poetry of the West* (1860); H. H. Bancroft, *Literary Industries* (1890); Alfred Powers, *A History of Oregon Literature* (1935); AmWom; ApCAB; DcAmB; LibW: NatCAB 13; NotAW; REnAW;

TwCBDA; WhAmHS; Alli; Alli Supp.; AmAu; AmAu&B; BiD&SB; DcAmAu; Dc-
NAA; HsB&A; OhA&B; REnAL; AmWomWr; *Bio-Base.* Her papers and manuscripts
are in the Oregon Historical Society Library and Bancroft Library, University of California.

W

WALKOWITZ, JUDITH ROSENBERG
(1945–)
History of Women and Sexuality

Judith Rosenberg Walkowitz was born on September 13, 1945, in New York City, the daughter of lawyer parents. She attended P.S. 56 in the Bronx, then Baldwin Junior and Senior High Schools on Long Island, New York. The excitement of the history department at the University of Rochester, where she attended college, in addition to a belief that social change was possible, encouraged Walkowitz to pursue a career as a historian. She received an undergraduate degree from the University of Rochester with high honors in 1967. She did her graduate work there as well, earning a master's degree in 1968 and a Ph.D. in 1974.

After completing her dissertation, which explored prostitution in the United States during the late nineteenth century, Walkowitz accepted a position as assistant professor of history at Rutgers University. She worked there until 1989, becoming associate professor in 1979 and professor in 1984. In 1983 she was visiting associate professor of history at the University of California at Irvine. Since 1989 Walkowitz has been professor of history and director of women's studies at Johns Hopkins University. She has taught on such varied subjects as the history of sexuality, witchcraft and magic, Victorian London, and crime and society in modern Europe.

Walkowitz is the author or editor of three books, all of which explore issues of sexuality from a historical perspective. Her most recent, *City of Dreadful Delight,* explores narratives of sexual danger in late-Victorian London. Another of her books, *Prostitution and Victorian Society: Women, Class and the State,* won the Berkshire Conference Book Prize. Walkowitz has also published ten scholarly articles on topics that include Jack the Ripper, feminist historiography, and the politics of prostitution. Among her current projects are an article on sexual harassment in Victorian London and a book on the cultural geography of London's West End.

Judith R. Walkowitz has been the recipient of numerous awards and fellowships, including those from the Guggenheim Foundation, the National Endowment for the Humanities, the American Council of Learned Societies, and the Woodrow Wilson Foundation. She has served on the editorial board of *Victorian Studies* since 1992, was the co-organizer of the Gender and Nationalism Conference held at Bellagio, Italy, in 1992, and has served on the Speakers Bureau of the American Historical Association. She also currently serves on the editorial board of *Differences* and the *Journal of British Studies*. From 1987 to 1990 she served as the president of the Berkshire Conference on Women Historians, and she has also chaired the Committee on Women Historians of the American Historical Association. Walkowitz has served as a reviewer for the Rockefeller Foundation and the Woodrow Wilson Foundation, and as a consultant to the National Science Foundation.

Judith Rosenberg Walkowitz is married to Daniel J. Walkowitz and is the mother of one child, Rebecca. Her interests include swimming, tennis, snorkeling, theater, and film.

BOOKS BY JUDITH R. WALKOWITZ

City of Dreadful Delight: Narratives of Sexual Danger in Late-Victorian London. Chicago: University of Chicago Press, 1992.

Editor, with Judith Newton and Mary Ryan. *Sex and Class in Women's History: Essays from Feminist Studies.* London: Routledge and Kegan Paul, 1983.

Prostitution and Victorian Society: Women, Class and the State. New York: Cambridge University Press, 1980.

ADDITIONAL SOURCE

Questionnaire completed by the subject for *American Women Historians, 1700s–1990s: A Biographical Dictionary.*

WALWORTH, ELLEN HARDIN
(1832–1915)
Historic Preservation

Ellen Hardin Walworth was born on October 20, 1832, to John J. and Sarah Ellen (Smith) Hardin. Her paternal grandfather, Martin D. Hardin, was a United States Senator from Kentucky, and her father was a lawyer and Whig member of Congress from 1843 to 1845; he was killed at the battle of Buena Vista in the Mexican War in 1847. Ellen attended Jacksonville Academy until her mother married Reuben Hyde Walworth, the last chancellor of New York State. The family moved to Saratoga Springs, New York, and Ellen was married a year later to a stepbrother, Mansfield Tracy Walworth, a lawyer and eventually a minor novelist. Ellen converted to Roman Catholicism and had six children in the first nine years of marriage despite the fact that her husband became increasingly violent and unstable. She left her husband in 1861, and over the next ten years reconciled, separated, secured a government clerkship in Washington, and reconciled again when she lost her job. When he physically abused her during her eighth pregnancy, she left permanently in January 1871 and returned to Saratoga to secure what she called a "limited divorce." Walworth opened a girls' boarding school and operated it for fifteen years before returning to Washington for health reasons. Meanwhile, her former husband continued to harass her. Eventually her oldest son, Frank, shot his father to death in a New York City hotel room on June 3, 1873. Frank was sentenced to life imprisonment, but Ellen studied law and secured his release in 1877 by reason of insanity.

During her lifetime, Walworth continued to be extremely active in various organizations, local and national, and pursued the art of becoming the first woman in several different organizations. She joined the American Association for the Advancement of Science in 1876, the first woman to become active in this organization. She was one of the first women in New York State to hold a position on the board of education, where she encouraged the study of history. In 1876 she helped raised funds for the restoration of Mount Vernon and began an eighteen-year stint as the only woman trustee of the Saratoga Monument Association. She was named chair of the committee on tablets and completed research on every episode of the Revolutionary battle of Saratoga. She then located descendants of participants and obtained funds for marking the sites. She published a visitors' guidebook for Saratoga in 1877 and wrote a history of the association in 1891. She often delivered speeches and published historical papers, and in 1893 was one of the first to urge the establishment of a National Archives. In 1890 she was one of three women that founded the Daughters of the American Revolution and was its first secretary general. She was also the first editor of the *American Monthly Magazine* in 1892. Ellen Walworth died in Georgetown University Hospital in Washington of an obstruction caused by gallstones on June 23, 1915.

ADDITIONAL SOURCES

Clarence A. Walworth, *The Walworths of America* (1897); Reginald Wellington Walworth, *Walworth-Walsworth Genealogy* (1962); WhoAm 1914–15; Biographical Dictionary of America, 10 (1906); obituaries in *Evening Star* (Washington), June 23, 1915; *Washington Post* and NewYT, June 24, 1915; *American Monthly Magazine,* July 1893; *Americana,* Oct. 1935; Walworth Memorial Museum in Congress Park, Saratoga Springs; NatCAB; DcAmAu; InWom; TwCBDA; Alli Supp.; AmAu&B; DcNAA; HarEnUS; AmWom; ApCAB; NotAW; WhAm 1; WomWWA 14; *Bio-Base;* the divorce, murder, and trial are covered in NewYT, June 4–July 14, 1873; Phoebe Hannaford, *Daughters of America: Women of the Century* (Augusta, ME: True and Co., 1883).

WARE, CAROLINE F.
(1899–1990)
Economic History

Caroline F. Ware was born on August 14, 1899, in Brookline, Massachusetts, to Henry and Louisa Ware. Caroline's great-great-grandfather was dean of Harvard University Divinity School, and her father was a lawyer and a graduate of Harvard College and Harvard Law School. She attended Vassar in 1916, where she studied under Lucy Salmon and graduated in 1920. She taught at the Baldwin School, a private institution for girls in Bryn Mawr, Pennsylvania, and in 1922 was part of the tutorial staff at the Bryn Mawr Summer School for Women Workers, which resulted in a lifelong interest in the working class. Ware spent the 1922–1923 school year at Oxford University until her mother's illness forced her to return to Boston. Her fascination with Frederick Jackson Turner led her to Harvard for the fall 1923 term. The school had just obtained the papers of the Boston Manufacturing Company in Waltham, and this became Ware's dissertation topic, which in turn resulted in *The Early New England Cotton Manufacture.* The book earned the Hart, Schaffner and Marx prize for the outstanding book in economics in 1929. Meanwhile, she had married Gardiner Means, also a student at the university, in 1927. (Ware decided to keep her own name because she had a bigger reputation than he and she didn't want to lose the momentum.) She obtained an academic position at Vassar College. In 1931 she agreed to direct a Columbia project on the study of Greenwich Village. In 1935 the results were published as *Greenwich Village 1920–1930: A Comment on American Civilization in the Post War Years.* As she became more immersed in teaching, Ware's writing was put aside until the late 1950s, when she coauthored and edited a volume of the United Nations' *History of the Cultural and Scientific Development of Mankind* with Dutch historian Jan Romein and Indian historian K. M. Panikkar. This proved to be Caroline Ware's last publication, though she remained intellectually active until her death in 1990.

ADDITIONAL SOURCES

Caroline F. Ware Papers in Franklin Delano Roosevelt Library, Hyde Park, New York; Ellen Fitzpatrick, "Caroline F. Ware and the Cultural Approach to History," *American Quarterly* 43 (June 1991): 173–198; obituary in *Washington Post,* Apr. 7, 1990; WhE&EA; WhoAm 74, 76; *Bio-Base*; WhoAmW 58, 64, 66, 68, 70, 72.

WARREN, MERCY OTIS
(1728–1814)
History of the American Revolution

Mercy Otis Warren was born in Barnstable, Massachusetts, to James Otis, a lawyer, farmer, merchant, and judge, and Mary (Allyne) Otis. While the Otis sons were educated, the daughters received no formal education. On November 14, 1754, Mercy married James Warren of Plymouth, also a merchant and farmer. In 1759 she began writing poems and eventually political satire as the Revolutionary War became imminent. Despite personal tragedies (her brother James died from being struck by lightning; a son, James, returned from the Revolution mentally and physically impaired; another son, Charles, died of consumption; and her husband's political career failed), Warren continued to write and in the late 1770s began her most famous work, the three-volume *History of the Rise, Progress and Termination of the American Revolution. Interspersed with Biographical, Political and Moral Observations,* which was published in 1805. The book has been valuable because it contains personal opinions of people and events to whom she had access. Otis's friendship with John Adams was hurt by accusations in the book; while the two were eventually reconciled in 1812, Adams insisted that he and his wife, Abigail, regretted encouraging Warren to write her book, saying, "History is not the Province of the Ladies." Mercy Otis Warren died in Plymouth, Massachusetts, on October 19, 1814.

ADDITIONAL SOURCES

Collections at the Massachusetts Historical Society; portrait by John Singleton Copley in the Museum of Fine Arts, Boston; Alice Brown, *Mercy Warren* (1896); Katherine Anthony, *First Lady of the Revolution: The Life of Mercy Otis Warren* (1958); *William and Mary Quarterly,* July 1953; Worthington C. Ford, "Mrs. Warren's 'The Group,' " Massachusetts Historical Society, *Proceedings* 42 (1930): 15–22; Charles Warren, "Elbridge Gerry, James Warren, Mercy Warren and the Ratification of the Federal Constitution in Mass.," Massachusetts Historical Society, *Proceedings* 44 (1932): 143–164; William R. Smith, *History as Argument: Three Patriot Historians of the American Revolution* (1966); Lester H. Cohen, "Explaining the Revolution: Ideology and Ethics in Mercy Otis Warren's Historical Theory," *William and Mary Quarterly,* 3rd series, 37 (Apr. 1980): 200–218; Benjamin Franklin V, Introduction to *The Plays and Poems of Mercy Otis Warren,* 1980, pp. vii–xxx; Maud Macdonald Hutcheson, "Mercy Warren 1728–1814," *William and Mary Quarterly,* 3rd series, 10 (July 1953): 378–401; Charles H. Lippy, "Independence and Identity: Mercy Otis Warren Interprets the Revolution," *Ohio Journal of Religious Studies* 4, no. 2 (1976): 66–76; Emily Stipes Watts, *The Poetry of American Women from 1632 to 1945* (1977), pp. 39–44; Gerald Weales, "The Quality of Mercy, or Mrs. Warren's Profession," *Georgia Review* 33 (Winter 1979): 881–894; AmWomWr; WebAB 1979; *Bio-Base.*

WATERS, CLARA ERSKINE CLEMENT
(1834–1916)
Art History

Clara Erskine Clement Waters was born in St. Louis, Missouri, to John Erskine, a businessman, and Harriet Bethiah (Godfrey) Erskine. Clara was privately tutored and on August 3, 1852, married James Hazen Clement, also a businessman. The family moved to Newton, Massachusetts. While there Clara began traveling and writing a series of art handbooks: *A Handbook of Legendary and Mythological Art* (1871), *Painters, Sculptors, Architects, Engravers, and Their Works* (1874), and, with Laurence Hutton, *Artists of the Nineteenth Century and Their Works* (1879). She wrote a novel, *Eleanor Maitland,* in 1881, and a biography of the actress Charlotte Cushman the next year. During this time, her husband died; in 1882 she married Edwin Forbes Waters, owner of the *Boston Daily Advertiser* and an author himself. She continued to travel abroad and made a trip around the world in 1883–1884. In 1886 she wrote *A Handbook of Christian Symbols and Stories of the Saints as Illustrated in Art,* followed by *Stories of Art and Artists,* published the next year. In the early 1890s she concentrated on books on foreign cities: *Venice the Queen of the Adriatic* (1893), *Naples*

(1894), and *Rome the Eternal City* and *Constantinople* (both 1896). She wrote *Angels in Art* in 1898, *Saints in Art* the following year, *Heroines of the Bible in Art* in 1900, and *Women in the Fine Arts* in 1904. Waters continued to travel, climbing the Great Pyramid at the age of sixty-six. She died on February 29, 1916, in Brookline, Massachusetts, of chronic myocarditis.

ADDITIONAL SOURCES

Obituary in *Boston Transcript,* Feb. 21, 1916; Frances E. Willard and Mary A. Livermore, eds., *A Woman of the Century* (1893); Adin Ballou, *History of the Town of Milford* (1882); Alli Supp.; AmAu&B; AmWom; BbD; BiD&SB; DcAmAu; DcNAA; InWom; NotAW; WhAm 1; *Bio-Base.*

WERGELAND, AGNES MATHILDE
(1857–1914)
World History

Agnes Mathilde Wergeland was born on May 8, 1857, in Christiania (Oslo), Norway, to Sverre Nicolai and Anne Margrete (Larsen) Wergeland. She attended a school for young ladies in Christiania in 1879 and in 1883 studied Old Norse and Icelandic law under famous jurist Konrad Mauer in Munich, Germany. She then attended the University of Zurich and became the first woman from Norway to receive a Ph.D. She received a fellowship in history from Bryn Mawr College in Pennsylvania in 1890 and lectured there for two years before lecturing at the University of Illinois in 1893. She was a docent in history at the University of Chicago from 1896 to 1902 and nonresident instructor from 1902 to 1908. In 1902 Wergeland was offered the position of chair of the department of history at the University of Wyoming, and she became a United States citizen in 1904. She wrote *Ameriká og Andre Digte* (1912) and *Efterladte Digte* (1914). In 1916 *History of the Working Classes in France, Leaders in Norway and Other Essays, Slavery in Germanic Society During the Middle Ages,* and *Early Christian Romanesque and Gothic Archictecture* were all published posthumously. Agnes Wergeland died on March 6, 1914, in Laramie, Wyoming. A $5,000 endowment fund was given as a memorial to the Royal Frederik's University at Christiania for Norwegian women students to study history and economics in the United States. A scholarship in history was also donated to the University of Wyoming in her honor.

ADDITIONAL SOURCES

WomWWA 1914–15; Maren Michelet, *Glimpses from Agnes Mathilde Wergeland's Life* (1916); *American Educators of Norwegian Origin* (1931); *Laramie Daily Boomerang,* March 7, 1914; DcAmB.

WERTHEIMER, BARBARA MAYER
(1926–1983)
U.S. Labor History

Barbara Mayer Wertheimer was born in New York City in 1926. She received a B.A. from Oberlin College in Ohio in 1946 and an M.A. from New York

University in 1960. She married Valentin Wertheimer, who was eventually vice-president of Amalgamated Clothing Workers. The two moved to Pennsylvania, where they served as an organizing team for the Amalgamated Clothing Workers of America. Barbara became associate, then acting national education director from 1947 to 1958. Following this, she served as a consultant for the American Labor Education Service from 1960 to 1961. She was community services consultant for the New York State Division of Housing and Community Renewal from 1961 to 1966 and senior extension associate and labor program specialist at the New York State School of Industrial and Labor Relations for Cornell University from 1966 to 1972.

Wertheimer wrote *Exploring the Arts: Handbook for Trade Union Program Planners* in 1968 and *Handbook for Consumer Counselors: A Resource and Training Manual* in 1970. She then became director of the Trade Union Women's Studies and senior extension associate from 1972 to 1977. She wrote *Trade Union Women: A Study of Their Participation in New York City Locals* with Anne H. Nelson in 1975 and *We Were There: The Story of Working Women in America* in 1977. She was associate professor and director of the Institute for Women and Work from 1977 to 1983. She was editor of *Labor Education for Women Workers* in 1981 and wrote *Education Needs of Union Women*, a monograph, in 1982. She was also a member of the editorial board of *Labor History* and past commissioner, later "Friend of the Commission," of the New York City Commission on the Status of Women. She was on the advisory committee for "Twentieth Century Union Woman: Vehicle for Social Change" at the University of Michigan for the National Oral History Project, funded by the Rockefeller Foundation. Wertheimer was also on the advisory committee for "Life and Times of Rosie the Riveter," a film project, and editor of the *Newsletter* of the Committee on Programs for Union Women. She was president and founding member of the New York State Labor History Association. Barbara Wertheimer died of lung cancer on September 20, 1983, at her summer home in Lakeville, Connecticut. At the time of her death she had received a Ford Foundation fellowship and was writing *Our Century, Our Time: A Narrative History of Working Women from World War I to the Present.*

ADDITIONAL SOURCES

ConAu 110; obituary in NewYT, Sept. 22, 1983, p. B-16; obituary in NewYTBS 14: 1148, Sept. 1983.

WHARTON, ANNE HOLLINGSWORTH
(1845–1928)
Popular History

Anne Hollingsworth Wharton was born on December 15, 1845, in Southampton Furnace, Cumberland County, Pennsylvania, to Charles Wharton, a merchant in the iron trade, and Mary McLanahan (Boggs) Wharton. Anne attended a private school in Philadelphia and became interested in colonial and Revolutionary history. In 1880 she published *Genealogy of the Wharton Family of Philadelphia, 1664 to 1880.* She then began writing on life in the seventeenth and eighteenth centuries, beginning with *Through Colonial Doorways* in 1893. This was followed by *Colonial Days and Dames* in 1895; *A Last Century Maid* in 1896; *Martha Washington* in 1897; *Heirlooms in Miniatures* in 1898; *Salons Colonial and Republican* in 1900; and *Social Life in the Early Republic* in 1902. She then took time out from writing history to write a series of travel books (containing some history): *Italian Days and Ways* (1906); *An English Honeymoon* (1908); *In Chateau Land* (1911); *A Rose of Old Quebec* (1913); and *English Ancestral Homes of Noted Americans* (1915). She was an associate editor for the book *Furnaces and Forges in the Province of Pennsylvania,* which was published in 1914. Her last book was *In Old Pennsylvania Towns* (1920).

Wharton was selected to judge the American colonial exhibit at the World's Columbian Exposition at Chicago and was a founder of the Pennsylvania Society of Colonial Dames of America as well as being first historian of the National Society of the Colonial Dames. She died on July 29, 1928.

ADDITIONAL SOURCES

WhoAm 1928–29; J. W. Jordan, *Colonial Families of Philadelphia,* v. 1 (1911); obituary in *Public Ledger* (Philadelphia), July 30, 1928.

WILLIAMS, AMELIA WORTHINGTON
(1876–1958)
History of Texas

Amelia Worthington Williams was born in Maysfield, Texas, on March 25, 1876, to Thomas Herbert Williams, a merchant and cotton planter, and Emma (Massengale) Williams. She attended Stuart Seminary in Austin, Texas, and Ward Seminary (later the Ward-Belmont School) in Nashville, Tennessee, where she received a liberal arts degree in 1895. She also received a B.A. degree at Southwest Texas State Normal School (later State College) in 1922 and a B.A. and M.A. in 1926 and a Ph.D. in 1931 from the University of Texas. From 1904 to 1925 she taught history and English in several Texas schools. In 1925 she began teaching American and English history at the University of Texas, where she became professor in 1931. She taught there until her retirement in 1951.

Williams's specialty was Texas history. Her doctoral dissertation, "A Critical Study of the Siege of the Alamo and of the Personnel of Its Defenders," made her the authority on the subject at that time. She also wrote *Following General Sam Houston* in 1935 and edited, with Eugene C. D. Barker, eight volumes of *The Writings of Sam Houston, 1813–1863* (1938–1943). She was a member of the Daughters of the Republic of Texas, the Daughters of the American Revolution, United Daughters of the Confederacy, and the Order of the Eastern Star. Amelia Williams died in Austin, Texas, on August 14, 1958.

ADDITIONAL SOURCES

TexWr; BiIn 6; NatCAB 44.

WILLIAMS, CATHARINE READ ARNOLD
(1787–1872)
Local History

Catharine Read Arnold Williams was born on December 31, 1787, to Capt. Alfred and Amey R. Arnold in Providence, Rhode Island. Her mother died when she was young, and since her father was a sea captain, she was sent to live with two maiden aunts who tutored her at home. On September 28, 1824, she married Horatio N. Williams in New York City. The Williamses lived in western New York state for approximately two years before Catharine returned to Providence with her infant daughter and divorced her husband. She tried running a school, but poor health forced her to turn to writing to support herself and her child. She began with poetry and fiction, then turned to nonfiction with *Tales, National and Revolutionary* in 1830, followed by *Fall River, an Authentic Record* published in 1833, which described a sensational murder by Rev. Ephraim K. Avery. *Biography of Revolutionary Heroes* was published in 1839, and *The Neutral French, or the Exiles of Nova Scotia* came out in 1841 after research in the Canadian provinces. Between 1843 and 1845 Williams wrote a two-volume collection called *Annals of the Aristocracy; Being a Series of Anecdotes of Some of the Principal Families of Rhode Island.* In 1849 she went to Brooklyn, New York, to care for an aged aunt and returned after the aunt's death to Providence. Catharine Williams died on October 11, 1872.
ADDITIONAL SOURCES
NatCAB; DcAmAu; HarEnUS; Alli; OxCan; *Bio-Base.*

WILLIAMS, MARY WILHELMINE
(1878–1944)
History of Latin America

Mary Wilhelmine Williams was born in Stanislaus County, California, on May 14, 1878, to Carl Wilhelm Salander (later Charles Williams) and Caroline Madsen. Her mother had been born in Denmark and her father in Sweden. She attended local schools and at eighteen went to the San Jose (California) State Normal School. She graduated in 1901, but was not able to attend college until three years later, when she gave up teaching to enter Stanford University. She received a B.A. degree three years later and an M.A. in 1908. She returned to teaching from 1908 to 1911 and studied at the University of Chicago during the summer. She traveled to Europe in 1911–1912 to research her doctoral dissertation at the Public Record Office in London. She became an instructor in history at Stanford and received a Ph.D. in 1914 with her dissertation, *Anglo-American Isthmian Diplomacy, 1815–1915,* which was published in 1916. It won the Justin Winsor Prize of the American Historical Association. In 1914–1915 Williams became an instructor in history at Wellesley College. She then taught at Goucher College in Baltimore as assistant professor, associate professor (1919), and professor (1920).

Williams was responsible for forming the first collegiate course in Canadian history in the United States in 1916. While she contributed to the *Dictionary of American Biography* and wrote two books on Scandinavia, her specialty was Latin American history. She was on the board of editors of the *Hispanic American Historical Review* from 1927 to 1933 and was secretary of the Conference on Latin American History in 1928 and 1934. She also served on the American Historical Association's executive council from 1922 to 1926. Her biographical sketch of John Middleton Clayton, who signed the Clayton-Bulwer Treaty for the Isthmian canal, appeared in Volume 6 of *American Secretaries of State and Their Diplomacy* in 1928. She published *The People and Politics of Latin America,* which became a standard work for college students, in 1930. Her biography *Dom Pedro the Magnanimous, Second Emperor of Brazil* (1937) was the first written on the subject in English.

From 1918 to 1919 Williams was a cartographic, geographic, and historical expert for the government of Honduras, and in 1926–1927 she completed a survey for the American Association of University Women in fifteen Latin American countries on their facilities for higher education for women. Aviator Charles A. Lindbergh consulted with Williams in 1928 before setting out on a tour of South America, and she was appointed by the State Department to serve on various committees on Latin American problems. She received a decoration from the Dominican government in 1940 recognizing her work furthering understanding between the two countries. Mary Williams retired in 1940 and died on March 10, 1944, in Palo Alto, California, of a stroke. Her ashes were buried in Alta Mesa, Palo Alto. Her grave is marked as she wished—"Teacher, Historian, Pacifist, Feminist."

ADDITIONAL SOURCES

Papers on correspondence, biographical, and bibliographical data are in the Office of the President, Goucher College; obituary in *Palo Alto* (California) *Times,* Mar. 11, 1944; obituary in *Hispanic American Historical Review,* Aug. 1944; NotAW; AmAu&B; DcNAA; WhAm 2; WhNAA; *Bio-Base.*

WINSLOW, OLA ELIZABETH
(1885?–1977)
Colonial Religious History

Ola Elizabeth Winslow was born around 1885 in Grant City, Missouri, to William and Hattie Elizabeth (Colby) Winslow. She received a B.A. from Stanford University in 1906 and an M.A. in 1914. She earned her Ph.D. from the University of Chicago in 1922. From 1909 to 1914 she was an instructor at the College of the Pacific (now University of the Pacific), in San Jose, California. She then became professor of English and head of the department from 1914 to 1944 at Goucher College in Baltimore, Maryland; she was assistant dean from 1919 to 1921. She was professor at Wellesley College, Wellesley, Massachusetts, from 1944 to 1950 and professor emeritus from 1950 to 1977. She was also professor of English from 1950 to 1962 at Radcliffe College, Cambridge, Massachusetts. She received a D.Litt. from Goucher College in 1951.

During her teaching years, Ola Winslow wrote a number of books, many of them historical. Her first historical biography, *Jonathan Edwards, 1703–1758* (1940), won a Pulitzer Prize in biography the next year. She then wrote *Meetinghouse Hill, 1630–1783* (1952), *Master Roger Williams* (1957), *John Bunyan* (1961), *Samuel Sewall of Boston* (1964), and *Portsmouth, the Life of a Town* (1966), and was editor of Jonathan Edwards, *Basic Writings* (1966). She also wrote *John Eliot: Apostle to the Indians* (1968), *"And Plead for the Rights of All": Old South Church in Boston, 1669–1969* (1970), and *A Destroying Angel: The Conquest of Smallpox in Colonial Boston* (1974). Ola Winslow died in Damariscotta, Maine, on September 27, 1977.

ADDITIONAL SOURCES

New York Times Book Review, May 8, 1966; *Christian Century,* Sept. 11, 1968; *Wall Street Journal,* Sept. 17, 1968; *Christian Science Monitor,* Oct. 9, 1968; *Virginia Quarterly Review,* Summer 1974; *New England Quarterly,* Sept. 1974; DrAS 74H; DrAS 78H; WhoAm 74 and 76; WhoAmW 58, 64, 66, 68, 70, 72, 74; NewYTBS 77; WhAm 7; ConAu 1R; OxAm; REnAL; TwCA; TwCA Supp.; AmWomWr; ConAu 3NR; ConAu 73; BiIn 2, 4; *Bio-Base.*

WISCHNITZER, RACHEL BERNSTEIN
(1885–1989)
Jewish Architectural History

Rachel Bernstein Wischnitzer was born on April 14, 1885, in Minsk (White Russia) to Vladimir Grigorivitch Berstein, a lumber merchant (mother unlisted). She attended the University of Heidelberg, then graduated in 1907 from the Ecole Speciale d'Architecture in Paris, as one of the first women to receive a degree in architecture. She then attended the University of Munich from 1909 to 1910 and upon graduation returned to Russia, where editors in St. Petersburg commissioned her to write about synagogue architecture for the *Evrreiskaia Entsiklopediia.* There she met Mark Wischnitzer, the encyclopedia's editor for European Jewish history, and they were married in 1912. They moved to Berlin in the 1920s and from 1922 to 1924 co-edited the Hebrew and Yiddish periodical *Rimon.*

In 1933 Rachel Wischnitzer began a pioneering project which would establish a photo archive of all the illuminated Hebrew manuscripts in the Berlin Staats- und Universitatsbibliothek. Because of the approaching Holocaust, she found one day that she was not allowed to enter the library, and the project had to be abandoned, although the results of her research were published in scholarly Jewish periodicals. She also wrote *Symbole and Gestalten der Judischen Kunst* in 1935, which studied the significance of Jewish symbols used in synagogue floor mosaics and wall paintings, illuminated manuscripts, and ceremonial objects. Wischnitzer also assisted directors and curators of the Berlin Jewish Museum from 1936 until it was closed in 1938. Wischnitzer and her only child,

Leonard, fled first to Paris, then to New York in 1940. She received a master's degree from New York University in 1944. She returned to her writing career with *Synagogue Architecture in the United States* in 1955. That same year Wischnitzer was appointed lecturer in Jewish Art at Stern College of Yeshiva University in New York. In 1964 she published *The Architecture of the European Synagogue.* She retired from Stern College in 1968, at the age of eighty-three, and was awarded a doctorate "honoris causa." She continued to write, and when 100 years old published new insights into Picasso's painting of Guernica. Rachel Wischnitzer died in 1989.

ADDITIONAL SOURCES

Obituaries in NewYTBS 20: 1131, Nov. 1989; *Jewish Art* 16/17: 186–187, 1990–1991; WhoWorJ 72, 78.

WOODBURY, HELEN LAURA SUMNER
(1876–1933)
U.S. Labor History

Helen Laura Sumner was born in Sheboygan, Wisconsin, to George True Sumner, a lawyer, and Katharine Eudora (Marsh) Sumner on March 12, 1876. The family moved to Durango, Colorado, when she was five, and her father became a judge. In 1889 the family moved to Denver, where Helen attended East Denver High School. She received a B.A. in 1898 from Wellesley College, where Katharine Coman was a professor. Her first publication was a novel, *The White Slave, or "The Cross of Gold,"* published in 1896. Sumner attended the University of Wisconsin in 1902 for graduate study, where she was named honorary fellow in political economy in 1904–1906 and studied American history under Frederick Jackson Turner and Ulrich B. Phillips. During that time, she wrote on labor, contributing a chapter to John R. Commons's *Trade Unionism and Labor Problems* (1905) and collaborating with Thomas S. Adams on a textbook called *Labor Problems,* also in 1905.

In 1906 Sumner left the university to complete a fifteen-month field investigation of woman suffrage in Colorado for the Collegiate Equal Suffrage League of New York State. The result was a report entitled *Equal Suffrage* (1909). She returned to the University of Wisconsin to collaborate with Commons in the American Bureau of Industrial Research and edit the eleven-volume *Documentary History of American Industrial Society* (1910–1911). Her dissertation, "The Labor Movement in America, 1827–1837," resulted in a Ph.D. in political economy and American history in 1908, and it became a major part of *History of Labour in the United States* by a group headed by Commons. Sumner became a part of that group, which was said to have dominated labor research for decades. Another of her works, "History of Women in Industry in the United States," was incorporated in the Commons volumes. Sponsored by the United States Bureau of Labor Statistics, it was published as Volume 9 in 1910 as *Report on Condition of Woman and Child Wage-Earners in the United States.*

After her temporary employment with Commons ended in 1909, Sumner lived with her widowed mother in Washington, D.C., and worked on contract studies for federal bureaus and other scholarly projects. In 1910 the Bureau of Labor Statistics sent her to Europe; the result was *Industrial Courts in France, Germany, and Switzerland* (Bureau Bulletin No. 98). In 1913 she joined the Children's Bureau, created by Julia Lathrop, and worked there until 1918. While at the bureau she compiled several studies of child labor problems. After her marriage in 1918 to Robert Morse Woodbury, a Ph.D. graduate of Cornell, she worked on contract only until she and her husband became members of the staff of the Institute of Economics (Brookings Institution) in 1924; they remained until their retirement in 1926. In 1928 Woodbury was appointed associate editor of *Social Science Abstracts,* and the pair moved to New York City. Helen Woodbury died at her home in New York of heart disease on March 10, 1933.

ADDITIONAL SOURCES

NewYT, Mar. 12, 1933; WhAm 1912–13 to 1932–33; University of Wisconsin Archives; William S. Appleton, *Record of the Descendants of William Sumner of Dorchester, Mass.* (1879); collection of papers at the State Historical Society of Wisconsin; DcAmAu; NotAW.

WOODWARD, GRACE STEELE
(1899–   )
Biography

Grace Steele Woodward was born on September 14, 1899, in Joplin, Missouri, to John Thomas and Dora Elizabeth (Sims) Steele. She attended the University of Missouri in 1917–1918, the University of Oklahoma from 1918 to 1919, and Columbia University from 1919 to 1920. She married attorney Guy Hendon Woodward on September 8, 1920. Woodward began writing quite late in life, starting with *The Man Who Conquered Pain: A Biography of William Thomas Green Morton* in 1962. She wrote *The Cherokee* in 1963 and *Pocahontas* in 1969. *Pocahontas* won first prize from the Oklahoma State Writers. Woodward was a member of the Daughters of the American Colonists and Daughters of the American Revolution.

ADDITIONAL SOURCES

Tulsa World, Feb. 16, 1962, Sept. 13, 1962, Oct. 14, 1962, Oct. 13, 1963; *Muskogee-Phoenix,* Sept. 23, 1962; *Boston Sunday Globe,* Oct. 14, 1962; *Personal Book Guide,* Nov. 1962; *Watchman Examiner,* Nov. 22, 1962; *Townsman,* Nov. 22, 1962; *Bulletin* of the Tulsa County Medical Society, Dec. 1962; *Charleston* (WV) *Sunday Gazette,* Dec. 16, 1962; *Current Medical Digest,* Jan. 1963; *Joplin Globe,* Feb. 24, 1963; *Webb City Sentinel,* Mar. 15, 1963; *American Journal of the Medical Sciences,* Apr. 1963; *Atlanta-Journal Constitution,* Apr. 7, 1963; *Oklahoma Today,* Spring 1963; *Saturday Review,* June 15, 1963; *Northside News,* July 4, 1963; *Anesthesia and Analgesia,* July-Aug. 1963; *Colonial Courier,* Aug. 1, 1963; *Bixby Bulletin,* Oct. 18, 1963; *Tulsa Herald,* v. 34, no. 3; *Book World,* Sept. 28, 1969; WhoAmW 66, 68, 70; ConAu P-1.

WRIGHT, IRENE ALOHA
(1879–1972)
Caribbean History

Irene Aloha Wright, historian of the Caribbean, was born in Lake City, Colorado, on December 19, 1879, to Henri Edward and Letitia O. (Ballard) Wright. At age sixteen she decided she wanted to see the world and left Colorado for Mexico with the $300 her mother had sewn into the seams of her flannel petticoat. She worked as an English teacher for a wealthy Mexican family and studied Spanish and history. She returned to the United States and graduated from Virginia College for Young Ladies in Roanoke, Virginia, in 1898 and from Stanford University in 1904. Wright was a special writer for the *Havana Post* in Havana, Cuba, in 1904–1905. She was also city editor of the *Havana Telegraph* from 1905 to 1907 and owned and edited the *Cuban Magazine* from 1908 to 1914.

Wright became interested in Caribbean history and began researching in the Archives of the Indies in Seville, Spain. (She expected to remain one year and ended up living there for twenty-two years.) She wrote *Documented History of Havana in the Sixteenth Century* in 1927, followed by *English Voyages to the Spanish Main, 1569–1580* in 1932. She compiled original reports of the early Dutch slave trade for the Dutch government, represented the Library of Congress in Spain from 1932 to 1936, and was associate archivist of the United States National Archives from 1936 to 1938. In 1938 she became foreign affairs specialist for the Department of State, a position she held until her retirement in 1952. In 1949 she wrote *English Voyages to the Caribbean, 1580–1592.* She was decorated by the Spanish and Cuban governments and received gold medals from the Havana Academy of History and the Women Geographers of Washington. (She was one of only four selected to receive the Gold Medal in 1950, for the three-volume *English Voyages to the Spanish Main.*) She was president of the Society of Women Geographers at age seventy-four. She was a member of the Royal Historical Societies of England and the Netherlands. Irene Wright died on April 6, 1972.

ADDITIONAL SOURCES
BiIn 3, 9; WhoAmW 58, 61, 64, 66; AmAu&B; ConAu 33R; WhAm 5; WhNAA; G. Smith, "And Life Still Unfolds," InWom 33: 446–448, Dec. 1954; obituary in *Washington Post,* Apr. 8, 1972; obituary in NewYT, Apr. 8, 1972; obituary in NewYTBE 72; *Bio-Base.*

WRIGHT, MARCIA
(1935–   )
African History

Marcia Wright was born on May 26, 1935, in New Rochelle, New York, of Anglo-American ancestry. Her father was a business executive; her mother was a full-time homemaker. Wright attended public schools in Larchmont and Mamaroneck, New York, graduating from Mamaroneck High School. Her early influences included attending a cosmopolitan junior high and high school, her family, with its deep roots in New England, her church, and, as she puts it, "survival as the fourth of five children."

Wright attended Wellesley College, where she earned a bachelor's degree in 1957. She received the master's degree at Yale University in 1958 and the Ph.D. from the University of London in 1966. She was motivated to pursue the study of history because of early exposure to historical sites, an ability to appreciate and retain historical material, encouragement in the way of prizes and mentoring by teachers and professors, and a conviction that history has contemporary ramifications at all levels.

From 1964 to 1965 Wright taught as an instructor at Wellesley College. When she completed her doctorate she took an appointment as assistant professor at Columbia University, where she has been since 1966: as assistant professor from 1966 to 1972, as associate professor from 1972 to 1978, and as professor since 1978. She also spent a year, from 1974 to 1975, as visiting associate professor at the University of Dar es Salaam.

Marcia Wright is the author or co-editor of four books and the author of over thirty scholarly articles. She was one of the first U.S. scholars to conduct historical research on women in Africa. Wright's most recent book, *Strategies of Slaves and Women: Life Stories from East/Central Africa,* was published in 1993 and continues her work on East and Central Africa. She has also written on women, health issues, and work issues in southern Africa. Aside from her publications, Wright takes pride in having helped found the National Archives of Tanzania.

Wright has been the recipient of grants and fellowships from the Fulbright, Rockefeller, and MacArthur Foundations, the Social Sciences Research Council, and Columbia University. Since 1991 she has served as chair of the Taskforce on Africa and the Core for Columbia College, and she serves or has served on the editorial boards of *African Affairs, American Historical Review,* and *Canadian Journal of African Studies.* She has acted as a member of the selection committee for the Fulbright Hayes Predoctoral Fellowships in Africa and has provided professional service to the American Historical Association and the Institute for Research in History. From 1985 to 1990 Wright was the co-convener of the Project on Poverty, Health and the State in Southern Africa, at Columbia University.

Marcia Wright's interests outside of her work include environmental conservation, sports, and observing human value systems and identities. Wright's family includes herself and an aunt.

BOOKS BY MARCIA WRIGHT

Strategies of Slaves and Women: Life Stories from East/Central Africa. New York: Barber, 1993.

Editor, with Zena Stein. *Women's Health and Apartheid.* New York: Columbia Health Project, 1988.

Editor, with M. J. Hay. *African Women and the Law: Historical Perspectives.* Boston: Boston University African Studies, 1982.

German Missions in Tanganyika, 1891–1941: Lutherans and Moravians in the Southern Highlands. Oxford: Clarendon Press, 1971.

ADDITIONAL SOURCES

Questionnaire completed by the subject for *American Women Historians, 1700s–1990s: A Biographical Dictionary.*

WRIGHT, MARY CLABAUGH
(1917–1970)
Chinese History

Mary Clabaugh Wright was born in Tuscaloosa, Alabama, to Samuel Francis Clabaugh, a business executive, and Mary Bacon (Duncan) Clabaugh, a graduate of the University of Alabama. She was student body president and member of the National Honor Society at Ramsay High School in Birmingham, Alabama, before receiving a scholarship to Vassar College in 1934. While attending Vassar, Wright was president of the student Political Union and a member of Phi Beta Kappa; she graduated in 1938. She attended Radcliffe College for her postgraduate studies in European history but soon began concentrating on China; she received her master's in 1939. In 1940 she married Arthur Wright, who was studying Chinese and Japanese at Harvard. Immediately after their wedding, the two left for Kyoto for a year of doctoral research financed by fellowships. In June 1941 the Wrights moved to Peking (then Peiping) and lived in what was once a part of a prince's palace. They stayed on after the bombing of Pearl Harbor and were placed in an internment camp in 1943. They were evacuated from Wei-hsien on October 17, 1945, and returned to Peking and their research. The Wrights became the representatives for the Hoover Library, which had begun a new program to collect contemporary materials on the Chinese Revolution. They began a series of travels throughout China during 1946, meeting with Mao Tse-tung and Chu Te. Mary Wright managed to obtain 3,000 volumes from the Nationalist government offices. The collection grew until the two returned to the United States in April 1947. Arthur Wright completed his Ph.D. at Harvard and became a professor of history at Stanford. Mary became China curator at the Hoover Library and completed her Ph.D. in 1951. Her thesis was published in book form in 1957 as *The Last Stand of Chinese Conservatism: The T'ung-Chih Restoration, 1862–1874;* it immediately became the standard text on the subject.

Meanwhile, Wright had become an assistant professor of the Hoover Library in 1951 and associate professor in 1954. She completed several bibliographic studies of major Chinese topics. In 1959 the Wrights became members of the Yale faculty; Arthur became a professor and Mary became an associate professor and the first tenured woman in the faculty of arts and sciences. In 1955 Mary Wright presided over a research conference on the Chinese Revolution of 1911, which resulted in a book in 1968, *China in Revolution: The First Phase, 1900–*

1913. She also founded the Society for Ch'ing Studies and its journal, *Ch'ing-Shih Wen-T'i.* She was a member of the central developmental agency, the Joint Committee on Contemporary China. She received honorary degrees from Wheaton College, Western College, and Smith College and was also the first woman trustee of Wesleyan University at Middletown, Connecticut. In late 1969 Mary Wright developed inoperable lung cancer; she died in Guilford, Connecticut, on June 18, 1970.

ADDITIONAL SOURCES

Archives of Stanford University for papers of the Asian Survey Project; Radcliffe College Archives for letters from Japan and China from 1940 to 1945; NewYT, Nov. 4, 1956 and May 7, 1964; WhAm, v.5 (1973); obituary by John K. Fairbank in *American Historical Review* Oct. 1970, pp. 1885–1886; obituary by Jonathan Spence in *Journal of Asian Studies,* Nov. 1970, p. 131; obituary in NewYT, June 19, 1970; AmWomWr; NotAW: Mod; *Bio-Base.*

WRIGHT, MURIEL HAZEL
(1889–1975)
Local History

Muriel Hazel Wright was born on March 31, 1889, to Eliphalet Nott and Ida Belle (Richards) Wright near Lehigh, Choctaw Nation (later Coal County, Oklahoma). Her father was half Choctaw Indian (his father having been chief of the Choctaw Nation from 1866 to 1870 and responsible for suggesting the name Oklahoma for the Indian Territory) and was company physician for the Missouri-Pacific Coal Mines. Her mother was a Presbyterian missionary and a graduate of Lindenwood College in St. Charles, Missouri. In 1895 the family moved to Atoka so that Muriel could attend Presbyterian and Baptist elementary schools. In 1902, when the family returned to their home, Ida Wright tutored her two girls at home. In 1906 Muriel entered Wheaton Seminary (later Wheaton College) in Norton, Massachusetts. Her family moved to Washington, D.C., in 1908, when her father became a resident delegate of the Choctaw Nation to the United States government. Muriel studied at home until 1911, when she entered East Central State Normal School in Ada, Oklahoma. She graduated the next year and began teaching in Wapanucka, Oklahoma, then in Tishomingo. She returned to Wapanucka in 1914 as the school principal.

In 1916 Muriel Wright began her master's degree in history and English at Columbia in New York; her studies were interrupted by World War I, and she returned to education. From 1922 to 1928 she was secretary of the Choctaw Committee, that oversaw the many economic and business affairs of the tribe, and she also helped organize the Choctaw Advisory Council and was secretary from 1934 to 1944. With George Shirk, she worked to initiate a statewide historical marker program and blocked an attempt to remove the Choctaw Council House from Tuskahoma. She was inducted into the Oklahoma Hall of Fame in 1940.

From 1924 to 1942, when Muriel Wright returned briefly to teaching, she researched and wrote about the history of Oklahoma Indians. In 1929 she published a four-volume work with Joseph B. Thorburn, *Oklahoma: A History of the State and Its People;* that same year she published a school textbook, *The Story of Oklahoma.* From 1929 to 1931 the Oklahoma Historical Society employed her to research the history of the Five Civilized Tribes. She edited *The Chronicles of Oklahoma,* a quarterly journal of the Oklahoma Historical Society to which she had often contributed articles, holding the position of associate editor from 1943 to 1955 and that of editor from 1955 to 1973. She published articles in other periodicals as well, and she received a Rockefeller Foundation grant which resulted in *A Guide to the Indian Tribes of Oklahoma* in 1951. The book won praise from the American Association for State and Local History. She received a Distinguished Service Citation from the University of Oklahoma in 1949 for her historical writing and work on behalf of the state and her tribe, and in 1964 she was awarded an honorary doctor of humanities degree by Oklahoma City University. She was a member of the Mayflower Descendants, Daughters of the American Revolution, Colonial Dames of XVII Century, United Daughters of the Confederacy, and the National League of American Penwomen.

In 1971 Wright was recognized as the outstanding Indian woman of the twentieth century by the North American Indian Women's Association. Toward the end of her life, she maintained an office at the Oklahoma Historical Society to continue her writing. Muriel Wright died of a stroke in 1975 in Oklahoma City.

ADDITIONAL SOURCES

The Oklahoma Historical Society Division of Library Resources has a collection of papers; LeRoy H. Fischer, "Muriel H. Wright, Historian of Oklahoma," *Chronicles of Oklahoma,* Spring 1974, pp. 3–21; Lucy A. Shirk, "Muriel H. Wright: A Legend," *Chronicles of Oklahoma,* Fall 1975, pp. 397–399; *Who's Who in Oklahoma,* 1964; Lu Celia Wise, *Indian Values Past and Present* (1978); obituary in *Daily Oklahoman,* Feb. 28, 1975; NotAw: Mod, pp. 751–752; *Oklahoma: A Handbook of Oklahoma Writers* and *First Families of America: Handbook of American Genealogy;* BiIn 8, 9, 12; NewYTBE, 1970; WhoAmW 68A; ConAu 109; WhoAmW 58, 61, 68, 70, 72; WhAm 5; *Bio-Base.*

Y

YOUNG, MARY
(1929–)
Native American History

Mary Young was born December 16, 1929, in Utica, New York, of English, Scotch-Irish, French, and Dutch ancestry. Her father was a college professor; her mother was an accountant. She attended elementary school and two years of high school in Hamilton, New York, then graduated from high school in Marietta, Georgia. Her early influences were mainly parental. Young lived a block from a graveyard and became interested in the headstones. She wondered at the differences in viewpoint expressed by her parents and her paternal grandmother, and she was fascinated, at age nine, with Henrik Willem Van Loon's *Story of Mankind.* Young attended Oberlin College, earning a bachelor's degree in 1950. She then attended Cornell University, where she completed the Ph.D. in 1955.

Young taught at Ithaca College as an instructor from 1954 to 1955, and at Ohio State University from 1955 to 1973, where she moved up the ranks from instructor to professor. Since 1973 she has been at the University of Rochester as professor of history. She has also served as acting chair of the history department and director of undergraduate studies in history at the University of Rochester.

Mary Young has written two books and nearly twenty articles. Much of her scholarship focuses on Cherokee history, particularly Cherokee land rights; she has also written on the historiography of the Indian frontier, the metaphysics of Indian-white relations, women and the Indian question, and war and culture on the frontier. Her current research, "Four Perspectives on Cherokee Removal," focuses on violent and nonviolent conflict resolution on the Indian frontier.

Mary Young is an elected member of the American Antiquarian Society. She has received the Ray Allen Billington Award, the Pelzer Prize of the Organization of American Historians, the American Studies Association Prize, and the University Mentor Award. She has received grants from the Social Sciences Research Council and the Schalkenback Foundation, and was an Ezra Cornell fellow.

Young currently serves on the editorial boards of *Journal of Social History, Ohio History,* and *Journal of American Ethnic History,* and she previously served on the boards of *Journal of American History, Journal of the Early Republic,* and *Marxist Perspectives.* She has provided service to the Organization of American Historians by serving on the executive board and by serving on and chairing the Frederick Jackson Turner Prize Committee and the Program Committee. She has also served on the awards selection committees for the Woodrow Wilson Foundation and the National Endowment for the Humanities. From 1994 to 1995 Young was president of the Society for Historians of the Early Republic, after having served that organization as a member of the advisory council from 1981 to 1985.

Mary Young's hobbies include reading murder mysteries, walking, travel, and arguing.

BOOKS BY MARY YOUNG

Friends of the Indian. I. Your Great Father, the President. II. The Christian Party in Politics. Staunton, VA: Mary Baldwin College, 1981.

Rednecks, Ruffleshirts and Rednecks: Indian Allotments in Alabama and Mississippi 1830–1860. Norman: University of Oklahoma Press, 1961.

ADDITIONAL SOURCE

Questionnaire completed by the subject for *American Women Historians, 1700s–1990s: A Biographical Dictionary.*

BIBLIOGRAPHY

Adams, Oscar Fay. *A Dictionary of American Authors*. 5th ed., revised and enlarged. New York: Houghton Mifflin, 1904.

Adams, William D. *Dictionary of English Literature*. New York: Gordon Press, 1972.

Adelson, Roger. "Interview with Afaf Lutfi al-Sayyid Marsot." *The Historian* 54 (Winter 1992): 225–242.

———. "Interview with Darlene Clark Hine." *The Historian* 57 (Winter 1995): 258–274.

———. "Interview with Joan Jensen." *The Historian* 56 (Winter 1994): 245–258.

———. "Interview with Natalie Zemon Davis." *The Historian* 53 (Spring 1991): 405–422.

Allibone, S. Austin. *A Critical Dictionary of English Literature and British and American Authors Living and Deceased from the Earliest Accounts to the Latter Half of the Nineteenth Century*. 3 vols. Philadelphia: J. B. Lippincott, 1858–1891.

American Literary Yearbook. New York: Gordon Press, 1976.

Anderson, Owanah. *Ohoyo One Thousand: A Resource Guide of American Indian/Alaska Native Women*. Wichita Falls, TX: Ohoyo Resource Center, 1982.

Author's and Writer's Who's Who. London: Burke's Peerage, Limited, 1934–1971.

Babb, Francis H. "Abby Maria Hemenway (1828–1890)." Master's thesis, University of Maine, 1939.

Bain, Robert, Joseph M. Flora, and Louis D. Rubin, Jr. *Southern Writers: A Biographical Dictionary*. Baton Rouge: Louisiana State University Press, 1979.

Barns, Florence Elberta. *Texas Writers of Today*. Dallas, TX: Tardy Publishing Company, 1935.

Bataille, Gretchen M., ed. *Native American Women: A Biographical Dictionary*. New York: Garland, 1993.

Bawden, Liz-Anne. *The Oxford Companion to Film*. New York: Oxford University Press, 1976.

Baym, Nina. *American Women Writers and the Work of History, 1790–1860*. New Brunswick, NJ: Rutgers University Press, 1995.

Bellot, H. Hale. *American History and American Historians.* Norman: University of Oklahoma Press, 1952.

Bent, William Rose. *The Reader's Encyclopedia.* New York: Thomas Y. Crowell, 1965.

Bibliography of Asian Studies. Ann Arbor, MI: The Association for Asian Studies, 1995.

Bigelow, Barbara Carlisle, ed. *Contemporary Black Biography.* Detroit: Gale Research, 1994.

Bio-Base: A Periodic Cumulative Master Index on Microfiche to Sketches Found in About 500 Current and Historical Biographical Dictionaries. Detroit: Gale Research, 1984.

Biographical Directory of Librarians in the United States and Canada. Chicago: American Library Association, 1970.

The Biographical Encyclopedia and Who's Who of the American Theatre. (See Notable Names in the American Theatre.)

Biographical Index. New York: W. W. Wilson, 1937–1996.

Bittons, Davis, and Leonard J. Arrington. *Mormons and Their Historians.* Salt Lake City: University of Utah Press, 1988.

Blain, Virginia, Patricia Clements, and Isobell Grundy. *The Feminist Companion to Literature in English: Women Writers from the Middle Ages to the Present.* New Haven, CT: Yale University Press, 1990.

Boia, Lucian, ed. *Great Historians of the Modern Age: An International Dictionary.* Westport, CT: Greenwood Press, 1991.

Boslough, John. "The Landmark Hunter." *Historical Preservation,* 38 (Apr. 1986): 46–51.

Boyer, Mary. *Arizona in Literature.* Phoenix, AZ: Haskell, 1935.

Browning, David Clayton. *Everyman's Dictionary of Literary Biography, English and American.* Comp. after John W. Cousin. Rev. ed. New York: Dutton, 1960.

Burke, W. J., and Will D. Howe. *American Authors and Books, 1640 to the Present Day.* 3rd rev. ed., revision by Irving Weiss. New York: Crown, 1962.

Cameron, Mabel W. *The Biographical Encyclopedia of American Women.* Reprint of 1924 edition. Detroit: Omnigraphics, 1992.

Celebrity International Staff. *Celebrity Register.* New York: Celebrity Services International, 1989.

Center for the American Woman & Politics Staff. *Women in Public Office: A Biographical Directory & Statistical Analysis.* Metuchen, NJ: Scarecrow Press, 1978.

Commire, Anne, ed. *Yesterday's Authors of Books for Children.* Detroit: Gale Research, 1977.

Concise Dictionary of American Biography. New York: Scribner's, 1980.

Concise Dictionary of American Literary Biography. Detroit: Gale Research Company, 1987.

Contemporary Authors: A Bio-bibliographical Guide to Current Authors and Their Work. Vol. 1– . Detroit: Gale Research, 1962– .

Coyle, William. *Ohio Authors and Their Books.* Cleveland, OH: World Publishing, 1962.

Crawford, Ann Fears. *Women in Texas: Their Lives, Their Experiences, Their Accomplishments.* Austin, TX: State House Press, 1992.

Current Biography. Vol. 1– . New York: Wilson, 1940– .

Davis, Dorothy R., ed. *The Carolyn Sherwin Bailey Historical Collection of Children's Books: A Catalogue.* New Haven: Southern Connecticut State College, 1966.

Davis, Marianna W. *Contributions of Black Women to America.* Vol. 2. Columbia, SC: Kenday Press, 1981.

Delaney, John J., and James Edward Tobin. *Dictionary of Catholic Biography.* Garden City, NY: Doubleday, 1961.

Dexter, Elisabeth Anthony. *Career Women of America, 1776–1840.* Clifton, NJ: August M. Kelley, 1972.

Dictionary of American Biography. New York: Scribner's, 1928–1937.

Dictionary of American Scholars. NY: R. R. Bowker, 1963.

Dominguez, Francisco J. "Interview with Dr. Vicki Ruiz on the Chicana Feminist Struggle." *Third World Forum,* Apr. 30, 1990, 6–7, 11.

Drake, Francis Samuel. *Dictionary of American Biography.* Boston: J. R. Osgood, 1872.

Duke, Maurice, Jackson R. Bryer, and M. Thomas Inge. *American Women Writers: Bibliographical Essays.* Westport, CT: Greenwood Press, 1983.

Duyckinck, Evert Augustus, and G. L. Duyckinck. *Cyclopaedia of American Literature.* Edited by M. L. Simmons. Philadelphia: Baxter, 1875.

Fink, L. C. *Biographical Dictionary of American Labor.* Westport, CT: Greenwood Press, 1984.

Foremost Women in Communications. New York: Foremost American Publishing, 1970.

Foremost Women of the Twentieth Century. New York: Melrose, 1987.

Frankel, Noralee, comp. *Directory of Women Historians.* Washington, DC: American Historical Association, 1988.

Fuller, Muriel. *More Junior Authors.* New York: Wilson, 1963.

Garrety, John Arthur, ed. *Encyclopedia of American Biography.* New York: Harper and Row, 1974.

Golemba, Beverly E. *Lesser-Known Women: A Biographical Dictionary.* Boulder: Lynne Rienner, 1992.

Halliwell, Leslie. *The Filmgoer's Companion.* New York: Hill and Wang, 1974.

Hannaford, Phoebe. *Daughters of America: Women of the Century.* Augusta, ME: True and Co., 1883.

Harris, Joseph E. "Professor Merze Tate (1905–   ): A Profile." *Profiles* (Howard University Graduate School of Arts and Sciences) (Dec. 1981): 1–24.

Hart, James David. *The Oxford Companion to American Literature.* New York: Oxford University Press, 1983.

Hart, John Seely. *Female Prose Writers of America.* Philadelphia: E. H. Butler and Co., 1855.

Heller, Scott. "Getting It Right: Historian Shepherds Her 'Midwife's Tale' Through Filming." *Chronicle of Higher Education* 41 (Jan. 13, 1995): A7, A13.

Herman, Kali. *Women in Particular: An Index to American Women.* Phoenix, AZ: Oryx Press, 1984.

Hersh, Amy. "Julie Harris Among Winners of National Medal of Arts." *Backstage* 35 (Oct. 14, 1994): 1.

Herzberg, Max J. *The Reader's Encyclopedia of American Literature.* New York: Thomas Y. Crowell, 1962.

Hesseltime, William B., and Louis Kaplan. "Women Doctors of Philosophy in History." *Journal of Higher Education* 14 (1943): 256.

Hinds, Katherine. "Joan Wallach Scott: Breaking New Ground for Women." *Change* 17 (July/Aug. 1985): 48–53.

Hine, Darlene Clark, Elsa Barkley Brown, and Rosalyn Terborg-Penn, eds. *Black Women in America: An Historical Encyclopedia.* 2 vols. Brooklyn, NY: Carlson Publishers, 1993.

Hoehn, Matthew, ed. *Catholic Authors.* Newark, NJ: St. Mary's Abbey, 1947.

Hoes, Durwood. *American Women 1935–1940: A Composite Biographical Dictionary.* Detroit: Gale Research, 1981.

Huber, Miriam. *Story and Verse for Children.* New York: Macmillan, 1965.

International Author's and Writer's Who's Who. Cambridge, England: International Biographical Center, 1976.

International Bibliophile Society Staff. *The Bibliophile Dictionary: A Biographical Record of the Great Authors.* New York: Garden Press. 1972.

International Who's Who of Women. Detroit: Europa Publications, 1992.

Ireland, Norma O., ed. *Index to Women of the Modern World, from Ancient to Modern Times.* Metuchen, NJ: Scarecrow Press, 1970.

James, Edward T. et. al, eds. *Notable American Women 1607–1950.* Cambridge, MA: The Belknap Press of Harvard University, 1971.

Johnson, Edna et. al. *Anthology of Children's Literature.* Boston: Houghton Mifflin, 1959.

Johnson, Rossiter. *The Twentieth Century Biographical Dictionary of Notable Americans.* New York: Gordon Press, 1972.

Johannsen, Albert. *The House of Beadle and Adam and Its Dime and Nickel Novels.* Norman: University of Oklahoma Press, 1950.

Kessler-Harris, Alice. "Equal Opportunity Employment Commission v. Sears Roebuck and Co.: A Personal Account." *Radical History Review* 35 (1986): 57–79.

Kirk, John Foster. *A Supplement to Allibone's Critical Dictionary of British and American Authors.* 2 vols. Philadelphia: J. B. Lippincott, 1891.

Knight, Lucien Lamarr, comp. *Biographical Dictionary of Southern Authors.* Atlanta: Martin and Hoyt Co., 1929. Reprint. Detroit: Gale Research, 1978.

Kunitz, Stanley Jasspon, and Howard Haycraft. *American Authors 1600–1900: A Biographical Dictionary of American Literature. Complete in One Volume with 1300 Biographies and 400 Portraits.* New York: Wilson, 1938.

Kunitz, Stanley J., and Howard Haycraft. *The Junior Book of Authors.* New York: Wilson, 1951.

————. *Twentieth-Century Authors: A Biographical Dictionary of Modern Literature, Complete in One Volume with 1850 Biographies and 1700 Portraits.* New York: Wilson, 1942.

Kunitz, Stanley J., Howard Haycraft, and Vineta Colby. *Twentieth-Century Authors. First Supplement.* New York: Wilson, 1955.

Lamar, Howard R., ed. *The Reader's Encyclopedia of the American West.* New York: Thomas Y. Crowell, 1977.

Lanker, Brian. *I Dream a World.* New York: Stewart, Tabori and Chang, 1989.

Lauretis, Teresa de. *Feminist Studies-Critical Studies.* Bloomington: Indiana University Press, 1986.

Leasher, Evelyn. *Oregon Women.* Corvallis: Oregon State University Press, 1980.

Leonard, John W. *Who's Who in America: A Biographical Dictionary of Notable Men and Women of the United States, 1899–1900.* Reprint of the 1900 ed. New York: AMS Press, 1974.

Lerner, Gerda. "Editor's Introduction." *Scholarship in Women's History: Rediscovered and New.* 11 vols. Brooklyn, NY: Carlson Publishing, 1994.

Levernier, James A., and Douglas R. Wilmes, eds. *American Writers Before 1800: A Biographical and Critical Dictionary.* Westport, CT: Greenwood Press, 1983.

Levy, Daniel S. "Outracing the Bulldozers." *Time,* Aug. 6, 1990, 80.

Lincoln Library of Language Arts. Columbus, OH: Frontier Press, 1978.

Lincoln Library of Social Studies. Buffalo, NY: Frontier Press, 1968.

Logan, Mrs. John A. *The Part Taken by Women in American History.* Wilmington, DE: Perry-Nalle Publishing, 1912.

Logan, Rayford W., and Michael R. Winston. *Dictionary of American Negro Biography.* New York: Norton, 1982.

Lossing, Benson J. *Harper's Encyclopedia of United States History, from 458* A.D. to 1905. Detroit: Omnigraphics, 1974.

Low, W. Augustus, ed. *Encyclopedia of Black Americans.* New York: McGraw-Hill, 1986.

McGraw-Hill Encyclopedia of World Biography. New York: McGraw-Hill, 1975.

McHenry, Robert, ed. *Liberty's Women.* Springfield, MA: G & G Merriam, 1980.

Mainiero, Lina, ed. *American Women Writers: A Critical Reference Guide from Colonial Times to the Present.* 5 vols. New York: Ungar, 1979–1994.

Malinowski, Sharon, ed. *Notable Native Americans.* Detroit: Gale Research, 1995.

Meier, Matt S. *Mexican American Biographies: A Historical Dictionary, 1836–1987.* Westport, CT: Greenwood Press, 1988.

Meier, Matt S., and Felichiano Rivera, eds. *Dictionary of Mexican American History.* Westport, CT: Greenwood Press, 1981.

Moulton, Charles W. *Library of Literary Criticism of English and American Authors.* Buffalo, NY: Moulton Publishing Co., 1901–1905. 8 vols. Reprint. Gloucester, MA: Peter Smith, 1959.

————. *Library of Literary Criticism of English and American Authors Through the Beginning of the Twentieth Century.* New York: Ungar, 1966.

Myers, Robin. *A Dictionary of Literature in the English Language from Chaucer to 1940.* Oxford: Pergamon, 1970.

Nakamura, Joyce, ed. *Something about the Author.* Detroit: Gale Research, 1987.

National Cyclopaedia of American Biography. New York: J. T. White, 1892.

New York Times Biographical Service: A Compilation of Current Biographical Information of General Interest. v. 1, no. 1– , Jan. 7, 1970– . New York: Times Books, 1970.

Nieto, Eva M., ed. *Notable Hispanic American Women.* Detroit: Gale Research Company, 1993.

Notable American Women, 1607–1950: A Biographical Dictionary. Cambridge, MA: Belknap Press of Harvard University Press, 1971.

Notable Names in the American Theatre: A New and Revised Edition of the Biographical Encyclopedia and Who's Who of the American Theatre. Clifton, NJ: J. T. White, 1976.

Ohles, John, ed. *Biographical Dictionary of American Educators.* Westport, CT: Greenwood Press, 1978.

Organization of American Historians Committee on the Status of Minority Historians and Minority History. *Directory of Minority Historians, 1995.* Bloomington, IN: Organization of American Historians, 1994.

Pascal, Francine. *Who's Who.* New York: Bantam, 1990.

Phelps, Shirelle, ed. *Who's Who Among Black Americans.* Detroit: Gale Research, 1995.

Philip, Gordon. *Artists of the American West.* Secaucus, NJ: Castle Books, 1980.

Powell, Allan Kent. *Utah History Encyclopedia.* Salt Lake City: University of Utah Press, 1994.

Preston, Wheeler. *American Biographies.* Reprint of the 1940 edition. Detroit: Omnigraphics, 1975.

Raven, Susan. *Women of Achievement: Thirty-five Centuries of History.* New York: Harmony Books, 1981.

Reginald, R. *Science Fiction and Fantasy Literature.* Detroit: Gale Research, 1979.

Roberson, Glenda, and Mary A. Johnson. *Leaders in Education: Their Views on Controversial Issues.* Lanham, MD: University Press of America, 1988.

Romig, Walter, ed. *The Book of Catholic Authors.* Stratford, NH: Ayer Publishers, 1977.

Ruiz, Vicki. "The Quest for Balance." Paper presented to American Historical Association Committee on Women Historians, San Francisco, CA, 1994.

Rush, Theressa Gunnels, Carol Fairbanks Myers, and Esther Spring Arata. *Black American Writers, Past and Present: A Biographical and Bibliographical Dictionary.* Metuchen, NJ: Scarecrow Press, 1975.

Salem, Dorothy C., ed. *African American Women: A Biographical Dictionary.* New York: Garland, 1993.

Sanchez Korrol, Virginia. "A Personal Journey Towards a Multicultural Curriculum." Paper prepared for the Multicultural Conference, Brooklyn College, CUNY, April 1995.

Schapsmeir, Frederick H., and Edward L. Schapsmeir. *Encyclopedia of American Agricultural History.* Westport, CT: Greenwood Press, 1976.

Schockley, Ann Allen. *Afro-American Women Writers, 1746–1933: An Anthology and Critical Guide.* Boston: G. K. Hall, 1988.

Scott, Anne Firor. "A Historian's Odyssey." In her *Making the Invisible Woman Visible.* Urbana: University of Illinois Press, 1984, xi–xxvii.

Scott, Joan W. *Gender and the Politics of History.* New York: Columbia University Press, 1988.

Sicherman, Barbara, et al., eds. *Notable American Women: The Modern Period.* Cambridge, MA: Belknap Press of Harvard University Press, 1980.

Siegel, Mary-Ellen. *Her Way: A Guide to Biographies of Women for Young People.* Chicago: American Library Association, 1984.

Smith, Jessie Carney. *Notable Black American Women.* Detroit: Gale Research, 1992.

Spiller, Robert E., et al., eds. *Literary History of the United States.* New York: Macmillan, 1974.

Stewart, Doug. "She Can Size Up Your Old Building in a Heartbeat." *Smithsonian* 24 (Apr. 1993): 127–136.

Telgen, Diane, and Jim Kamp, eds. *Notable Hispanic American Women.* Detroit: Gale Research, 1993.

Thomas, Clara. *Canadian Novelists, 1920–1945.* Folecroft, PA: Folecroft Library Editions, 1970.

Tinling, Marion. *Women Remembered: A Guide to Landmarks of Women's History in the United States.* Westport, CT: Greenwood Press, 1986.

Titus, William A. *Wisconsin Writers.* Detroit: Gale Research, 1974.

Todd, Janet, ed. *A Dictionary of British and American Women Writers, 1660–1800.* Totowa, NJ: Roman and Allanheld, 1985.

Toye, William. *The Oxford Companion to Canadian History and Literature*. New York: Oxford University Press, 1983.

Trent, William Peterfield, John Erskine, Stuart P. Sherman, and Carl Van Doren, eds. *Cambridge History of American Literature*. New York: Putnam, 1917–1921.

Uglow, Jennifer. *The International Dictionary of Women's Biography*. New York: Continuum, 1982.

Unterburger, Amy, ed. *Who's Who Among Asian Americans, 1994/95*. Detroit: Gale Research, 1995.

Vinson, James, ed. *American Writers Since 1900*. Chicago: St. James Press, 1983.

Wakeman, John, and Stanley J. Kunitz. *World Authors*. New York: H. W. Wilson, 1975.

Wallace, W. Stewart, comp. *A Dictionary of North American Writers Deceased Before 1950*. Toronto: Ryerson Press, 1951.

Ward, Martha E. *Authors of Books for Young People*. Metuchen, NJ: Scarecrow, 1990.

Ward, Robert E. *A Bio-Bibliography of German-American Writers, 1670–1970*. White Plains, NY: Kraus International Publications, 1985.

Warner, C. D. *Biographical Dictionary and Synopsis of Books, Ancient and Modern*. New York: Gordon Press, 1972.

Webster's American Biographies. New York: Merriam-Webster, 1975.

Who's Who in America. Chicago: Marquis Who's Who, 1934– .

Who's Who in American Art, 1991–1992. NY: R. R. Bowker, 1991.

Who's Who in American Education. New Providence, NJ: Marquis, 1995.

Who's Who in American Jewry. Los Angeles, CA: Standard Who's Who, 1980.

Who's Who in Government. Chicago: Marquis Who's Who, 1972/73–1977.

Who's Who in the East. Chicago: Marquis Who's Who, 1967.

Who's Who in the World. Ed. 1– , 1971/72– . Chicago: Marquis, 1970.

Who's Who in World Jewry. 1955– . New York: Pitman, 1955– .

Who's Who of American Women. New Providence, NJ: Marquis, 1958–1995.

Who Was Who Among English and European Authors, 1931–1949. Detroit: Gale Research, 1978.

Who Was Who Among North American Authors, 1921–1939. Detroit: Gale Research, 1976.

Who Was Who in America: A Companion Biographical Reference Work to Who's Who in America. Chicago: Marquis, 1942–1981, v. 1–7.

Who Was Who in America: Historical Volume, 1607–1896. A Component Volume of Who's Who in American History. Chicago: Marquis, 1963.

Who Was Who in Literature: Nineteen Six to Nineteen Thirty-Four. Detroit: Gale Research, 1979.

Willard, Frances Elizabeth, and Mary A. Livermore. *A Woman of the Century: 1470 Biographical Sketches Accompanied by Portraits of Leading American Women in All Walks of Life*. Buffalo, NY: Charles Wells Moulton, 1893.

Williams, Ora, ed. *American Black Women in the Arts and Social Sciences*. Metuchen, NJ: Scarecrow Press, 1994.

Wilson, Clyde N., ed. *American Historians, 1607–1865*. Detroit: Gale Research, 1984.

Wilson, James Grant, ed. *Appleton's Cyclopaedia of American Biography*. New York: D. Appleton and Co., 1901. Reprint. Detroit: Gale Research, 1968.

Winkler, Karen J. "A Prize-Winning Historian in Spite of Herself." *Chronicle of Higher Education* 37 (June 26, 1991): A3.

World Almanac Editors. *The Good Housekeeping Woman's Almanac.* New York: Newspaper Enterprise Association, 1977.

Wright, Frances Valentine, ed. *Who's Who Among Pacific Northwest Authors.* Missoula, MT: Pacific Northwest Library Association, 1969.

Writer's Directory. New York: St. Martin's Press, 1983.

Wunder, John R. *Historians of the American Frontier: A Bio-Bibliographical Sourcebook.* Westport, CT: Greenwood Press, 1985.

Zophy, Angela Howard, and Frances M. Kavenik. *Handbook of American Women's History.* New York: Garland, 1990.

INDEX

Page numbers in **boldface** type refer to the main entry for each American woman historian.

About the Authors

JENNIFER SCANLON, trained in U.S. women's history, is Associate Professor and Director of Women's Studies at SUNY Plattsburgh. She is author of *Inarticulate Longings: The Ladies' Home Journal, Gender, and the Promise of Consumer Culture* (1995).

SHAARON COSNER has taught English and Journalism at Arizona State University and currently teaches at Corona del Sol High School in Tempe, Arizona. She is author of ten books.

ISBN 0-313-29664-2

90000>

9 780313 296642

HARDCOVER BAR CODE

FOR REFERENCE

NOT TO BE TAKEN FROM THIS ROOM